DEPENDABILITY BENCHMARKING FOR COMPUTER SYSTEMS

DEPENDABILITY BENCHMARKING FOR COMPUTER SYSTEMS

Edited by

Karama Kanoun
Lisa Spainhower

A JOHN WILEY & SONS, INC., PUBLICATION

Published by John Wiley & Sons, Inc., Hoboken, New Jersey
Published simultaneously in Canada.

For general information on our other products and services please contact our Customer Care Department
within the U.S. at 877-762-2974, outside the U.S. at 317-572-3993 or fax 317-572-4002.

Wiley also publishes its books in a variety of electronic formats. Some content that appears in print, however,
may not be available in electronic format.

Library of Congress Cataloging-in-Publication Data is available.

ISBN 978-0470-23055-8

Printed in the United States of America.

10 9 8 7 6 5 4 3 2 1

CONTENTS

PREFACE

The book is written for engineers and researchers working in the field of dependability and, more generally, in the field of system engineering. The book could be adopted as an advanced undergraduate, graduate, or continuing education textbook. The variety of benchmarks presented provide useful starting points for further research in dependability benchmarking.

This book consists of sixteen chapters, prepared by researchers and engineers working in the dependability field for several years and, more specifically, on dependability benchmarking during the more recent years. These chapters illustrate the current multiplicity of approaches to dependability benchmarking, and the diversity of benchmark measures that can be evaluated.

Chapters 1 through 6 examine system-level benchmarks that focus on various aspects of dependability using different measurement methods. Chapters 7 to 16 focus on benchmarks for system components: control algorithms (Chapter 7), intrusion detectors (Chapter 8), fault-tolerance algorithms (Chapter 9), operating systems (Chapters 10 to 15), and microprocessors (Chapter 16).

Chapter 1 describes an autonomic computing benchmark that measures system resiliency. In common with other benchmarks, it has a quantitative throughput metric to capture the impact of disturbances. The autonomic computing benchmark also has a qualitative metric representing the level of human interaction needed to detect, analyze, and recover from disturbances.

Chapter 2 contains three benchmarks that analytically measure reliability, availability, and serviceability of a system. All three are intended to allow a consistent dependability feature versus cost analysis for widely varying system architectures.

Chapter 3 covers two quantitative benchmarks that concentrate on the recovery of standalone systems and enterprise clusters. Recovery is broadly defined to be the time required for a system to return to service. For each benchmark, a scoring and weighting methodology is described.

The benchmark in Chapter 4 changes the physical environment around the system in order to quantitatively measure susceptibility to silent data corruption.

Chapters 5 and 6 include performance measurements in the presence of faults, providing performance degradation (due to faults) and availability measures to end users of on-line transaction processing and Web serving systems. Chapter 5 discusses a benchmark for on-line transaction processing that focuses on availability using direct experimental measures. Chapter 6 includes a measurement-based benchmark for Web servers that encompasses availability, accuracy, resilience, and service degradation.

Chapter 7 is dedicated to the benchmarking of automotive control applications running inside engine control units. It addresses the safety of the software applications from the perspective of the engine they control. It is aimed at supporting the selection or the purchase of automotive applications for electronic controller units.

In Chapters 8 and 9, the systems under benchmarks are, respectively, the intrusion-detection mechanisms and fault-tolerance algorithms.

Chapter 8 discusses issues that should be addressed when benchmarking intrusion detectors in the cyber domain. It is worth mentioning that no intrusion detector benchmark is currently available, and that this chapter does not develop a benchmark per se.

Chapter 9 addresses Byzantine protocols dedicated to Byzantine-fault tolerance. The benchmark is aimed at assessing the effectiveness of Byzantine-fault tolerance implementation. It is illustrated by a specific protocol, the Castro–Liskov protocol.

Chapters 10–15 exemplify the multifaceted feature of dependability benchmarking, illustrated by operating systems. The benchmarks presented differ mainly in the nature of the faults considered: Chapter 10 addresses internal faults, whereas chapters 11–15 are concerned with external faults. Chapters 11, 12, and 13 address faults in the software application, Chapter 14 addresses faults in device drivers, and Chapter 15 addresses faults in hardware platforms.

Chapter 10 defines a benchmark that captures the user's expectations of product reliability during common user experiences. Although the benchmark can be applied to any software product, this chapter focuses on the application of this benchmark for operating-systems development. Its aim is to help the operating-system developer to improve, during its development, the operating system's reliability.

Chapters 11–14 present benchmarks based on experimentation. They consider the operating system as a black box, examine it only through its available inputs, and observe its behavior only through the operating-system outputs. The ultimate objective of end-user's benchmarks is to improve the application software, the device drivers, or the hardware platform. However, the benchmark results may indicate weaknesses in the operating system that the operating-system developer may use, with further analyses, to improve the operating system.

Chapter 11 is dedicated to the Ballista project, the first operating-system robustness-testing approach. It reexamines the design decisions made and the lessons learned from a decade of robustness-testing research.

Chapter 12 elaborates on the Ballista approach and develops a benchmark evaluating, in addition to the operating-system robustness, two measures: the system response time and restart time in the presence of faults.

Chapter 13 focuses on real-time kernels. It characterizes the response time predictability, based on the divergence of the response time in the presence of fault, and the frequency of out-of-boundary responses times.

Chapter 14 concentrates on failures modes of the operating systems induced by faulty drivers. Additionally, it evaluates three complementary measures: responsiveness, availability, and workload safety.

Chapter 15 considers in a first step the operating system as a black box and develops an end-user benchmark, then shows how this benchmark can be complemented to help the operating-system developer improve the operating system's dependability.

Chapter 16 is dedicated to microprocessor benchmarks with respect to electrical charge induced by high-energy particles, referred to as soft errors. As the benchmark presented does not require any specific knowledge about the microprocessors, it can be used by the manufacturers or end users.

ACKNOWLEDGMENTS

Beyond the acknowledgements contained in the chapters of this book, we would like to especially thank:

- The European Commission, which has partially financed the work achieved within the DBench project, and, particularly, Angelo Marino, the scientific officer of the project, for his continual support and advice;
- IFIP, the International Federation for Information Processing, and, particularly, the 10.4 Working Group on Dependable Computing and Fault Tolerance, which created the Special Interest Group on Dependability Benchmarking (SIGDeB). In particular, Jean Arlat was the Working Group Chair who fostered the SIGDeB's creation;
- Carnegie Mellon University, IBM, LAAS-CNRS, and Sun Microsystems, who provided support for the SIGDeB meetings; and
- All SIGDeB members and DBench partners, who contributed to preparing the way for the benchmarks presented in the book. Particularly active members beyond the authors represented in this book include: Wendy Bartlett (Hewlett Packard), Jean-Paul Blanquart (EADS-Astrium), Mario Dal Cin (retired from Friedrich Alexander University, Erlangen-Nürnberg), Jean-Claude Laprie (LAAS-CNRS), Brendan Murphy (Microsoft), and Don Wilson (retired from Hewlett Packard).

Finally, we would like to acknowledge Jim Gray, who inspired work in this area and actively nurtured both research groups and individuals in this field of research.

KARAMA KANOUN
LISA SPAINHOWER

Toulouse, France
Poughkeepsie, New York
May 2008

CONTRIBUTORS

Arnaud Albinet, LAAS-CNRS, University of Toulouse, Toulouse, France

Jean Arlat, LAAS-CNRS, University of Toulouse, Toulouse, France

Ricardo Barbosa, Critical Software, S. A., Coimbra, Portugal

William Bryson, Sun Microsystems, Inc., Santa Clara, California,

Joyce Coleman, IBM Toronto Laboratory, Markham, Ontario, Canada

Cristian Constantinescu, AMD, Fort Collins, Colorado

Diamantino Costa, Critical Software, S. A., Coimbra, Portugal

Yves Crouzet, LAAS-CNRS, University of Toulouse, Toulouse, France

David de-Andres, ITACA, Technical University of Valencia, Valencia, Spain

John DeVale, Applied Physics Laboratory, Johns Hopkins University, Laurel, Maryland

Kobey DeVale, Department of Electrical and Computer Engineering, Carnegie Mellon University, Pittsburgh, Pennsylvania

João Durães, ISEC/CISUC, University of Coimbra, Coimbra, Portugal

Richard Elling, Sun Microsystems, Inc., San Diego, California

Jean-Charles Fabre, LAAS-CNRS, University of Toulouse, Toulouse, France

Mario R. Garzia, Microsoft Corporation, Redmond, Washington

Pedro Gil, ITACA, Technical University of Valencia, Valencia, Spain

Weining Gu, Coordinated Science Laboratory, University of Illinois at Urbana-Champaign, Urbana, Illinois

Ravishankar Iyer, Coordinated Science Laboratory, University of Illinois at Urbana-Champaign, Urbana, Illinois

Ali Kalakech, LAAS-CNRS, University of Toulouse, Toulouse, France

Zbigniew Kalbarczyk, Coordinated Science Laboratory, University of Illinois at Urbana-Champaign, Urbana, Illinois

Karama Kanoun, LAAS-CNRS, University of Toulouse, Toulouse, France

Philip Koopman, Department of Electrical and Computer Engineering, Carnegie Mellon University, Pittsburgh, Pennsylvania

Tony Lau, IBM Toronto Laboratory, Markham, Ontario, Canada

Bhushan Lokhande, IBM Rochester Laboratory, Rochester, Minnesota

Henrique Madeira, DEI/CISUC, University of Coimbra, Coimbra, Portugal

James Mauro, Sun Microsystems, Inc., Somerset, New Jersey

Ricardo Maia, Critical Software, S. A., Coimbra, Portugal

Roy A. Maxion, Computer Science Department, Carnegie Mellon University, Pittsburgh, Pennsylvania

Francisco Moreira, Critical Software, S. A., Coimbra, Portugal

Priya Narasimhan, Electrical and Computer Engineering Department, Carnegie Mellon University, Pittsburgh, Pennsylvania

Ira Pramanick, Sun Microsystems, Inc., Menlo Park, California

Juan-Carlos Ruiz, ITACA, Technical University of Valencia, Valencia, Spain

Ana-Elena Rugina, LAAS-CNRS, University of Toulouse, Toulouse, France

Peter Shum, IBM Toronto Laboratory, Markham, Ontario, Canada

Lisa Spainhower, IBM, Poughkeepsie, New York

Dong Tang, Sun Microsystems, Inc., Santa Clara, California

Kymie M. C. Tan, Computer Science Department, Carnegie Mellon University, Pittsburgh, Pennsylvania

Marco Vieira, DEI/CISUC, University of Coimbra, Coimbra, Portugal

Robert Wisniewski, IBM Rochester Laboratory, Rochester, Minnesota

Sonya J. Wierman, Electrical and Computer Engineering Department, Carnegie Mellon University, Pittsburgh, Pennsylvania

Mary Peterson Yost, IBM, Software Group, Somers, New York

Pedro Yuste, ITACA, Technical University of Valencia, Valencia, Spain

PROLOGUE
DEPENDABILITY
BENCHMARKING:
A REALITY OR A DREAM?

Karama Kanoun, Philip Koopman, Henrique Madeira,
and Lisa Spainhower

Until recently, for computer systems, a benchmark referred implicitly to a performance benchmark. For example, the seminal handbook on database and transactional systems benchmarking, published in the early 1990s [Gray 1993], was totally dedicated to performance benchmarks. The handbook title does not even mention "performance" benchmarking. De facto, a benchmark has been a performance benchmark.

Many factors converge to raise the importance of dependability of today's computer-based systems. These include global 24/7 operations, on-line businesses, and the increasing complexity of systems. At the same time, high levels of performance are available at rapidly decreasing cost, decreasing the predominance of absolute performance and relative price/performance as indicators of customer satisfaction. Dependability is more and more playing a determinant role. However, although industry standard benchmarks are easily and widely used to measure computer performance in a deterministic and reproducible manner, dependability benchmarking is in its infancy. Nonetheless, although far from the maturity of current performance benchmarks, dependability benchmarking is making definite progress, as demonstrated by efforts in industry and academia illustrated in this book.

A dependability benchmark is intended to characterize system behavior in the presence of faults that could be internal or external to the system being benchmarked. Potential faults include component failures, hardware or software design flaws, faults in other systems interacting with the benchmarked systems, operator errors, and perturbations in the environment. Benchmarking the dependability of a system consists of evaluating dependability or dependability-and-performance-related measures in the presence of faults, in a well-structured and standardized way. Measures may characterize the system in a comprehensive way; that is, they may address the service delivery level and take into account the occurrence of various events impacting its behavior and their consequences. On the other hand, they may characterize specific features of the system such as coverage provided by fault tolerance mechanisms, time to restart the system, or time to system backup. As a consequence, numerous benchmarking measures are of interest.

The key aspect that distinguishes benchmarking from existing evaluation and validation techniques is that a benchmark fundamentally represents an agreement (explicit or tacit) that is accepted by those who make and sell computers and those who purchase them. This technical agreement states the measures, the way the measures are obtained, and the domain (e.g., application area) in which these measures are considered valid and meaningful. In other words, a real benchmark is something that the user community and the computer industry accept as representative enough of a given application domain to be deemed useful, and to be generally used as a way of measuring specific features of a computer system and, consequently, a way to compare different systems.

Currently, several organizations and research groups are carrying out promising work on dependability benchmarking, and, as a result, a great variety of benchmarks has been defined and implemented in the last decade. Many of these dependability benchmarks resulted from work performed by single institutions (proprietary benchmarks defined in response to internal needs, or work on particular aspects of dependability benchmarking). A few other benchmarks resulted from coordinated and concerted work between several institutions. Even though standard, well established, and widely agreed on dependability benchmarks, approved by recognized consortiums as in the case of performance benchmarks, do not really exist, the dependability benchmarks developed so far are paving the way for such standard benchmarks.

The results of a dependability benchmark are aimed at either characterizing system dependability capabilities in a qualitative manner (e.g., on the basis of the dependability features supported or claimed, such as the on-line error detection, fail-silent failure mode), or quantitatively assessing these properties. Dependability benchmark results can be useful for both the end users and vendors to:

- Characterize the dependability of a component or a system, qualitatively or quantitatively
- Track dependability evolution for successive versions of a product
- Identify weak parts of a system, requiring more attention and perhaps needing some improvements by tuning a component to enhance its dependability, or by tuning the system architecture (e.g., adding fault tolerance) to ensure a suitable dependability level
- Compare the dependability of alternative or competitive solutions according to one or several dependability attributes

A dependability benchmark can be performed in various phases of the system life cycle. The measures obtained for a specific phase are then helpful for the current or subsequent phases. The purpose of a benchmark may vary significantly along the system life cycle. For example:

- During the very early design phases, a dependability benchmark could support the decision whether to purchase a particular hardware or software component or platform that is to be integrated into a particular application.

- During development, results could be used to reveal weak points and to monitor the improvement actually achieved by fault removal activities (e.g., regression testing).
- For operational life, benchmark results could be useful to evaluate the impact of faults (hardware, software, or operator faults) on system dependability.

With many current systems, the traditional role of dependability assessment methods in the development life cycle of computing systems and applications (i.e., measuring used as an inherent step of the improvement process, and as a verification and validation facilitator) must be expanded in order to address the technical problems resulting from current component-based development practices involving intensive reuse of components. The use of dependability benchmarks is an important step in that direction. In fact, it is now a common practice for large-scale software development to reuse preexisting ("off-the-shelf") components (normally, general-purpose components possibly from the open-source community or components easily adapted to the requirements of the new system) and to develop from scratch only such further components and "glue" code as are also needed. Given the high costs of designing and implementing new software, vendors see the reuse of components as a way to reduce development effort and to achieve rapid time to market. However, component reuse introduces unknown risks of failure, as the new operational conditions may differ substantially from those that the components were initially designed for, and the new operational conditions may cause the activation of unknown residual faults or produce new component interaction faults. The use of dependability benchmarking in the development/integration of such composite systems seems very useful for component selection and to assess dependability measures of the whole system.

The benchmark performer (i.e., the person or entity actually performing the benchmark) can be a system manufacturer (or vendor), a system integrator, a third party, or an end user. These entities have different visions of the target system and, as a consequence, they have diverse expectations of the benchmark results. For example, system vendors have low-level access and observation points, whereas other entities usually can only make use of available inputs and outputs to interact with the system and observe its behavior to assess its dependability.

To sum up, dependability benchmarks allow objective characterization of system dependability. Therefore, they can provide a good means for fair comparison between alternative systems. They can also be used for guiding development efforts of system providers, and for supporting acquisition choices of system purchasers, or for comparing the dependability of new versions of a system with respect to previous ones.

Due to the above various aspects of dependability benchmarks, a range of approaches for dependability benchmarking has been followed. This book reflects these varieties. Some of them address the end-user points of view and others address primarily the vendor point of view (even though the user point of view is always there). Additionally, these benchmarks are at different maturity stages.

Benchmarking a system or a component is typically based on experimentation, or modeling, or on both. Experimental results may be obtained from controlled experiments defined in the benchmark or from the observation of the system in the field, under its operational conditions. Controlled experimentation consists of applying a workload and a faultload to the system being benchmarked to obtain the benchmark measures; they are based on fault injection techniques. All the benchmarks presented in this book can be understood in terms of the reference model for implementing dependability benchmarks illustrated in Figure 1. However, some work focuses mainly on the controlled experimenta-

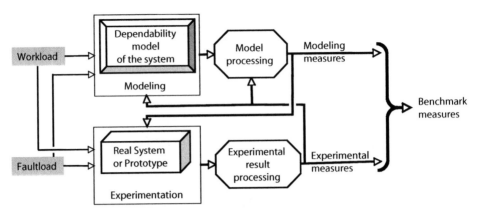

<u>Figure 1.</u> Reference model for implementing dependability benchmarks.

tion parts (putting effort into the selection of the workload, faultload, and experimental measures), some work gives more importance to modeling, whereas other work emphasizes obtaining experimental results from system observation.

In general, it is clear that dependability benchmarking is still a developing art. It took decades for performance benchmarking to mature, progressing from measures such as Whetstones, Dhrystones, and Livermore Loops to multiple generations of SPEC benchmarks. Primary technical challenges were in the areas of representativeness of the workloads, scalability of benchmarks to larger systems, and vulnerability of benchmarks to performance optimizations by either system design and tuning or aggressive compiler optimizations. It should, therefore, be reasonable to expect that dependability benchmarking will similarly take many years to reach maturity.

There are some aspects of dependability benchmarking that are likely to prove even more challenging than achieving well-accepted performance benchmarks. First, actual performance is something that can be measured in a reasonably short amount of time (hours or days) in an actual production system. Thus, the accuracy of a performance prediction can be validated fairly quickly with respect to a particular user's everyday experience. On the other hand, measuring achieved dependability requires operating for a long enough period of time to observe how the system responds to real failure. Given a reasonably reliable system, it could take months or years to find out if a dependability benchmarking prediction bears any resemblance to actual experience for a given system.

An additional complication with creating a good dependability benchmark is the public unavailability of comprehensive fault and failure data from which to create a faultload. Addressing this lack will at the very least be analogous to the process by which performance benchmarking gathered representative user programs through the creation of the SPEC (Standard Performance Evaluation Corporation) consortium. However, collecting faultloads is likely to be more challenging because many faults depend heavily on implementation and operating environment (they are not portable in the way source programs are). Furthermore, many of the best sources of such data have justifiable competitive disincentives to make data available on what has gone wrong with their systems.

Current trends in computing system design contribute to making dependability benchmarking increasingly difficult. For instance, the highly dynamic nature of most systems and the constant adaptation to changes in the environment, particularly in large networked systems composed of heterogeneous nodes that demand online deployment of services, runtime reconfiguration, and upgrading, make the benchmarking of dependability attributes a difficult, but extremely important technical challenge. However, the change from single computing nodes to networked systems of systems has also been a challenge for traditional performance benchmarking. Like performance benchmarks, dependability benchmarks will need to continually evolve to keep pace with the changing nature of the computing world.

We expect that eventually there will be a solid set of accepted, standardized, and validated dependability benchmarks. As with performance benchmarking, success will be a journey of continually improving benchmarks to keep up with technological changes, but the rewards of such a journey will be plentiful.

The idea of preparing this book arose during the completion of DBench, a European project on dependability benchmarking, partially supported by the European Commission during 2000–2004 [DBench], and has matured and evolved within the Special Interest Group on Dependability Benchmarking [SIGDeB], founded in 1999 by the IFIP Working Group 10.4 on Dependable Computing and Fault Tolerance.

DBench developed a framework for defining dependability benchmarks for computer systems, with emphasis on off-the-shelf components (commercial or not) and on systems based on off-the-shelf components, via experimentation and modeling [Kanoun et al. 2001]. To exemplify how the benchmarking issues can actually be handled in different application domains, a set of benchmarks and their associated implementations has been developed. They concern general-purpose operating systems, embedded systems (automotive and space applications), and transactional systems. These benchmarks are presented in this book. They address specifically the end-user and the system integrator points of view. They share the following common characteristics:

- The benchmark performer is the system purchaser or a third party who has no in-depth knowledge about the benchmark target and who is aiming at obtaining valuable information about the target system dependability.
- The primary users of the benchmark results are the end users of the benchmark target or the *integrators* of the system including the benchmark target.

On the other hand, the work of the Special Interest Group on Dependability Benchmarking started with an open-ended mission of exploration [Koopman and Madeira 1999], but evolved to consider a system vendor point of view [Wilson et al. 2002]. The benchmark performer, who is the system developer, has access to detailed information on the system that is not available for system purchasers. The work has identified a set of standardized classes for characterizing the dependability of computer systems. The classification seeks to enable comparison of different computer systems in the dimensions of availability, data integrity, disaster recovery, and security. Different sets of criteria have been proposed for computer systems that are used for different application types (e.g., transaction processing and process control).

Pioneer work on dependability benchmarking is published in [Tsai et al. 1996] for fault tolerant systems, in [Mukherjee and Siewiorek 1997] for software systems, and in [Brown and Patterson 2000] for Software RAID systems. The first open workshop on the topic was held by the Special Interest Group on Dependability Benchmarking in 2002 [Workshop 2002]. Much of the work on dependability benchmarking was published after 2000, authored primarily by institutions and individuals contributing to this book.

REFERENCES

[Brown and Patterson 2000] A. Brown and D. A. Patterson, "Towards Availability Benchmarks: A Case Study of Software RAID Systems," in *Proceedings 2000 USENIX Annual Technical Conference,* San Diego, CA, USA, USENIX Association, 2000.

[DBench] http://www.laas.fr/DBench.

[Gray 1993] Jim Gray (Editor), *The Benchmark Handbook for Database and Transaction Systems* (2nd Edition), Morgan Kaufmann, 1993.

[Kanoun et al. 2001] K. Kanoun, J. Arlat, D. Costa, M. Dalcin, P. Gil, J.-C. Laprie, H. Madeira, and N. Suri, "DBench—Dependability Benchmarking," in *Supplement of the International Conference on Dependable Systems and Networks,* Göteborg, Sweden, 2001, pp. D.12–D.15.

[Koopman and Madeira 1999] P. Koopman and H. Madeira, "Dependability Benchmarking & Prediction: A Grand Challenge Technology Problem," in *First International Workshop on Real-Time Mission-Critical Systems: Grand Challenge Problems,* Phoenix, November 1999.

[Mukherjee and Siewiorek 1997] A. Mukherjee and D. P. Siewiorek, "Measuring Software Dependability by Robustness Benchmarking," *IEEE Transactions of Software Engineering,* vol. 23 no. 6, pp. 366–376, 1997.

[SIGDeB] http://www.laas.fr/~kanoun/ifip_wg_10_4_sigdeb/.

[Tsai et al. 1996] T. K. Tsai, R. K. Iyer, and D. Jewitt, "An Approach Towards Benchmarking of Fault-Tolerant Commercial Systems," in *Proceedings 26th International Symposium on Fault-Tolerant Computing (FTCS-26),* Sendai, Japan, pp. 314–323, IEEE Computer Science Press, Los Alamitos, CA, 1996.

[Wilson et al. 2002] D. Wilson, B. Murphy, and L. Spainhower, "Progress on Defining Standardized Classes for Comparing the Dependability of Computer Systems," in *Workshop on Dependability Benchmarking,* pp. F1–F5, Washington, DC, 2002.

[Workshop 2002] Workshop on Dependability Benchmarking, Supplement Volume of 2002 *International Conference on Dependable Systems and Networks (DSN),* July 2002, pp. F1–F36, IEEE Computer Society Press. Also, papers are available at: http://www.laas.fr/~kanoun/ifip_wg_10_4_sigdeb/external/02-06-25/index.html.

1

THE AUTONOMIC COMPUTING BENCHMARK

Joyce Coleman, Tony Lau, Bhushan Lokhande, Peter Shum,
Robert Wisniewski, and Mary Peterson Yost

1.1. INTRODUCTION TO THE AUTONOMIC COMPUTING BENCHMARK

In 2001, IBM initiated a project to revolutionize the self-managing capability of IT systems [Horn 2001]. The company formed a new business unit to execute this mission. Five years later, IBM has achieved great progress in standards evolution, technology innovation, and product deliveries from IBM and throughout the IT industry. One of the key questions we asked in 2001 was, "How can we measure autonomic capability?" A team was assembled with performance benchmarking experts from several product areas to address this question, and the Autonomic Computing Benchmark project was initiated.

This project resulted in the development of the Autonomic Computing Benchmark, which is one of the first benchmarks designed to measure the system resiliency of an enterprise environment. Just as other industry benchmarks allow standardized comparisons between product offerings from competing vendors, we hope that this benchmark will help in quantifying the self-healing capabilities of systems. We believe that this type of quantification is necessary to enable customers to accurately assess resiliency claims from vendors, and to assist vendors in identifying key areas in which they can improve the resiliency characteristics of their products.

The Autonomic Computing Benchmark uses a fault injection methodology and five

Dependability Benchmarking for Computer Systems. Edited by Karama Kanoun and Lisa Spainhower
Copyright © 2008 IEEE Computer Society

categories of faults or disturbances.* The initial system under test is composed of a multitier Java™ 2 Platform—Enterprise Edition (J2EE) environment that includes Web server, application server, message server, and database server components. Two metrics are used to evaluate the system resiliency: a quantitative *throughput index* that represents the impact of the disturbances on quality of service, and a qualitative *maturity index* that represents the level of human interaction needed to detect, analyze, and recover from a disturbance, as defined by the IBM Autonomic Maturity Model [IBM 2001].

In this chapter, we describe our experiences designing and executing the Autonomic Computing Benchmark. In Section 1.2, we discuss the requirements that guided our benchmark design. Section 1.3 gives an overview of the Autonomic Computing Benchmark methodology, disturbances, and metrics. Section 1.4 explains how to interpret the results of the benchmark. In Section 1.5, we explain some of the potential uses of the benchmark. Section 1.6 discusses some challenges that we faced during the design and execution of the benchmark. In Section 1.7 we present our conclusions.

1.2. BENCHMARK REQUIREMENTS

Before we set out to develop the Autonomic Computing Benchmark, we agreed that there are several key characteristics and requirements that would ensure an effective and reliable benchmark.†

1.2.1. Concise Metrics

One of the most important requirements guiding the design of the Autonomic Computing Benchmark was that it should produce a small set of metrics that are easily interpreted. These metrics would be used in many ways, such as to compare the same system over time, or to compare different systems with the same business function.

1.2.2. Diverse Levels of Autonomic Maturity

The benchmark should be applicable to systems at any level of autonomic maturity since it might be many years before autonomic features are widely available. This requirement also means that initial testing and results may rank very low on indexes that are measured against "ideal" behavior that is not currently available or even possible with current industry offerings.

In addition, this wide maturity capacity would allow maximum applicability to a diverse range of applications and business needs. Similar to the need for different availability levels based on the importance of an application, we would also want to differentiate maturity based on the requirements of the enterprise system.

---

*In this chapter, we use the words "fault" and "disturbance" interchangeably. The word "fault" often implies an invalid operation and is the common term used in the dependability literature. The word "disturbance" conveys a broader meaning that covers invalid operations, intrusions, interruptions, and events that could alter the state of the system under test. For example, a load surge of ten times the number of users accessing a system is not an invalid operation but could cause a detrimental impact on the system. However, we continue to use the terms "fault injection" and "performance under fault" because they are commonly used and because they sound better than "disturbance injection" and "performance under disturbance."

The views expressed in this chapter are those of the authors and do not necessarily represent the views of IBM Corporation.

†Sections 1.2.1 through 1.2.4 are adapted from [Lightstone et al. 2003].

1.2.3. Benchmark Suites

Autonomic computing is intended to address a large range of business scenarios and tech-nology elements. The broad implication is that a suite of benchmarks would be needed to cover scenarios such as Web-based e-commerce, data warehousing and decision support, and e-mail. Thus, we define a reference framework that defines phases and metrics for all Autonomic Computing Benchmarks to be included in the suite, based on the notion of a reference workload. A reference workload accommodates the particular business require-ments in a scenario, such as the number of transactions processed by a business-to-busi-ness (B2B) application, or the number of e-mails processed by a messaging server that match a business scenario. By adding reference workloads to the benchmark specifica-tion, the framework is extended to a large number of business classes over well-defined and accepted workloads and schemas.

In addition to the diverse workloads, unique environments also create the need for unique disturbances and administrative interactions. The reference framework should provide the capacity to easily and effectively interact with and fail new components with-in the system under test.

1.2.4. Low Cost

Benchmarks are very costly to develop. A particular concern was that the Autonomic Computing Benchmark would not be run if the costs were too high. Thus, it is essential to leverage the resources and skills used for existing performance benchmarks in the con-struction of autonomic computing benchmarks.

1.2.5. Administrative Interactions

Since the very essence of the testing in this scenario is interacting with and many times disabling components in the system under test, it was necessary for the reference frame-work to provide the capability to restore the system to its previous state and prepare it for further testing.

Measuring the effects of these disturbances may require hours of observation and tim-ing within the system, and, therefore, the ability to fully automate the construction, prepa-ration, and recovery of the system would be required in order to make the toolkit usable and economical. This could be accomplished with a "write once" interaction that could be registered with the framework to perform tasks such as collecting and restoring log infor-mation or restarting servers and processes.

1.2.6. The Autonomic Computing Benchmark

The Autonomic Computing Benchmark was designed to meet the five requirements de-scribed in Sections 1.2.1 through 1.2.5:

1. The benchmark offers a qualitative, comparable, and concise measurement of auto-nomic capability that uses two metrics: a quantitative *throughput index* that repre-sents the impact of the disturbances on quality of service, and a qualitative *maturity index* that represents the level of human interaction needed to detect, analyze, and recover from a disturbance, as defined by the IBM Autonomic Maturity Model [IBM 2001].

2. The benchmark is capable of measuring a wide variety of autonomic levels because

of the granularity of the Autonomic Maturity Model. As expected, we have seen low maturity scores in the initial runs because the maturity model leaves room for vast improvement in autonomic features and products over what is currently possible.

3. Because the Autonomic Computing Benchmark is designed to wrap around a reference workload, it is applicable to a number of scenarios. For our initial reference implementation, we selected the SPECjAppServer2004 Performance Benchmark, a popular J2EE performance benchmark from the SPEC organization [SPECj 2004]. Since then, we have extended the Autonomic Computing Benchmark to other workloads and benchmarks.

5. Our use of existing performance benchmarks and workloads makes the Autonomic Computing Benchmark inexpensive to set up and run. The infrastructure required to run the benchmark is simple and lightweight.

6. The Autonomic Computing Benchmark is designed with the capability to automate virtually all administrative tasks in the system under test. Log records can be automatically stored so that, after a run has ended, a benchmark operator can verify that a disturbance ran correctly and investigate how the system under test responded to the disturbance.

1.3. OVERVIEW OF THE AUTONOMIC COMPUTING BENCHMARK

1.3.1. Methodology

The Autonomic Computing Benchmark approaches the task of measurement by using an existing performance benchmark workload, injecting disturbance as the workload is executing, and measuring the performance under fault as compared to a stable environment.

The benchmark methodology consists of three phases, as outlined in Figure 1.1. These are the baseline phase, the test phase, and the check phase. Note that prior to running a baseline phase or test phase, the workload must be allowed to ramp up to steady state, in which the workload runs at a consistent level of performance.

The baseline phase determines the operational characteristics of the system in the absence of the injected perturbations. The running of this phase must comply with all requirements defined by the performance workload.

The test phase determines the operational characteristics of the system when the workload is run in the presence of the disturbances. This phase uses the same setup and configuration as the baseline phase. The test phase is divided into a number of consecutive *fault injection slots*. These fault injection slots are run one after another in a specified sequence.

The check phase ensures that the reaction of the system to the disturbances did not af-

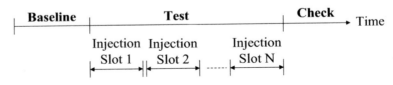

Figure 1.1. Autonomic Computing Benchmark phases.

fect the integrity of the system. During this phase, a check is made to ensure that the system is in a consistent state.*

During each injection slot, the benchmark driver initiates the injection of a disturbance into the system under test (SUT). Ideally, the SUT detects the problem and responds to it. This response can consist of either fixing the problem or bypassing the problem by transferring work to a standby machine without resolving the original problem. If the SUT is not capable of detecting and then either fixing or bypassing the problem automatically, the benchmark driver waits an appropriate interval of time, to simulate the time it takes for human operator intervention, and initiates an appropriate human-simulated operation to recover from the problem.

As Figure 1.2 demonstrates, each injection slot consists of five subintervals:

1. The *injection interval* is the predefined time that the system is allowed to run at steady state before a particular disturbance is injected into the SUT. The benchmark driver waits for the predefined injection interval before injecting the disturbance. The purpose of the injection interval is to demonstrate that the system is functioning correctly before any disturbance is injected.

2. The *detection interval* is the time from when a disturbance is injected to the time when a disturbance is detected. For a SUT that is not capable of detecting a disturbance automatically, the driver will be configured to wait for a predefined detection interval before initiating a recovery action. This is to simulate the time it takes for the human operator to detect a disturbance.

3. The *recovery-initiation interval* is the time from when a disturbance is detected to the time when a recovery action begins. For an SUT that is not capable of detecting the disturbance or initiating a recovery action automatically, the driver will be configured to wait for a predefined recovery-initiation interval before initiating the recovery action. This is to simulate the time it takes for a human operator to initiate recovery.

4. The *recovery interval* is the time that it takes the system to perform recovery. Because the system is allowed to recover during every fault injection slot, all disturbances are considered independently of one another, rather than cumulatively.

*For example, in industry benchmarks such as TPC-C and SPECjAppServer2004, the specifications include requirements to verify that the transaction summary in the workload driver matches the row counts of various tables in the database under test.

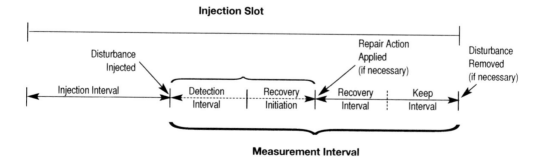

Figure 1.2. Injection slot subintervals.

In other words, no more than one disturbance affects the system at any given time.

5. The *keep interval* is the time to ramp up again and run at steady state after the recovery. This is the time remaining in a measurement interval. It is valid to run the steady state at a different throughput from that used in the injection time period.

It is important to note two things. First, the breakdown of the slot interval into subintervals is for expository purposes only. During a benchmark run, the benchmark driver only distinguishes the boundaries of these subintervals when the system under test requires simulated human intervention. Second, only the operations processed during the last four of the five intervals are part of the measurement interval and are, therefore, counted when calculating the throughput for the run.

1.3.1.1. Practical Considerations Relating to the Methodology.

In our implementation of the Autonomic Computing Benchmark, we made one modification to the methodology described in Section 1.3.1. Our initial design goal was to run all of the fault injection slots one after another in a specified sequence. In our experience, however, we found that running multiple disturbances in sequence had the undesirable effect of requiring that the database tier recover for all prior transactions from previous injection slots if it had to perform recovery during the current slot. Therefore, we prefer to run injection slots in isolation, with a check phase following each injection slot.

Regarding the interval lengths that we commonly use, we find that a 50-minute phase interval provides a balance between efficiency and the need to allow a system under test sufficient time to detect and recover from the injected disturbances. Therefore, for a baseline run we allow the system to warm up for 5 minutes, and then use a 50-minute baseline phase. For a test run, we allow the system to warm up for 5 minutes, and then use a 50-minute test phase, which is broken up into 10 minutes for the injection interval, 20 minutes for the combined detection interval and recovery-initiation interval, and 20 minutes for recovery interval and keep interval.

1.3.1.2. Comparison to the DBench-OLTP Methodology.

The methodology for our benchmark is in many ways similar to that of DBench-OLTP, a dependability benchmark for OLTP application environments that is one of several benchmark prototypes being developed within the DBench community [DBench 2003]; see also Chapter 5 of this book. Both the Autonomic Computing Benchmark and DBench-OLTP are based on the idea of injecting faults while a workload is executing, and measuring the performance under fault as compared to a stable environment. However, as described by Brown and Shum [2005], there are several important differences between the Autonomic Computing Benchmark and DBench:

- The reference workload for DBench-OLTP is TPC-C. The Autonomic Computing Benchmark, in contrast, can be extended to work with any workload and workload driver, as long as the output is in the form of throughput over time (for example, a count of successful operations every 10 seconds). The Autonomic Computing Benchmark has already been used with SPECjAppServer2004 and with Trade 6, a J2EE workload, using both the IBM WebSphere® Studio Workload Simulator and Rational® Performance Tester to drive the Trade 6 workload.

- DBench-OLTP has a single-component focus, such as a database management server. The Autonomic Computing Benchmark is used to test a multicomponent environment, such as a J2EE environment, which allows it to more realistically simulate a customer environment.

- Both DBench-OLTP and the Autonomic Computing Benchmark quantify and measure the performance impact of a fault or disturbance, but the Autonomic Computing Benchmark also quantifies and measures the level of human interaction needed to detect, analyze, and recover from a disturbance.

- DBench-OLTP uses a number of quantitative metrics, including the number of transactions executed per minute in the presence of faults, the price per transaction in the presence of faults, the number of data errors, and two measures of availability. The Autonomic Computing Benchmark uses a single quantitative metric based on throughput.

1.3.2. Disturbance

The disturbances in our execution runs were developed based on customer surveys and internal problem management reports. This list is not intended to be comprehensive, and we intend to refresh it based on customer feedback and experience. Also, we did not orient our work to security issues. System security is a specific discipline that should be addressed fully by experts in this area.

In the next sections, we present the five disturbance categories and describe the disturbances in detail.

1.3.2.1. Unexpected Shutdown. Disturbances in this category simulate the unexpected shutdown of an operating system, one or more application processes, or the network link between components in the SUT (Table 1.1).

TABLE 1.1. Unexpected shutdown faults

Fault name	Description
Abrupt OS shutdown for DBMS, application, HTTP, and messaging servers	This disturbance scenario represents the shutdown of the server operating system. It is intended to simulate the situation in which an operator accidentally issues an operating system shutdown command either remotely or at the console. All the processes on the server are stopped and the operating system is halted gracefully. This is different from the well-known blue screen situation on the Windows® platform (which is considered a software bug), a power failure (which is tied to the hardware), or accidentally shutting down by using the power switch.
Abrupt process shutdown for DBMS, application, HTTP, and messaging servers	This disturbance scenario represents the shutdown of one or more processes supplying the component of the SUT. It is intended to simulate the situation in which an operator accidentally issues an operating system command to end the processes. This is different from issuing a command to the processes to inform them of the need to terminate. The only alert provided to the processes that "the end is near" is that supplied by the operating system to all processes that are to be ended (i.e., signal 9 in Linux).
Network shutdown for DBMS, application, HTTP, and messaging servers	This disturbance scenario represents the shutdown of the network link between critical components of the SUT. It is intended to simulate the situation in which the network becomes unavailable because of a pulled cable, faulty switch, or operating-system-level loss of network control.

1.3.2.2. Resource Contention. Disturbances in this category simulate the case in which resources on a machine in the SUT are exhausted because of an unexpected process, user action, or application error (Table 1.2).

1.3.2.3. Loss of Data. Disturbances in this category simulate a scenario in which business-critical data is lost (Table 1.3).

1.3.2.4. Load Resolution. Disturbances in this category simulate a sudden increase in the workload on the system (Table 1.4).

1.3.2.5. Detection of Restart Failure. Disturbances in this category simulate a situation in which an application or machine is corrupted and cannot be restarted (Table 1.5).

1.3.3. Metrics

Two metrics are used to capture the effect of a disturbance on the SUT: throughput index and maturity index.

1.3.3.1. Throughput Index. The throughput index is a quantitative measure of the quality of service under fault. It describes the relationship between the throughput when the system is infected with a disturbance and the throughput when it is not infected:

$$\text{Throughput index}_i = P_i/P_{\text{base}}$$

where P_i = number of transactions completed without error during fault injection interval i and P_{base} = number of transactions completed without error during baseline interval (no disturbance).

The overall throughput index is calculated by taking the average of the throughput indexes for each individual injection slot. It is a value from zero to one.

It is important to emphasize that the throughput index should not be considered as an availability score. Availability scores are typically well above 99% because they include the concept of mean time to failure. In other words, they are estimated over a long period of time, when the failure of any component in a system is highly unlikely. When the Autonomic Computing Benchmark is run, in contrast, we ensure that a component fails, and measure the throughput over a very short period of time immediately after this planned failure.

1.3.3.2. Maturity Index. The maturity index is a qualitative measure of the degree of autonomic capability. It is calculated based on questions answered by the test operator. The questions relate to the human involvement in the detection, analysis, and recovery of the disturbance (Table 1.6). The scoring system is derived from the IBM Autonomic Computing Maturity Model [IBM 2001]. For each disturbance, the evaluation is based on how the problem is detected, analyzed, and resolved according to a set of questions, using the following scale:

- A is awarded 0 points (basic)
- B0 is awarded 0.5 points (basic/managed)

TABLE 1.2. Faults due to resource exhaustion

CPU hog on DBMS, application, HTTP, and messaging servers	This disturbance scenario represents the case in which the CPU resource on the system is exhausted. It is intended to simulate the situation in which a certain process in the machine stops being a good citizen and takes over all the CPU cycles. All the CPUs on the system are driven to 100% utilization by the hog process.
Memory hog on DBMS, application, HTTP, and messaging servers	This disturbance scenario represents the case in which all the physical memory on the system is exhausted. It is intended to simulate the situation in which a certain process in the machine stops being a good citizen and takes over all the physical memory. All the free physical memory of the system is taken up by the hog process. This disturbance is complicated by the virtual memory system, so the current implementation is to request all physical memory and randomly access within this memory to simulate page requests.
I/O hog on DBMS server	This disturbance scenario represents the case in which the disk bandwidth of the physical drive containing the business data is saturated. It is intended to simulate the situation in which a certain process in the machine stops being a good citizen and creates unplanned heavy disk I/O activities. The disk actuator is busy servicing read or write requests all the time. This should not be confused with the case in which the bandwidth of the I/O bus is saturated.
DBMS runaway query	This disturbance scenario represents the case in which the DBMS is servicing a runaway query. It is intended to simulate the situation in which a long-running, resource-intensive query is accidentally kicked off during operation hours. It should not be confused with a batch of smaller queries being executed.
Messaging server poison message flood	This disturbance scenario represents the case in which the message queue is flooded with many poison messages. A poison message is a message that the receiving application is unable to process, possibly because of an unexpected message format. It is intended to simulate the situation in which the operator configures a wrong queue destination. A large number of poison messages are sent to the message queue. This should not be confused with the case in which the application is causing a queue overflow.
DBMS and messaging server storage exhaustion	This disturbance scenario represents the case in which the system runs out of disk space. It is intended to simulate the situation in which a certain process in the machine stops being a good citizen and abuses the disk quota. All the disk space of the drives containing the business data is taken up by the hog process.
Network hog on HTTP, application, DBMS, and messaging servers	This disturbance scenario represents the case in which the network link between two systems in the SUT is saturated with network traffic. It is intended to simulate the situation in which a certain process in the machine stops being a good citizen and transfers excessive data on a critical network link.
Deadlock on DBMS server	This disturbance scenario represents the case in which a deadlock involving one or more applications leaves a significant number of resources (rows or tables) in the DBMS locked, making them inaccessible to all applications. Any queries on the DBMS that require these locked resources will not complete successfully.
Memory leak in a user application	This disturbance scenario represents the case in which a user application causes a memory leak that exhausts all available memory on the system. It is intended to simulate the case in which a poorly written application is deployed on an application server.

TABLE 1.3. Loss of data

DBMS loss of data	This disturbance scenario represents the loss of a database table. It is intended to simulate the case in which an operator with a connection to the database issues a simple DROP TABLE command accidentally. The table definition and all the data in the table are lost.
DBMS loss of file	This disturbance scenario represents the loss of a database file that contains critical business data. It is intended to simulate the situation in which an operator accidentally issues an operating system command to delete one or more database files that contain data for a particular table. The DBMS can no longer address the file from the file system. This is different from an operating system file-handle loss, which is considered a bug in the operating system
DBMS and messaging loss of disk	This disturbance scenario represents the loss of a physical hard drive that contains the business data. It is intended to simulate the case in which a hard drive is damaged such that the disk controller marks the targeted hard drive as offline.

TABLE 1.4. Load resolution

Moderate load handling and resolution	This disturbance scenario represents the case in which the load on the SUT increases moderately (generally about two times the previous load). It is intended to simulate the situation in which a heavy load is introduced because of a peak season or marketing campaign. The optimal result for this disturbance is to handle the entirety of the new load with the same response time and results as were seen with the previous load. This can be validly accomplished by overplanning the infrastructure, but a more attractive solution is to share the extra infrastructure with a separate system that is not seeing the increased load.
Significantly increased load handling and resolution	This disturbance scenario represents the case in which the load on the SUT increases drastically (generally about 10 times the previous load). It is intended to simulate the situation in which a significantly heavy load is introduced because of a catastrophic event or failure of the primary system. The optimal result for this disturbance is to handle the same amount of business as before without being overwhelmed by the extreme increase in requests. Technologies that illustrate this characteristic are flow control and quality of service monitors.

TABLE 1.5. Restart failure

OS restart failure of DBMS, application, HTTP, and messaging servers	This disturbance scenario represents the case in which the operating system has been damaged and does not restart. It is intended to simulate the case in which a key file or data that is required during the boot process is lost. When the operating system is rebooted, it fails at the point where the key file cannot be loaded.
Process restart failure of DBMS, application, HTTP, and messaging servers	This disturbance scenario represents the case in which the software component fails to restart. It is intended to simulate the case in which a key file or data that is required during the startup process is lost. When the software program is restarted, it fails at the point where the key file or data cannot be loaded.

TABLE 1.6. Maturity index

Autonomic level	Description
Basic	Rely on reports, product, and manual actions to manage IT components
Managed	Management software in place to provide facilitation and automation of IT tasks
Predictive	Individual components and systems management tools able to analyze changes and recommend actions
Adaptive	IT components collectively able to monitor, analyze, and take action with minimal human intervention
Autonomic	IT components collectively and automatically managed by business rules and policies

- B is awarded 1 point (managed)
- C is awarded 2 points (predictive)
- D is awarded 4 points (adaptive)
- E is awarded 8 points (autonomic)

Note that this scale is nonlinear in order to take into account the difficulty of implementing a system that meets the higher autonomic levels.

The questions used are as follows.

How is the disturbance detected?

A. The help desk calls the operators to tell them about a rash of complaints.
B0. The operators detect the problem themselves by monitoring multiple data sources.
B. The operators detect the problem themselves by monitoring a single data source.
C. The autonomic manager notifies the operator of a possible problem.
D. The autonomic manager detects the problem without human involvement.

How is the disturbance analyzed?

A. The operator collects and analyzes multiple sources of system-generated data.
B. The operator analyzes data from a single management tool.
C. The system monitors and correlates data that leads to recommended recovery actions.
D. The system monitors and correlates data that allows actions to be taken without human involvement.
E. The system monitors and correlates data based on business rules and policies that allow actions to be taken without human involvement.

What is the action taken?

A. The operator performs the required procedures and issues the commands on each affected resource individually.
B. The operator performs the required procedures and issues the commands on a centralized management console.

C. The operator approves and initiates the recovery actions.

D. The autonomic system initiates the recovery actions. No human action is needed.

The overall maturity index is the average score of all injection slots normalized to the highest autonomic level possible. It is a value from zero to one. A value of zero indicates that the autonomic capabilities of the system are basic (manually managed by reports, product manuals, and manual actions). A value of one indicates that the system is autonomic (automatically manages itself to achieve business objectives).

1.4. SAMPLE RESULTS

In this section, we present sample results that were obtained during a run of the Autonomic Computing Benchmark using Trade 6, a J2EE workload, as the reference workload.

1.4.1. Baseline Run

Figure 1.3 shows a sample baseline result. The throughput calculated during the baseline phase is used to calculate the throughput index for each disturbance run during the test phase.

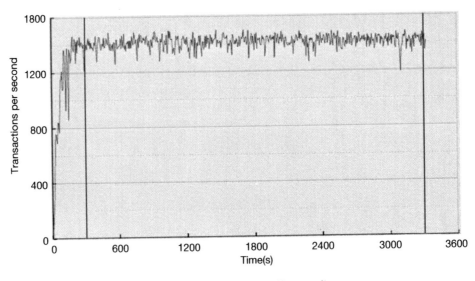

Figure 1.3. Sample baseline result.

1.4.2. Sample Disturbance #1

Figure 1.4 illustrates results that were obtained from a sample test phase run of the Autonomic Computing Benchmark. At the time indicated by the second vertical line, a disturbance that targets one component is injected into the SUT. In this example, the system is not able to remove the effect of the disturbance, and throughput remains close to zero until the third vertical line, when the disturbance is removed from the system (for example, by killing a resource-hog process or by restarting an application that was abruptly shut

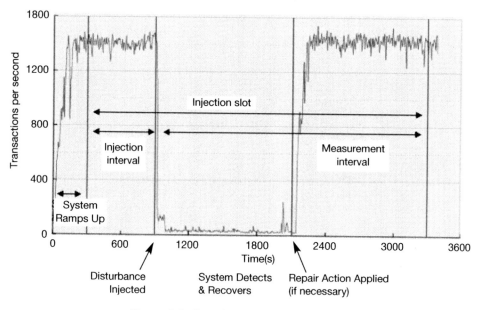

Figure 1.4. Sample disturbance result #1.

down). However, the good news for this SUT is that once the disturbance is removed from the system, throughput quickly returns to normal levels. Note that this might not always be the case. For example, in some cases a disturbance might cause a component in the system so many problems that it is unable to continue processing work even when the disturbance has been removed.

The throughput is calculated by counting the number of successful operations that take place during the measurement interval, and then dividing by the duration of the injection slot. In this example, assume that the throughput is calculated at an average of 700 operations per second. To calculate the throughput index, this value is divided by the value for an equivalent baseline phase. From Figure 1.3, we see that the average throughput during the baseline phase was approximately 1400 operations per second. Therefore, we obtain a throughput index of 0.50. Note that this throughput index is highly dependent on the timings chosen for the benchmark run. If we had kept the same injection interval but shortened the detection initiation interval (i.e., applied the repair action earlier), we would have obtained a higher throughput index. Benchmark runs are, therefore, only comparable when the same intervals are used in each run.

The operator running the benchmark then calculates the maturity index by considering the qualitative response of the system to the disturbance. In this example, it is clear that the SUT is not initiating a recovery action of any kind, but it might still obtain a non-zero maturity index if it detects the problem and perhaps provides a recommendation to the user about a possible recovery action that the user could manually execute.

1.4.3. Sample Disturbance #2

Figure 1.5 demonstrates a repeated execution of the same disturbance, but this time a monitoring product is used to detect the disturbance and initiate a recovery action. It might do this in one of several ways. It might terminate a rogue process that was hogging

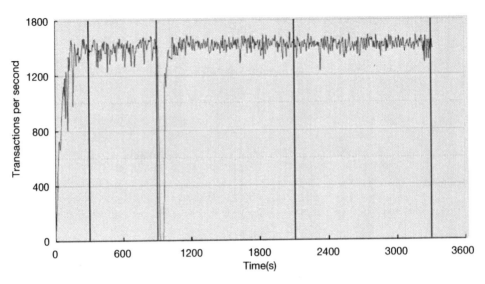

Figure 1.5. Sample disturbance result #2.

a resource in the system (repair), or it might shift work to a standby machine without re-solving the original problem (bypass).

In this example, we see that the throughput index will be somewhere on the order of 0.95, since the throughput was zero only briefly. And we will also see a higher maturity score than in the previous example, since the SUT is clearly detecting the disturbance and initiating a recovery action of some kind.

1.4.4. Comparison of Results from Benchmark Runs

One of the possible applications of the Autonomic Computing Benchmark is to assess the value added by an autonomic product to a system under test. In the following example, we compare two executions of the benchmark, using Trade 6 as the reference workload. In the first execution, a set of disturbances was run in a basic SUT. The SUT was then en-hanced by adding an autonomic product and the benchmark was executed a second time. The results obtained are shown in Figure 1.6.

From the figure, it can be seen that the enhancement added some value to the SUT. In terms of the throughput index, it had a small but measurable impact, and although the in-crease in the maturity index might seem small, remember that the scale is nonlinear. In this case, the enhancement raised the SUT from a managed level to a predictive level, which represents a significant improvement in the ability of the SUT to manage itself. A managed system only provides some tools that allow a user to monitor the system and ini-tiate actions, whereas a predictive system is one that can analyze incoming data and make recommendations to the user about possible actions to take.

An analysis of the above results could be that the enhancement increased the maturi-ty level significantly by detecting and analyzing the disturbances, but did not have a significant impact on throughput because it could not initiate automatic recovery ac-tions. In other words, this particular enhancement can simplify the work of human op-erators monitoring the system, but is not able on its own to replace those human opera-tors.

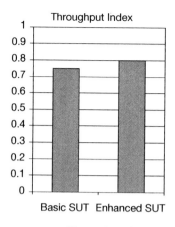
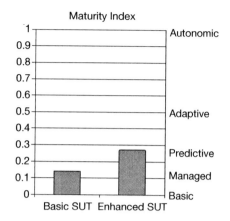

Figure 1.6. Comparison of basic SUT and enhanced SUT.

1.5. APPLICATIONS OF THE AUTONOMIC COMPUTING BENCHMARK

We believe that the Autonomic Computing Benchmark has a number of potential uses for a variety of different types of users.

IT infrastructure specialists could use the benchmark to:

- Test the resiliency of new applications (whether developed in-house or purchased)
- Automate testing in their environment to determine areas of weakness
- Set and evaluate resiliency goals for products

Vendors could use the benchmark to:

- Measure version-to-version improvements in their products
- Focus their development efforts on designing state-of-the-art autonomic features that target the areas of greatest need
- Generate marketing metrics and statistics that demonstrate the resiliency of their products
- Publish results in order to highlight strengths as compared to other vendors

System integrators could

- Measure cross-product resiliency
- Compare a system with and without a component (for example, a monitoring product or failover support) in order to quantitatively assess the value added by the feature

1.6. CHALLENGES AND PITFALLS

Although the benchmark provides an excellent way of quantifying the resiliency of a system, it also presents a number of challenges.*

*Sections 1.6.1, 1.6.3, and the introduction to 1.6.4 are borrowed from [Brown et al. 2004]. Sections 1.6.4.1 through Section 1.6.4.3 are based on an unpublished draft article that was abbreviated and converted into the poster paper [Brown and Redlin 2005].

1.6.1. Design of Disturbances

There are three keys challenges in designing disturbances. The first is to select the set of disturbances to implement so that they are meaningful and relevant to customer scenarios. The second is to ensure that the benchmark remains reproducible despite injecting the disturbance. We must ensure that individual disturbances can be injected reproducibly, and must coordinate injected disturbances with the applied workload. The third challenge concerns the representativeness of the injected disturbances. Unlike a performance workload, which can be simulated in isolation, environmental disturbances might require a large-scale simulation infrastructure. Significant resources may be needed to successfully inject these disturbances, unless tricks can be found to simulate their effects with fewer resources.

We have responded to these challenges by basing our set of disturbances on customer surveys and internal problem management reports, and by having subject-matter experts from each of the components in the SUT design and implement the disturbances. Through several iterations of the benchmark on different SUTs, we have found that well-designed disturbances can be injected reproducibly. In some cases, we have faced difficulties in injecting large-scale disturbances, and we continue to search for methods of simulating disturbances without necessitating significant resources.

1.6.2. Comparing Results

The flexibility of the Autonomic Computing Benchmark raises the question of what types of comparisons between results are meaningful. In order to compare the resiliency of two SUTs, the reference workload, disturbances, and timing parameters used in the runs must clearly be identical. But what if, for example, the user wishes to compare how the products from vendors A and B react to an abrupt shutdown? It will be necessary to write two product-specific implementations of the abrupt shutdown disturbance. Judgment is required to ensure that the two implementations are similar enough in design that the comparison is fair to both products.

Another consideration is how systems of different scale can be compared. A large, high-throughput system will take longer to crash, and will require a longer interval in which to recover after the crash. A possible solution to this problem is to create classes of SUTs based on throughput or on different scaling factors in the workload, such as number of users and number of products, and to compare only results from within a single class.

A third factor complicating the comparison of results is the absence of a cost component in the metric, which makes it possible for an operator to artificially inflate a resiliency score by overprovisioning hardware and software components in the SUT. Currently, we require only that a benchmark result include a list of hardware and software components used to achieve that result. One way to minimize overprovisioning as well as to ensure that the system under test is reasonably stressed is to require a minimal level of utilization from the key components.

1.6.3. Handling Partially Autonomic Systems

Partially autonomic systems include some autonomic capabilities, but still require some human administrative involvement to adapt fully. For example, a system might diagnose a problem and suggest a course of action, but wait for an administrator's approval before completing the self-healing process. An autonomic computing benchmark should provide useful metrics for such systems so that we can quantify the steps toward a fully autonomic system. But the benchmark cannot easily simulate a representative, reproducible human administrator to complete the SUT's autonomic loop. Human involvement in the benchmark process itself may need to be considered, in which case the benchmark scope expands to include aspects of human-user studies, with statistical techniques used to provide reproducibility. An alternative approach is to break the benchmark into separate phases such that human intervention is only required between phases. Each phase would then be scored individually, with a scorecard-based penalty applied according to the amount of interphase human support needed. This phase-based approach also may help with benchmarking of systems that crash or fail in response to injected changes, because failure in one phase can be treated independently from behavior in other phases.

1.6.4. Metrics and Scoring

Autonomic benchmarks must quantitatively capture four dimensions of a system's autonomic response:

- The level of the response (how much human administrative support is still needed)
- The quality of the response (whether it accomplishes the necessary adaptation)
- The impact of the response on the system's users
- The cost of any extra resources needed to support the autonomic response

The quality and impact dimensions can be quantified relatively easily by measuring end-user-visible performance, integrity, and availability both during and after the system's autonomic response. The level dimension is harder to quantify, as it requires an assessment of human involvement with the system.

There are a number of challenges surrounding the issue of metrics and scoring. In the following sections, we expand on several metric-related issues.

1.6.4.1. Quantifying the Impact of a Disturbance on an SUT. A key issue when measuring self-healing involves the details of how to quantify the impact of the injected disturbance on the SUT. In a non-self-healing SUT, the impact will be visible in the quality of the SUT's response, motivating use of a quality of service (QoS) metric. But measuring QoS has many subtleties, and the benchmark designer has to make choices. There are many possible QoS metrics—throughput, response time, correctness, and so on. Which should be used? Should the benchmark measure the SUT's response as a pass/fail test against a predefined QoS limit, or should it compute the degree of QoS degradation? Should the QoS evaluation be done against a single, fixed level of applied workload (e.g., a certain number of requests per second chosen to drive the SUT at a predefined fraction of its full capacity), or should the benchmark instead test a full range of workloads in order to expose how the SUT's behavior varies at different utilization levels?

To measure the impact of a disturbance to the SUT's delivered QoS, we chose to measure QoS in terms of throughput, using a fixed applied workload. This kind of throughput measure is often known as "goodput."

We measure throughput relative to a workload generated by a constant number of simulated users each making requests at a fixed maximum rate. Note that each simulated user runs on its own thread (or threads) of execution. When a disturbance causes the SUT to slow down to the point where it cannot satisfy the maximum rate of incoming requests, some threads will block and the request rate will decrease to match the SUT's capacity. In our experiments, we chose the number of users to generate a throughput that matches the capacity of a system that has one fewer cluster member than the SUT being exercised. This choice prevents the SUT from saturating when some of the disturbances are applied. This choice of a workload allows a distinction to be made between those disturbances that significantly reduce the capacity of the SUT, those that result in a total loss of service, and those that do not impact the ability of the SUT to service requests. Our QoS measure is also able to provide insights into which disturbances take a long time for recovery.

1.6.4.2. Quantifying the Level of Autonomic Maturity.
One crucial aspect of autonomic computing is the ability of the SUT to self-heal automatically. Since very few SUTs will have purely autonomic or purely manual healing processes, the benchmark must be able to quantify how close the SUT is to fully automated self-healing. Conversely, it must quantify the degree of involvement of human administrators in the healing process. Figuring out how to quantify the level of autonomic maturity is probably the most challenging of the issues. Solutions range from qualitative, subjective approaches like scoring a questionnaire filled out by the benchmark user, to quantitative but still subjective approaches like assigning numerical scores to each human action required in an SUT's healing response, to quantitative and objective approaches like measuring the configuration complexity of healing tasks [Brown and Hellerstein 2004].

We chose a subjective measure in the form of a questionnaire to identify the activities required for discovering and recovering from the various disturbances. We classified the activities according to a management model representing five levels of maturity, and assigned a nonlinear point scale to the classifications (reflecting the relatively greater impact of higher levels of maturity). The levels in this scale are based on the IBM Autonomic Computing Maturity Model, and were discussed in Section 1.3.3. For each disturbance that the benchmark injects, the operator running the benchmark fills out a list of questions that help to determine into which classification the SUT falls. The results of the questionnaire are used to determine the maturity level of the autonomic computing capabilities for each disturbance (and, hence, the number of points assigned).

However, because of the subjectivity of our questionnaire, we sometimes have difficulty reaching consensus on how particular disturbances should be scored. In some cases, we find that the IBM Autonomic Computing Maturity Model does not provide enough guidance about how a disturbance should be graded. For example, the difference between an adaptive and autonomic analysis is that an autonomic analysis is "based on business rules and policies," but insufficient guidelines are given about what these business rules and policies should look like.

Another observation from our experiment is that the nonlinear scoring of the autonomic maturity level is too idealistic. Although in theory this is intended to distinguish the relatively greater impact and difficulties of achieving the adaptive and autonomic level, in practice we have found that systems do quite well if they achieve the predictive level. The current nonlinear scale does not give enough credit to the predictive level. In the future, we will experiment with replacing the nonlinear scale (e.g., 0, 1, 2, 4, 8) with a linear scale instead (e.g., 0, 2, 4, 6, 8).

1.6.4.3. Quantifying the Quality of a Self-Healing Action.
One more dimension to determine the maturity is to quantify the quality of a self-healing action. In some cases, a self-healing system has no observable impact from a disturbance due to it being a

nonsignificant experiment. In other cases, a self-healing system simply tolerates a disturbance with no adverse effects, such as when a runaway SQL query is prevented from hogging the CPU due to either the design of the operating system's scheduler or the workload management facility of the database system. In yet other cases, self-healing can involve a multistage healing process; the resource affected by the disturbance is first bypassed, so that the effects of the disturbance are no longer visible to users of the system. Next, the affected resource is repaired, and then it is finally reintegrated back into the SUT.

As an example, consider a self-healing storage system based on a redundant array of independent disks (RAID). After a disk failure (the disturbance), the RAID array can bypass the problem by servicing requests from the remaining disks. If the healing process ends here, the RAID array continues to operate, but at a lower level of redundancy, making it susceptible to future disturbances. If the healing process continues, the array initiates repair by reconstructing the failed disk's data on a standby spare disk. Finally, it reintegrates the reconstructed disk back into the system, restoring full redundancy.

Unlike the RAID example, not all SUTs will provide the full set of self-healing stages. Some may simply bypass problems, leaving themselves unprotected against future disturbances. Others may jump straight to recovery. And reintegration may or may not be automatic. A self-healing benchmark must decide how it will handle this panoply of SUT behaviors: should it distinguish between the self-healing stages or measure them as a unit? If they are treated as a unit, how will the benchmark fairly compare an SUT that only does bypass with an SUT that does bypass, repair, and reintegration? If they are measured individually, how will the benchmark draw the dividing line between stages?

We resolve this issue by judging that merely bypassing a problem does not constitute a full recovery. In the case of disturbances for which our SUT can bypass the problem, we calculate the maturity index by taking the average of two scores: one based on the quality of the bypass action, and one based on what repair action (if any) is performed on the initially damaged resources. We base this method on the observation that when no repair occurs, the original set of resources is no longer available at the end of the injection slot. Even if the throughput has returned to its predisturbance level, the state of the SUT is inferior to its original state since it would be unable to withstand a subsequent injection of the disturbance under study.

Regarding the case of a disturbance that is non-significant or is tolerated by an SUT, we currently assign a throughput index of 1.00 and a maturity index of "N/A." We assign this score because the disturbance has no visible impact on the SUT, and, therefore, there is no need for the SUT to either detect or recover from the disturbance. However, this also means that systems that are immune to a particular disturbance by design will receive no credit in the maturity score. In the future, we intend to reevaluate our approach to scoring this kind of scenario.

1.7. CONCLUSION

We have demonstrated a working and effective benchmark for measuring the autonomic self-healing capability of a J2EE-based computing system. Our benchmark quantifies the ability of the SUT to adapt to disturbances injected into its environment in an autonomic way. The benchmark has the potential to play a key role in the engineering of autonomic systems, as it provides the quantitative guidance needed to evaluate new and proposed autonomic technologies, to set goals and development targets, and to assess and validate autonomic progress.

In the future, we hope to accomplish three goals. First, we would like to extend our set of disturbances in order to keep them meaningful and current. This will involve soliciting input from customers and probing the marketplace in order to determine new or existing problem scenarios that could potentially cause customers to experience outages. Second, we would like to drive the lessons learned from our benchmark runs into formal requirements for the next generation of autonomic solutions throughout the industry. (For information on IBM's current autonomic efforts, see [IBM 2006].) And third, we hope to promote the standardization of the field of autonomics by encouraging the adoption of the Autonomic Computing Benchmark by teams within and outside of IBM.

We have identified significant opportunities for refinement and improvement, and have laid out a roadmap for the next generation of autonomic solutions. We look forward to seeing increasingly sophisticated benchmarks for autonomic capability being used widely in autonomic engineering efforts.

ACKNOWLEDGMENT

Note that some of the material from Sections 1.2 and Sections 1.6 is adapted directly from earlier articles by members of the Autonomic Computing team, including [Lightstone et al. 2003], [Brown et al. 2004], and [Brown and Redlin 2005]. We have made minor modifications to the text from these articles and in some cases expanded on it. Within the chapter, we indicate which sections were drawn from the earlier articles. We thank the authors of these articles for allowing us to use their words.

REFERENCES

[Brown et al. 2004] A.B. Brown, J. Hellerstein, M. Hogstrom, T. Lau, S. Lightstone, P. Shum, and M.P. Yost, "Benchmarking Autonomic Capabilities: Promises and Pitfalls," in *Proceedings of the 1st International Conference on Autonomic Computing (ICAC 2004)*, pp. 266–267, New York, May 2004.

[Brown and Hellerstein 2004] A.B. Brown and J. Hellerstein, "An Approach to Benchmarking Configuration Complexity," in *Proceedings of the 11th ACM SIGOPS European Workshop*, Leuven, Belgium, September 2004.

[Brown and Redlin 2005] A.B. Brown and C. Redlin, "Measuring the Effectiveness of Self-Healing Autonomic Systems," in *Proceedings of the 2nd International Conference on Autonomic Computing (ICAC 2005)*, pp. 328–329, Seattle, June 2005.

[Brown and Shum 2005] A.B. Brown and P. Shum, "Measuring Resiliency of IT Systems," presentation to the Workshop on Dependability Benchmarking organized by the Special Interest Group on Dependability Benchmarking (SIGDeB), Chicago, November 2005, http://www.laas. fr/~kanoun/Ws_SIGDeB/5-IBM.pdf.

[DBench 2003] "DBench-OLTP: A Dependability Benchmark for OLTP Application Environments—Benchmark Specification," Version 1.1,0, http://www.dbench.org/benchmarks/DBench-OLTP.D1.1.0.pdf, 2003.

[Horn 2001] P. Horn, "Autonomic Computing: IBM's Perspective on the State of Information Technology," http://www-03.ibm.com/autonomic/pdfs/autonomic_computing.pdf, 2001.

[IBM 2001] IBM Corporation, "Autonomic Computing Concepts," http://www.ibm.com/autonomic/pdfs/AC_Concepts.pdf, 2001.

[IBM 2006] IBM Corporation, "IBM Autonomic Computing Library," http://www.ibm.com/autonomic/library.shtml, 2006.

[Lightstone et al. 2003] S. Lightstone, J. Hellerstein, W. Tetzlaff, P. Janson, E. Lassettre, C. Norton, B. Rajaraman, and L. Spainhower, "Towards Benchmarking Autonomic Computing Maturity," in *IEEE International Conference on Industrial Informatics (INDIN 2003): Proceedings,* pp 51–59, Banff, Alberta, Canada, 2003.

[SPECj 2004] "SPECjAppServer2004 Design Document", Version 1.00, http://www.spec. org/jAppServer2004/docs/DesignDocument.html, 2004.

2

ANALYTICAL RELIABILITY, AVAILABILITY, AND SERVICEABILITY BENCHMARKS

Richard Elling, Ira Pramanick, James Mauro,
William Bryson, and Dong Tang

2.1. INTRODUCTION

Performance benchmarking has a history of evolution toward specialization. The first widely measured benchmarks were simple and intended to represent the speed of a computer. Today, there are many performance benchmarks that reward specialized performance features or domains. For example, the Standard Performance Evaluation Corporation [SPEC] provides performance benchmarks for CPUs, graphics, high-performance computing (HPC), Java client/server, e-mail, Web servers, and the Network File System (NFS). Interestingly, no single system or vendor dominates all SPEC benchmarks. Each system has strengths and weaknesses due to the decisions and trade-offs made during design. Consumers can use the SPEC benchmark suites to evaluate different systems to meet their specific requirements.

However, there are few benchmarks that compare the availability characteristics of a system. Availability requirements are described as a probability number (mathematical definition of availability), or the percentage of available system operational time, where 100% is the maximum achievable availability. Desire for a "five-nines" (99.999%) availability probability is common. This desire poses a problem for system designers and service providers; even a simple design has many unknowns in real-world implementations, which could negatively impact system availability. Many of these unknowns are beyond the scope of hardware or software design. The desire for five-nines availability does not translate easily into design requirements.

Another problem with the probability specifications is that they do not differentiate a highly reliable system from a highly robust system or a rapidly recoverable system. If an availability budget allows five minutes (better than five-nines) of outage per year, does that mean that a system requiring fifteen minutes of downtime to repair must have a reliability characteristic such that it will not sustain an outage for three years? Or does it mean that a system that can recover from an outage in one minute can accept five outages per year as reasonable? Since we accept that equipment can and does break over time, does scheduled maintenance and its associated outage count against the five minutes budget? If so, what can the designers do to decrease the maintenance outage duration or defer the maintenance to a later time?

As in performance benchmarking, different systems and vendors take different approaches to solving the availability problem. However, unlike performance benchmarking, there are no widely accepted industry standard benchmarks that can be used to evaluate systems for availability attributes. Sun Microsystems is working with industry and academia to develop benchmarks intended to discriminate a system's availability attributes. These benchmarks are designed to be portable to a variety of hardware and software architectures, allowing comparison of diverse systems.

Reliability, availability, and serviceability (RAS) analysis and benchmarking can use both measurement-based [Dbench, Mauro et al. 2004, Pramanick et al. 2003, Zhu et al. 2002b] and analytical benchmarks [Mauro et al. 2003]. Measurement-based benchmarks are often used for performance analysis in which the system under test is subjected to a workload and its performance is directly measured as a function of operations per time interval. Chapter 3, System Recovery Benchmarks, describes several measurement-based benchmarks. Analytical benchmarks evaluate the capabilities of a system. This evaluation can be made without putting a system under test. By analogy, a measurement-based benchmark for a truck would measure the horsepower, maximum speed, or acceleration. An analytical RAS benchmark for the same truck may determine whether the failure of a tire will cause a disruption in the operation of the truck. Not surprisingly, some trucks have tandem wheel configurations to provide both load sharing and robustness in the face of tire failure.

2.2. DIVIDING THE AVAILABILITY PROBLEM

We can describe the steady-state availability of a system as a function of the mean time to fail (MTTF) and mean time to repair (MTTR):

$$\text{Availability} = \frac{\text{MTTF}}{(\text{MTTF} \times \text{MTTR})}$$

Mathematically, we can increase the availability by increasing MTTF to infinity or decreasing the MTTR to zero. In practice, neither of these extremes is likely to be found in a modern computing system.

We can divide the availability problem into three classifications of attributes [Zhu et al. 2002a]:

- *Rate* is analogous to MTTF; we measure or project the expected failure rate. We commonly measure these as failures in time (FIT), where a single FIT is one failure per billion hours.
- *Recovery* is analogous to the MTTR. Obviously, a rapid recovery from faults is highly desirable. Recovery can be measured quantitatively.

- *Robustness* is a measure of a system's ability to survive failures. A common example of a robust design would include redundancy for those components that have high FIT rates. Design robustness can be examined analytically.

By examining these attributes separately, we can discriminate between different systems and their approaches to reaching high availability. In this chapter, we look at analytical benchmarks that can be used to evaluate robustness characteristics of system designs.

2.3. FAILURE RATES

Hardware failure rates for systems and components are often predicted using industry-standard reliability-prediction models. Commonly used models are MIL-HDBK-217F [MIL-STDS] and Telcordia SR-332 [Telcordia]. These models were developed over many years by studying the failure rates of many system components under various stress conditions. Predictions can also be improved by correlating these methods to actual field measurements, as in the case of a major company, like Sun Microsystems, which uses both prediction and field measurements to improve the failure rate analysis of systems and components.

We use failure rate information when evaluating the robustness attributes of a system. However, we do not concern ourselves with the overall FIT rate of a system for analytical RAS benchmark purposes. This is because the FIT rate has a direct relationship to the number of components in a system. If we use the overall FIT rate, then a simple, small, nonrobust system would always win over a complex, large, robust system. Rather, we use the failure rate information to describe the expected distribution of failures across the components of a system. For example, a hypothetical system with predicted failure rate distribution is shown in Table 2.1. The contribution of each component's failure rate is described as the percentage failure rate (PFR) for the system. The total for all components in the system is 100%:

$$\sum_{i=1}^{N} PFR_i = 100\%$$

where PFR_i is the percentage-of-failure rate for component I and N is the number of components in the system.

The failure rate distribution of components is used for analytical robustness benchmarks. When analyzing the robustness of a system, we need to know the probability that a

TABLE 2.1. Predicted percentage of failure rates for a hypothetical system

Components	Percentage of failure rate (%)
Disks	10
Power supplies	15
CPU and memory boards	20
Other boards	20
Memory	25
Fans	5
Miscellaneous and cables	5

given component will fail, as well as the level of robustness designed into the system to compensate for the failure. For example, if a component has a very low failure rate, then it may be difficult to justify adding redundancy. However, a component that shows a high failure rate would need a robust design to achieve high system availability. By knowing the PFR for components, we can analyze robustness techniques and how they contribute to the overall system robustness.

2.4. ROBUSTNESS BENCHMARKS

We can analyze the robustness of a system by observing how the system reacts to the loss of a component. We have created two benchmarks for robustness: the Fault Robustness Benchmark (FRB-A) and the Maintenance Robustness Benchmark (MRB-A). These benchmarks use similar analysis techniques: get the failure rate of all components in the system, classify the effect on the system for the loss of the component, and sum the products of the percentage failure rate and the class.

The FRB-A and MRB-A show two different aspects of the robustness of a system. The FRB-A benchmark describes the robustness of the system in response to a component failure. The MRB-A benchmark describes the robustness of the system during the repair activity. FRB-A will reward systems that can accept failures without causing outages. MRB-A will reward systems that can be repaired without causing outages. For example, FRB-A will reward mirroring disk drives so that a drive failure will not cause an outage. MRB-A will reward hot-pluggable disk drives that can be repaired without causing an outage.

We classify the reactions as:

- *Fully disruptive.* The failure of a component causes the system to be unavailable until the repair is complete. We assign a scalar weight value of 1 to the component that falls into this class.
- *Semidisruptive.* The failure of a component causes the system to be unavailable during a portion of the recovery/repair activity, but not the entire duration of the activity. We assign a scalar weight value of 10 to the component that falls into this class.
- *Nondisruptive.* The failure of a component does not cause any unavailability. We assign a scalar weight value of 100 to the component that falls into this class.

The classification of system reactions to events is done from the perspective of a single service, or the service provided by a single operating system instance. In this case, a fully disruptive event would mean that the operating system is not running, a semidisruptive event indicates an automatic reboot, and nondisruptive events do not cause an operating system restart, for the failure classes used in FRB. Robustness benchmarks developed based on this classification are not appropriate for evaluating systems with multiple operating systems, such as clusters or blade-style server farms. A higher-level perspective could be chosen for evaluating clusters; however, in such cases it can be trivial to attain high scores with relatively simple designs using unreliable components.

The scalar weight values of 1, 10, and 100 are intended to create a wider spread of results as we expect more systems to implement robustness techniques over time. These choices penalize semidisruptive techniques and favor nondisruptive techniques. Experience has shown that many computer systems designed for a particular market tend to score in a narrow range and this spreading technique more clearly exposes their differences. The benchmarks could be extended to include additional scalar weight values in the future.

Given the above failure effect classification, each component is assigned two scores: FR_i, which represents the scalar weight value for fault robustness for component i, and MR_i, which represents the scalar weight value for maintenance robustness for component i. Then, the FRB-A and MRB-A are calculated as follows:

$$\text{FRB-A} = \sum_{i=1}^{N} PFR_i \times FR_i$$

$$\text{MRB-A} = \sum_{i=1}^{N} PFR_i \times MR_i$$

where PFR_i is the percentage of failure rate for component i and N is the number of components in the system.

The FRB-A and MRB-A results will be a number between 1 and 100. To achieve a perfect score of 100, the system would have to cause no disruptions for any component failure (FRB-A) or replacement of any component (MRB-A). On the other hand, a fragile system with a score of 1 would cause a disruption for any failure or maintenance event. Most commercial computing systems are somewhere between these extremes.

Using the hypothetical example above, we might consider the effect of mirroring disks, dynamic reconfiguration (DR), and the self-healing feature CPU offlining. DR allows components to be attached or detached from a running system without causing fully disruptive outages. CPU offlining allows a processor to be dynamically removed from service without causing any disruption. Table 2.2 shows such an analysis. Note that this is a simplified view of system components. Most modern computer systems have dozens of field replaceable units (FRU), each of which may have different robustness characteristics.

TABLE 2.2. Example FRB-A and MRB-A scores

Components	Predicted failure rate (%)	FRB class scalar weight (FR_i)		MRB class scalar weight (MR_i)	
		Less robust	Mirroring, DR, CPU offlining	Less robust	Mirroring, DR, CPU offlining
Disks	10	1	100	1	100
Power supplies	15	100	100	100	100
CPU and memory boards	20	1	10	1	100
Others boards	20	1	1	1	1
Memory	25	10	100	1	100
Fans	5	100	100	100	100
Miscellaneous and cables	5	1	1	1	1
Score		FRB-A = 23.1	FRB-A = 57.25	MRB-A = 20.8	MRB-A = 75.3

The robustness of a system can be described by the fault (FRB-A) and maintenance (MRB-A) robustness benchmarks. These benchmarks can be used to evaluate the merits of robustness features. Both are needed to show robustness against failures and the repair of failed parts.

The results of FRB-A and MRB-A benchmarks on three selected system configurations are shown in Table 2.3. These results clearly show the system architecture differences among Sun Fire™ T1000, Sun Fire™ V490, and Sun Fire™ E25K servers.

The FRB-A scores are very similar, even though the number of redundant components is much greater on the E25K server. This is due to the scalar values assigned to the redundant components. Component failures that result in a semi-disruptive outage, such as automatic reboot, are assigned a scalar value of 10. In modern computing systems, many components fall into this category. It is expected that FRB-A scores near the theoretical maximum can only be achieved by fully fault-tolerant systems. Similarly, to build a system with no fault robustness is also unusual in the enterprise-server market. Robustness techniques such as error-correcting codes (ECC) for main memory are rewarded by the FRB-A benchmark and are standard for enterprise-class servers.

The MRB-A score shows the benefit of the E25K server design using hot pluggable components and dynamic reconfiguration. Components that are hot pluggable and dynamically reconfigurable are of the nondisruptive maintenance class. Almost all of the components in an E25K server fall into this category, and the MRB-A score is near the theoretical maximum for the benchmark. By contrast, the T1000 has an MRB-A score of 1. The T1000 MRB-A score is consistent with very small form factor and blade servers as physical size makes full hardware redundancy impractical and the service model considers redundancy at the server level, allowing servers to be considered as FRUs.

The E25K is designed such that nearly all components are redundant and can be replaced without causing an outage. This design decision is reflected in the robustness benchmark scores.

2.5. SERVICE COMPLEXITY BENCHMARK

In general, simple systems tend to be more dependable than complex systems. Analytical RAS benchmarks can describe the relative complexity of systems. The most useful of such benchmarks deal with interfaces between system components or the human/computer interface. For example, the internal complexity of a field replaceable unit (FRU) has less of an impact on the service complexity than its relationship to other FRUs in the system.

The Service Complexity Benchmark version A, SCB-A, has been developed to evaluate the mechanical service complexity of a system at the FRU level. The predicted failure

TABLE 2.3. Benchmark results

System	T1000	V490	E25K
CPU sockets	1	4	72
Memory (GBytes)	8 @ 1 GBytes	32 @ 1 GBytes	576 @ 1 GBytes
Disks	1 @ 80 GBytes	2 @ 73 GBytes	4 @ 73 GBytes
FRB-A	46.7	70.5	71.3
MRB-A	1	13.3	99.9

rates for each FRU are calculated and the removal complexity of servicing the FRU is measured.

This failure-rate-based weighting method used for FRB-A and MRB-A is also used for SCB-A, that is, the percentage of failure rate is used as a weight for each FRU. MRB-A and FRB-A may need to consider the failure rate of components that may or may not constitute FRU boundaries. This is because the effect of different failure modes in a FRU may be different, such as correctable errors and uncorrectable errors generated by different DIMM failure modes. Since SCB-A is concerned with actual service, it is reasonable to consider complexity at the FRU level rather than lower-level components.

Again, the overall failure rate of the system is unimportant for this benchmark. This weighting rewards systems for which the FRUs that are most likely to fail are also the FRUs that are easiest to service. FRUs that are difficult to service are not penalized unless they are also relatively more likely to fail than other FRUs.

Table 2.4 shows an example system with 14 component FRUs. This example shows the importance of weighting the FRUs based on their probability of failure. Some FRUs have few or zero active components and thus are considered highly reliable.

2.5.1. Removal Complexity

To measure the removal complexity of servicing a component FRU, the benchmark counts the number of fasteners, cable ends, and other components that must be removed in order to replace each component. The FRU itself is also counted.

- Other components or parts that will penalize systems that have components physically obstructed by other components are counted. Access covers or bezels are not counted, as that would unfairly penalize systems with protective coverings.
- Cable ends that will penalize systems that require many cables are counted. This will reward those systems that have few cables and whose components are easily pluggable.

TABLE 2.4. Example SCB-A failure rate weighting by FRU

Component	Failure rate (FITs)	Quantity	Subtotal (FITs)	PFR(%)
AC/DC	1000	2	2000	8.9
HDD	1250	2	2500	11.1
Floppy drive	1666	1	1666	7.4
CD/DVD	1666	1	1666	7.4
LED/media board	98	1	98	0.4
LED pass-thru board	2	1	2	0.0
Front display	118	1	118	0.5
Fans	333	8	2666	11.9
CPU/memory board	1838	4	7352	32.7
Memory DIMMs	206	16	3296	14.7
Front fan tray	0	1	0	0.0
SCSI riser board	92	1	92	0.4
Rear fan tray	0	1	0	0.0
Motherboard	1023	1	1023	4.6
Total			22480	100.0

- Fasteners include loose screws, clips, and zip ties. SCB-A does not count levers, captive screws, latches, release buttons, and so on. Only noncaptive fasteners are counted. This has the effect of penalizing those systems that have many loose fasteners and rewarding those systems that use levers or other captive fasteners.

Table 2.5 shows the removal complexity measurements for the same example system. It is obvious from the cable ends and fasteners counts that this system is designed such that most of the FRUs are pluggable and there are few loose cables. The only FRU that requires fasteners is the motherboard. Such modular systems tend to be simple to service.

2.5.2. SCB-A Score

We define SCB-A as follows:

$$SCB\text{-}A = \sum_{i=1}^{N} PFR_i \times RC_i$$

where RC_i is the removal complexity measure for FRU i as shown in the Total column in Table 2.5, PFR_i is the percentage of failure rate for component i, and N is the number of components in the system.

The SCB-A score indicates the serviceability complexity of a computer system. A low score indicates that a system is simple and a large score indicates that a system is complex. The minimum possible score is one, since we count the FRU being replaced. There is no mathematical maximum score, though in practice most computer systems have scores well below 100.

Table 2.6 shows the SCB-A scoring summary. A spreadsheet is used to conveniently automate the calculations.

2.5.3. Comparing Computer Systems Using SCB-A

When comparing computer systems, the detailed FRU information is not very useful. However, the weighted average of other components, cable ends, and fasteners can reveal

TABLE 2.5. Example removal complexity measurement

Component	Parts (FRU + other)	Cable ends	Fasteners	Total
AC/DC power supply	3	0	0	3
Hard disk drive	1	0	0	1
Fan tray 0	1	1	0	2
Fan tray 1	1	0	0	1
Memory (DIMMs)	3	0	0	3
CPU/memory board	1	0	0	1
PCI riser board	1	4	2	7
System controller	1	0	1	2
FC-AL backplane board	2	1	0	3
Center plane board	7	1	9	17
Power distribution board	12	5	15	32

TABLE 2.6. Example SCB-A scoring summary

| Component | Service measurements | | | System configuration | | Normalized average | | |
	Other parts	Cable ends	Fasteners	Qty.	PFR (%)	Other parts	Cable ends	Fasteners
AC/DC power supply	3	0	0	2	10.12	0.30	0.00	0.00
Hard disk drive	1	0	0	2	12.65	0.13	0.00	0.00
Fan tray 0	1	1	0	1	5.63	0.06	0.06	0.00
Fan tray 1	1	0	0	1	3.52	0.04	0.00	0.00
Memory (DIMMs)	3	0	0	32	33.35	1.00	0.00	0.00
CPU/memory board	1	0	0	2	25.54	0.26	0.00	0.00
PCI riser board	1	4	2	1	1.42	0.01	0.06	0.03
System controller	1	0	1	1	0.92	0.01	0.00	0.01
FC-AL backplane board	2	1	0	1	0.26	0.01	0.00	0.00
Center plane board	7	1	9	1	3.63	0.25	0.04	0.33
Power distribution board	12	5	15	1	2.97	0.36	0.15	0.45
Subtotals					100	2.42	0.30	0.81
SCB-A Score								3.53

the design decisions used. Knowledge of the design decisions may influence a comparison, especially for specific environments in which loose fasteners pose a safety risk or cable replacements are difficult due to limited dexterity constraints.

Figure 2.1 shows a SCB-A score comparison for six computer systems of similar size configurations. A lower SCB-A score is better. The stacked bars clearly show the design decisions made by the various manufacturers. All of the systems measured have some FRUs that are physically obscured by other FRUs. This is typical for this style of system. System 3 and System 4 have almost no loose fasteners. It is likely that these systems are very modular and make good use of levers and captive fasteners. System 2, System 4, and System 6 have a number of loose cables that need to be unplugged for servicing. System 1 is the system used in the examples above and has only two cables that connect to highly reliable components.

None of the systems shown in Figure 2.1 are "blade servers." A common characteristic of blade server designs is that there are no cables or fasteners. Each blade plugs into a chassis that provides infrastructure connectivity through a single connector. Blade server designs should score very well on the SCB-A benchmark.

2.6. CONCLUSION

Performance benchmarking uses many different benchmarks to describe system performance. The same technique can be used to evaluate the RAS characteristics of computer systems. Sun Microsystems has defined a methodology based on a set of analytical RAS benchmarks designed to characterize the rate of failures, robustness of design, and service complexity of computer systems. These benchmarks provide a means of comparing the

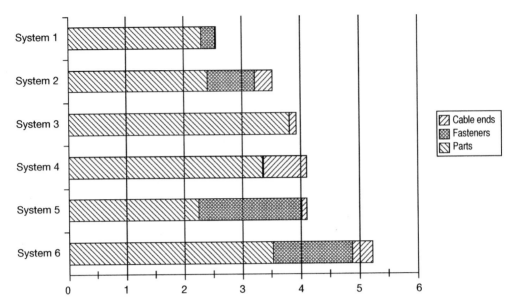

Figure 2.1. SCB-A comparison for six computer systems.

characteristics of large and small computing systems, quantification of areas for improvement, and insight into the design decisions that impact system RAS.

The percent-of-fault rate (PFR) for each component in the system is determined. This is used as a weighting factor to determine which components are more likely to fail than other components in a system. The overall failure rate is not used for these analytical benchmarks.

The Fault Robustness Benchmark version A, FRB-A, is used to evaluate the robustness techniques designed to reduce the effect of component failures from the perspective of an operating system platform. This benchmark rewards system designs in which the components most likely to fail are made redundant. Making relatively reliable components more redundant does not significantly improve the score. The FRB-A benchmark also rewards systems that allow the operating system to continue without causing a reboot. In practice, this tends to reward designs in which the operating system and hardware design work together to improve robustness.

The Maintenance Robustness Benchmark version A, MRB-A, is used to evaluate the effect of hardware maintenance activity from the perspective of an operating system platform. This benchmark rewards system designs in which the components most likely to fail are easily replaced without causing an outage. This benchmark rewards those systems that can be serviced while online, without causing a system outage.

The Service Complexity Benchmark version A, SCB-A, is used to evaluate the complexity of servicing components of computer systems. The SCB-A benchmark rewards systems in which the less-reliable components are easily replaced without requiring the removal of other components or fasteners, or disconnecting cables. The SCB-A benchmark does not penalize systems in which some highly reliable components may be more difficult to service. The goal of the SCB-A benchmark is to encourage computer system designers to build systems in which the component parts are easily serviced.

REFERENCES

[DBench] Dependability Benchmarking Project, European Union Information Society Technologies, http://www.laas.fr/DBench/.

[Mauro et al. 2003] James Mauro, Ji Zhu, and Ira Pramanick, "Robustness Benchmarking for Hardware Maintenance Events," in *Proceedings of the 2003 International Conference on Dependable Systems and Networks (DSN 03)*, San Francisco, pp. 115–122, 2003.

[Mauro et al. 2004] James Mauro, Ji Zhu, and Ira Pramanick, "The System Recovery Benchmark," in *IEEE Pacific Rim International Symposium on Dependable Computing (PRDC 04)*, Papeete, Tahiti, French Polynesia, pp. 271–280, 2004.

[MIL-STDS] U.S. Military Standard MIL-HDBK-217F, Reliability Prediction of Electronic Equipment, http://store.mil-standards.com/index.asp?PageAction=VIEWPROD&ProdID=13.

[Pramanick et al. 2003] Ira Pramanick, James Mauro, and Ji Zhu, "A System Recovery Benchmark for Clusters," in *IEEE International Conference on Cluster Computing (CLUSTER 03)*, Hong Kong, pp. 387–394, 2003.

[SPEC] Standard Performance Evaluation Corporation (SPEC), http://www.spec.org.

[Telcordia] Telcordia, SR-332, Reliability Prediction Procedure for Electronic Equipment, http://telecom-info.telcordia.com/site-cgi/ido/index.html.

[Zhu et al. 2002a] Ji Zhu, James Mauro, and Ira Pramanick, "R-Cubed: Rate, Robustness and Recovery—An Availability Benchmark Framework," Sun Microsystems Technical Report, TR-2002-109, September 2002, http://research.sun.com/techrep/2002/smli_tr-2002-109.pdf.

[Zhu et al. 2002b] Ji Zhu, James Mauro, and Ira Pramanick, "System Recovery Benchmarking—An Approach to Measuring System Recovery," in *Supplementary Proceedings of the Dependable Systems and Networks (DSN 02)*, Washington, DC, pp. 488–492, June 2002.

SYSTEM RECOVERY
BENCHMARKS

Richard Elling, Ira Pramanick, James Mauro,
William Bryson, and Dong Tang

3.1. INTRODUCTION

Benchmarking computer systems is an exercise in measurement, focused traditionally on providing a metric that describes performance in some meaningful way, either by the performance of a particular subsystem (processor, I/O) [SPEC] or by the system as a whole (TPC benchmarks) [TPC]. Such benchmarks are intended to provide a relatively objective set of data that can be used to compare systems from different vendors. Performance, however, is not the only attribute of a computer system that is evaluated in the selection process. System availability, or uptime, is often the more critical factor in choosing a platform. Assessing availability involves examining the features of the hardware and software designed to keep the system running, since an agreed-upon industry benchmark for measuring availability does not exist. The lack of such a benchmark continues to leave a gap in the evaluation process, and it is generally agreed throughout the industry that a method for benchmarking availability is needed.

In this chapter, we first describe System Recovery Benchmarks (SRBs), a generic framework for developing benchmarks that measure automated recovery, and two SRB implementations: SRB-A and SRB-X.

The System Recovery Benchmarks are complementary to the analytical Fault and Maintenance Robustness Benchmarks (FRB-A and MRB-A) and the Service Complexity Benchmark (SCB-A) as described in Chapter 2. The fundamental difference between these benchmarks is that the analytical benchmarks do not require the existence of an actual system, whereas the recovery benchmarks are measured on actual, running systems. The recovery benchmarks are measurement-based and characterize system behavior. In

Dependability Benchmarking for Computer Systems. Edited by Karama Kanoun and Lisa Spainhower
Copyright © 2008 IEEE Computer Society

this regard, the recovery benchmarks resemble the majority of performance benchmarks currently in use.

3.2. MOTIVATION AND BACKGROUND

Three key attributes that apply to system availability—*rate, robustness,* and *recovery*—are discussed in the R-Cubed (R^3) framework [Zhu et al. 2002a]. *Rate* is the number of fault and maintenance events that occur on a system over a given period of time. *Robustness* represents a system's ability to detect and handle faults, maintenance, and system-external events. *Recovery* is the speed with which a system returns to operation following an outage. Of these attributes, rate and robustness can be quantified using analytical methods [Mauro et al. 2003] and characterized under laboratory conditions, whereas recovery can be accurately measured under laboratory conditions.

In recent years, quality research has been done in the area of benchmarking availability. An early study evaluating the robustness of a system through fault injection was [Miller et al. 1990], which evaluated the behaviour of UNIX systems by passing invalid argument strings to various utilities. A similar characterization effort was described in [Dingman 1995] and [Koopman et al. 1997]. [Seiwiorek et al. 1993] extended the concept of a robustness benchmark with performance benchmarking. A robustness benchmark for Tandem fault-tolerant computers is described in [Tsai et al. 1996]. A common component of the described robustness benchmarks is the use of fault injection, which is extended to a faultload and workload model in [Madeira and Koopman 2001]. Several of these efforts were examined in [Mukherjee and Seiwiorek 1997], which described the desirable features of a system robustness benchmark and proposed a hierarchal approach to building a robustness benchmark. [Brown and Patterson 2000] measured robustness by examining the variations in system quality of service metrics over time. Whereas these studies examined the robustness of single systems, [Stott et al. 2000] looked at assessing the robustness of distributed systems.

The focus of this work has been system robustness—an important attribute of availability. In our SRB work, we focus on the recovery attribute. We consider the fact that general purpose computers implement rapid recovery designs that enable a system to often reboot to an operational level, albeit in a degraded state, following a fatal fault event. Typical designs implement automatic system recovery (ASR) to disable failed hardware yet allow the system to boot without requiring human intervention. More modern designs allow disabling faulty hardware without causing a reboot, which complements and extends ASR techniques. These rapid reboot and recovery mechanisms tend to execute the same sequence of steps and, thus, are both consistent and measurable. Predictability is important to mission-critical computing, and system recovery time is an important component of the overall availability picture. Thus, there is real value in quantifying recovery time. These assertions and the general need for advanced benchmarking availability features and capabilities provide sufficient justification for system recovery benchmarking.

3.3. OVERVIEW OF THE SRB FRAMEWORK

The SRB framework is designed to measure the recovery time of general purpose computing servers and clusters. Recovery, in this context, is the time required for a system to return to service following a system fault. The framework provides specific language describing a return to service, and the requirements for injected faults:

- Return to service means that the system is restored to a working, usable state.
- The return to service must be automatic and occur without human intervention.
- The fault must be fatal to the service.
- The fault must be detected automatically and immediately such that the recovery methods are invoked within seconds of the fault injection (e.g., modifying a kernel hot path that causes a system panic). A fault that results in a relatively gradual deterioration of the system will not meet SRB requirements.

For clustered systems, recovery and the return to service take on a somewhat different meaning. Clusters can provide multiple levels of service redundancy and a fatal condition may not result in a complete service disruption.

Each SRB benchmark specification details a method of measuring system startup, restart, and recovery events. A well-defined method of representing the results of the measurements is also given. It is a goal of the SRB framework that the specification and methodology be applicable to a broad range of computer systems, such that comparisons can be made across different platforms. Just as industry-standard performance benchmarks (TPC, SPEC) are used to compare the performance characteristics of different computer systems, the SRB results can be used to compare the recovery times and attributes of various systems.

3.3.1. System-Recovery Benchmarks

A typical production computer system can be viewed as having several layers; each layer has some level of dependency on the layers below. Table 3.1 shows the layering that has been adopted to drive specific SRBs and the name of the benchmark associated with each stack layer. The stack layers are defined, from the top down, as follows:

- *Cluster.*
- *Application.* The specific software components that exist at this layer will vary dramatically from system to system. For our purposes, the application layer is the software running on the system that provides a service and relies on the lower levels for services. If the system is using a database, the application may call on the database for data services. Other applications may call directly on the operating system (e.g., UNIX systems calls) for services. The startup and recovery of this layer is applica-

TABLE 3.1. System stack layers and benchmarks

System layer	Benchmark
Cluster	SRB-X
Application	SRB-D
Database or data service	SRB-C
Disk management (RAID)	SRB-B
Operating system	SRB-A
Hardware	SRB-A

tion-specific, but requires that the underlying services are also available to support startup and recovery processes.

- *Database.* Many systems implement a database as a persistent data service. The use of database systems in computing is ubiquitous and warrants inclusion in the SRB framework. Examples include relational database management systems such as the Oracle and DB2 databases. Data services may also be file services (e.g., QFS or NFS) or based on custom data management code. There are often variables that affect the recovery and startup of this layer, many of which are specific to the data service.

- *Disk Management.* This category includes host-based RAID software such as the Solaris™ Volume Manager software and so-called "hardware RAID" arrays. Again, there are many variables that affect the startup and recovery time of the logical management software. In fact, disk volume configuration can be a significant contributor to overall startup and recovery time.

- *Operating System.* This is the base operating system kernel running on the system. Thus far, we have defined only the general-purpose operating system. Virtual machines are a subset of the operating system as they do not represent an end-user service.

- *Hardware.* This refers to the hardware platform and its bootstrap support.

The context of the recovery—the state that represents the system providing a service—is determined by the layer on the system stack targeted for measurement. More succinctly, a specific SRB benchmark will be defined that targets measurements of a specific layer in the stack. However, not all of the layers described lend themselves to a benchmark specification. For example, an application layer benchmark specification that could apply to any arbitrary application is not possible. Developing a benchmark for the database and disk management layers offers some unique challenges as well.

The SRB benchmarks are being developed serially, starting with the SRB-A benchmark. SRB-A targets the operating system as providing the measured service. The SRB-X benchmark has also been defined. Additional work on the remaining benchmarks is under consideration.

3.4. SRB-A: SYSTEM-RECOVERY BENCHMARK FOR OPERATING SYSTEM AND HARDWARE

In this section, we will describe the implementation details of the SRB-A benchmark. The issues of formalizing a general benchmark specification that accommodates different system types and operating systems are noted. The specific items that will cause startup and recovery time to vary, how they are addressed, and the benchmark methodology and metrics are discussed.

Every benchmark, at its core, measures something, and the SRB-A is no different. SRB, in general, is concerned with measuring system outage duration, or the amount of elapsed time from fault injection until the system returns to a usable state. For SRB-A, a fatal fault is a fault that results in a reboot of the operating system. For consistent measurement, the nature of the injected fault is such that it is detected in a short period of time—less than one second. The fault is also such that the system will automatically reboot and achieve the usable state.

3.4.1. Defining a System

We tend to think of a computer system as a tightly integrated collection of processors, memory, and I/O managed by a single instance of an operating system (kernel). Traditionally, a single system was housed in a single cabinet, or several smaller systems were installed in a rack enclosure. In either case, the boundaries of the system were clearly defined and understood.

Modern computing systems have evolved such that the actual boundaries of what constitutes a system must be clearly delineated. There are three primary features found in systems today that complicate the system description: virtualization, dynamic system domains (DSD), and control consoles.

3.4.1.1. Virtualization. One of the more popular buzzwords in the computer industry today is virtualization. In effect, the old model of an OS running on a processor is no longer valid. Virtualization software is inserted between the hardware and the OS in order to allow multiple OSes to run on the same hardware concurrently. In essence, the virtualization software looks like hardware to the guest OS, and looks like an OS to the hardware.

Virtualization does impact the reboot time of many systems. For instance, during a guest OS reboot the power on self-test (POST) for the hardware is not required, as the virtualization software provides the view of the hardware to the OS. This should reduce the boot time for the OS, but adds the risk that the virtualization software contains defects or deficiencies—a likely scenario.

There are two popular methods for implementing virtualization: using a hypervisor and using a host OS. Hypervisors are special-purpose software designed to augment or replace the traditional bootstrap firmware. In many ways, we can consider the hypervisor to be simply a fancy version of traditional OpenBoot PROM (OBP) or Basic Input/Output Software (BIOS). A host OS implementation of the virtualization layer is very different. We consider a host/guest OS relationship to be more like the OS/application relationship. It is unclear at this time how best to accommodate these forms of virtualization in the SRB-A specification. In order to provide a clear link between SRB-A and the goal of measuring the time to recover from an OS-level fault, we may need to create a separate benchmark to handle the host/guest OS virtualization style.

3.4.1.2. Dynamic System Domains. We use the description of Sun Microsystem's Dynamic System Domains (DSD) to categorize the features provided by hardware vendors that are used to create multiple, independent hardware platforms which can then run independent OS images. This is different from virtualization in that there is no software layer between the OS and hardware. The OS has direct access to the hardware in the traditional sense, but the hardware can be changed dynamically—new processors, memory, or I/O may be added or removed from the running OS. Naturally, these dynamic changes must be accommodated by the OS and impact the reboot time, which varies based upon the hardware configuration of the domain during boot.

The SRB specifications will define a system as a single instance of the underlying OS (kernel) that provides the generic OS-level services. If a vendor chooses to measure the boot and recovery time of a domain, the system is defined as an instance of the kernel, and all of the underlying hardware that the kernel instance controls.

3.4.1.3. Control Consoles. Another feature commonly found on modern computers is a control console. Long ago, the control console for a computer system was a physically attached terminal device. This evolved into a keyboard and monitor for desktop computers and a serial port for servers. Today, servers often use a microprocessor-based system controller that provides a control console across a network transport. As the control console is an intelligent device, it has its own startup characteristics, which are independent of the system it is controlling. Additionally, it is necessary that the control console be operational prior to the main system bootstrap initiation. Such control consoles are found on both single- and multiple-domain systems, but are the control points for managing multiple domains.

For the purpose of these benchmarks, the assumption is made that the control console is in a state of readiness for all measurements, that is, the SRB-A benchmark will not include measuring of the boot or recovery time of the control console. This assertion will be explicitly stated in the specification. The rationale is simple—control consoles typically do not require rebooting or restarting in production environments. This also implies that the traditional notion of "cold boot" is not measured in the SRB-A benchmark.

3.4.2. Defining Recovery

As with any benchmark, the defined state of what is being measured must be clear and precise. The goal of system recovery benchmarks is to measure the time required to recover. Mauro and coworkers [2004] use the default multiuser state, init level 3, for the Solaris™ Operating System as the measurement mark for system services. However, this init level does not work for the Solaris™ 10 Operating System, which does not use the SVR4 notion of init levels. Also, some Linux distributions and other operating systems use other methods to start services at boot time. In order to provide a consistent indicator of an operating system being ready for service, we use the log-in prompt readiness as the indication that the system is up and ready for users to log in. This works well for all multiuser operating systems, as well as modern, single-user desktop operating systems such as Mac OSX and Microsoft Windows XP. The measurement is simply the time between fault injection and log-in prompt ready.

3.4.3. SRB-A Measurements.

The SRB-A benchmark measures two system events on a standalone system:

1. Clean system reboot: operator-initiated shutdown and automatic boot.
2. Unclean system reboot: a fatal fault injected, followed by automatic boot.

The decision to measure these events is based on the observation of live production systems and an analysis of metrics that would be both useful and meaningful. The measurement of a clean system reboot provides a baseline metric that is useful when compared to the recovery measurements. Since a system shutdown results in system services transitioning from an available to unavailable state, and thus is a factor in the downtime duration for a clean shutdown/reboot event, the shutdown time is included in the metric.

The unclean reboot test involves injecting a fault into the system under test, which will result in an unclean kernel exit, and measuring the elapsed time until the system is ready for log in. Many operating systems have a method for inducing unclean shutdown from a user. For example, in the Solaris Operating System, the uadmin(1m) command can be used to call the kernel's panic() function, which initiates an unclean kernel shutdown.

Other operating systems have similar kernel functions that can be called via utilities or, in the worst case, by programs specifically written for the purpose.

Measuring both clean and unclean reboot time also has the effect of driving optimization for the entire shutdown and reboot process. Some techniques that may improve booting may require storing the state to persistent storage. This would normally be part of the clean shutdown process. By causing an unclean shutdown, these techniques will be forced to enter a state reconciliation process that will likely consume time and, therefore, negatively impact the benchmark score. To achieve a good score, the operating system and hardware designers must work together to reduce the recovery time.

3.4.4. Variables Impacting Recovery

There are several factors that impact the amount of time required for a system to boot. The primary factors that affect the SRB-A measurements are:

- System size
- Bootstrap software or firmware and diagnostics settings
- Operating system startup procedures
- File system initialization

To meet the goal of being able to compare widely varying computer systems, these factors must be addressed.

3.4.4.1. System Size. The system size has a direct and potentially linear affect on system startup and recovery time. The system size components are:

- Number of processors that can run OS services. Many systems today use multiprocessor hardware, including large symmetrical multiprocessor (SMP) systems as well as dual-core laptops. The number of physical processors does not seem to impact the SRB-A measurements. However, the number of processors, virtual or physical, that can be scheduled by the OS to run services does impact the initialization time of both the OS and the collection of services running on the OS.
- Amount of physical memory. System memory testing and initialization tends to scale linearly with the amount of physical memory on the system.
- Number of I/O channels. I/O interfaces vary somewhat across computer platforms, so a generic term, I/O channels, is used to describe the scale of the I/O subsystem. This may require further refinement as we develop the SRB-A benchmark.
- Number of disk logical units (LUNs). Experience, observations, and measurements have shown that the scale of the storage subsystem impacts the system initialization and recovery time. During boot, each LUN must be probed to determine if it contains data that must be recovered or brought online to support system services. The probe, recovery, and initialization time can impact overall boot time. Writing cached data and cleanly closing LUNs can impact the clean shutdown time.

The current method of addressing the system size factor in the SRB-A benchmark is by use of a scale factor, discussed in Section 4.7.1.

3.4.4.2. Firmware Settings. Modern computing systems implement firmware that is executed when the system is booted and prior to starting the operating system. In general, the firmware runs diagnostics, initialization, and loads the operating system image into memory for execution. It is common for this firmware to have options that change the diagnostics level or initialization methods for the hardware. For example, the Sun Fire™ servers have diagnostics options for minimum or maximum diagnostics testing, often with several intermediate levels of tests.

In order to address these potential variances, and in the interest of keeping the benchmark simple, the specification will state simply that the benchmark should run with the factory default settings of the systems firmware tunable parameters. More precisely, the values used for testing should be the same values used when system installation and verification is completed at a customer site. The benchmark report will include the list of possible parameters and their settings.

3.4.4.3. Operating System Startup Parameters. In some cases, it is necessary or desirable to set operating system variables to adjust the resources used by the operating system or the services started at boot time. These settings can affect the system boot time as resources are allocated and initialized, and as services are started. It is not feasible to define all of the possible iterations of systems parameters in the benchmark. Thus, we take an approach similar to that with the firmware settings. The SRB-A benchmark will be measured using the default operating system startup parameters as shipped from the factory. In the case in which the operating system is not installed in the factory, and is installed at a customer site, the default parameters for a full operating system installation are used. The benchmark report will include the list of parameters and installed services.

3.4.4.4. Logical Units and File Systems. File system integrity is vital to the availability and correctness of modern computer systems. A facility for verifying and, if needed, repairing file systems exists to help ensure correctness. For example, the `fsck_ufs(1m)` program in the Solaris Operating System is responsible for verifying and repairing damage to the UNIX file system (UFS) that is used as the default file system containing the bootable operating system when booting from a local disk. This verification and repair can significantly impact boot time, and improvements were made as disks grew and file system checking began to dominate boot time. In general, the file system checking process is impacted by a number of variables:

- The number of file systems.
- The size of the file systems.
- The extent of potential damage and the techniques used to minimize damage. For example, metadata logging was implemented to reduce the time required to verify and repair file system structures. This reduces the extent of potential damage to the file system.
- The I/O performance of the LUNs.

The bad news is that these factors vary wildly from system to system and incident to incident, making generic benchmarking of this component of the boot time difficult. To account for this, multiple benchmark runs will be conducted and statistical methods will be used to identify the mean recovery time and variance.

The specification will also state that all of the file systems required to accommodate an end-user login will be mounted at boot time. For example, some Sun customers use separate root (/) and varying files (/var) file systems. If the system being benchmarked has these separate file systems, then both must be mounted to complete the requirements for the benchmark.

3.4.5. Workload Dependency

The next consideration is workload, and what workload the system should be under, if any, when the fault is injected. Does a system running a heavy workload generate different SRB-A results than an idle system? If yes, does varying the workload also vary results? If yes, then what workload should be defined in the benchmark specification?

The workload dependency on recovery has a direct correlation to the system layers being measured. For example, if the measurement includes the recovery of a database, the workload will have a significant impact on the recovery. This is generally true for a measurement that includes the upper stack layers: disk management, data service, or application. However, for the lower system layers that are measured by SRB-A, our experience and testing has shown that recovery time does not significantly vary between a loaded and idle system.

The underlying reasons for the lack of significant variance between the recovery of an idle versus loaded system can be explained by considering what constitutes a busy system and what occurs during the reboot process. We will describe a busy system as one in which all of the hardware subsystems are doing work—processors are executing threads and the main and virtual memory system, network traffic, and disk I/O are actively used. The kernel does not actively attempt to save state to persistent storage, aside from file system writes done on behalf of the workload. The SRB-A benchmark measures the hardware and kernel layers and not the application-specific layers. When the fault is injected, the system enters an error-handling routine, such as the UNIX `panic()` function, and the workload stops. Restarting the hardware and OS layers to a usable state does not involve restarting the workload. Thus, the kernel does not reload and restore the state of the workload.

We have performed experiments using a TPC-C-like workload. This workload causes significant CPU, memory, network, and disk utilization. The variance on recovery time between the idle system and the system running the database workload varied by less than 1%. The idle system recovered in 724 seconds, versus 732 seconds for the loaded condition.

For the SRB-A benchmark, the fault injection during an idle workload is chosen.

3.4.6. Running the SRB-A Benchmark

SRB-A measurements are simple and can be made using a stopwatch. Indeed, this method may be the best way for a neutral party to run the benchmark. However, the stopwatch method is not sufficient to drive product improvement, nor does it lend itself to multiunit testing as is often found in companies that develop operating system software. Mauro and coworkers [2004] refer to automation efforts using `logger(1)` to identify milestones during the test process. Currently at Sun Microsystems, we use a set of Dtrace [Dtrace] scripts to record high resolution time and event identification. The Dtrace collectors also show what processes are active, the resource utilization, and the duration of the process life. This detailed information has resulted in identifying areas of improvement at the operating system level. Identifying opportunities for improvement at the firmware level remains for future work.

3.4.7. SRB-A Results Metrics

Benchmark results should be meaningful, easy to understand, and unambiguous. Also, the SRB-A metric must represent the size of the benchmarked system. It is desirable to have the result represented as a single numeric value, as opposed to a result and a separate value representing system size. Given these goals of simplicity and fairness, the SRB-A specification will define the method for calculating the scale factor, and the use of the scale factor in calculating the benchmark result.

3.4.7.1. Scale Factor. A scale factor is used to represent the size of the system under test. It is calculated using an algebraic formula with these variables:

- C = number of virtual processors
- M = size of physical main memory in gigabytes
- I = number of I/O channels
- D = number of attached disk LUNs

Each variable is multiplied by a weighting factor and summed to derive the scale factor. The weighting factors are based on our experience in measuring system boot and recovery time for a wide variety of computer systems [Mauro et al. 2004]. We tested systems with 8, 24, and 64 processors; memory sizes of 24, 196, and 512 GBytes; and the number of attached disk LUNs ranging from 500–1,000. This testing used instrumented start scripts and the code with facilitated profiling to determine where the time was spent during the boot and recovery process. The data and preliminary models from this work are shown in Table 3.2.

The scale factor is derived as

$$SF = 0.1C + 0.4M + 0.05I + 0.45D$$

For example, a system with 24 virtual processors, 196 GBytes of memory, 8 I/O channels, and 540 attached disk LUNs would have a scale factor of

$$SF = (0.1 \cdot 24) + (0.4 \cdot 196) + (0.05 \cdot 8) + (0.45 \cdot 540)$$

$$SF = 2.4 + 78.4 + 0.4 + 243$$

$$SF = 324.2$$

TABLE 3.2. SRB-A scale factor weights

Variable	Weight	Description
C	0.1	Number of virtual processors
M	0.4	Amount of memory
I	0.05	Number of I/O channels
D	0.45	Number of attached disk LUNs

3.4.7.2. Calculating the SRB-A Score. The SRB-A score is calculated as

$$\text{SRB-A} = \frac{SF}{(T_{\text{cleanboot}} + T_{\text{uncleanboot}})}$$

where $T_{\text{cleanboot}}$ is the time in minutes measured for the clean shutdown and boot, and $T_{\text{uncleanboot}}$ is the time in minutes measured for the unclean shutdown and boot. For the example system described, the $T_{\text{cleanboot}}$ was measured as 16.25 minutes and the $T_{\text{uncleanboot}}$ was 20.47 minutes. Thus, the SRB-A score is calculated as

$$\text{SRB-A} = \frac{324.2}{(16.25 + 20.47)}$$

$$\text{SRB-A} = 8.83$$

The SRB-A score has the property that bigger scores are better. You can achieve a bigger score by increasing the size of the system or decreasing the recovery time.

3.4.7.3. Caveat Emptor. As of the time of this writing, we have not been able to demonstrate that the scale factor applies to a large population of machines. The work presented in [Mauro et al. 2004] focused on a specific family of Sun servers running the same OS version. Subsequent tests on other hardware platforms and operating systems have raised questions about the weighting factors as empirically derived. This is an area for continued work. Regardless of the scale factor calculation, improving the clean and unclean reboot time is valuable to reduce the operating system recovery time.

3.5. SRB-X: SYSTEM RECOVERY BENCHMARK FOR CLUSTERS

The System Recovery Benchmark for Clusters, SRB-X, is designed to measure the recovery time for failure modes that are specific to multinode clusters. The SRB-X benchmark is currently in development and being refined. This section describes the benchmark and its design philosophy.

3.5.1. Cluster Definitions

A typical cluster consists of several computers that are referred to as *nodes* in this chapter. These nodes are connected together and share resources to provide highly available services. Each node runs its own operating system. A *service* in a cluster is typically configured to be potentially hosted on one or more nodes in the cluster, to render the service highly available (HA) in the case of node failure. The service can be implemented as either a *failover service* or a *scalable service*. A failover service is actively hosted on a single node at any given time. A scalable service may be actively hosted on multiple nodes simultaneously.

HA clusters can be broadly categorized into two different classes: enterprise clusters and telecommunications clusters. Enterprise clusters, sometimes called data center clusters, typically share data and provide a single view of the data to all clients. Enterprise clusters have stringent guarantees ensuring preservation and correctness of the data. Telecommunications clusters often do not share data, though the data may be replicated. These two classes of clusters have different recovery criteria and, thus, are difficult to compare directly. The SRB-X benchmark is intended for enterprise clusters for which a single, consistent view of shared data is required and, therefore, the data may need to be validated and corrected during the fault recovery process. Highly available data and data integrity are requirements for the clustered service.

3.5.2. Cluster Layers

Figure 3.1 shows the various layers in a typical enterprise cluster stack. The blocks represent logical layers, with some mapping to physical hardware. Starting from the bottom of the stack, each node in the cluster has both shared and nonshared hardware. The shared hardware is typically persistent storage, usually disks. Each node runs its own operating system, which must be capable of managing both the shared and nonshared hardware. The cluster framework is distributed across all of the nodes in the cluster and controls the configuration of the hardware via the operating systems. The cluster framework provides a unified view of the hardware resources upon which an application-specific cluster service is implemented. The application views the clustered service as providing a consistent platform regardless of faults in the underlying layers.

The SRB-X benchmark measures recovery at the cluster framework layer. The recovery of the application and clustered service depends upon the actions taken by the cluster framework when faults occur. Recovery at the cluster framework layer includes both the shared and nonshared hardware, as well as the operating system and any logical volume management system. Also, it is the cluster framework layer that manages the view of the shared hardware to the upper layers, so it makes sense to understand and benchmark the cluster framework layer. Clustered, application-specific benchmarks may be developed later.

3.5.3. Cluster Outage Modes

The outage modes in a cluster fall into two broad categories: unplanned and planned. Unplanned outages are caused by failures in one or more of the components in the stack.

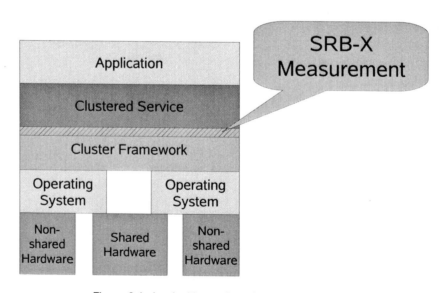

Figure 3.1. Logical layers in a data center cluster.

Planned outages are initiated by administrative action. For an HA cluster, an outage may lead the cluster framework to initiate a *failover* to allow the application to be recovered on another node. An outage may also cause the cluster framework to *reconfigure* the cluster. For example, a faulted node will cause the cluster framework to reconfigure itself such that the node resources are no longer available and shared hardware that was owned by the node has its ownership changed to a surviving node. Similarly, adding a node back into the cluster, usually a planned activity, results in a cluster reconfiguration as the cluster framework recognizes the node and manages its access by the clustered services.

Common outage modes include:

- *Switchover*—a planned action where an application is moved from one node to another. In most cases, the application is brought down in an orderly manner and the application is restarted without requiring data recovery.
- *Failover*—an unplanned action by which an application is moved from one node to another. Since this is an unplanned action, the application may need to recover data.
- *Cluster reboot*—the entire cluster is rebooted.
- *Node shutdown*—a single node is shut down and the cluster is reconfigured.
- *Node rejoin*—a node that was down is brought up and rejoins the operational cluster.
- *Cluster partitioning*—a fault occurs that splits the cluster into two or more subclusters. Such splits are undesirable because they risk corruption of the shared data. The Sun Cluster™ framework will ensure that only one cluster exists at any given time, thus protecting access to the shared data.
- *Application failure*—the application supported by the clustered service fails. Such failures may or may not require a cluster reconfiguration.

SRB-X will measure the system outage when a cluster node fails, resulting in a cluster reconfiguration. This outage is referred to as a *cluster reconfiguration outage.* The other outage modes are possible candidates for other SRB cluster benchmarks. The cluster reconfiguration outage applies to both failover and scalable services. For failover services, the node hosting the application is faulted and the failover process is used to restart the application on another node. The failover service suffers an outage during this process. Scalable services, although simultaneously hosted by more than one node in a cluster, also suffer a potential outage when an active node is faulted, as the remaining nodes must reconfigure.

The fault that is injected to cause a failover is referred to as an *outage trigger.* SRB-X measures the duration of an outage when an active node goes down. This outage is referred to as a cluster reconfiguration outage.

3.5.4. SRB-X Recovery Measurement

A service is considered to have recovered if the system is restored to a working, usable state and the service is operational. Since SRB-X is focused on enterprise clusters, it follows that the definition of recovery must be done in the context of a service that accesses shared data. The access to be measured is a write operation that will eliminate accesses that may be potentially cached in a node. This write operation must be initiated by a client external to the cluster. This client should be connected to the cluster via a dedicated network. Figure 3.2 shows a logical view of the cluster under test and the client.

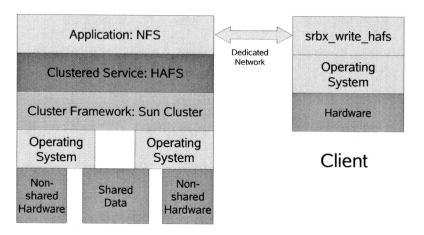

Figure 3.2. Logical view of SRB-X measurement setup

The write operation should be executed in a loop, with a fixed, small time period, such that a write is initiated just before the outage trigger injection. The write command issued by the client is referred to as srbx_write_hafs in the remainder of this chapter.

The HA data service being measured should be minimal in size and represent a file service, such as the Network File System (NFS). This minimal data service is referred to as the highly available file system (HAFS). The rationale for this is that SRB-X aims to measure cluster framework recovery and not clustered file system recovery. Thus, a minimal file service is suitable. If it is desired to measure the file service itself, then a different SRB is more appropriate. The minimal file service is used by SRB-X to measure the framework recovery as a means of establishing the readiness of the cluster framework. After an SRB-X outage trigger, the completion of a write request by the file service indicates that the minimal service is up. This in turn, indicates that the cluster framework has completed its reconfiguration steps needed to host the clustered service.

The HA nature of the HAFS necessarily implies that the file system data is shared by nodes in the cluster. However, it does not specify the actual implementation of the service. For example, some clusters may provide a global file system implementation whereby any or all nodes of the cluster may share concurrent, direct access to the shared storage. Other clusters may allow read access by many nodes but write access by only one node. Other clusters may require that all read and write access to shared storage is managed by only one node. Each of these implementation styles has merit, and SRB-X may be useful in determining their recovery characteristics.

For SRB-X, the cluster is considered to be recovered after the injection of the outage trigger, when the srbx_write_hafs command completes. This write must be issued against a file system residing on shared storage in the cluster.

3.5.5. Reconfiguration Outage Triggers

The reconfiguration outage trigger should result in an immediate node outage, as opposed to a gradual deterioration in service delivery. A trigger that is generally available on all platforms and satisfies this requirement is to switch off power to the node servicing the client's srbx_write_hafs commands. Software outage triggers also exist that can be generically applied across many platforms, such as the UNIX kernel panic() function.

The reconfiguration outage trigger may cause a node to go down abruptly. However, this node outage may not cause the cluster framework to immediately begin reconfiguration. This node outage must be detected by the surviving nodes prior to initiating the cluster reconfiguration. This detection is a key component of the automatic recovery capabilities of a cluster, and different clustering solutions have different detection algorithms and policies. Thus, detection of an outage trigger needs to be measured by the SRB-X benchmark. In the case in which detection algorithms are tunable, the default values should be used. The appropriate configuration parameter settings are included in the benchmark report.

3.5.6. Cluster Configuration Details

The configuration of a cluster can vary significantly based on the service level or business requirements. This section lists some cluster configuration details and the policy that SRB-X uses to help ensure that SRB-X results can be relevantly compared.

3.5.6.1. Number of Cluster Nodes.
A typical number of nodes in an enterprise cluster is two, although single-node clusters exist and some cluster frameworks allow dozens of nodes. We believe that the number of nodes in a cluster impacts the reconfiguration time of the cluster and may be proportional to the number of nodes. SRB-X should not restrict the number of nodes and the results from clusters with different numbers of nodes should not be directly compared. The SRB-X policy is that comparisons of SRB-X results should only be made for those clusters with the same number of nodes.

3.5.6.2. Node Size and Type.
Many cluster frameworks support multiple node sizes and types. For example, the Sun Cluster™ software allows a cluster to contain nodes with a single processor along with multiprocessor nodes. The lowest common denominator is that all nodes are of the same size and type. By specifying that SRB-X clusters have nodes that are the same size and type, we can eliminate any dependency of the recovery due to size or type dependencies. Also, it seems common for customers to implement clusters using nodes of the same size and type.

3.5.6.3. Shared Hardware.
Enterprise clusters often share disk storage and network infrastructure. Cluster recovery is dependent on the shared hardware. It is not desirable to define the benchmark such that it must account for all of the possible combinations of shared hardware components available. To help keep the benchmark simple, SRB-X will require the minimum configuration of shared hardware needed to provide the HAFS service to a networked client.

3.5.7. Variables Impacting SRB-X Recovery

SRB-X measures the outage duration experienced by a client-initiated write command on an HAFS service. The main components of a reconfiguration outage as milestones are shown in Figure 3.3. In this example, the cluster node hosting the active HAFS service will be shut down as a result of the outage trigger. The outage trigger starts the measurement, and a successful write by the client completes the measurement.

The measured outage time can be decomposed into a generic set of processes. The outage detection time is the process for ensuring the health of the cluster nodes, often implemented using heartbeat messages. The surviving nodes must agree that the down node is

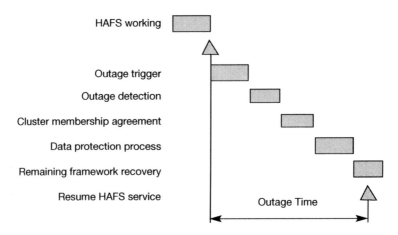

Figure 3.3. SRB-X measurement timeline.

really down, and what the new cluster membership and configuration will be. The data protection process ensures that only the surviving nodes have access to the shared data. Next, the shared data and logical network addresses must be moved to the surviving node, which will host the HAFS service along with any other remaining framework recovery procedures. Once the framework recovery is complete, the HAFS service can resume. Shortly thereafter, the client write operation will complete successfully. Most of these processes have tunable parameters that affect their completion times. The SRB-X benchmark requires that these variables be set to their default value and that the values be described in the benchmark report.

3.5.8. Client Workload

Empirically, the SRB-X measurements are impacted by the workload on the HAFS service. For simplicity, during the SRB-X measurements, no other services should be running on the cluster. The HAFS workload can be varied by adding clients. Real-world clusters would likely be subjected to the load of many clients. We have decided to take both a no-load measurement and a loaded measurement to represent the optimal case and a more typical case. The no-load measurement uses a single client issuing `srbx_write_hafs` commands. The loaded measurement should use a known, standard file system benchmark-load generator such as that used by the SPECsfs benchmark. A statistically significant number of benchmark runs are executed and the mean time is used to calculate the SRB-X score.

3.5.9. SRB-X Score

It is desirable to have the SRB-X score represented as a single number where higher numbers indicate improved recovery times. In other words, the score is inversely proportional to the measured recovery time. The proposed SRB-X score calculation is:

$$\text{SFB-X} = \frac{3600}{(T_{\text{noload}} + T_{\text{load}})}$$

where T_{noload} is the mean time in seconds for the tests with only a single client and a single workload stream, and T_{load} is the mean time in seconds for the tests with multiple client workloads. The numerator is the value of one hour in seconds. The recovery times tend to be on the order of tens of seconds, and using 3600 seconds as the numerator results in scores that have a value greater than one. This provides scores in a range that are easy to communicate and compare. This method also has the benefit that if a system reduces its recovery time by half, the score will double.

The rationale for taking the average of the recovery times from the synthetic loads, T_{load}, and then adding that directly to T_{noload} instead of taking the average across all the synthetic loads and no-load cases, is as follows. The no-load run represents a baseline value, and should be given the same weight as an average synthetic load scenario. An average across all runs, including the no-load and syn-load ones, would give a larger weight to the synthetic load scenarios, depending on the number of such scenarios in the specification. Taking the average across the synthetic load runs, and then adding that to the no-load run value gives equal weight to the no-load and synthetic load scenarios.

Clearly, this choice of score calculation is a point of contention for benchmark development. The behavior we wish to drive with the benchmark is improvement of cluster framework recovery time. Any measured improvements will result in a better (larger) score and, thus, the score will drive the desired improvements. Other mathematical calculations could be used, and we are open to discussion on this topic.

Using artificial cluster examples, we can calculate the scores and compare the results. Table 3.3 shows the results.

In this example, cluster A is clearly superior to clusters B and C. The no-load time of cluster C is better than cluster A, but the loaded time is worse. This may be explained by the capacity differences between the cluster nodes. We do not wish to reward those systems that are not properly sized to handle the workload, and this is reflected in the contribution of the loaded recovery time to the score.

3.6. SUMMARY AND FUTURE WORK

In this chapter, we have described a family of recovery benchmarks that measure the time for a system to recover from an injected fault. To date, two benchmarks have matured to the point of being useful for product design and improvement. The SRB-A benchmark measures the recovery time of an operating system and hardware for a clean and unclean reboot event. The SRB-X benchmark measures the recovery time of a enterprise cluster framework when an active node of the cluster is abruptly shutdown.

The benchmarks described here are still in the development stage. However, we have been using these benchmarks at Sun Microsystems to drive product improvement for suc-

TABLE 3.3. Example SRB-X scores

Cluster	T_{noload} (seconds)	T_{load} (seconds)	SRB-X Score
A	65	90	23.2
B	90	140	15.7
C	45	140	19.5

cessive generations of products. SRB-A is used to drive reduction in the boot time for the Solaris Operating System and the SRB-X benchmark is used to drive reduction in the recovery time for the Sun Cluster software. Since these benchmarks actually test multiple layers of a solution stack, we use them to drive improvements in other Sun products, such as hardware and logical volume management. We believe in the usefulness of these benchmarks and welcome efforts to spread their use.

REFERENCES

[Brown and Patterson 2000] A. Brown and D. A. Patterson, "Towards Availability Benchmarks: A Case Study of Software RAID Systems," presented at USENIX 2000.

[DBench] Dependability Benchmarking Project, European Union Information Society Technologies, http://www.laas.fr/DBench/.

[Dtrace] Solaris Dynamic Tracing Guide, http://docs.sun.com/app/docs/doc/817-6223.

[Dingman et al. 1995] C. Dingman, "Measuring Robustness of a Fault Tolerant Aerospace System," in *Proceedings of the 25th International Symposium on Fault-Tolerant Computing*, pp. 522–527, June 1995.

[Koopman et al. 1997] P. Koopman, C. Dingman, D. Siewiorek, and T. Mart, "Comparing Operating Systems Using Robust Benchmarks," in *Proceedings of the 16th Symposium on Reliable Distributed Systems*, pp. 72–79, October 1997.

[Madeira and Koopman 2001] H. Madeira and P. Koopman, "Dependability Benchmarking: Making Choices is an N-Dimensional Problem Space," in *Proceedings of the First Workshop on Evaluating and Architecting System Dependency*, Göteborg, Sweden, 2001.

[Mauro et al. 2003] James Mauro, Ji Zhu, and Ira Pramanick, "Robustness Benchmarking for Hardware Maintenance Events," in *Proceedings of the 2003 International Conference on Dependable Systems and Networks (DSN 03)*, San Francisco, pp. 115–122, 2003.

[Mauro et al. 2004] James Mauro, Ji Zhu, and Ira Pramanick, "The System Recovery Benchmark," presented at IEEE Pacific Rim International Symposium on Dependable Computing (PRDC 04), Papeete, Tahiti, French Polynesia, pp. 271–280, 2004.

[Miller et al. 1990] B. Miller, L. Fredriksen, and B. So, "An Empirical Study of Reliability of UNIX Utilities," *Communications of the ACM*, vol. 33, no. 12. pp. 32–43, December 1990.

[Mukherjee and Seiwiorek 1997] A. Mukherjee and D. P. Siewiorek, "Measuring Software Dependability by Robustness Benchmarking," *IEEE Transactions on Software Engineering*, vol. 23, no. 6, June 1997.

[Pramanick et al. 2003] Ira Pramanick, James Mauro, and Ji Zhu, "A System Recovery Benchmark for Clusters," presented at IEEE International Conference on Cluster Computing (CLUSTER 03), Hong Kong, pp. 387–394, 2003.

[Seiwiorek et al. 1993] D. P. Seiwiorek, J. Hudak, B. Suh, and F. Segal, "Development of a Benchmark to Measure System Robustness," in *Proceedings of the 1993 International Symposium on Fault-Tolerant Computing*, pp. 88–97, Toulouse, France, June 1993.

[SPEC] Standard Performance Evaluation Corporation (SPEC), http://www.spec.org.

[Stott et al. 2000] D. T. Stott et al., "NFTAPE: A Framework for Assessing Dependability in Distributed Systems with Lightweight Fault Injectors," in *Proceedings of the IEEE International Computer Performance and Dependability Symposium*, pp. 91–100, March 2000.

[Tsai et al. 1996] T. Tsai, R. K. Iyer, and D. Jewitt, "An Approach Towards Benchmarking of Fault Tolerant Commercial Systems," in *Proceedings of the 1996 Symposium on Fault-Tolerant Computing*, pp. 314–323, Sendai, Japan, June 1996.

[Zhu et al. 2002a] Ji Zhu, James Mauro, and Ira Pramanick, "R-Cubed: Rate, Robustness and Recovery—An Availability Benchmark Framework," Sun Microsystems Technical Report, TR-2002-109, September 2002, http://research.sun.com/techrep/2002/smli_tr-2002-109.pdf,

[Zhu et al. 2002b] Ji Zhu, James Mauro, and Ira Pramanick, "System Recovery Benchmarking—An Approach to Measuring System Recovery," in *Supplementary Proceedings of the Dependable Systems and Networks Conference (DSN 02),* Washington, DC, pp. 488–492, June 2002.

DEPENDABILITY BENCHMARKING USING ENVIRONMENTAL TEST TOOLS

Cristian Constantinescu

4.1. INTRODUCTION

The need for high computer dependability has increased as constantly larger numbers of users rely on the correct operation of these devices. However, cost considerations have led to the wide use of commercial-off-the-shelf (COTS) components, even in the case of business- and life-critical applications. Under these circumstances, both manufacturers and users need to measure and compare dependability of different competing products.

R. C. Camp defines benchmarking as the "process of measuring products, services and practices against the toughest competitors" [Camp 1989]. Experience has shown that devising suitable tools for measuring computer dependability is far from trivial. Fault injection experiments are among the most notable efforts for dependability benchmarking. Commonly, fault injection relies on simulation [Berrojo et al. 2002; Constantinescu 2003; Folkesson 1998; Kim and Somani 2002], software [Ademaj et al. 2002; Aidemark et al. 2001; Carreira et al. 1998; Scott et al. 1998; Durães and Madeira, 2002], and hardware [Constantinescu 2000; Constantinescu 2003; Madeira et al. 1994; Martínez et al. 1999] techniques. Power disturbances were used for the injection of transient faults, as shown in [Karlsson et al. 1991; Wagner and McCluskey 1985]. Scan-chain implementation [Folkesson 1998] and laser fault injection [Samson et al. 1998] have been also successful. An extensive analysis of fault injection techniques is available in [Arlat et al. 2003]. However, in-depth knowledge of the tested system is usually required for effectively using fault injection as a benchmarking tool. As a result, these techniques are more feasible for developers and manufacturers.

The content of this chapter was presented at the IEEE Annual Reliability and Maintainability Symposium, [Constantinescu 2005].

Another important aspect that has to be taken into consideration when addressing benchmarking is the impact of technology on dependability. The semiconductor industry has evolved at a very rapid pace over the last decades. The International Technology Roadmap for Semiconductors (ITRS) predicts significant improvements for all major types of integrated circuits [ITRS 2003]. For instance, by 2018, microprocessor unit (MPU) physical gate length will be as low as 7 nm, the voltage will drop to 0.5 V, and the clock frequency will approach 30,000 MHz. These impressive technological gains have led to improved performance and, at the same time, increased likelihood of occurrence of intermittent and transient faults [Constantinescu 2002; Hareland et al. 2001; Shivakumar et al. 2002; Stathis 2001]. Last but not least, physical and simulated fault injection proved that transients and intermittents, in particular, are capable of inducing undetected computational errors or corrupt memory stored information [Constantinescu 2000; 2003]. These undetected errors are commonly referred to as silent data corruption (SDC).

The benchmarking approach presented herein employs environmental test tools. Systems under evaluation execute the Linpack benchmark, which is capable of detecting numerical errors such as silent corruption of the data. First, a temperature and voltage operating test, also referred to as the four corners test, is used for evaluating ten prototype systems. Second, an electrostatic discharge (ESD) test is carried out on four servers, produced by two manufacturers.

The chapter is organized as follows. Section 4.2 shows that SDC is a real threat to dependability, as proved by error data collected from production servers, failure analysis results, and physical and simulated fault injection. Section 4.3 describes the four corners test and provides the results of the experiments. The ESD test is presented in Section 4.4, along with the measurement results. Section 4.5 provides conclusions.

4.2. IS SILENT DATA CORRUPTION A REAL THREAT?

SDC is an elusive phenomenon. As the name suggests, it occurs when data is corrupted and no error is signalled. SDC may take place while data is processed within the arithmetic/logic unit, when results are stored in a buffer or memory array, or when data is transferred from one subsystem to another, over an interconnect. Error correcting codes (ECC), cyclical redundancy codes (CRC), and parity are widely used to protect data integrity. However, complexity of the design and validation, cost issues, and time-to-market considerations make full chip and system protection against SDC difficult to achieve, in particular in the case of COTS-based computers. The following example shows in what circumstances SDC may occur.

Field reports indicated that two servers experienced large numbers of single-bit errors. These errors were detected on the data path of the processor bus, corrected by ECC, and logged by the processor machine check architecture. Table 4.1 shows the number of er-

TABLE 4.1. Single-bit correctable errors on the processor bus

Server 1				Server 2			
P0	P1	P2	P3	P0	P1	P2	P3
3264	15	0	0	108	121	97	101
7104	20	0	0	—	—	—	—

rors reported by each processor of the two servers. The fist server experienced two large bursts of errors, totalling 10,403 events. Processors P0 and P1 reported 3264 and 15 errors in the first burst, respectively. The second burst was even more severe; P0 and P1 reported 7104 and 20 errors, respectively. 427 errors were detected and corrected on the processor bus of the second server. They were reported by all processors, P0–P3.

Failure analysis determined that intermittent contacts, at solder joints of two printed circuit boards, were the root cause of the errors. No errors were reported after the failing boards were replaced. However, neither error logs nor failure analysis could provide accurate estimates of the period of time for which the intermittent faults were active.

At this point, an obvious "what if" question had to be answered: What would have happened if similar faults had affected a control signal instead of the ECC protected data path? Extensive physical and simulated fault injection experiments were conducted to answer this question. In the first stage of the study, faults were physically injected into control signals of the processor bus. The duration of the faults was varied in a wide range, as no accurate information was available about the activation time of the intermittent faults in the field. The system under test was running a Linpack benchmark, capable of deriving the residues of the matrix computations. The value of the residues is an indication of the correctness of the mathematical operations, that is, large residues signal computational errors. Fault injection revealed very low error detection coverage, especially in the case of faults activated for a short period of time. Figure 4.1 provides the 90% confidence intervals of the error detection coverage, as a function of fault duration [open squares and triangles show the results of physical fault injection (PFI), carried out on the initial system]. LCL and UCL represent the lower and upper confidence limits, respectively. The undetected errors represent SDC and occurred predominantly in the 25 ns–8 ms fault duration range. In the second stage of the experiment, simulated fault injection (SFI) was performed to evaluate the effectiveness of a checking for protocol violations (CPV) based error detection mechanism. A temporal language, which models the behavior of complex devices as a series of timed expressions, was used to accurately reproduce the CPV functionality. Traces from the processor bus of the system used for PFI were collected as the Linpack benchmark was executed. These traces were used as inputs of the simulation. The type, duration, and number of faults injected during SFI were identical to those used in PFI. The plots marked by solid triangles and squares in Figure 4.1, depict the 90% confidence intervals of the CPV error detection coverage. Although error detection significantly improved with CPV, SDC still occurred in the case of faults activated for a short time, in particular within the 25 ns–2 ms range. Taking into account both the field error data and the results of the fault injection experiments, we believe that SDC is a serious threat to the dependability of computing systems. Readers may find details on the fault injection techniques, the types and number of injected faults, and the methodology used for statistical analysis in [Constantinescu 2003].

4.3. TEMPERATURE AND VOLTAGE OPERATING TEST

The purpose of temperature and voltage operating tests, also referred to as four corners tests, is to ensure that computer systems function properly within given environmental limits. The experiment described herein was devised for evaluating the occurrence of SDC events. The operating temperature of the systems undergoing testing was varied between –10°C and 70°C. The test started at the nominal voltage and continued at –5%, –6%, –10%, +5%, +6%, and +10% of the nominal voltage. Figure 4.2 shows the profile of

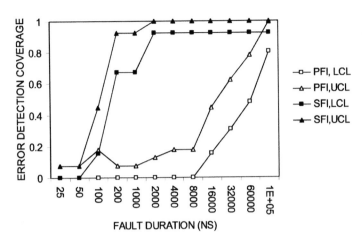

<u>Figure 4.1.</u> 90% confidence intervals of error detection coverage for a control signal of the processor bus (CPV is used in the case of SFI only).

the four corners test and the time duration of each test segment (i.e., the period of time the system operated at a constant voltage). The systems under test run the Linpack benchmark and the correctness of matrix computations was checked by deriving the residues. It has to be stressed that Linpack benchmark primarily exercises the processor, memory controller, and, partially, the system memory. Specific tests have to be executed for discovering SDC in other subsystems. For instance, test techniques for dynamic memory devices are discussed in [Vollrath 2000].

Ten prototype systems were tested for SDC using the profile showed in Figure 4.2. The total number of errors observed was 148. Nine out of ten systems experienced SDC. The types and the number of errors were:

- 134 SDC events (90.5%)
- 14 detected errors* (9.5%): 2 reboot, 5 blue screen, 7 system hang

Most of the SDC events, i.e., 125, occurred at the "corners" of the test, as Figure 4.3 shows. The number of SDC events and the detected errors, per operating voltage and temperature range, is provided in Tables 4.2 and 4.3, respectively. Ninety-five of the SDC events (71%) were observed at +5% and +6% voltages. The same number of SDC events occurred in the 60°C to 70°C range, whereas 32 events (24%) occurred in the 0°C to 30°C temperature range. An interesting observation was that SDC events occurred in bursts, most of the time, suggesting the existence of intermittent faults. Failure analysis showed that a memory controller experienced setup-time and hold-time violations that led to single- and multibit data errors. Redesign of the controller was required for eliminating SDC.

The experiments also showed that SDC events occurred while the temperature was rising or dropping, not at a constant level. For instance, the Linpack benchmark was run at 55°C on four systems for 162 hours (total 648 system hours), and no SDC was observed. Note that the systems that experienced the higher number of errors, under the four corners

---

*Reboots and system hangs were considered detected errors, in contrast with SDC. Blue screens provide limited information on error type and location.

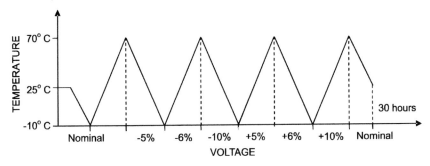

Figure 4.2. Profile of the temperature and voltage operating test.

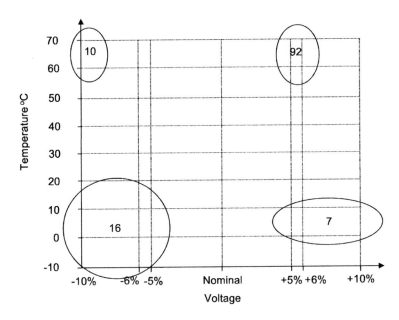

Figure 4.3. Distribution of the SDC events.

TABLE 4.2. Number of errors per operating voltage

Voltage	Nominal	−5%	−6%	−10%	+5%	+6%	+10%
SDC	8	10	5	14	21	74	2
Reboot	0	0	0	0	0	0	2
Blue Screen	0	1	0	0	0	0	4
Hang	1	0	1	4	0	0	1

TABLE 4.3. Number of errors per operating temperature range

Temperature, °C	−10 to 0	0 to 10	10 to 20	20 to 30	30 to 40	40 to 50	50 to 60	60 to 70
SDC	5	14	13	5	1	0	1	95
Reboot	1	0	0	0	0	0	0	1
Blue Screen	0	0	0	0	0	0	0	5
Hang	1	0	1	0	0	0	0	5

test, were selected for this experiment. As a consequence, we consider that tests exercising the system at a constant elevated temperature, commonly used by computer manufacturers, have a lower chance of detecting faults that induce SDC.

4.4. ELECTROSTATIC DISCHARGE OPERATING TEST

The purpose of ESD tests is to demonstrate that computers properly function when electrostatic discharges occur under normal operating conditions. Development of an ESD test begins with identifying the test points. Only surfaces that are accessible to the users or maintenance personnel during normal operation are selected. These include power keys, reset buttons, disk drives, LEDs, cable connectors, and so forth. The next step is to select the voltage levels of the discharge. Usually, air discharges are performed in the 2 kV–15 kV range, whereas contact discharges use 2 kV–8 kV voltages. A climatically controlled room and properly calibrated ESD guns are required [IEC 2006].

The experiments described in this chapter were carried out on four servers, produced by two manufacturers. Thirty test points were selected for each server, on the front, back, sides and top surfaces. 4 kV, 6 kV, 8 kV, 12 kV, and 15 kV voltages were used for air discharges and 8 kV for contact discharges. Twenty positive and 20 negative discharges were applied to each test point. All servers were running the Linpack benchmark. Three servers passed the ESD tests. One experienced SDC when 15 kV air discharges were targeted to the front disk bay. Three (3) out of 40 discharges (7.5%) were SDC events. Follow-up ESD tests of the disk bay showed that about 8% of the discharges induced SDC. This experiment proved that simple operations, like on-line adding and removing or replacing a disk drive in a computer system, have the potential of corrupting the results provided by the machine.

4.5. CONCLUSIONS

The presented benchmarking techniques employed environmental test tools. The computing systems under evaluation executed the Linpack benchmark, which is capable of detecting numerical errors, that is, silent corruption of the data.

The four corners test was performed on ten prototype systems and revealed that over 90% of the errors were SDC events. Failure analysis determined that setup-time and hold-time violations, experienced by a memory controller, induced the errors. The ESD test was carried out on four servers, produced by two manufacturers. One of the servers experienced SDC when electrostatic discharges were targeted at the disk bay area. This means that very common maintenance operations have the potential of silently corrupting the computational results. To the author's best knowledge, this is the first reported case of SDC events induced by ESD in a commercially available server under normal operating conditions.

The advantages of using environmental tools for dependability benchmarking are twofold. First, no proprietary data about the systems under test is necessary and, as a result, this approach may be used both by manufacturers and independent evaluators. Second, the Linpack benchmark, as well as other test programs, are widely available for exercising the systems under evaluation. As a consequence, we consider that environmental test tools are capable of playing a significant role in dependability benchmarking of computing systems and, in particular, in the measurement of SDC.

ACKNOWLEDGMENT

The author thanks John Blair and Scott Scheuneman for their support in setting up and running the environmental tests.

REFERENCES

[Ademaj et al. 2002] A. Ademaj, P. Grillinger, P. Herout, and J. Hlavicka, "Fault Tolerance Evaluation Using Two Software Based Fault Injection Methods," in *Proceedings of the Eighth IEEE International On-Line Testing Workshop,* pp. 21–25, 2002.

[Aidemark et al. 2001] J. Aidemark, J. Vinter, P. Folkesson, and J. Karlsson, "GOOFI: Generic Object-Oriented Fault Injection Tool," in *Proceedings of the International Conference on Dependable Systems and Networks,* pp. 83–88, 2001.

[Arlat et al. 2003] J. Arlat, Y. Crouzet, J. Karlsson, P. Folkesson, E. Fuchs, and G. H. Leber, "Comparison of Physical and Software-Implemented Fault Injection Techniques," *IEEE Transactions on Computers,* vol. 52, no. 8, pp. 1115–1133, 2003.

[Berrojo et al. 2002] L. Berrojo, F. Corno, L. Entrena, I. González, C. Lopez, M. Sonza Reorda, and G. Squillero, "An Industrial Environment for High-Level Fault-Tolerant Structures Insertion and Validation," in *Proceedings of the 20th VLSI Test Symposium,* Monterey, CA, pp. 229–236, IEEE Computer Science Press, Los Alamitos, CA, 2002.

[Camp 1989] R. C. Camp, "Benchmarking: The Search for Industries Best Practices that Lead to Superior Performance," Quality Press, 1989.

[Carreira et al. 1998] J. Carreira, H. Madeira, and J. G. Silva, "Xception: A Technique for the Experimental Evaluation of Dependability in Modern Computers," *IEEE Transactions on Software Engineering,* February, pp. 125–136, 1998.

[Constantinescu 2000] C. Constantinescu, "Teraflops Supercomputer: Architecture and Validation of the Fault Tolerance Mechanisms," *IEEE Transactions on Computers,* vol. 49, no. 9, pp. 886–894, 2000.

[Constantinescu 2002] C. Constantinescu, "Impact of Deep Submicron Technology on Dependability of VLSI Circuits," in *Proceedings of the International Conference on Dependable Systems and Networks,* pp. 205–209, 2002.

[Constantinescu 2003] C. Constantinescu, "Experimental Evaluation of Error-Detection Mechanisms," *IEEE Transactions on Reliability,* vol. 52, no. 1, pp. 53–57, March 2003.

[Constantinescu 2005] "Dependability Benchmarking Using Environmental Test Tools," in *Proceedings of IEEE Annual Reliability and Maintainability Symposium,* pp. 567–571, 2005.

[Durães and Madeira, 2002] J. Durães and H. Madeira, "Emulation of Software Faults by Selective Mutations at Machine-code Level," in *Proceedings of the 13th International Symposium on Software Reliability Engineering,* Annapolis, MD, pp. 329–340, 2002.

[Folkesson 1998] P. Folkesson, S. Svensson, and J. Karlsson, "A Comparison of Simulated Based and Scan Chain Implemented Fault Injection," in *Proceedings of 28th FTCS Symposium,* pp. 284–293, 1998.

[Hareland et al. 2001] S. Hareland, J. Maiz, M. Alavi, K. Mistry, S. Walsta, and C. Hong, "Impact of CMOS Process Scaling and SOI on the Soft Error Rates of Logic Processes," in *IEEE Symposium on VLSI Technology,* pp. 73–74, 2001.

[IEC 2006] International Electrotechnical Commission (IEC), http://www.iec.ch.

[ITRS] International Technology Roadmap for Semiconductors (ITRS), http://public.itrs.net.

[Karlsson et al. 1991] J. Karlsson, U. Gunneflo, P. Lidén, and J. Torin, "Two Fault Injection Techniques for Test of Fault Handling Mechanisms," in *Proceedings of the 1991 International Test Conference,* Nashville, TN, pp. 140–149, 1991.

[Kim and Somani 2002] S. Kim and A. K. Somani, "Soft Error Sensitivity Characterization of Microprocessor Dependability Enhancement Strategy," in *Proceedings of the International Conference on Dependable Systems and Networks,* pp. 416–425, 2002.

[Madeira et al. 1994] H. Madeira, M. Rela, F. Moreira, and J. G. Silva, "A General Purpose Pin-level Fault Injector," in *Proceedings of 1st European Dependable Computing Conference,* pp. 199–216, Germany, 1994.

[Martínez et al. 1999] R. J. Martínez, P. J. Gil, G. Martín, C. Pérez, and J. J. Serrano, "Experimental Validation of High-Speed Fault-Tolerant Systems Using Physical Fault Injection," in *Proceedings of Dependable Computing for Critical Applications,* San Jose, CA, pp. 249–265, 1999.

[Samson et al. 1998] J. R. Samson Jr., W. Moreno, and F. Falquez, "A Technique for Automated Validation of Fault Tolerant Designs Using Laser Fault Injection (LFI)," in *Proceedings of 28th FTCS Symposium,* pp. 162–167, 1998.

[Scott et al. 1998] D. T. Scott, G. Ries, M. Hsueh, and R. K. Iyer, "Dependability Analysis of a High-Speed Network Using Software-implemented Fault Injected and Simulated Fault Injection," *IEEE Transactions on Computers,* vol. 47, no. 1, pp. 108–119, 1998.

[Shivakumar et al. 2002] P. Shivakumar, M. Kistler, S. W. Keckler, D. Burger, and L. Alivi, "Modeling the Effect of Technology Trends on the Soft Error Rate of Combinatorial Logic," in *Proceedings of the International Conference on Dependable Systems and Networks,* pp. 389–398, 2002.

[Stathis 2001] J. H. Stathis, "Physical and Predictive Models of Ultrathin Oxide Reliability in CMOS Devices and Circuits," *IEEE Transactions on Device and Materials Reliability,* vol. 1, no. 1, pp. 43–99, 2001.

[Vollrath 2000] J. Vollrath, "Tutorial: Synchronous Dynamic Memory Test Construction—A Field Approach," in *IEEE International Workshop on Memory Technology, Design and Testing,* pp. 59–64, 2000.

[Wagner and McCluskey 1985] K. D. Wagner and E. J. McCluskey, "Effect of Supply Voltage on Circuit Propagation Delay and Test Application," in *Proceedings of the International Conference on Computer-Aided Design,* Santa Clara, CA, pp. 42–44, 1985.

5

DEPENDABILITY BENCHMARKS FOR OLTP SYSTEMS

Marco Vieira, João Durães, and Henrique Madeira

5.1. INTRODUCTION

On-line transaction processing (OLTP) systems constitute the core of the information systems of most organizations. Database management systems (DBMS), which are the key components of OLTP systems, have a long tradition of high dependability, particularly concerning data integrity and recovery aspects. However, although OLTP systems comprise the best examples of complex business-critical systems, no practical way has been proposed so far to assess their dependability or, at least, to characterize the innumerous alternative solutions available. Unfortunately, this is also the scenario for other computer applications domains.

Computer benchmarks are standard tools that allow evaluating and comparing different systems or components according to specific characteristics (e.g., performance). The transactional systems industry has a reputed infrastructure for performance evaluation, and the set of benchmarks managed by the Transaction Processing Performance Council (TPC) [TPC] are recognized as one of the most successful benchmarking initiatives of the computer industry. Nevertheless, dependability evaluation and comparison have been absent from the TPC benchmarking efforts.

The TPC Benchmark™ C (TPC-C) [TPC-C 2005] is one of the most important and well-established performance benchmarks for OLTP systems. This benchmark includes a mixture of read-only and update-intensive transactions that simulate the activities found in complex OLTP application environments. TPC-C specifies that data recovery features of the system under benchmarking must ensure that data can be recovered from any point in time during the benchmark execution. However, the benchmark specification does not

Dependability Benchmarking for Computer Systems. Edited by Karama Kanoun and Lisa Spainhower
Copyright © 2008 IEEE Computer Society

include any procedure to confirm that these mechanisms are working efficiently or to measure the impact of faults on the system dependability.

Performance benchmarks such as TPC-C have contributed to improving the performance of successive generations of DBMS, but in many cases the systems and configurations used to achieve the best performance are very different from the ones that are actually used in the field. The major problem is that the results tend to portray rather artificial scenarios, as recovery mechanisms are configured for minimum impact on performance and the effectiveness of dependability features is normally relaxed.

The fact that many businesses require very high availability for their database servers, including small servers used in many e-commerce applications, shows that it is necessary to shift the focus from measuring pure performance to the measurement of both performance and dependability. This way, the tight dependence between performance and dependability in modern DBMS requires the definition of practical methods to characterize a given configuration or to compare different products in a more realistic scenario. Above all, it is important to include in the benchmarks new measures that show the benefit of adding better mechanisms to the system or configuring the available mechanisms to achieve the best dependability, even if the performance is slightly reduced.

In spite of the pertinence of having dependability benchmarks for transactional systems, the reality is that no dependability benchmark (or even a really practical approach to characterize dependability characteristics such as availability) has been proposed so far, in clear contrast with the benchmarking of performance, for which TPC started a very successful initiative long ago.

A dependability benchmark is a specification of a standard procedure to measure both dependability and performance of computer systems or components. The main goal is to provide a standardized way to compare different systems or components from a dependability point of view. As performance benchmarks have contributed to improving the performance of systems, we believe that a new dependability benchmark represents a possible way to improve the dependability of future systems. A dependability benchmark for OLTP environments seems to be useful in several scenarios:

- Help end-users and system administrators to choose the system that best fits their requirements by comparing the dependability features of alternative systems.
- Help system integrators to choose the best components for a given solution.
- Assist system vendors in promoting their products. In addition, a dependability benchmark may be a very important tool to help the system vendors detect possible dependability problems on their computer systems/components.
- Provide researchers with a tool to evaluate new prototypes.

Our proposal for dependability benchmarking is mainly inspired by measurement-based techniques. This way, compared to typical performance benchmarks such as the TPC benchmarks, which consist mainly of a workload and a set of performance measures, our approach to dependability benchmarks adds two new elements: (1) measures related to dependability, and (2) a faultload that emulates real faults experienced by systems in the field. This chapter presents the first dependability benchmark for OLTP application environments (called DBench-OLTP) following this approach. The DBench-OLTP benchmark consists of a document that specifies all the steps required to experimentally evaluate performance and dependability measures of OLTP systems. This benchmark adopts the basic experimental setup, the workload, and the performance measures from

TPC-C [TPC-C 2005] and specifies the new measures related to dependability and a faultload that includes a representative set of operator faults, software faults, and high-level hardware failures. This chapter provides an overview of the key aspects of the DBench-OLTP benchmark. A more detailed discussion can be found in [Vieira 2005, Vieira and Madeira 2005, Vieira and Madeira 2003] and the complete specification is available at [Vieira and Madeira 2004c] for public use.

The chapter has five sections. Section 5.2 discusses the key components and the main properties of a dependability benchmark for OLTP systems. Section 5.3 presents the DBench-OLTP dependability benchmark. Section 5.4 shows a dependability benchmarking example and Section 5.5 concludes the chapter.

5.2. SPECIFYING DEPENDABILITY BENCHMARKS FOR OLTP SYSTEMS

A typical OLTP environment consists of a number of users managing their transactions via a terminal or a desktop computer connected to a DBMS using a local area network or through the Web. An OLTP system is thus a typical client–server system or a multitier system. In a simplified approach, the server is composed of three main components: the hardware platform (including the disk subsystem), the operating system, and the transactional engine. Most of the transactional systems available today use a DBMS as transactional engine, which is in practice the main component of any OLTP system, assuring not only the transactional properties but also the recovery mechanisms.

Dependability is an integrative concept that includes the following attributes [Laprie 1995]: availability, reliability, safety, confidentiality, integrity, and maintainability. Among all the possible dependability attributes, availability is one of the most relevant in databases and OLTP systems in general. Thus, our approach to dependability benchmarking of OLTP systems is particularly focused on the availability attribute.

The computer system/component that is characterized by the benchmark is called the system under benchmark (SUB).* However, the SUB can be larger than the component or subsystem directly targeted by the benchmark [which we call the benchmark target (BT)]. For example, in an OLTP system the SUB could be the whole server (including the database management system, the operating system, the hardware, etc.), whereas the benchmark target is the transactional engine. This is also the approach used in typical performance benchmarks from TPC and SPEC (Standard Performance Evaluation Corporation). For example, although the TPC-C benchmark [TPC-C 2005] targets the database engine, it characterizes the system under test (SUT), which consists of all hardware (including one or more processing units, network components, data storage, etc.) and software supporting the database employed in the benchmark.

Performance benchmarks include two major components: a workload that represents the work that the system must perform during the benchmark run and a set of performance measures that characterizes the performance of the system under benchmarking. Our approach to dependability benchmarking adds two new elements: measures related to dependability, which characterize the dependability of the system under benchmarking, and a faultload, which represents a set of faults and stressful conditions that emulate real faults experienced by OLTP systems in the field.

---

*The term system under benchmark (SUB) has been generally adopted in the context of the DBench Project [DBench]. It is equivalent to the term system under test (SUT) commonly used in TPC benchmarks [TPC].

In addition to the measures, workload, and faultload, the benchmark must also specify the procedure and rules that have to be followed during the benchmark implementation and execution. Furthermore, the components of the experimental setup needed to run the benchmark must also be defined.

5.2.1. Specifying the Dependability Benchmark Components

A dependability benchmark for OLTP systems consists of a document specifying the benchmark components. The benchmark users must be able to implement the benchmark from that specification. Obviously, the specification may include source code samples or even tools to facilitate the benchmark implementation. We propose the following general steps to specify a dependability benchmark:

1. The first step is the identification of the benchmark domain. The division of the application spectrum into well-defined domains is necessary to cope with the huge diversity of systems and applications and to make it possible to make choices on the definition of benchmark components. In fact, most of the components are very dependent on the benchmark domain. For example, the benchmark measures, the most common (external) faults that may affect the system, and the workload, just to name a few, are very dependent on the domain.

2. The second step is the characterization of the SUB in terms of typical functionalities and features, including dependability features that are expected to be found in the set of possible targets addressed in the benchmark. For example, for transactional applications one can assume that the SUB can be any system able to execute transactions according to the typical transaction properties (known as ACID properties [Ramakrishnan and Gehrke 2002]), which include, for example, data recovery features.

3. The third step is the definition of the measures, which is the first component to be specified, as the definition of the other components may be very dependent on the measures.

4. The remaining components (workload, faultload, procedures and rules, and experimental setup) are defined in the last step. Although the specification of these components is not always directly dependent on the benchmark measures, some dependencies are expected. That is, the definitions of the workload and faultload, for example, are normally related to the measures of interest.

The following sections present and discuss how to define each component of a dependability benchmark for OLTP application environments.

5.2.1.1. Measures. Two classes of measures can be considered in dependability evaluation:

1. *Direct experimental measures*—measures that characterize the service provided by the system in the presence of faults (e.g., transaction rate and service availability) and measures that characterize, in value and time domains, the efficiency of the fault tolerance mechanisms available (e.g., error detection coverage and recovery efficiency).

2. *Unconditional measures on dependability attributes*—measures that characterize the system dependability in a global way, taking into account the occurrence of the

and so on. These measures include availability, reliability, safety, confidentiality, integrity, and maintainability.

As suggested by the name, direct experimental measures can be obtained directly from the experimental results. The unconditional measures have to be estimated using modeling techniques with the help of external data such as fault rates and mean time between failures (MTBF). It is worth noting that models of complex systems are difficult to define and the external data is difficult to obtain.

The benchmarking approach proposed in this chapter considers only direct experimental measures, following the traditional benchmarking philosophy based on a purely experimental approach. These measures are related to the conditions disclosed in the benchmark report and can be used for system comparison or for system/component improvement and tuning. This is similar to what happens with performance benchmarking results, as the performance measures do not represent an absolute measure of performance, since the main goal is to compare computer performance in a meaningful way. In a similar manner, the measures for a dependability benchmark must be understood as benchmark results that can be useful to characterize system dependability in a relative fashion (e.g., to compare alternative systems or components) or to improve/tune system dependability.

Our proposal is to select the measures for a dependability benchmark for OLTP environments in order to meet the following characteristics/goals:

- Measures should be based on the service provided by the OLTP system during the benchmark run and must be independent of the system structure (to allow the comparison of different systems).
- Focus on an end-to-end perspective (e.g., the point of view of the end users).
- Allow the characterization of both dependability and performance features.
- It should be easy to implement and understand by database users and database administrators.
- Measures should not be extrapolated or inferred; measures must be directly computed based on the information collected during the benchmark execution.

5.2.1.2. Experimental Setup and Benchmark Procedure and Rules. The experimental setup describes the setup required to run the benchmark. We propose the following key elements for the experimental setup of a dependability benchmark for OLTP systems:

- *Benchmark Target (BT)*. Represents the system or component that the benchmark user wants to characterize. In a transactional system, the benchmark target is normally the transactional engine, which does not mean that the benchmark cannot be used to characterize other components of the transactional environment (e.g., operating system, hardware, etc).
- *System under Benchmarking (SUB)*. In practice, to evaluate the benchmark target it is often necessary to include it in a wider system, which is called the system under benchmarking. This way, the SUB provides all the support needed to run the workload and represents the system for which the measures apply. In a transactional system, the SUB includes all the hardware and software components needed to execute the workload.

- *Benchmark Management System (BMS).* This is the system in charge of managing all the experiments. The goal is to make the execution of the benchmark a completely automated process.

The procedures and rules that must be followed during the benchmark execution have to be defined. This is, of course, dependent on the specific benchmark but the following points give some guidelines on specific aspects needed in most of the cases:

- Procedures for "translating" the workload and faultload defined in the benchmark specification into the actual workload and faultload that will apply to the SUB
- Uniform conditions to build the setup and run the dependability benchmark
- Rules related to the collection of the experimental results
- Rules for the production of the final measures from the direct experimental results
- Scaling rules to adapt the same benchmark to systems of very different sizes
- System configuration disclosures required to interpret the benchmark results
- Rules to avoid optimistic or biased results

5.2.1.3. Workload and Faultload. The definition of the workload is considerably simplified by the existence of workloads from standard performance benchmarks (e.g., [TPC]). Obviously, these already established workloads are the natural choice for an OLTP dependability benchmark. However, when adopting an existing workload some changes may be required in order to target specific system features.

The faultload represents a set of faults and stressful conditions that emulate real faults experienced by OLTP systems in the field. Among the main components needed to define a dependability benchmark for OLTP application environments, the faultload is clearly the most obscure one due to the complex nature of faults. Our proposal is to define the faultload by considering one or more of the following classes of faults:*

- *Operator faults.* Operator faults in database systems are database administrator mistakes [Brown and Patterson 2001, Vieira and Madeira 2002, Vieira and Madeira 2004a]. The great complexity of database administration tasks and the need for tuning and administration on a daily basis, clearly explains why operator faults (i.e., wrong database administrator actions) are prevalent in database systems.
- *Software Faults.* Software faults (i.e., software bugs) are recognized as an important source of system outages [Gray 1990, Lee and Iyer 1995] and, given the huge complexity of today's software, the predominance of software faults tends to increase. Recent results have shown that it is possible to emulate software faults according to the software fault classes most often found in field data [Durães and Madeira 2002a, Durães and Madeira 2003].
- *Hardware faults.* Traditional hardware faults, such as bit flips and stuck-ats, are not generally considered an important class of faults in OLTP systems. On the other hand, high-level hardware failures such as hard disk failures, network interface failures, or failures of the interconnection network itself are quite frequent. In fact, most of the DBMS available have recovery mechanisms explicitly developed to recover from hardware components failures [Ramakrishnan and Gehrke 2002].

*An important aspect is that these three classes represent our proposal for the classification of computer faults for dependability benchmarking. Other classifications could have been considered.

Two properties are particularly relevant in the faultload definition: *fault representativeness* and *fault portability*. To be useful, a faultload must be representative of real faults and, at the same time, it must define the faults in a way that it makes them portable among the possible target systems. Several studies on the representativeness and portability of operator faults [Brown and Patterson 2001, Vieira and Madeira 2002, Vieira and Madeira 2004a], software faults [Christmansson and Chillarege 1996, Madeira et al. 2000, Durães and Madeira 2003], and hardware faults [Zhu et al. 2003a, Zhu et al. 2003b] can be found in literature.

5.2.2. Properties of a Dependability Benchmark for OLTP Systems

A dependability benchmark for transactional systems must be representative, portable, repeatable, scalable, nonintrusive, and simple to use. This way, properties validation is a fundamental step toward the acceptance of emerging benchmarks as actual standards. The following paragraphs present some key aspects concerning each property of a dependability benchmark for OLTP systems:

- *Representativeness.* A benchmark must represent real-world scenarios in a realistic way. In dependability benchmarking, representativeness is mainly influenced by the workload and faultload characteristics. Concerning the workload, it is essential to verify if the profile of the transactions includes a mixture that simulates (in a realistic way) the activities found in real OLTP systems. Concerning the faultload, field data should be used to validate if the set of faults considered in the faultload represent real faults from the field. However, this may be a hard task as field data on the underlying causes of computer failures is not generally available. Previous works in the literature are probably the best source to assess the representativeness of a given faultload.

- *Portability.* A benchmark must allow the comparison of different systems in a given domain. The best way to assess portability is to implement the benchmark in different systems. Different DBMS and operating systems must be considered in the validation of a dependability benchmark for OLTP environments, as some classes of faults may depend on the transactional engine and others on the operating system.

- *Repeatability.* A dependability benchmark must report similar results when run more than once in the same environment. Repeatability has to be understood in statistical terms, as it is virtually impossible to reproduce exactly the same conditions concerning target-system state during the benchmark run. In practice, small deviations in the measures in successive runs are normal and just reflect the asynchronous nature of transactions in an OLTP system. The benchmark repeatability can be verified by running the benchmark several times in the same SUB.

- *Scalability.* Tthe benchmark must be able to evaluate systems of different sizes. The best way to assess scalability is to implement the benchmark in systems of different sizes. Concerning the workload, it must have a scale factor that allows scaling the size of the data storage and the number of transactions submitted according to the size of the system under benchmarking. On the other hand, the size of the faultload may depend on the complexity of the system (e.g., more disks means more faults). Therefore, it is necessary to evaluate if for very complex systems so the size of the faultload does not become impractical.

- *Nonintrusiveness.* The benchmark must require minimum changes (or no changes at all) in the target system. Intrusiveness may be assessed during the benchmark implementation. If the implementation of the workload or faultload introduces significant changes in the SUB (either in the structure or in the behavior) it means that the benchmark is intrusive and its results are not valid.
- *Simplicity of Use.* The benchmark must be as easy to implement and run as possible. During the benchmarking process, it is possible to evaluate the complexity of the benchmark implementation and execution. The time needed to implement and run the benchmark should also be assessed. Ideally, the benchmark execution should take only a few hours per system; however, due to the complexity of transactional systems a few days is acceptable.

As we can see, although some properties can be verified through a detailed analysis of the benchmark components, others may require the execution of experiments. The word *validation* is used in the sense that it is possible to gain enough confidence in the benchmark properties through a set of representative experiments complemented by a detailed analysis of the benchmark components.

5.3. DBENCH-OLTP: A DEPENDABILITY BENCHMARK FOR TRANSACTIONAL SYSTEMS

The DBench-OLTP dependability benchmark uses the basic setup, workload, and performance measures specified by TPC-C and introduces new components mentioned before: measures related to dependability and faultload. The DBench-OLTP specification [Vieira and Madeira 2004c] follows the well-accepted style of the TPC specifications and is structured in clauses that define and specify how to implement the different components of the benchmark. This section presents and discusses the DBench-OLTP dependability benchmark, with particular emphasis on the new components (see DBench-OLTP specification [Vieira and Madeira 2004c] for details).

5.3.1. Measures

The DBench-OLTP dependability benchmark measures are computed from the information collected during the benchmark run and are collected from the point of view of the emulated users. As we are interested in characterizing both performance and dependability, the DBench-OLTP measures are divided into three groups: baseline performance measures, performance measures in the presence of the faultload, and dependability measures.

The *baseline performance measures* are inherited from the TPC-C performance benchmark and include the number of transactions executed per minute (tpmC) and price per transaction ($/tpmC) without (artificial) faults. The number of transactions executed per minute represents the total number of completed *new-order* transactions (one of the five types of TPC-C transactions) divided by the elapsed time of the measurement interval. The price per transaction is the ratio between the price and the SUB performance. The system price is calculated based on a set of pricing rules provided in TPC-C specification. In the context of DBench-OLTP, these measures represent a baseline performance instead of optimized pure performance (as is the case of TPC-C), and should be considered a good compromise between performance and dependability.

The *performance measures in the presence of the faultload* are:

- *Tf*—number of transactions executed per minute in the presence of the faultload. It measures the impact of faults in the performance and favors systems with higher capability of tolerating faults, fast recovery time, and so on.
- *$/Tf*—price-per-transaction in the presence of the faultload. It measures the relative benefit of including fault handling mechanisms in the target systems in terms of the price.

The *dependability measures* reported are:

- *Ne*—number of data errors detected by consistency tests and metadata tests. It measures the impact of faults on the data integrity.
- *AvtS*—service availability* from the SUB point of view in the presence of the faultload. It measures the amount of time the system is available from the SUB point of view. The system is available when it is able to respond to at least one terminal within the minimum response time defined for each type of transaction by TPC-C. The system is unavailable when it is not able to respond to any terminal.
- *AvtC*—service availability from the end users' (terminals) point of view in the presence of the faultload. It measures the amount of time the system is available from the client's point of view. The system is available for one terminal if it responds to a submitted transaction within the minimum response time defined for that type of transaction by the TPC-C benchmark. The system is unavailable for that terminal if there is no response within that time or if an error is returned.

It is worth noting that AvtC and AvtS are defined based on the service provided by the system. Therefore, the system is considered available when it is able to provide the service defined by the transactions. For example, from the client's point of view the system is not available if it submits a transaction and gets no answer within the specified time (see transaction profile in the TPC-C specification [TPC-C 2005]) or gets an error. In this case, the unavailability period is counted from the moment when a given client submits a transaction that fails until the moment when it submits a transaction that succeeds. From the server point of view, the system is available when it is able to execute transactions submitted by the clients. The measures AvtS and AvtC are given as a ratio of the amount of time the system is available and the experiment duration (refer to the benchmark specification [Vieira and Madeira 2004c] for details on the calculation of AvtS and AvtC).

5.3.2. Experimental Setup

As proposed previously, the main elements are the system under benchmarking (SUB) and the benchmark management system (BMS). The goal of the BMS is to emulate the TPC-C client applications and respective users and control all the aspects of the benchmark run. In addition, the BMS handles the insertion of the faultload and records the raw data needed to calculate the measures (measures are computed afterward by analyzing the information collected during the benchmark run).

---

*In the context of DBench-OLTP, we use the term "availability" to refer to the readiness of the service provided by the system during a benchmarking experiment. It does not take into account the occurrence of the various events impacting its behavior (e.g., fault occurrence rates and mean time to repair)

The SUB represents a system fully configured to run the workload, and whose performance and dependability are to be evaluated. From the benchmark point of view, the SUB is the set of processing units used to run the workload and to store all the data processed. That is, given the huge variety of systems and configurations used in practice to run OLTP applications, the definition of the SUB is tied to the transactional workload instead of being defined in a structural way.

5.3.3. Benchmark Procedure and Rules

A DBench-OLTP run includes two main phases:

1. *Phase 1.* This is the first run of the workload without any artificial faults. This phase corresponds to a typical TPC-C measurement interval (see [TPC-C 2005]), and follows the requirements specified in the TPC-C standard specification. Phase 1 is used to collect the baseline performance measures, and the idea is to use them together with other measures (see below) to characterize both the system performance and dependability.

2. *Phase 2.* In this phase, the workload is run in the presence of the faultload to collect the performance measures in the presence of the faultload and dependability measures. The goal is to assess the impact of faults on the transaction execution and to evaluate specific aspects of the SUB dependability. As shown in Figure 5.1, Phase 2 is composed of several independent injection slots. An injection slot is a measurement interval during which the workload is run and one or more faults from the faultload are injected. The same configuration of the SUB must be used in both Phase 1 and Phase 2.

In order to assure that each injection slot portray a realistic scenario as much as possible, and at the same time assures that important properties such as repeatability and representativeness of results are met by the DBench-OLTP benchmark, the definition of the profile of the injection slot has to follow several rules. The following points briefly summarize those rules (see also Figure 5.1):

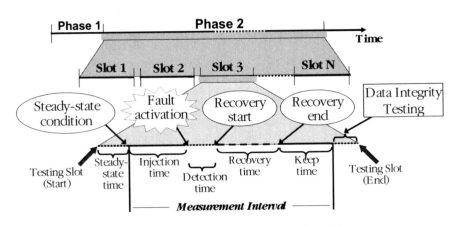

<u>Figure 5.1.</u> Benchmark run and injection slots.

1. The SUB state must be explicitly restored at the beginning of each injection slot in order to prevent the effects of the faults from accumulating across different slots.

2. The tests are conducted with the SUB in a steady-state condition that represents the state in which the system is able to maintain its maximum transaction processing throughput. The system achieves a steady-state condition after a given time executing transactions (*steady-state time*).

3. Operator faults and high-level hardware failures are injected a certain amount of time (*injection time*) after the steady-state condition has been achieved. This time is defined in the benchmark specification and is specific for each fault in the faultload. For operator faults and high-level hardware failures, only one fault is injected in each slot.

4. Software faults are injected at the beginning of the measurement interval (i.e., the injection time is equal to zero) and ten faults are injected in each slot (see Subsection 5.4.5.3).

5. For operator faults and high-level hardware failures, a diagnostic procedure must be executed after a given *detection time*. The goal is to evaluate the effects of the faults and start the required recovery procedure. The DBench-OLTP benchmark defines the detection times to be used for each of the types of operator faults and high-level hardware failures considered. For the systems with built-in detection capabilities, the diagnostic procedure is executed if the system does not react to the faults before the end of the detection time.

6. For software faults the detection time has a different objective. In this case, the recovery procedure is always started some time after the injection of the faults as some software faults can have latent effects that cannot be easily detected (e.g., performance degradation, deadlocks, etc).

7. The *recovery time* represents the time needed to execute the recovery procedure. For operator faults and high-level hardware failures, if no recovery is needed, then the recovery time is not considered (it is equal to zero). For software faults, the recovery procedure must always be executed.

8. When the recovery procedure completes, the workload must continue to run during a *keep time* in order to evaluate the system speedup after recovery.

9. After the workload end, a set of application consistency tests must be run to check possible data integrity violations caused by the fault injected. The integrity tests are performed on the application data (i.e., the data in the database tables after running the workload) and use both business rules and the database metadata to assure a comprehensive test.

It is worth noting that the duration of each injection slot depends on the fault injected and corresponding times (steady-state time, injection time, detection time, recovery time, and keep time). However, the workload must run for at least 15 minutes after the steady-state condition has been achieved, to assure that the database is run under realistic conditions concerning memory and disk accesses.

5.3.4. Workload

The DBench-OLTP dependability benchmark adopts the workload of the well-established TPC-C performance benchmark, which represents a typical database installation and is well accepted as a realistic OLTP scenario. The business represented by TPC-C is a wholesale supplier having a number of warehouses and their associated sales districts. This workload includes a mixture of read-only and update-intensive transactions that simulate the activities of most OLTP application environments, including transactions resulting from human operators working on interactive sessions.

5.3.5. Faultload

As proposed before, three classes of faults can be considered in a dependability benchmark for OLTP systems: (1) operator faults, (2) software faults, or (3) high-level hardware failures. Although faults from different classes may be included in a single faultload, our approach is to define a different faultload for each class. In fact, trying to combine several classes in the same faultload just increases the complexity of the problem, which makes it difficult to fulfill key benchmarking properties such as representativeness, portability, and scalability. The DBench-OLTP benchmark can then be used by considering three different faultloads, each one based on a different class of faults.

5.3.5.1. Faultload Based on Operator Faults.
The problem of operator faults in OLTP systems is essentially a problem of database administrator mistakes. End-user errors are not considered, as the end-user actions do not affect directly the dependability of a DBMS. Database administrators manage all aspects of a DBMS. In spite of constant efforts to introduce self-maintaining and self-administering features in a DBMS, database administration is still a job heavily based on human operators. This way, the injection of operator faults in a DBMS can be easily achieved by reproducing common database administrator mistakes.

Different DBMS include different sets of administration tasks and, consequently, have different sets of possible operator faults. In [Vieira and Madeira 2002, Vieira and Madeira 2004a], we propose a set of general guidelines for the definition of faultloads based on operator faults. Based on those works, we have performed the following general steps to define the faultload based on operator faults:

1. Identify all the administration tasks for the core administration functionalities, considering a representative set of DBMS with different sizes and functionalities (Oracle 9i, Sybase Adaptive Server 12.5, Informix Dynamic Server 9.3, and PostgreSQL 7.3).
2. Identify the administration tasks that are common to all the DBMS considered in step 1. This consists of establishing equivalence between the administration tasks identified and then selecting the ones that exist in all the DBMS.
3. Identify all the types of operator faults that may occur when executing each of the administration tasks identified in the previous step.
4. Identify the types of operator faults that are common to all the DBMS considered. This is done by establishing equivalence between the fault types and then selecting the common ones.
5. Assign weights to each fault type according to the number of times the correspondent administration task is executed.
6. The faultload includes the most representative types of faults identified in step 5 (see Table 5.1).

The rules to identify the set of faults to be injected and the correspondent injection and detection times are presented in Table 5.1. The types of faults considered and the correspondent rules and times have been postulated based on DBA experience and considering practical aspects such as the time needed to run the benchmark, the impact of each type of faults in the several DBMS, the different types of recovery required, and the fault's portability. Note that, in most of the cases, operator faults can only be detected by the system administrator or by the users, which means that the detection time is highly human depen-

TABLE 5.1. Types of operator faults

Fault type	Description	Detection time
Abrupt operating system shutdown	Ten faults injected at the following injection times: 3, 5, 7, 9, 10, 11, 12, 13, 14, and 15 minutes. Note that the injection time is counted only after the steady-state condition has been achieved (see Figure 5.3).	0 sec.
Abrupt transactional engine shutdown	Ten faults injected at the following injection times: 3, 5, 7, 9, 10, 11, 12, 13, 14, and 15 minutes.	30 sec.
Kill a set of user sessions	Five faults injected at the following injection times: 3, 7, 10, 13, and 15 minutes. The set of sessions to be killed in each fault injection must be randomly selected during the benchmark run and consist of 50% of all the active sessions from the users holding the TPC-C tables.	0 sec.
Delete a table	Three faults injected for each one of the following TPC-C tables: order, new-order, order-line, and ware (a total of 12 faults). The injection times are the following: 3, 10, and 15 minutes.	2 min.
Delete a user schema	Three faults injected at following injection times: 3, 10, and 15 minutes. The schema to be considered is the one that holds the TPC-C tables. If the objects are distributed among several users, then all schemes holding TPC-C tables must be deleted.	1 min.
Delete a file from disk	The set of faults to be injected are defined performing the following steps for each TPC-C table: 1. Select randomly 10% of the disk files containing data from the TPC-C table being considered (a minimum of 1). 2. Inject three faults for each disk file selected before in the following injection times: 3, 10, and 15 minutes.	4 min.
Delete a set of files from disk	Three faults for each set of files containing each TPC-C table (nine TPC-C tables, which correspond to a total of 27 faults). The injection times are the following: 3, 10, and 15 minutes. The sets of files to be deleted are chosen randomly.	2 min.
Delete all files from a disk	The set of faults to be injected must be defined performing the following steps: 1. Select randomly 10% of the disks containing data from any TPC-C table (in a minimum of 1). 2. Inject three faults for each disk selected before in the following injection times: 3, 10, and 15 minutes.	1 min.

dent. To reduce the time needed to execute the benchmark, the injection and detection times were scaled down. An important aspect is that the use of estimated times still guarantees a fair evaluation as all SUBs are benchmarked under similar conditions.

As shown in Table 5.1, the faultload is composed of a set of faults from each of the selected types injected in different instants (i.e., with different injection times). The number of faults from each type is mainly dependent on the size and configuration of the data storage of the system under benchmarking. For systems with identical data storage configurations in terms of the number of files and disks, the faultload is equivalent. Like the TPC-C benchmark, DBench-OLTP has been defined to compare system of similar sizes. In fact, it is not advisable to use TPC-C or DBench-OLTP to compare systems with hundreds of processors and disks with systems with only one processor and two or three disks.

Each fault in the faultload is injected in a different slot at different injection times. As a large number of injection slots could make the time needed to execute the benchmark impractical, an important goal in the definition of this faultload was to keep the number of injection slots within acceptable limits. Nevertheless, although we try to define the faultload based on a small set of fault types, the objective is to consider a set of types that represent the whole spectrum of recovery causes, evoced in diverse circumstances. It is worth noting that each fault type corresponds in practice to many concrete faults. For instance, for the type "Delete all files from one disk" the number of faults depends on the number of disks in the system.

Fault injection is distributed over time because two faults of the same type injected at different moments may cause the system to behave in different ways. In other words, different injection times are considered in order to inject faults during different stages of the execution of the workload. This improves the benchmark representativeness in the sense that recovery is performed considering different load conditions and different distances from past checkpoints. Injecting the faults at well-defined moments (i.e., very specific injection times) also increases the benchmark repeatability.

5.3.5.2. Faultload Based on High-Level Hardware Failures.
High-level hardware component failures are mainly related to the hardware components of the transactional server and each type of failure is normally associated with a specific hardware component. Among other components, a typical server contains mother board, CPU, RAM, hard disks, disk controllers, network interfaces, and power adapters. This way, some examples of typical types of high-level hardware failures include CPU failures, RAM failures, hard disk failures (complete disk failure or corruption of portions of the stored data), disk controller failures, network interface failures, failures on the interconnection network, and power source failures.

To define the faultload based on high-level hardware failures, we have first identified the hardware components that compose a typical database server and then obtained the types of high-level hardware failures that may occur in each component. This resulted in the selection of the types of failures presented in Table 5.2, which represent the most frequent high-level hardware failures found in the field [Kuhn 1997, Somany and Vaidya 1997]. It is worth noting that many types of high-level hardware failures are too difficult (or even impossible) to emulate in a benchmarking context (e.g., CPU failures, memory failures, and mother board failures).

Table 5.2 presents the rules used to identify the set of faults to be injected and the corresponding injection and detection times. The reasoning behind the definition of these rules is similar to the faultload based on operator faults (see Section 5.4.5.1). Thus, the

TABLE 5.2. Types of high-level hardware failures

Fault type	Description	Detection time
Power failure	Ten faults must be injected at the following injection times: 3, 5, 7, 9, 10, 11, 12, 13, 14, and 15 minutes.	0 sec.
Disk failure	The set of faults of the type "Disk failure" to be injected must be defined by performing the following steps for each TPC-C table: 1. Select randomly 20% of the disks containing data from the table being considered (a minimum of two except if there is only one disk). 2. Inject three faults for each disk selected before, using the following injection times: 3, 10, and 15 minutes.	1 min.
Corruption of storage media	The set of faults to be injected must be defined by performing the following steps for each TPC-C table: 1. Select randomly 10% of the disk files containing data from the table being considered (a minimum of 1). 2. Inject three faults for each disk file selected before, using the following injection times: 3, 10, and 15 minutes.	4 min.

number of faults of each type depends on the number of disks and files in the SUB, as systems with many disks and files are normally more prone to faults related to the data storage. As for operator faults, the injection times are distributed over time in order to cover different stages of the execution of the workload. The detection times take into account the impact of each type of faults in several DBMS.

5.3.5.2. Software Faults.
In [Durães and Madeira 2004a], a methodology to define faultloads based on software faults for dependability benchmarking is proposed. This methodology is based on previous field data studies meant to identify the most representative types of software faults [Christmansson and Chillarege 1996, Durães and Madeira 2003] and on a generic technique for the injection of software faults [Durães and Madeira 2002a, Durães and Madeira 2003]. This technique, named G-SWFIT (Generic Software Fault Injection Technique), consists of the modification during runtime of the binary code of software modules by introducing specific changes that correspond to the code that would be generated by the compiler if the software faults were in the high-level source code. A library of mutations, previously defined for the target platform and operating system (see [Durães and Madeira 2004a]), is used for the injection of the faults. The target application code is scanned for specific low-level instruction patterns and mutations are performed on those patterns to emulate related high-level faults.

The G-SWFIT emulation technique and the guidelines proposed in [Durães and Madeira 2004a] are used in the DBench-OLTP faultload based on software faults. It is worth noting that this is the first dependability benchmark using a faultload based on software faults. Table 5.3 summarizes the types of software faults considered, which represent the most frequent types of faults found in the field study presented in [Duraes03], covering more than 50% of the most common faults observed (the remaining faults are dispersed through a large number of fault types, each one responsible for a reduced number of fault occurrences, and, thus, are not as interesting for fault injection from a representativeness point of view [Durães and Madeira 2003]).

TABLE 5.3. Types of software faults

Fault types	Description	% observed in field study
MIFS	Missing "if (condition) { statement(s) }"	9.96 %
MFC	Missing function call	8.64 %
MLAC	Missing "AND EXPR" in expression used as branch condition	7.89 %
MIA	Missing "if (condition)" surrounding statement(s)	4.32 %
MLPC	Missing small and localized part of the algorithm	3.19 %
MVAE	Missing variable assignment using an expression	3.00 %
WLEC	Wrong logical expression used as branch condition	3.00 %
WVAV	Wrong value assigned to a value	2.44 %
MVI	Missing variable initialization	2.25 %
MVAV	Missing variable assignment using a value	2.25 %
WAEP	Wrong arithmetic expression used in parameter of function call	2.25 %
WPFV	Wrong variable used in parameter of function call	1.50 %
Total faults coverage		50.69 %

Software faults are not injected into the benchmark target (the DBMS). As the injection of software faults implies the modification of the target code, any conclusion drawn afterward might not apply to the original benchmark target. We use the notion of the fault injection farget (FIT), which is a component of the SUB other than the benchmark target. The best option for the FIT in the DBench-OLTP context is the operating system (OS) itself, as the OS is indispensable in a transactional server.

As the OS is very large, specific portions were previously selected as prime candidates for fault injection. For example, in Windows operating systems these portions correspond to the code of the API most used by typical applications, which are the kernel32 and ntdll system modules. This represents an additional advantage as, normally, all applications under Windows have these two modules mapped into its address space, which improves the portability of the faultload. For other families of operating systems (e.g., Linux) similar approaches are followed.

After knowing the types of software faults to be considered, two important questions concerning the benchmark procedure and rules were investigated:

1. *Profile for the injection of software faults.* Ten faults are injected at the beginning of the measurement interval, as soon as the system achieves the steady-state condition. The DBMS is restarted 5 minutes after the injection of the faults, independently of the visible effects of those faults (to remove any latent fault effects). This time has been postulated based on experiments to identify the average fault activation time of the types of software faults presented in Table 5.3. The DBMS is always restarted because some faults may have effects that cannot be directly identified by typical error diagnosis procedures (e.g., performance degradation, deadlocks, etc).

2. *Number of faults injected in each slot.* To identify the number of faults to be injected in each slot, a set of experiments has been performed considering different systems. For one fault per slot (or a very small number of faults per slot), the fault activation rate is quite small (less than 10%), which would require a large number of injection slots to get results statistically representative because, in most of the slots, the faults injected would not cause visible effects. On the other hand, for a high number of faults per slot the activation rate is too high, getting gradually closer to

100% as the number of faults increases. After performing some experiments, we have observed that by injecting 10 faults per slot an acceptable activation rate is obtained (approximately 33%).

The faultload based on software faults allows the evaluation of a DBMS running on top of an operating system containing software bugs (e.g., incorrect resource management, wrong API results etc.). In fact, the faults injected emulate a software bug in the operating system code, whereas the benchmark measures the impact of these faults on the DBMS. This is a realistic scenario as it is a well-known fact that operating systems contain residual software faults [Koopman et al. 97, Voas et al. 97, Fabre et al. 99]. Even so, the DBMS should behave in an acceptable manner. For example, it should preserve the integrity of the database, allow recovery if needed, and so on. However, this faultload can only be used to compare the behavior of different DBMS running on top of a given operating system. As faults are injected at the OS level, the comparison among operating systems is not possible. The sets of faults to be injected is specific to a given OS and not to the DBMS.

As the injection of software faults is quite complex, the set of software faults to be injected and the tool needed to inject those faults are provided with the benchmark specification. The idea is to simply download the G-SWFIT tool and the library and use them in the benchmark environment.

5.4. DEPENDABILITY BENCHMARKING EXAMPLES USING DBENCH-OLTP

This section describes a practical example of the use of the DBench-OLTP dependability benchmark. The goal of the benchmarking experiments conducted is to compare and rank several transactional systems. These systems represent possible alternatives for small- and medium-size OLTP applications such as typical client–server database applications or e-commerce applications. In this sense, the benchmarking experiments presented answer the following question: Which system is the best choice for a typical OLTP application, when considering both performance and dependability aspects?

As presented in Section 4, the DBench-OLTP benchmark can be used by considering three different faultloads. In the experiments presented in this section, we have used only the faultload based on operator faults. Some examples using software faults and high-level hardware failures are presented in [Vieira and Madeira 2004b], as part of a set of the experiments meant to validate the benchmark.

5.4.1. Systems under Benchmarking

Table 5.4 shows the systems under benchmarking (letters in the left-most column will be used later to refer to each system). Three different DBMS (Oracle 8i, Oracle 9i, and PostgreSQL 7.3), three different operating systems (Windows 2K, Windows Xp, and SuSE Linux 7.3), and two different hardware platforms (one based on a 800 MHz Pentium III with 256 MB of RAM and the other on a 2 GHz Pentium IV with 512 MB of RAM) have been used.

Two configurations have been chosen for the Oracle 8i and Oracle 9i DBMS (Configuration A and Configuration B in Table 5.4) based on database administration experience. The goal is to show the impact of different tuning on the benchmark results. The main difference between these two configurations is the size of the redo log files (100 MB for

TABLE 5.4. Systems under benchmarking

System	Operating system	DBMS	DBMS configuration	Hardware
A	Windows 2K Prof. SP 3	Oracle 8i R2 (8.1.7)	Configuration A	Processor: Intel Pentium III
B	Windows 2K Prof. SP 3	Oracle 9i R2 (9.0.2)	Configuration A	800 MHz
C	Windows Xp Prof. SP 1	Oracle 8i R2 (8.1.7)	Configuration A	Memory: 256 MB
D	Windows Xp Prof. SP 1	Oracle 9i R2 (9.0.2)	Configuration A	Hard Disks: Four
E	Windows 2K Prof. SP 3	Oracle 8i R2 (8.1.7)	Configuration B	20 GB/7200 rpm
F	Windows 2K Prof. SP 3	Oracle 9i R2 (9.0.2)	Configuration B	Network: Fast Ethernet
G	SuSE Linux 7.3	Oracle 8i R2 (8.1.7)	Configuration A	
H	SuSE Linux 7.3	Oracle 9i R2 (9.0.2)	Configuration A	
I	SuSE Linux 7.3	PostgreSQL 7.3	—	
J	Windows 2K Prof. SP 3	Oracle 8i R2 (8.1.7)	Configuration A	Processor: Intel Pentium IV 2 GHz
K	Windows 2K Prof. SP 3	Oracle 9i R2 (9.0.2)	Configuration A	Memory: 512 MB

Configuration A and 1MB for Configuration B) and the checkpoint frequency (approximately 6 minutes for Configuration A and 4 seconds for Configuration B).

As mentioned in Section 5.4, the number of faults in the faultload based on operator faults is dependent on the size and configuration of the data storage of the system under benchmarking. In the present benchmarking experiments, the size of the database tables and the distribution of files among the available disks is equivalent for all systems, therefore, the faultload used to benchmark a given system is equivalent to the faultloads used in the others. Table 5.5 presents the faultloads considered.

5.4.2. Benchmarking Results

In order to understand the effects on the measures of a given component of the SUB, it is necessary to perform benchmarking in several SUB configurations in which the only difference between each configuration is the component under study. The following sections present and discuss the results in a way that compares different alternatives for each one of the main components that comprise a transactional system (the DBMS, the operating system, and the hardware platform) and for the DBMS configuration. Section 5.5.2.5 proposes a ranking for the systems under benchmarking.

TABLE 5.5. Faultload based on operator faults used in the benchmarking example

Type of fault		# of faults	% of faults
F1	Abrupt operating system shutdown	10	10.3
F2	Abrupt transactional engine shutdown	10	10.3
F3	Kill set of user sessions	5	5.2
F4	Delete table	12	12.4
F5	Delete user schema	3	3.1
F6	Delete file from disk	27	27.8
F7	Delete set of files from disk	27	27.8
F8	Delete all files from one disk	3	3.1
	Total	97	100

5.4.2.1. *Comparing Different DBMS.* This section presents the results regarding six different transactional systems: systems A, B, C, D, G, H, and I from Table 5.4. These systems use three different DBMS, three different operating systems, and the same hardware platform. The goal is to compare the different DBMS (Oracle 8i, Oracle 9i, and PostgreSQL 7.3) running on top of different operating systems and using the same hardware and similar DBMS configurations (Configuration A from Table 5.4). Figure 5.2 presents the results.

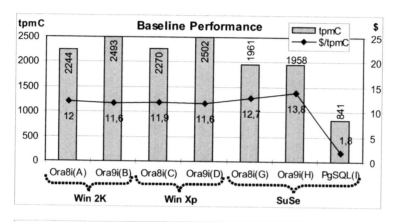

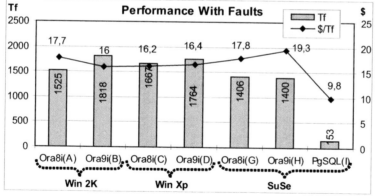

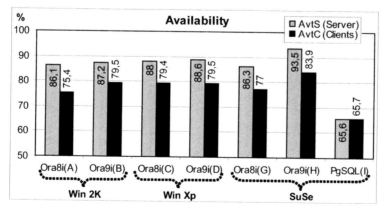

Figure 5.2. Benchmarking results for systems using different DBMS.

As we can see, the baseline performance (tpmC) strongly depends on the DBMS and systems of the same family may provide similar or different performance results depending on the operating system used. In fact, for the systems using Windows, the baseline performance using Oracle 9i is higher than using Oracle 8i. On the other hand, for the systems based on the SuSE Linux operating system, the baseline performance is similar for Oracle 8i and Oracle9i. Finally, for PostgreSQL the baseline performance is quite low.

In terms of the price per transaction ($/tpmC), the systems based on Oracle running over SuSE Linux present the higher prices (due to the poor performance reached). Considering systems only running Windows, the most expensive ones (based on the Oracle 9i) present a lower price-per-transaction than the less expensive ones (based on the Oracle 8i), due to the better performance achieved.

For the performance measures in the presence of faults, results show that the number of transactions executed per minute (Tf) also depends on the DBMS used. In fact, the Oracle9i DBMS is clearly more effective than Oracle 8i except when running on top of SuSe Linux. On the other hand, and similarly to baseline performance, the transactional system based on the PostgreSQL presents very poor results, due to the poor recovery mechanisms available in this DBMS.

Regarding the dependability measures, results show that the availability observed for the systems running the Oracle9i DBMS is better than for systems using Oracle 8i. The system based on Oracle 9i running over SuSE Linux (system H) presents a much higher availability than any other system, which means that, although it is a slow system, it recovers from faults faster than the others, thus increasing the availability time.

An important aspect concerning the dependability features of the systems is that no data integrity errors (Ne) were detected, which shows that the transactional engines considered (Oracle and PostgreSQL) are very effective in guarantying data integrity even in the presence of operator faults.

5.4.2.2. Comparing Different Operating Systems.

Although DBench-OLTP is naturally oriented for DBMS comparison, the benchmark can also be used to select alternative operating systems for transactional environments.

As shown by the results presented in Figure 5.2, the baseline performance (tpmC) also depends on the operating system used. A considerable difference in the baseline performance is observed for systems based on the same DBMS running over different operating systems. In fact, the same DBMS using Windows achieves a better number of transactions executed per minute than by using SuSE Linux.

The number of transactions executed per minute (Tf) is also influenced by the operating system. For the systems running Oracle8i the Windows Xp operating system is clearly more effective than Windows 2K and for the systems running Oracle 9i the reverse seems to occur. However, the small difference in the results for the systems using Oracle 9i does not allow a solid conclusion.

Regarding the dependability measures, results show that the availability observed for the systems running the Oracle8i DBMS over Windows Xp is better than over SuSE Linux, which in turn is better than Windows 2K. An important aspect is that Oracle 9i running over SuSE Linux presents a much higher availability than any other system.

5.4.2.3. Comparing Different DBMS Configurations.

The goal of this section is to demonstrate the use of the DBench-OLTP benchmark to compare transactional systems using the same hardware and software, but considering different DBMS configurations. Figure 5.3 compares four different transactional systems using two versions of the Oracle DBMS (Oracle 8i and Oracle 9i) running over the Windows 2K operating system and using the same hardware platform (systems A, B, E, and F from Table 5.4). In these experiments, each of the Oracle DBMS was tested using two different configurations of the recovery mechanisms. As mentioned before, the main difference between these two configurations is that one provides better recovery capabilities (Configuration A) than the other (Configuration B).

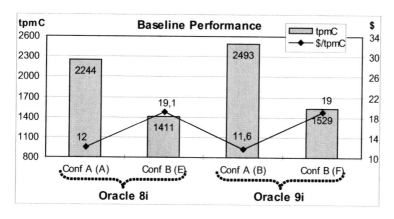

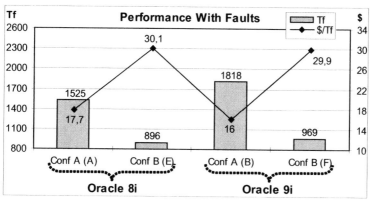

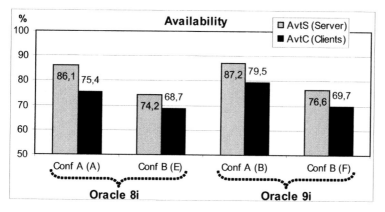

Figure 5.3. Benchmarking results for systems using two different DBMS configurations.

As expected, results show that Configuration A is better than Configuration B in both the Oracle 8i and Oracle 9i DBMS, which indicates that DBench-OLTP can help database administrators in selecting the best DBMS configuration according to their needs.

5.4.2.4. Systems Ranking. In the previous sections, we have compared different alternatives for each one of the main components of an OLTP system (the hardware platform, the operating system, and the DBMS). Table 5.6 summarizes the system ranking

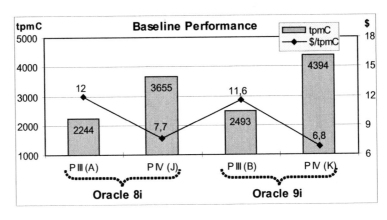

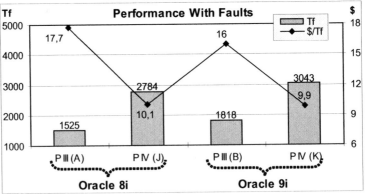

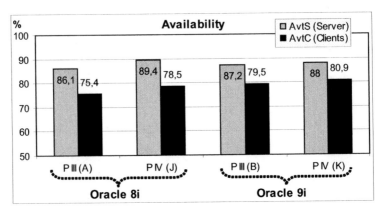

Figure 5.4. Benchmarking results for systems using different hardware.

TABLE 5.6. Systems ranking according to several criteria

Criteria	System ranking (best to worst)
Baseline performance (tpmC)	K, J, D, B, C, A, G, H, F, E, I
Performance with faults (Tf)	K, J, B, D, C, A, G, H, F, E, I
Availability (AvtS and AvtC)	H, J, D, K, C, B, G, A, F, E, I

proposed according to three different criteria: baseline performance, performance with faults, and availability.

Concerning a global ranking, the analysis of Table 5.6 and all the results presented before allow us to propose the following order (from the best to the worst): J, K, D, B, C, H, G, A, F, E, and I. It is important to note that the global ranking always depends on the benchmark performer point of view (i.e., it depends on what is being looked for). In our case, we were particularly interested in the best compromise among the three criteria presented in Table 5.6.

5.4.3. Using the Benchmark to Obtain More Specific Results

Typically, benchmarks provide a small set of measures easy to understand and compare. The DBench-OLTP benchmark follows this well-established measuring philosophy, but it can also be used to obtain more specific results that allow a detailed characterization of the SUB behavior concerning performance and dependability. For space reasons, in this section we give just one example of the large set of specific results that can be obtained.

Figure 5.5 shows an example of the availability variation across the several injection slots, considering two systems (systems A and B from Table 5.4). The availability at each moment represents the average availability during the corresponding injection slot and that is why the availability never reaches zero. Obviously, at some moments the system is completely unavailable during the recovery of some faults, but this is not visible because the charts show average availability for each injection slot. As we can see, system B presents a higher and more regular availability across time than system A, which means that Oracle 9i is more stable in the presence of faults than its predecessor.

5.4.4. Benchmark Properties Discussion

The following sections discuss some important aspects concerning the properties of the DBench-OLTP benchmark using the faultload based on operator faults.

5.4.4.1. Representativeness. In dependability benchmarking, representativeness is mainly influenced by the workload and faultload characteristics. As we have adopted the TPC-C workload, which is well accepted as a realistic OLTP scenario, the representativeness of the workload is assured. In terms of the faultload, available studies clearly point to operator faults as one of the most frequent causes for computer failures [Gray 1990, Sullivan and Chillarege 1992, Lee and Iyer 1995, Brown and Patterson 2001]. In order to improve the representativeness of the faultload based on operator faults, the types of faults considered have been chosen based on field experience with database systems administration, the ability of the faults to emulate the effects of other types of faults, the diversity of impact on the system, and the complexity of the required recovery. Thus, the type of erro-

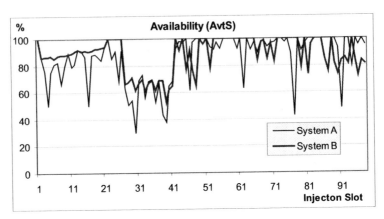

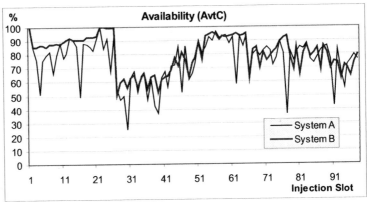

Figure 5.5. Availability variation during the benchmark run.

neous behavior induced by the injected faults and the kind of recovery procedure required represent quite well the typical recovery scenarios experienced by DBMS in the field.

5.4.4.2. Portability. Different DBMS may include different sets of administration tasks and, consequently, have different sets of possible operator faults. However, as shown in [Vieira and Madeira 2002, Vieira and Madeira 2004a], it is possible to establish equivalence among many operator faults in different DBMS. The results presented in this chapter also show that it is possible to implement the faultload based on operator faults in different operating systems and DBMS.

5.4.4.3. Repeatability. To evaluate repeatability, we have executed the benchmark three times in each system. The results obtained show that the results variation for the baseline performance (tpmC) is inside the interval defined by the TPC-C specification (2%). Concerning performance in the presence of faults (Tf), the variation is a little bit higher (but always less than 4%). The variation on the availability measures is below 0.5%. These seem to be quite fine intervals.

5.4.4.4. Scalability. As mentioned in this chapter, the faultload based on operator faults is dependent on the size and configuration of the data storage of the system under benchmarking. For large systems with many disks and files, the number of faults to consider may become extremely high. In those cases, although the DBench-OLTP benchmark continues to apply, the time needed to conduct the benchmarking process may increase considerably.

5.4.4.5. Nonintrusiveness. The emulation of operator faults in a DBMS can be easily achieved by reproducing common database administrator mistakes. Those mistakes can be reproduced by submitting normal SQL commands to the target system so there is no need for changes in the target system to introduce this faultload.

5.4.4.6. Simplicity of Use. The implementation of the DBench-OLTP benchmark using operator faults is quite simple (in part, because the emulation of operator faults is a very easy task). Concerning the time needed to conduct all the benchmarking process, the effort is very low. In fact, we have been able to implement the DBench-OLTP benchmark (using operator faults) in 10 days and to execute 11 benchmarking experiments in about 33 days (a ratio of 3 days per benchmarking experiment).

5.5. CONCLUSIONS

This chapter proposes a new dependability benchmark for OLTP application environments—the Dbench-OLTP dependability benchmark. This benchmark specifies the measures and all the steps required to evaluate both the performance and key dependability features of OLTP systems. The DBench-OLTP uses the basic setup, workload, and performance measures specified in the TPC-C performance benchmark, and adds two new elements: (1) measures related to dependability and (2) a faultload based on operator faults.

Several different transactional systems have been benchmarked using the DBench-OLTP benchmark. Three different DBMS (Oracle 8i, Oracle 9i, and PostgreSQL 7.3), three different operating systems (Windows 2000, Windows Xp, and SuSE Linux 7.3), and two different hardware platforms have been used. The experimental results were analyzed and discussed in detail. These results allow us to rank the systems under benchmarking concerning both performance and dependability and clearly show that dependability benchmarking can be successfully applied to OLTP application environments. In fact, from the practical benchmarking example presented we can confirm that DBench-OLTP can be used to select the main components for an OLTP system. Although the main goal is the comparison of DBMS, DBench-OLTP can also be used to select operating systems and hardware for transactional environments. In addition, this benchmark can also help the database administrator tuning the DBMS configuration parameters to achieve the adequate compromise for performance and dependability. Finally, results show that DBench-OLTP can be very useful to provide a detailed analysis of the SUB behavior concerning performance and dependability.

REFERENCES

[Brown and Patterson 2000] A. Brown and D. A. Patterson, "Towards Availability Benchmarks: A Cases Study of Software RAID Systems," in *Proceedings of the 2000 USENIX Annual Technical Conference,* San Diego, CA, USENIX Association, 2000.

[Brown and Patterson 2001] A. Brown and D. A. Patterson, "To Err is Human," presented at First Workshop on Evaluating and Architecting System Dependability (EASY), Göteborg, Sweden, July 2001.

[Brown et al. 2002] A. Brown, L. C. Chung, and D. A. Patterson. "Including the Human Factor in Dependability Benchmarks," in *Workshop on Dependability Benchmarking,* Supplemental Volume of DSN 2002, pp. F-9–14, Washington, D.C., 2002.

[Brown et al. 2004] A. Brown, L. Chung, W. Kakes, C. Ling, and D. A. Patterson, "Dependability Benchmarking of Human-Assisted Recovery Processes," in *IEEE/IFIP International Conference on Dependable Systems and Networks,* DSN 2004, Florence, Italy, June 2004.

[Buchacker et al. 2003] K. Buchacker, M. Dal Cin, H.-J. Hoxer, R. Karch, V. Sieh, and O. Tschache, "Reproducible Dependability Benchmarking Experiments Based on Unambiguous Benchmark Setup Descriptions," in *IEEE/IFIP International Conference on Dependable Systems and Networks,* DSN 2003, San Francisco, June 22–25, 2003.

[Christmansson and Chillarege 1996] J. Christmansson and R. Chillarege, "Generation of an Error Set that Emulates Software Faults," in *Proceedings of the 26th IEEE Fault Tolerant Computing Symposium,* FTCS-26, Sendai, Japan, pp. 304–313, June 1996.

[DBench] DBench Project, Project funded by the European Community under the "Information Society Technology" Programme (1998–2002), http://www.dbench.org/.

[Durães and Madeira 2002a] J. Durães and H. Madeira, "Emulation of Software Faults by Selective Mutations at Machine-code Level," in *Proceedings of the 13th IEEE International Symposium on Software Reliability Engineering,* ISSRE 2002, Annapolis, MD, November 2002.

[Durães and Madeira 2002b] J. Durães and H. Madeira, "Characterization of Operating Systems Behaviour in the Presence of Faulty Drivers through Software Fault Emulation," in *2002 Pacific Rim International Symposium on Dependable Computing,* PRDC-2002, pp. 201–209, Tsukuba, Japan, December 2002.

[Durães and Madeira 2003] J. Durães and H. Madeira, "Definition of Software Fault Emulation Operators: A Field Data Study," in *IEEE/IFIP International Conference on Dependable Systems and Networks, Dependable Computing and Communications,* DSN-DCC 2003, San Francisco, June 2003.

[Durães and Madeira 2004a] J. Durães and H. Madeira, "Generic Faultloads Based on Software Faults for Dependability Benchmarking," in *IEEE/IFIP International Conference on Dependable Systems and Networks,* DSN 2004, Florence, Italy, June, 2004.

[Durães and Madeira 2004b] J. Durães, M. Vieira, and H. Madeira, "Dependability Benchmarking of Web-Servers," in *Proceedings of the 23rd International Conference on Computer Safety, Reliability and Security,* SAFECOMP 2004, Potsdam, Germany, September, 2004.

[Fabre et al. 1999] J.-C. Fabre, F. Salles, M. Rodríguez Moreno, and J. Arlat, "Assessment of COTS Microkernels by Fault Injection," in *Proceedings 7th IFIP Working Conference on Dependable Computing for Critical Applications: DCCA-7,* San Jose, CA, pp. 25–44, January 1999.

[Gray 1990] J. Gray, "A Census of Tandem System Availability Between 1985 and 1990," *IEEE Transactions on Reliability,* vol. R-39, no. 4, pp. 409–418, 1990.

[Kalakech et al. 2004] A. Kalakech, K. Kanoun, Y. Crouzet, and A. Arlat, "Benchmarking the Dependability of Windows NT, 2000 and XP," in *Proceedings of the International Conference on Dependable Systems and Networks,* DSN 2004, Florence, Italy, 2004.

[Koopman et al. 1997] P. J. Koopman, J. Sung, C. Dingman, D. P. Siewiorek, and T. Marz, "Comparing Operating Systems using Robustness Benchmarks," in *Proceedings of the 16th International Symposium on Reliable Distributed Systems,* SRDS-16, Durham, NC, pp. 72–79, 1997.

[Kuhn 1997] D. R. Kuhn, "Sources of Failure in the Public Switched Telephone Network," *IEEE Computer,* vol. 30, no. 4, April 1997.

[Laprie 1995] J.-C. Laprie, "Dependable Computing: Concepts, Limits, Challenges," in *Proceedings of the 25th International Symposium on Fault-Tolerant Computing, FTCS-25,* Special Issue, Pasadena, CA, pp. 42–54, 1995.

[Lee and Iyer 1995] I. Lee and R. K. Iyer, "Software Dependability in the Tandem GUARDIAN System," *IEEE Transactions on Software Engineering,* vol. 21, no. 5, pp. 455–467, May 1995.

[Lightstone et al. 2003] S. Lightstone, J. Hellerstein, W. Tetzlaff, P. Janson, E. Lassettre, C. Norton, B. Rajaraman, and L. Spainhower. "Towards Benchmarking Autonomic Computing Maturity," in *Proceedings of the First IEEE Conference on Industrial Automatics (INDIN-2003),* Banff, Canada, August 2003.

[Madeira et al. 2000] H. Madeira, D. Costa, and M. Vieira, "On the Emulation of Software Faults by Software Fault Injection," in *Proceedings of the International Conference on Dependable Systems and Networks, DSN-2000,* New York, NY, pp. 417–426, 2000.

[Mauro et al. 2004] J. Mauro, J. Zhu, and I. Pramanick. "The System Recovery Benchmark," in *Proceedings of the 2004 Pacific Rim International Symposum on Dependable Computing, PRDC 2004,* Papeete, Tahiti, 2004.

[Moreira et al. 2003] F. Moreira, R. Maia, D. Costa, N. Duro, P. Rodríguez-Dapena, and K. Hjortnaes, "Static and Dynamic Verification of Critical Software for Space Applications," in *Proceedings of the Data Systems In Aerospace Conference, DASIA 2003,* June 2003.

[Ramakrishnan and Gehrke 2002] R. Ramakrishnan and J. Gehrke, *Database Management Systems,* 3rd ed. McGraw-Hill, 2002.

[Ruiz et al. 2004] J.-C. Ruiz, P. Yuste, P. Gil, and L. Lemus, "On Benchmarking the Dependability of Automotive Engine Control Applications," in *IEEE/IFIP International Conference on Dependable Systems and Networks, DSN 2004,* Florence, Italy, June 2004.

[Somany and Vaidya 1997] A. K. Somani and N. H. Vaidya, "Understanding Fault Tolerance and Reliability," *IEEE Computer,* vol. 30, no. 4, April 1997.

[SPECWeb99] Standard Performance Evaluation Corporation, "SPECweb99 Release 1.02 (Design Document)," http://www.spec.org/web99/, July 2000.

[Sullivan and Chillarege 1992] M. Sullivan and R. Chillarege, "Comparison of Software Defects in Database Management Systems and Operating Systems," in *Proceedings of the 22nd IEEE Fault Tolerant Computing Symposium, FTCS-22,* pp. 475–484, July 1992.

[TPC] Transaction Processing Performance Council, www.tpc.org.

[TPC-C 2005] Transaction Processing Performance Council, "TPC Benchmark C, Standard Specification, Version 5.4," 2005, available at http://www.tpc.org/tpcc/.

[Vieira 2005] M. Vieira, *Dependability Benchmarking for Transactional Systems,* PhD thesis, Faculty of Sciences and Technology of the University of Coimbra, July 2005, available at http://eden.dei.uc.pt/~mvieira/phd.

[Vieira and Madeira 2002] M. Vieira and H. Madeira, "Definition of Faultloads Based on Operator Faults for DMBS Recovery Benchmarking," in *Proceedings of the Pacific Rim International Symposium on Dependable Computing, PRDC2002,* Tsukuba, Japan, December 2002.

[Vieira and Madeira 2003] M. Vieira and H. Madeira, "A Dependability Benchmark for OLTP Application Environments," in *Proceedings of the 29th International Conference on Very Large Data Bases, VLDB 2003,* pp. 742–753, Berlin, Germany, 2003.

[Vieira and Madeira 2004a] M. Vieira and H. Madeira, "Portable Faultloads Based on Operator Faults for DBMS Dependability Benchmarking," in *Proceedings of the 28th Annual International Computer Software and Applications Conference, COMPSAC 2004,* Hong Kong, September 2004.

[Vieira and Madeira 2004b] M. Vieira, J. Durães, and H. Madeira, "How to Specify Dependability Benchmarks for OLTP Application Environments," in *Proceedings of the 9th Conference on Software Engineering and Databases, JISBD2004,* Malaga, Spain, November 2004.

[Vieira and Madeira 2004c] M. Vieira and H. Madeira, "DBench-OLTP Dependability Benchmark Specification (v1.2.0)," 2004, available at http://gbd.dei.uc.pt/downloads.php.

[Vieira and Madeira 2005] Marco Vieira, *Dependability Benchmarking for Transactional Systems,* Ph.D. thesis, Faculty of Sciences and Technology of the University of Coimbra, July 2005.

[Voas et al. 1997] J. Voas, F. Charron, G. McGraw, K. Miller, and M. Friedman, "Predicting How Badly 'Good' Software Can Behave," *IEEE Software,* vol. 14, no. 4, pp. 73–83, 1997.

[Wilson et al. 2002] D. Wilson, B. Murphy, and L. Spainhower. "Progress on Defining Standardized Classes of Computing the Dependability of Computer Systems," in *Proceedings of the DSN 2002 Workshop on Dependability Benchmarking,* pp. F1–5, Washington, DC, 2002.

[Zhu et al. 2003a] J. Zhu, J. Mauro, and I. Pramanick. "R3—A Framwork for Availability Benchmarking," in *Proceedings of the IEEE/IFIP International Conference on Dependable Systems and Networks, DSN 2003,* pp. B-86–87, San Francisco, 2003.

[Zhu et al. 2003b] J. Zhu, J. Mauro, and I. Pramanick, "Robustness Benchmarking for Hardware Maintenance Events," in *Proceedings of the IEEE/IFIP International Conference on Dependable Systems and Networks, DSN 2003,* pp. 115–122, San Francisco, 2003.

6

DEPENDABILITY BENCHMARKING OF WEB SERVERS

João Durães, Marco Vieira, and Henrique Madeira

6.1. INTRODUCTION

Web servers are increasingly becoming a strategic resource for data exchange and content distribution. Ranging from on-line stores to media corporations, Web servers are a key component of the information infrastructure. Given the swiftness of Web surfers when jumping from one site to the next, business may be easily lost if a corporate site is temporarily unavailable to its costumers. Thus, the deployment of a given Web server should be a matter of careful consideration and thought. Currently, when choosing from similar products (web servers), the decision is typically made mainly according to performance, cost, compatibility, and ease of deployment. However, dependability properties are at least as important. Performance benchmarks are typically used to assess performance and cost figures. Although performance benchmarks for Web servers are among the best examples of successful performance benchmarks (e.g., the SPECWeb benchmark suite [SPEC 2000]), dependability benchmarks for Web servers are still nonexistent.

Assessing system dependability is in fact a very difficult problem as it is dependent on fault probability, which in turn is dependent on many factors, either internal to the system (hardware and software) or external (environment or human made).

Dependability assessment has been addressed in the dependability research community by using both model-based and measurement-based techniques. The former include analytical [Trivedi et al. 1994] and simulation [Jenn et al. 1995] techniques. Measurement-based techniques include field measurement [Gray 1990], fault injection [Arlat et al. 1993], and robustness testing [Koopman and DeVale 1999], just to mention few examples.

Most of these dependability assessment techniques have been developed for mission-critical systems or for the high-end, business-critical area and, thus, make assumptions about design or operating environments that affect their direct porting to more mainstream computing systems. The goal of dependability benchmarking is, thus, to provide generic ways of characterizing the behavior of components and computer systems in the presence of faults, allowing for the quantification of dependability measures.

Following the well-established philosophy used in the performance benchmark world, the dependability benchmarking proposals are mainly inspired by measurement-based techniques. However, beyond existing techniques, such as fault injection and robustness testing, dependability benchmarking must provide a uniform, repeatable, and cost-effective way of performing this evaluation, especially for comparative evaluation of competing or alternative systems and/or components.

A dependability benchmark can then be defined as a specification of a standard procedure to assess dependability-related measures of a computer system or computer component [Madeira and Koopman 2001, Kanoun et al. 2004]. The main components of the dependability benchmark are [Koopman and Madeira 1999]:

- **Workload**—represents the work that the system must perform during the benchmark run.
- **Faultload**—represents a set of faults and stressful conditions that emulate real faults experienced in the field.
- **Measures**—characterize the performance and dependability of the system under benchmark in the presence of the faultload when executing the workload.
- **Experimental setup and benchmark procedure**—describes the setup required to run the benchmark and the set of procedures and rules that must be followed during the benchmark execution.

This chapter presents a dependability benchmark for Web servers (the WEB-DB) focusing on availability, accuracy, resilience, and service degradation. To the best of our knowledge, this is the first proposal of a dependability benchmark for this important class of systems.

In [Vieira and Madeira 2003] (see Chapter 5), a dependability benchmark is proposed for transactional systems—the DBench-OLTP dependability benchmark that considers a set of operator faults, software faults, and high-level hardware failures. A dependability benchmark for transactional systems regarding a faultload that considers a set of hardware faults is proposed by [Buchacker and Tschaeche 2003].

A dependability benchmark for operating systems (OSs) is proposed by [Kalakech et al. 2004] (see also Chapter 12). The goal of this benchmark is to characterize the OS behavior in the presence of application-related faults, and to evaluate performance-related measures in the presence of faults. A practical approach to characterize OS behavior in the presence of software faults in OS components such as faulty device drivers is presented in [Durães and Madeira 2002b]. This work proposes the use of a multidimensional perspective to evaluate different views of the results, allowing the comparison of operating systems according to multiple perspectives.

Research work developed at the University of California–Berkeley has lead to the proposal of a dependability benchmark to assess human-assisted recovery processes [Brown et al. 2002].

Sun Microsystems defined a high-level framework [Zhu et al. 2003a] (see Chapter 2) dedicated specifically to availability benchmarking. Within this framework, two specific benchmarks have been developed. One of them [Zhu et al. 2003b] addresses specific aspects of a system's robustness on handling maintenance events such as the replacement of a failed hardware component or the installation of a software patch. The other benchmark is related to system recovery [Zhu et al. 2004] (see also Chapter 3).

IBM has developed benchmarks to quantify a system's level of autonomic capability, addressing four main spaces of IBM's self-management: self-configuration, self-healing, self-optimization, and self-protection [Lightstone et al. 2003] (see also Chapter 1).

6.2. MEASURING THE DEPENDABILITY OF WEB SERVERS: A BENCHMARK PROPOSAL

A typical Web environment consists of several clients requesting or sending data via a Web browser to the Web server through the Internet. The concept of Web server can have different meanings across the industry and research communities. In the context of this benchmark, the terms *Web server* and *Web server program* refer to the HTTP daemon (i.e., a computer program). The term *Web server solution* refers to the complete solution required to run the HTTP daemon and includes all the necessary hardware, operating system, and the Web server itself (the HTTP daemon).

The WEB-DB dependability benchmark proposed in this chapter uses the basic experimental setup, the workload, and the performance measures specified in the SPECWeb99 benchmark [SPEC 2000]. The following subsections present the WEB-DB dependability benchmark, with particular emphasis on the new components.

6.2.1. Experimental Setup and Benchmark Procedure

Figure 6.1 presents the key elements of the experimental setup required to run the WEB-DB dependability benchmark. The key elements are the *system under benchmarking* (SUB) and the *benchmark management system* (BMS).

The SUB consists of a Web server solution, which includes all the hardware and software necessary to run the web server (the HTTP daemon). From the benchmark point of view, the SUB is the set of processing units needed to run the workload. It is important to

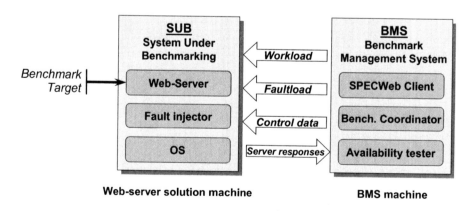

Figure 6.1. Experimental setup overview.

note that the SUB is larger than (and includes) the component directly targeted by the benchmark (named *benchmark target* or BT), which is the Web server program.

The BMS is a set of tools that control all aspects of the benchmark experiments. Its key functionalities are: submission of the workload, coordination and synchronization of the several components involved in the experiments, and collection of the raw data needed to produce the benchmark measures (measures are computed afterwards by analyzing the information collected during the benchmark run). Typically, the SUB and the BMS reside in separate machines, with the exception of the fault injector itself, which must be located in the same machine as the Web server program.

The execution of the WEB-DB dependability benchmark includes two main phases (Figure 6.2):

- **Phase 1.** This phase corresponds to the execution of the SPECWeb99 performance benchmark and is used to determine the *baseline performance* of the SUB. The baseline performance corresponds to the performance attainable by the SUB under normal operating conditions (that is, without artificial faults) but with the BMS tools running. A key notion implied here is that the BMS is considered as part of the workload submitted to the SUB. A second result of this phase is a measure of the intrusiveness of the BMS, which is directly given by the difference of the performance of the SUB with and without the BMS. Note that the execution of the SPECWeb99 benchmark includes three runs and the results reported are the average of the results from those runs.

- **Phase 2.** In this phase, the workload is run in the presence of the faultload to evaluate the impact of the faults on the SUB. As in Phase 1, this phase includes three runs and the results reported represent the average of the results from those runs. During each run, all faults defined in the faultload are applied.

As shown in Figure 6.2, each run is made up of several injection slots. An injection slot can be defined as a measurement interval during which the workload is run and some faults from the faultload are injected. The execution profile of each injection slot is close-

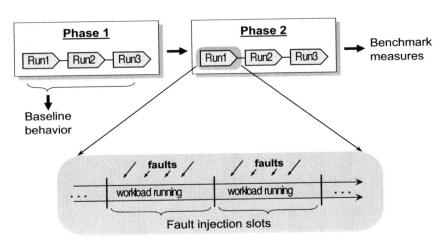

Figure 6.2. Benchmark execution profile.

ly related to the class of the faults to be injected (see subsection 6.2.4 for a detailed discussion on the execution profile of each slot).

6.2.2. Workload

The WEB-DB dependability benchmark adopts the workload of the well-established SPECWeb99 performance benchmark. This workload represents typical requests submitted to real Web servers. Its definition was based on the analysis of Web-based services in several real websites (see [SPEC 2000] for more details). The workload is composed of the typical operations allowed by the HTML (GET and POST operations, both static and dynamic). The workload also reproduces common actions such as on-line registration and advertisement serving.

6.2.3. Measures

The WEB-DB dependability benchmark measures are computed from the information collected during the benchmark run and follow the well-established measuring philosophy used in the performance benchmark world. In fact, the measures provided by existing performance benchmarks give relative measures of performance that can be used for system comparison or for system/component improvement and tuning. It is well known that performance benchmark results do not represent an absolute measure of performance and cannot be used for planning capacity or to predict the actual performance of the system in the field. In a similar way, the measures proposed for this first dependability benchmark must be understood as benchmark results that can be useful to characterize system dependability in a relative fashion (e.g., to compare two alternative systems) or to improve/tune the system dependability.

The WEB-DB measures are grouped into three categories: baseline performance measures, performance measures in the presence of faults, and dependability measures.

The *baseline performance measures,* inherited from the SPECWeb99 performance benchmark, are obtained during Phase 1 and include:

- **SPEC**—This is the main SPECWeb99 metric. It measures the number of simultaneous conforming connections. SPEC defines conforming connection as a connection with an average bit rate of at least 320 kbps and less than 1% of errors reported.
- **THR**—Reports the number of operations (e.g., GETs and POSTs) per second (throughput).
- **RTM**—Represents the average time in milliseconds that the operations requested by the client take to complete (mean response time).

The *performance measures in the presence of faults,* which represent the penalty in the performance of the Web server caused by the faults injected in Phase 2, include:

- **SPECf**—main SPEC measure in the presence of the faultload
- **THRf**—throughput in the presence of the faultload
- **RTMf**—response time in the presence of the faultload

The *dependability measures* reported are also collected in Phase 2 and include:

- **Resilience.** This measure gives an indication of the hardiness of the server when executing in a faulty environment. It is obtained through the observation of the number of times that the Web server had to be explicitly (externally) restarted. This happens when the Web server dies or stops providing useful service. This measure is computed using the following formula:

Resilience = 100 − (Number of explicit restarts/Number of faults injected) × 100

- **Accuracy.** Reports the error rate in the presence of the faultload. This measure is computed as:

Accuracy = 100 − (Number of requests with errors/Total number of request) × 100

- **Availability.** Represents the time the system is available to execute the workload. It is worth noting that in the context of the WEB-DB dependability benchmark, availability is defined based on the service provided by the system; the system is considered available when it is able to provide the service defined by the workload. In other words, the system is not available if the clients get no answer or get an error. For each run in Phase 2, this measure is given as a ratio between the amount of time the system is available and the total duration of that run.

6.2.4. Faultload

The faultload represents a set of faults and exceptional events that emulate real faults experienced by Web servers in the field. A faultload can be based on three major classes of faults: operator faults, software faults, and hardware faults.

The WEB-DB benchmark uses two different faultloads: one based on software faults that emulate realistic software defects (see [Durães and Madeira 2003, Durães and Madeira 2004]) and another based on operational faults that emulate the effects of hardware and operator faults. Of course, a general faultload that combines these two is also possible (and is in fact the best option). The following subsections present and discuss the two faultloads.

6.2.4.1. Faultload Based on Software Faults. This faultload is aimed at the emulation of software defects that typically exist in deployed software. A representative faultload based on software faults is one that contains only faults that are representative of real program errors that elude traditional software testing techniques and are left undiscovered in software products after shipment. The results presented in [Christmansson and Chillarege 1996, Durães and Madeira 2003] identify a clear trend in the software faults that usually exist in available systems: a small set of well-defined fault types is responsible for a large part of the total software faults. These fault types represent the faults that are more likely to exist in deployed software [Durães and Madeira 2003]. Using this set of fault types as a starting point for a faultload definition, in [Durães and Madeira 2004] a generic faultload based on software faults for dependability benchmarking is proposed. WEB-DB follows the guidelines defined in [Durães and Madeira 2004] in the definition of the faultload based on software faults. Table 6.1 presents the fault types that compose this faultload and reproduces the statistical information regarding the representativeness of the fault types according to the complete set of faults used in [Durães and Madeira 2003]. The fault coverage is based on the field study presented in [Durães and Madeira 2003], which also agrees in general with another study from IBM presented in [Christ-

TABLE 6.1. Types of software faults considered in the faultload

Fault types	Fault coverage
Missing variable initialization	2.25%
Missing variable assignment using a value	2.25%
Missing variable assignment using an expression	3.00%
Missing "if (cond)" surrounding statement(s)	4.32%
Missing "AND EXPR" in expression used as branch condition	7.89%
Missing function call	8.64%
Missing "If (cond) {statement(s)}"	9.96%
Missing small and localized part of the algorithm	3.19%
Wrong value assigned to a value	2.44%
Wrong logical expression used as branch condition	3.00%
Wrong arithmetic expression used in parameter of function call	2.25%
Wrong variable used in parameter of function call	1.50%
Total	50.69%

mansson and Chillarege 1996]. The software faults included in this faultload fall in the two following subclasses: *missing construct* and *wrong construct* (where construct is a programming element such as statements, logical expression, etc.). Previous research has shown that these two subclasses are responsible for half of the total software faults that are likely to exist in deployed software [Durães and Madeira 2003] (the remaining faults are dispersed through a large number of fault types, each one responsible for a reduced number of fault occurrences and, thus, not as interesting for fault injection from a representativeness point of view [Christmansson and Chillarege 1996, Durães and Madeira 2003]).

To emulate (inject) the software faults of Table 6.1, we use an implementation of the G-SWFIT technique [Durães and Madeira 2002a, Durães and Madeira 2003]. This technique emulates the software faults by reproducing directly at low-level code (i.e., inside the injection target code) the processor instruction sequences that represent programming errors. The instruction sequence inserted in the target code is equivalent to the code that would have been generated by a compiler if the emulated defect had been in fact present in the target original high-level source code. A library of emulation operators (previously defined) guides the entire process. This technique has the important advantage that it does not need the source code of the target, and provides good accuracy in the emulation of faults. Additionally, it provides a practical fault injection technique for dependability research, which is an important feature for the feasibility of the benchmark.

The G-SWFIT technique is based on a two-step methodology. In the first step, fault locations are identified (i.e., the faultload is generated); this is done prior to the actual experimentation. In the second step, the faults are actually injected.

Note that software faults must not be injected in the benchmark target (the Web server). As the injection of software faults implies the modification of the target code, any conclusion drawn afterward might not apply to the original BT. We use the notion of fault injection target (FIT) which is a component of the SUB other than the BT. The best option for the FIT in the WEB-DB context is the operating system itself, as the OS is indispensable in a Web server installation and its services are required for the execution of the workload. Because OS are typically very large, specific portions of the OS were previously selected as prime candidates for fault injection. These portions correspond to the code of the API most used by typical Web servers during the execution of the SPECWeb99 workload (mostly network and file management API). Thus, these faultloads subject the Web server to the conditions that are caused by an operating system containing software defects (e.g., incorrect resource management, wrong API results, etc.). The resulting faultloads are specific to a given OS and not to the Web server. Although the methodology used to build the faultload is presented in [Durães and Madeira 2004], WEB-DB provides predefined faultloads for the Windows OS family.

6.2.4.2. Faultload Based on Operational Faults.
This faultload is aimed at the emulation of faults existing (or caused) at the environment and operational level. This includes hardware and network faults, as well as the Web server administrator (operator) faults.

The types of faults considered have been chosen based on a estimation of the rate of occurrence, ability to emulate the effects of other types of faults (to improve the faultload representativeness), diversity of impact in the system, and portability. The faultload is composed by a set of faults of the types presented in Table 6.2 injected at different (and well-defined) instants.

The injection of the types of faults considered in this faultload is quite easy when compared to the injection of software faults. Simple applications can be developed to inject the hardware and operator faults considered. The rightmost column of Table 6.2 presents some examples on how to introduce each type of fault in the SUB.

6.2.4.3. Injection Slots Execution Profile.
After choosing the types of faults to inject and the technique to inject those faults, we have to define the profile for the injection of faults. As mentioned before, each execution of the WEB-DB benchmark is made of three runs and each run comprises several injection slots. Figure 6.3 shows the execution profile for each injection slot.

In order to assure that each injection slot portrays as realistic a scenario as possible, and at the same time assure that important properties such as result repeatability and representativeness of results are met, the definition of the profile of the injection slot has

TABLE 6.2. Types of environment faults considered in the faultload

Fault types	Fault injection
Network interface failure	Represents a failure in the server network card. This fault can be easily emulated by disabling the network interface at the operating system level.
Network connection failure	Represents a failure in a network connection and can be emulated by closing abruptly TCP sockets used to connect the Web server to the clients.
Unscheduled Web-server shutdown	Represents an operator/hardware fault that leads to the abrupt shutdown of the Web server. This fault can be emulated by killing the Web server processes at the operating system level.
Uscheduled server (machine) reboot	Represents an operator fault that leads to the abrupt and untimely reboot of the server. This fault can be emulated by rebooting the operating system.

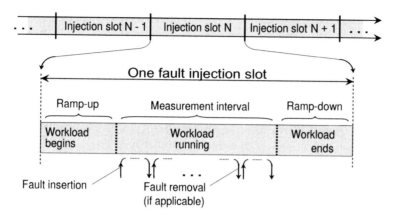

Figure 6.3. Injection slot execution profile.

to follow several rules. The following points summarize those rules (see also Figure 6.3):

- The SUB state must be explicitly restored at the beginning of each injection slot and the effects of the faults must not accumulate across different slots.

- The measurement interval starts when the system achieves the maximum processing throughput, which happens after a given time running the workload (ramp-up time). The ramp-down time at the end of each injection slot represents the time at which the SPECWeb99 workload needs to end. Note that no faults are injected during the SUB ramp-up and ramp-down. Ramp-up and ramp-down are 300 seconds long. These values are imposed by SPECWeb99 (see [SPEC 2000] for details).

- For the faultload based on software faults, faults are injected in intervals of 10 seconds and the measurement interval has a maximum duration of 20 minutes, which means that several slots may be needed to inject all the faults in the faultload, as the number of slots depends on the number of faults in the faultload. The 10-second injection intervals are heuristically established based on the SPECWeb99 workload operations, which on average take less than one second. Thus, inserting each fault for a period of 10 seconds is enough time to activate the fault. Before injecting the next fault, the previous one is undone (i.e., the original code is restored). It is worth noting that as the fault target for software faults is the operating system code, different Web servers are benchmarked with exactly the same faults, and the benchmark results compare the way the different Web servers behave in the presence of an unstable/faulty operating system.

- For the faultload based on operational faults, four injection slots are needed (i.e., one slot for each type of fault). Several faults from a given type are injected in each slot. The duration of the measurement interval is 20 minutes. The time between injections depends on the type of the faults and is as follows: 20 seconds for network connection failures, 40 seconds for network card failures, 10 seconds for abrupt Web server shutdowns, and 10 minutes for abrupt server reboots.

- After the injection of a fault, an error diagnostic procedure has to be executed to evaluate the effects of the fault (error detection) and to check if a recovery procedure is required. This recovery procedure is controlled by the BMS and represents the external intervention needed to restore the service of the Web server.

6.2.5. Benchmark Properties

A useful benchmark must be repeatable, portable, and representative [Gray 1993, Madeira and Koopman 2001]. To be credible, a dependability benchmark must report similar results when run more than once in the same environment. Concerning the WEB-DB benchmark, several tests have been done to confirm the fulfillment of this important requirement. However, repeatability has to be understood in statistical terms, as it is virtually impossible to reproduce exactly the same conditions concerning target system state during the benchmark run. In practice, small deviations in the measures in successive runs are normal and just reflect the asynchronous nature of Web environments. This is well known for SPECWeb99, as the results are obtained from the average of three workload executions.

Another important property is portability, as a benchmark must allow the comparison of different systems in a given application domain. Concerning dependability benchmarking, the faultload is the component that has more influence on portability. The WEB-DB portability is directly related to the portability of the G SWFIT technique. In the work presented in [Durães and Madeira 2002a], we have shown that G SWFIT is portable; the main issue is the definition of the mutation library. That task is mainly dependent on the target processor architecture. In fact, the programming language, the compiler, and the compiler optimization switches also have some influence on the library; however, such variations cause only the need for additional mutation specifications in the library. Different processor architectures usually require completely different libraries. When porting the mutation library to other processors, all that is required is the specification of new rules and mutations. The technique itself remains the same.

In order to report relevant results, a benchmark must represent real world scenarios in a realistic way. In dependability benchmarking, representativeness is mainly influenced by the workload and faultload characteristics. As we have adopted the SPECWeb99 workload, which is well accepted as a realistic workload, the representativeness is assured. In terms of the faultload, the type of faults considered have been chosen based on several studies on the representativeness and portability of operator faults [Brown and Patterson 2001, Vieira and Madeira 2004], software faults [Christmansson and Chillarege 1996, Madeira et al. 2000, Durães and Madeira 2002a, Durães and Madeira 2003], and hardware faults [Zhu et al. 2003b] that can be found in the literature.

6.3. APACHE VERSUS ABYSS: AN EXAMPLE OF DEPENDABILITY BENCHMARKING

Our case study is composed of two Web servers: Apache (www.apache.com) and Abyss (www.aprelium.com/abyssws). Each Web server was installed over three different operating systems: Windows 2000 (SP4), Windows XP (SP1) and Windows 2003 Server. This resulted in a total of six different SUB configurations.

The experiments were primarily intended to observe and quantify the differences between the two Web servers regarding dependability properties. However, the results can also be used to discover which of the three operating systems is most suitable to host a Web server, or which combination OS/Web server provides better dependability properties.

The remainder of this section presents the details of the experimental setup, the results observed, and an analysis of those results.

6.3.1. Experimental Setup

Each SUB configuration involves two computers connected via a 100 Mbps direct Ethernet connection. The SUB is entirely contained in one of the computers (the server computer). The BMS is composed of the following tools:

- The SPECWeb client, responsible for submitting the workload to the SUB and collecting measurements related to performance. This tool is placed in the client computer.
- The fault injector, responsible for all fault injection tasks. This tool is running in the server computer. The fault injector is also responsible for the assessment of the Web server process status. If the Web server process dies unexpectedly, or if it hangs or otherwise stops providing service, then it is restarted by the fault injector. These events are useful to obtain the resilience results.
- The availability evaluator, which continuously checks if the Web server is providing service by submitting a "GET" request and analyzing the result.

Figure 6.4 represents a client–server pair. All the computers used in our experiments have exactly the same configuration (1.6 GHz Pentium IV, 512 MB RAM, 7200 rpm IDE hard disc, 100 Mbps network interface). The software configuration of the client computers is the same for all SUBs (the SPECWeb client and the availability evaluator running on top of Windows XP). The server computers have six different configurations (i.e., six different SUBs: three OSes and two Web servers).

Because some of the BMS tools are also running on the same machine as the Web server, there is a small performance penalty. To keep our conclusions meaningful, we consider that the execution of the BMS tools is part of the workload subjected to the SUB, i.e., we want to observe the behavior variation induced by the presence of faults and not by the presence of the BMS tools. This means that the normal behavior of the SUB must be assessed with the BMS running but with no fault being injected (we call this the *baseline performance*). To that effect, our fault injector has a profile-only mode that executes all the tasks related to fault injection except the injection itself). Later, the behavior of the

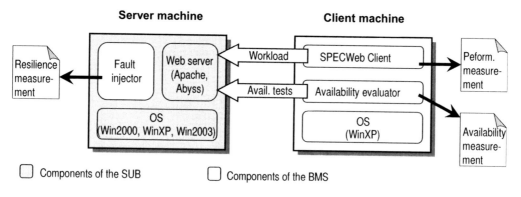

Figure 6.4. Experimental setup.

Web servers in the presence of faults will be compared to the behavior when the fault injector is running in profile mode.

We obtained the maximum performance attainable on our hardware configuration according to two guidelines:

- There was no specific effort toward custom performance optimization. Because our goal is the evaluation and comparison of dependability properties (instead of plain performance), we used a configuration that represents a setup likely to be used by system administrators when still deciding which server to use and prior to efforts toward optimization (which will be carried out after a choice has been made). Two factors contribute for a less than maximum performance of our setups (when compared to published results for similar hardware setups); the network interface has a maximum bandwidth of 100 Mbits and we used interpreted perl CGI scripts instead of compiled scripts.
- The heaviest workload subjected to each SUB was such that the conformance (as defined by SPEC) is 100%, which means that every connection that was submitted to that SUB was fulfilled in a timely fashion (see [SPEC 2000]). We also required that no errors be reported. The rationale behind the 100% conformance and 0% error requirements is that we are interested in observing a 100% clean (no errors) SUB behavior. Any errors that occur during the benchmark experiments can then be assigned to the presence of the faultloads.

The heaviest workload that a SUB is able to fulfill with 100% conformance, 0% errors, and no BMS tools running yields the maximum performance for that SUB (this configuration involves only the Web server and the SPECWeb client). The heaviest workload that a SUB is able to fulfill with 100% conformance, 0% errors, and the BMS tools running in profile mode yields the baseline performance for that SUB. Note that the requirement of the 100% conformance implies that the number of simultaneous connections submitted to the SUB for the baseline performance may be lower than the number of connections submitted in the maximum performance (when the SUB is unable to sustain the original number of connections with 100% conformance and 0% errors). Because fewer connections are submitted, the average operations per second per connection and the average bit rate per connection values may actually be higher in the baseline performance than in the maximum performance (and the response time lower). However, this does not mean that the baseline performance is greater: it is simply a consequence of the fact that fewer simultaneous connections were submitted.

Table 6.3 presents the maximum performance obtainable in our hardware configuration (row "Max Perf"), the baseline performance (row "Profile (BL)"), and a measurement of the intrusiveness caused by the BMS presence (row "Intrus (%)"). Columns CC% refer to the conformance percentage; columns "OSL" presents the number of operations per second per connection; columns "KBps" present the average bit rate. These three measures are specific to performance benchmark and are presented at this point solely to better assess the intrusion degree.

The intrusiveness represents the variation in performance due to the presence of the BMS. It is calculated (as a percentage) by simply dividing the performance measured when no BMS tools are running by the performance measured when the BMS tools are running. A positive value denotes a decrease in performance. Note that the intrusiveness values under the response time ("RTM"), the operations per second per connection

TABLE 6.3. Maximum performance attainable on the hardware platform, maximum performance attainable in presence of the BMS, and intrusion assessment*

	Apache						Abyss					
	SPC	CC%	THR	RTM	OSL	KBps	SPC	CC%	THR	RTM	OSL	KBps
Win2000												
Max Perf	32	100	92.7	354.7	2.92	345.3	29	100	82.9	351.3	2.86	338.6
Profile (BL)	31	100	90	354.9	2.9	346.7	28	100	82.7	344.4	2.95	348
Intrus (%)	3.12	0	2.91	−0.06	0.68	−0.41	3.45	0	0.24	1.96	−3.15	−2.78
WinXP												
Max Perf	27	100	78.6	342.5	2.91	346.1	26	100	75.2	348.9	2.89	345.5
Profile (BL)	26	100	74.5	348.9	2.87	342.7	25	100	73.3	343.4	2.93	338.6
Intrus (%)	3.7	0	5.22	−1.87	1.37	0.98	3.85	0	2.53	1.58	−1.38	2
Win2003												
Max Perf	30	100	85	353.2	2.83	343.9	25	100	71.9	345.4	2.88	348
Profile (BL)	30	100	82.4	363.9	2.75	333.1	24	100	79	345.8	2.92	341.3
Intrus (%)	0	0	3.06	−3.03	2.83	3.14	4	0	2.64	−0.12	−1.39	1.83

*See text for explanation.

("OSL"), and the bit rate ("KBps") must be analyzed in conjunction with and taking account of the SPEC index (SPC). A negative value in any of these figures should be interpreted as an increase in the performance if the number of simultaneous connections (given by the SPC figure) remains the same. According to our observations, all cases in which the intrusiveness is negative are related to a decrease in the number of simultaneous connections or with a decrease in the number of operations per connection, which explains the apparent increase in performance.

6.3.2. Benchmarking Results and Discussion

A complete benchmark experiment for a given SUB is composed of three complete executions for each faultload, following the SPECWeb99 style. The values for each benchmark measure are the average of the values obtained in each run for each measure.

Table 6.4 presents the results of each individual run for each faultload/SUB. These results show that the variations across different iterations for the same faultload/SUB combination are minimal. The resilience (RES%), availability (AVL%), and Accuracy (ACR%) are given as percentages; the throughput in the presence of faults (THRf) is given in operations per second, and the response time in the presence of faults (RTMf) is given in milliseconds. The SPEC measure in the presence of faults (SPECf) has no units. As we can see, the result variation across different iterations for the same faultload/SUB is small, confirming our previous claim that the benchmark is repeatable.

Table 6.5 presents results obtained for each faultload and the resulting average. To facilitate the comparison of the behavior of the SUB with and without faults, we also included in Table 6.5 the baseline performance for each SUB (row labeled "baseline").

Before analyzing the results, it is important to recall that the benchmark measures characterize the SUB. However, the SUB is the whole server (platform + operating system + Web server), which is larger than the component the Web-DB is meant to characterize (called benchmark target or BT), which is the Web server. The comparative analysis of different Web servers is achieved by comparing the results obtained in more than

TABLE 6.4. Results obtained in each individual iteration*

	Apache						Abyss					
	RES%	AVL%	SPECf	THRf	RTMf	ACR%	RES%	AVL%	SPECf	THRf	RTMf	ACR%
Windows 2000												
Software												
Iter. 1	92.12	96.59	10.15	83.57	361.4	94.38	90.49	95.74	5.15	76.362	357.9	89.69
Iter. 2	92.71	96.81	10.08	82.72	366.49	94.39	90.78	95.66	5.15	76.415	357.56	91.18
Iter. 3	93.06	96.75	11.69	84.67	358.66	95.14	90.84	95.43	4.62	75.115	363.63	89.33
Avg	92.63	96.72	10.64	83.65	362.18	94.627	90.7	95.61	4.97	75.964	359.7	90.07
Operational												
Iter. 1	96.31	94.4	17.25	73.325	446.95	99.788	97.74	96.9	15.50	75.7	368.83	99.51
Iter. 2	92.67	91.91	15	76.1	415.45	99.763	98.51	97.03	16.75	75.8	368.5	99.5
Iter. 3	96.99	95.22	18.75	75.075	370.03	99.808	97.81	97.36	14.75	76.375	366.68	99.44
Avg	95.32	93.84	17	74.833	402.23	99.786	98.02	97.09	15.67	75.958	367.75	99.48
Windows XP												
Software												
Iter. 1	93.75	97.9	13.83	71.90	356.05	94.71	93.78	96.62	10.78	68.71	356.15	87.19
Iter. 2	93.44	97.76	13.52	71.51	357.59	96.82	93.3	96.62	10.65	68.73	356.61	90.58
Iter. 3	98.85	97.86	14.04	71.61	357.72	95.16	93.44	96.62	10.78	68.65	357.27	90.49
Avg	93.68	97.84	13.80	71.67	357.12	95.563	93.51	96.62	10.74	68.70	356.68	89.42
Operational												
Iter. 1	97.55	97.87	20.25	71.15	363.93	99.613	98.35	97.51	14.5	67.20	369.98	99.6
Iter. 2	95.13	98.18	23	71.58	362.53	99.578	99.19	98.58	18.75	68.00	366.6	99.6
Iter. 3	99.16	98.08	23.75	71.55	362.05	99.968	97.74	97.92	16.75	67.53	367.43	99.52
Avg	97.28	98.04	22.33	71.59	362.33	99.629	98.43	96	16.667	67.74	367.4	99.57
Windows 2003												
Software												
Iter. 1	94.72	97.05	12.63	78.69	374.05	95.37	93.45	96.52	10.37	66.02	363.98	99.61
Iter. 2	94.72	97.65	14.89	77.59	372.8	95.14	93.37	96.72	10.37	65.94	355.23	92
Iter. 3	94.72	97.58	13.84	80.19	367.59	95.98	93.83	96.82	10.47	66.33	354.73	91.4
Avg	94.72	97.43	13.79	78.82	371.48	95.50	93.55	96.69	10.40	66.09	355.08	91.49
Operational												
Iter. 1	99.81	97.85	10	79.225	375.88	99.15	98.81	98.48	16.25	66.725	363.98	99.61
Iter. 2	98.81	97.6	7.75	79.275	376.3	99.085	98.81	98.28	15	66.175	363.03	99.57
Iter. 3	98.81	97.97	8.5	79.275	376.38	98.975	9.19	98.35	15	65.875	364.3	99.62
Avg	98.81	97.81	8.75	79.592	374.77	99.07	98.94	98.37	15.417	66.258	362.27	99.6

*See text for abbreviations.

one SUB, where the only difference between each SUB is the BT (e.g., we can only compare the results obtained for Apache and Abyss when each Web server is running on the same platform and operating system).

Because the benchmark comprises six different measures, it is inevitable that some of the measures favor one of the BTs, whereas the others measures favor other BTs. It is possible to recognize the best/worst BTs by analyzing the complete set of measures.

Different benchmark users may intend to deploy the Web servers in different environments. As such, the relative weight of each benchmark measure may have different relative weights across different benchmark users (e.g., user A may consider the availability more important than user B). In this case study, we assumed a general-purpose Web server scenario and assigned equal relevance to all six benchmark measures. To facilitate the identification of the SUB with the best dependability results, the values more favorable are presented with a gray background Table 6.5. The results presented in Table 6.5 sug-

TABLE 6.5. Benchmark measures results

	Apache						Abyss					
	RES%	AVL%	SPECf	THRf	RTMf	ACR%	RES%	AVL%	SPECf	THRf	RTMf	ACR%
2000												
(Baseline)	(100)	(100)	(31)	(90)	345.9	(100)	(100)	(100)	(28)	(82.7)	(344.4)	(100)
Software	92.63	96.72	10.64	83.65	362.18	96.63	90.7	95.61	4.97	75.96	359.69	90.07
Operation	95.32	93.84	17	74.83	402.23	99.79	98.02	97.09	15.67	75.96	367.75	99.48
Average	93.98	95.28	13.82	79.24	382.2	97.21	94.36	96.35	10.32	75.96	363.7	94.78
XP												
(Baseline)	(100)	(100)	(26)	(74.5)	(348.9)	(100)	(100)	(100)	(25)	(73.3)	(343.4)	(100)
Software	93.68	97.84	13.8	71.67	357.12	95.56	93.51	96.62	10.74	68.69	356.68	89.42
Operation	97.28	98.04	22.33	71.59	362.33	99.63	98.43	98	16.67	67.74	367.4	99.57
Average	95.48	97.94	18.07	71.63	359.7	97.6	95.97	97.31	13.71	68.22	362	94.5
2003												
(Baseline)	(100)	(100)	(30)	(82.4)	(363.9)	(100)	(100)	(100)	(24)	(70)	(354.8)	(100)
Software	94.72	97.43	13.79	78.82	371.48	95.5	93.55	96.69	10.4	66.09	355.08	91.49
Operation	98.81	97.81	8.75	79.59	374.77	99.07	98.94	98.37	15.42	66.26	362.27	99.6
Average	96.77	97.62	11.27	79.21	373.1	97.29	96.25	97.53	12.91	66.18	358.7	95.55

gest that Apache has better dependability properties than Abyss. Indeed, five out of six benchmark measures have their best values on the Apache side.

Although the benchmark is primarily intended for Web server comparison, the results can also be used to analyze the properties of the OSes or the entire SUB (OS + Web server). If we focus on one server, we can obtain information regarding which operating system provides better dependability properties for that server. According to our results and taking into account both faultloads and all six measures, Windows XP seems to provide the best platform for Apache and Windows 2003 the best for Abyss. The differences between XP and 2003 are smaller than the differences between 2000 and any of the other two OSs. On the other hand, if we focus on a given operating system we can determine which of the two observed Web servers provides the most dependable behavior. We can also extract information regarding which of the six SUBS presents the best dependability properties (considering all measures with the same weight); the combination Apache/XP seems to be the one for which the service degradation caused by faults is least noticeable.

The information contained in Table 6.5 can be best analyzed through the charts presented in Figures 6.5 through 6.7.

When in presence of software faults inside the operating system, Apache shows a clear advantage compared to Abyss. The only measure for which Apache does not behave better than Abyss is the response time in presence of faults (RTMf), in particular when the underlying OS is the Win2003. However, all the other five measures favor Apache.

When considering the faultload of operational faults, the differences between both servers are not as clear as when using the faultload of software faults. Apache presents a better overall behavior regarding resilience, SPECf, and THRf, but Abyss is superior when considering availability, accuracy, and RTMf. Should a benchmark end user use only this faultload, they would have to assign weight to each measure in order to better distinguish the behavior of the servers. The weight assigned to each measure would reflect the nature of the operational environment in which the Web server was deployed.

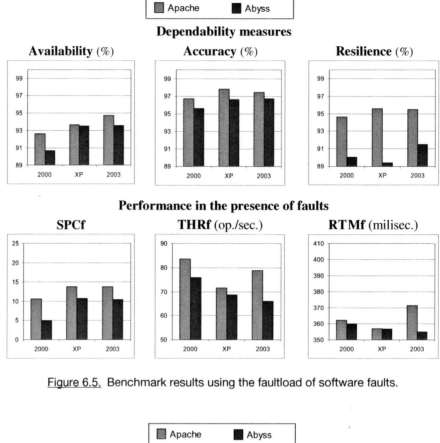

Figure 6.5. Benchmark results using the faultload of software faults.

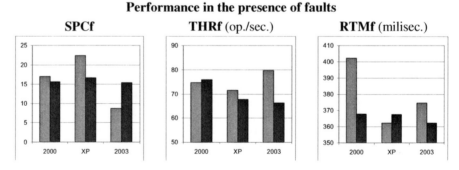

Figure 6.6. Benchmark results using the faultload of operational faults.

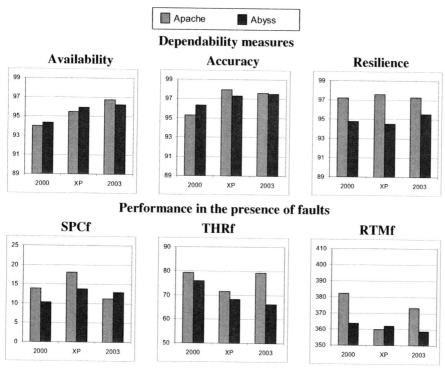

Figure 6.7. Global benchmark results.

When considering both faultloads, the difference between Apache and Abyss again becomes clear (Figure 6.7). Although Abyss is better for to availability and response time, Apache is superior regarding all other measures.

The following remarks are worth noting:

- The faultload based on software faults is the one that causes the largest number of process hangs and aborts (leading to lower resilience results). This is in agreement with the knowledge that the correctness of the OS is essential to the correct behavior of the applications.

- Abyss and Apache appear to have different internal strategies dealing with network mechanisms. Indeed, faults related to networks (network connection failure, network interface failure) cause larger behavior differences than other fault types. The difference in network fault tolerance is also indirectly behind the differences between the availability results; when Apache dies unexpectedly, its next instance has some trouble restoring the listening sockets. On the other hand, Abyss can restore its sockets more quickly in the same circumstances.

6.3.3. Benchmarking Execution Effort

The time involved in the execution of the benchmark for a given SUB is the sum of the time required for the setup procedures and the execution itself. The setup procedures are: OS and Web server installation, SPECWeb client, benchmark tools installation, and the faultload generation. The setup and configuration of the OS plus Web server plus tools take at most one hour. It is important to realize that we are interested in obtaining a basic, working Web server machine, not a customized specific-purpose portal; therefore, the configuration procedures are relatively simple.

The only faultload that may require specific preparation is the faultload based on software faults. This faultload is specific to each OS (see [Durães and Madeira 2004]) and, as such, may require specific generation. The generation of a faultload of software faults using G-SWFIT [Durães and Madeira 2002a, Durães and Madeira 2003] is an automated process that requires only simple parameter tuning. The entire process takes less than half an hour.

The execution of the benchmark is mainly dependent on the faultload size. Taking into account the three runs imposed by the SPECWeb99 rules and considering all slots needed to execute the complete faultload, the total benchmark execution time is 31 hours and 45 minutes (the worst-case scenarios are the SUBs involving Windows XP, which has a faultload of software faults of nearly 3000 faults) Adding the setup timing, the total time required by the benchmark is a less than one-and-a half day.

6.4. CONCLUSIONS

In this chapter, we presented a proposal for the dependability benchmarking of Web servers. To our knowledge, this is the first dependability benchmark specifically designed for Web servers. Given the central role that Web-based services play in today's society, the existence of a dependability benchmark aimed at the characterization of Web servers is a valuable tool to use when planning a Web-based information system. The results of the benchmark are especially useful when comparing several Web servers to decide which one is best suited to include in a larger information system.

The benchmark components were specifically designed to be representative of the typical Web-based services; the measurements address both user and system administrator perspectives and target all the key properties of the service expected from typical Web servers. The workload is composed of a standard widely accepted performance benchmark, which represents the typical requests submitted to Web servers. The faultload addresses the typical faults that exist in the operational environment surrounding Web servers, including software, hardware, operator (administrator), and network faults.

We illustrated the use of the benchmark through a case study involving two Web servers running on top of three different operating systems. The results show clear differences between the two Web servers and confirm that the benchmark can be used to differentiate the dependability properties of Web servers. This is valuable whenever there is the need to choose between several Web servers. Given the current industry trend to use commercial off-the-shelf components to build larger system, a tool to evaluate the dependability properties of such components (in our case, Web servers) is indispensable.

REFERENCES

[Arlat et al. 1993] J. Arlat, A. Costes, Y. Crouzet, J.-C. Laprie, and D. Powell, "Fault Injection and Dependability Evaluation of Fault-Tolerant Systems," *IEEE Transactions on Computers,* vol. 42, no. 8, pp. 913–923, 1993.

[Brown and Patterson 2001] A. Brown and D. Patterson, "To Err is Human," in *Proceedings of the First Workshop on Evaluating and Architecting System Dependability (EASY),* jointly organized with the International Conference on Dependable Systems and Networks, DSN'01, Göteborg, Sweden, 2001.

[Brown et al. 2002] A. Brown, L. Chung, W. Kakes, C. Ling, and D. A. Patterson, "Dependability Benchmarking of Human-Assisted Recovery Processes," in *Proceedings of the International Conference on Dependable Systems and Networks,* Florence, Italy, pp. 405–410, 2004.

[Buchacker and Tschaeche 2003] K. Buchacker and O. Tschaeche, "TPC Benchmark-c version 5.2 Dependability Benchmark Extensions," http://www.faumachine.org/papers/tpcc-depend.pdf, 2003.

[Christmansson and Chillarege 1996] J. Christmansson and R. Chillarege, "Generation of an Error Set that Emulates Software Faults," in *Proceedings of the 26th IEEE Fault Tolerant Computing Symposium, FTCS-26,* Sendai, Japan, pp. 304–313, June 1996.

[Durães and Madeira 2002a] J. Durães and H. Madeira, "Emulation of Software Faults by Educated Mutations at Machine-Code Level," in *Proceedings of the 13th International Symposium on Software Reliability Engineering,* ISSRE'02, Annapolis, MD, pp. 329–340, 2002.

[Durães and Madeira 2002b] J. Durães and H. Madeira, "Characterization of Operating Systems Behaviour in the Presence of Faulty Drivers through Software Fault Emulation," in *Proceedings of the 2002 Pacific Rim International Symposium on Dependable Computing (PRDC-2002),* pp. Tsukuba, 201–209, Japan, IEEE Computer Science Press, Los Alamitos, CA, 2002.

[Durães and Madeira 2003] J. Durães and H. Madeira, "Definition of Software Fault Emulation Operators: A Field Data Study," in *Proceedings of the International Conference on Dependable Systems and Networks, DSN2003,* San Francisco, pp. 22–25, 2003.

[Durães and Madeira 2004] J. Durães and H. Madeira, "Generic Faultloads Based on Software Faults for Dependability Benchmarking," in *Proceedings of the International Conference on Dependable Systems and Networks, DSN 2004,* Florence, Italy, June 2004.

[Gray 1990] J. Gray, "A Census of Tandem Systems Availability Between 1985 and 1990," *IEEE Transactions on Reliability,* vol. 39, pp. 409–418, 1990.

[Gray 1993] J. Gray, (Ed.), *The Benchmark Handbook for Database and Transaction Processing Systems,* Morgan Kaufmann, San Francisco, 1993.

[Jenn et al. 1995] E. Jenn, J. Arlat, M. Rimén, J. Ohlsson, and J. Karlsson, "Fault Injection into VHDL Models: The MEFISTO Tool," in *Predictably Dependable Computing Systems* (B. Randell, J.-C. Laprie, H. Kopetz, and B. Littlewood, Eds.), pp. 329–46, Springer, Berlin, 1995.

[Kalakech et al. 2004] A. Kalakech, K. Kanoun, Y. Crouzet, and A. Arlat. "Benchmarking the Dependability of Windows NT, 2000 and XP," in *Proceedings of the International Conference on Dependable Systems and Networks (DSN 2004),* Florence, Italy, IEEE Computer Science Press, Los Alamitos, CA, 2004.

[Kanoun et al. 2004] "Dependability Benchmarking Concepts," in K. Kanoun, H. Madeira, Y. Crouzet, M. D. Cin, F. Moreira, and J. C. R. García (Eds.), DBench, 2004. Project deliverable available at http://www.laas.fr/dbench/deliverables.

[Koopman and Madeira 1999] P. Koopman and H. Madeira, "Dependability Benchmarking and Prediction: A Grand Challenge Technology Problem," in *1st IEEE International Workshop on Real-Time Mission-Critical Systems: Grand Challenge Problems,* Phoenix, November 30, 1999.

[Koopman and DeVale 1999] P. Koopman and J. DeVale, "Comparing the Robustness of POSIX Operating Systems," in *Proceedings of the 29th International Symposium on Fault-Tolerant Computing (FTCS-29),* pp. 30–37, Madison, WI, EEE Computer Science Press, Los Alamitos, CA, 1999.

[Lightstone et al. 2003] S. Lightstone, J. Hellerstein, W. Tetzlaff, P. Janson, E. Lassettre, C. Norton, B. Rajaraman, and L. Spainhower. "Towards Benchmarking Autonomic Computing Maturity," in *Proceedings of the First IEEE Conference on Industrial Automatics (INDIN-2003),* Banff, Canada, August 2003.

[Madeira et al. 2000] H. Madeira, M. Vieira, and D. Costa, "On the Emulation of Software Faults by Software Fault Injection," in *Dependable Systems and Networks Conference—DSN-2000*, New York, June 2000.

[Madeira and Koopman 2001] H. Madeira and P. Koopman, "Dependability benchmarking: Making Choices in a n-dimensional Problem Space," in *Proceedings of the First Workshop on Evaluationg and Architecting System Dependability (EASY'01)*, jointly organized with the IEEE/ACM 28th Symposium on Computer Architecture and the IEEE International Conference on Dependable Systems and Networks, DSN'01, Göteborg, Sweeden, 2001.

[SPEC 2000] Standard Performance Evaluation Corporation, "SPECweb99 Release 1.02 (Design Document)," http://www.spec.org/web99/, July 2000.

[Trivedi et al. 1994] K. S. Trivedi, B. R. Haverkort, A. Rindos, and V. Mainkar, "Methods and Tools for Reliability and Performability: Problems and Perspectives," in *Proceedings of the 7th International Conference on Techniques and Tools for Computer Performance Evaluation* (G. Haring and G. Kotsis, Eds.), *Lecture Notes in Computer Science*, no. 794, pp. 1–24, Springer-Verlag, Vienna, 1994.

[Vieira and Madeira 2003] M. Vieira and H. Madeira, "A Dependability Benchmark for OLTP Application Environments," in *Proceedings of the 29th International Conference on Very Large Data Bases (VLDB 2003)*, Berlin, pp. 742–753, 2003.

[Vieira and Madeira 2004] M. Vieira and H. Madeira, "Portable Faultloads Based on Operator Faults for DBMS Dependability Benchmarking," in *Proceedings of the 28th Annual International Computer Software and Applications Conference, COMPSAC 2004*, Hong Kong, September 2004.

[Zhu et al. 2003a] J. Zhu, J. Mauro and I. Pramanick. "R3—A Framwork for Availability Benchmarking," in *Proceedings of the International Conference on Dependable Systems and Networks (DSN 2003)*, San Francisco, pp. B-86–87, 2003.

[Zhu et al. 2003b] J. Zhu, J. Mauro, and I. Pramanick, "Robustness Benchmarking for Hardware Maintenance Events," in *Proceedings of International Conference on Dependable Systems and Networks (DSN 2003)*, San Francisco, pp. 115–122, IEEE Computer Science Press, Los Alamitos, CA, 2003.

[Zhu et al. 2004] J. Mauro, J. Zhu and I. Pramanick. "The System Recovery Benchmark," in *Proceedings of the 2004 Pacific Rim International Symposium on Dependable Computing (PRDC 2004)*, Papeete, Tahiti, IEEE Computer Science Press, Los Alamitos, CA, 2004.

DEPENDABILITY BENCHMARKING OF AUTOMOTIVE CONTROL SYSTEMS

Juan-Carlos Ruiz, Pedro Gil, Pedro Yuste, and David de-Andrés

7.1. INTRODUCTION

In order to reduce temporal and economical development costs, automotive system developers are increasingly resorting to commercial off-the-shelf components (COTS), even when these components are to be integrated in critical parts of the vehicle. This situation motivates the need of new methodologies for quantifying, at least partially, the dependability of these components for comparison purposes, despite the lack of information issued from their developers.

Electronic control units (ECUs for short) are at the core of the development of most modern automotive control systems, such as engine control and antilock braking systems. These units are typically manufactured as systems-on-chip (SoC) in order to increase their scale of integration and their performance [Leen and Heffernan 2002]. Among other advantages, they are easier and cheaper to program, calibrate, and maintain than the older (most times mechanical) control systems. The wide spectrum of possibilities offered by these ECUs has led to their success in the automotive industry.

This chapter focuses on the specification of dependability benchmarks for automotive control applications running inside engine ECUs. The goal is to provide means to support the purchase/selection decisions made by automotive engineers when integrating such applications in the ECUs they produce. In order to perceive the importance of this work, one should understand that engine control applications are cornerstones in the construction of powertrain systems that harness the energy produced by the engine of a vehicle in order to produce motion. Their role in such systems is critical and it consists in managing the core of motor vehicles in order to maximize the power obtained from the combustion of air and fuel, while minimizing the production of pollutants [Heywood 1988]. Hence, incorrect control actions on the vehicle engine may not only damage the engine itself, but also have a negative impact on the safety of the vehicle passengers.

The importance of engine control applications in modern internal combustion vehicles motivates the need for methodologies and tools for evaluating the impact of their failures on the engines they control. In our context, the notion of dependability benchmarking must be thus understood as the evaluation of the safety of the ECU software from perspective of the engine. Most of the existing research in the domain concentrates on the verification of engine control algorithms according to their requirements [Fuchs et al. 1998; Leveson 2000]. Some research has also been performed on how to implement robust control strategies for tolerating the mechanical or electrical faults that may perturb the behavior of ECUs in general [Spooner and Passino 1997]. Robust engineering is another verification technique that has been proposed in order to improve ECU software testing techniques [Leaphart et al. 2006]. The idea is to use orthogonal array experiments to test control software against a range of inputs, including those perturbed by noise factors. However, the final goal of this work is limited to the verification of the functional requirements met by the tested software. The comparison of different candidates from a dependability point of view is out of the scope of the purposes of this work. More focused on benchmarking, the Embedded Microprocessor Benchmark Consortium (EEMBC) has developed a meaningful set of performance benchmarks for embedded processors and compilers. The EEMBC benchmarks are composed of dozens of algorithms organized into benchmark suites targeting telecommunications, networking, automotive and industrial, consumer, and office equipment products. Among these benchmarks, AutoMark [EEMC 2003] is devoted to the evaluation of the microprocessor performance when running automotive and industrial algorithms, such as road speed calculation and angle-to-time conversion. The main difference with the type of benchmark we consider relies on the fact that AutoMark focuses on the hardware regardless the software running inside the ECU. Another interesting benchmark is named Harstone [Donohoe et al. 1990]. This benchmark describes a series of timing requirements for testing a system's ability to handle hard real-time constraints. Since the ECU software must meet different real-time requirements, this benchmark can be of great interest when comparing different ECUs according to their real-time behavior. However, this benchmark does not provide any insights about how to compare engine control algorithms from a dependability perspective.

From our viewpoint, benchmarking the dependability (safety) of engine control solutions means, at least, studying (i) to what extent the external faults that may affect the execution of the ECU control algorithms may perturb the control produced by this unit, and (ii) the (eventual) impact of this faulty control over the controlled engine. It is obvious that this study is conditioned by the viewpoint of the expected benchmark users. As previously stated, the goal is, in our case, to support the selection decisions made by automotive engineers when integrating engine control software in their powertrain systems.

The rest of the chapter is structured as follows. Section 7.2 refines the notion of engine control applications introduced above and defines a general model for such applications. Section 7.3 exploits this model in order to specify a standard procedure to assess dependability-related measures of an engine control application. Then, Section 7.4 exemplifies this benchmark specification through a prototype implementation for diesel engine ECUs. Through this practical work, we illustrate the cost of implementing the proposed benchmark and the time required for its execution. Section 7.5 discusses to what extent the general properties described in the introductory chapter of this book are verified by our benchmark, and Section 7.6 presents conclusions.

7.2. BASICS OF AUTOMOTIVE ENGINE CONTROL SYSTEMS

Categorizing a dependability benchmark means specifying its benchmarking context. The number of different automotive embedded systems existing in today's vehicles and their heterogeneity prevent the definition of a unique methodology for benchmarking any sort of automotive control application. Thus, a first step toward the specification of useful automotive benchmarks must be the clear definition of the benchmarking context. This context defines (and restricts) the application domain of the resulting benchmark specification. Then, it is important to understand the characteristics of the automotive embedded systems included in the considered domain. This enables the definition of general models that are representative of a large spectrume of these automotive systems. These models are the abstractions on which dependability benchmarks for such systems can be then specified.

According to the above reasoning, this section introduces the basics required for understanding the type of automotive systems to which our benchmark can be applied. These systems are four-stroke diesel engines. Then it proposes a general model that captures the main characteristics of the control applications managing such systems.

7.2.1. How Engines Work

Engine control applications are responsible for the injection of a certain amount of fuel (gasoline or diesel) in a small, enclosed space and its combustion. As a result, a certain amount of energy is released in the form of expanding gas. Basically, an engine works in a cycle that allows setting off this combustion process thousands of times per minute. Then, the produced energy is harnessed in order to generate motion.

Most modern vehicles use engines with a four-stroke combustion cycle. These four strokes are intake, compression, combustion, and exhaust. The following points summarize what happens as the engine goes through its cycle:

1. *Intake.* The piston starts at the top, the intake valve opens, and the piston moves down to let the engine take in a cylinder-full of air. This happens in diesel and direct injection gasoline engines. In the other types of gasoline engines, the intake stroke fills the cylinder with a gasoline-air mixture.

2. *Compression.* The piston moves back up to compress the cylinder content. Compression makes the explosion more powerful. Diesel engine compression ratios are greater than gasoline ones.

3. *Combustion.* When the piston reaches the top of its stroke in a diesel engine, the fuel is injected into the compressed air. The heat of the compressed air lights the fuel spontaneously. In nondirect injection gasoline engines, the fuel has been already injected during the intake stroke. Thus, when the piston reaches the top of its stroke, the spark plug emits a spark to ignite the gasoline. In both gasoline and diesel engines, the combustion of the air/fuel mixture drives the piston down.

4. *Exhaust.* Once the piston hits the bottom of its stroke, the exhaust valve opens and the gas leaves the cylinder to go out the tail pipe. Now the engine is ready for the

next cycle, so it takes in, depending on the type of engine, another charge of air or air and fuel.

Typically, the linear motion of the piston is converted into rotational motion by the engine crankshaft, which is connected to the piston by a connecting rod (see Figure 7.1). The rotational motion is needed to rotate the car's wheels.

As this brief description shows, all four-stroke engines present similarities, despite the type of fuel (gasoline or diesel) they burn, which can be exploited in order to define a general model of the type of systems required to control them. Interested readers can find further details about how vehicle engines work in [Pulkrabek 1997].

7.2.2. Engine Control System Model

According to the general view of a four-stroke engine provided in the previous section, our goal here is to identify the main characteristics of the systems controlling these engines. These characteristics conform the general model on which the specification of our dependability benchmark is based (see Figure 7.2).

The notion of an engine ECU defined in the introduction of this chapter refers to the compound formed by the engine control application and the software and hardware supporting its execution. Typically, engine control applications run on top of a real-time operating system support and a microcontroller or DSP (Digital Signal Processor) based hardware platform [Miller et al. 1998]. As Figure 7.2 shows, these applications can be modeled as a set of control loops handling two types of input data: (i) the acceleration/deceleration data provided by the driver through the throttle, and (ii) the feedback data supplied by the set of sensors connected to the car engine. The first type of data is external to the engine and it defines the speed reference imposed by the vehicle driver. The second

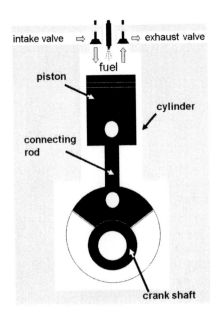

Figure 7.1. High-level view of a diesel engine.

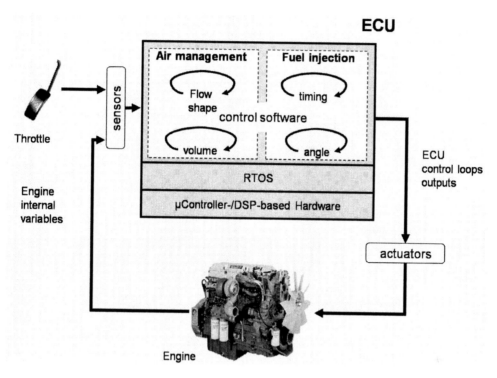

Figure 7.2. Model for an engine control system.

one is internal and it is used in order to monitor what is currently happening inside the vehicle engine.

The core of the engine control application can be characterized through four different control loops. On the one hand, the angle and the timing loops determine when the fuel injection must occur and how long it must last. On the other hand, the volume and the flow shape control loops manage the quantity of air and the way that air enters the cylinder. These four control loops are the ones that any (gasoline or diesel) engine control system should implement. However, one should notice that, due to their specific characteristics, each engine family also implements other specific control loops. Examples are, for instance, the EGR (exhaust gas recirculation) control loop of diesel engines and the spark control loop of gasoline engines. It is worth noting that this also happens in engines of the same family.

It is important to notice that engine control loops are typically designed to provide robust control. Although similar to fault tolerance, the notion of robust control only refers to the ability of a control algorithm to absorb perturbations in its inputs in order to compute correct outputs. In the automotive domain, this robustness is obtained by (i) applying filters to the inputs in order to eliminate the eventual perturbations and (ii) using predictive techniques that compute outputs based not only on the current set of inputs, but also on the previous state of the system and the dynamics the engine is supposed to follow. In that way, the impact of an incorrect input over the computed outputs is minimized. However, the question persists: what happens if the effect of an incorrect input (or other type of external fault) propagates to the computed control outputs? To the best of our knowledge, engine control applications do not integrate specific mechanisms to recover from the effects of such type of failures. As a result, if the consequence of a fault is the computation of an improper control output, then this output will be applied to the engine as it is. This is the type of unsafe situation whose consequences are evaluated by our dependability benchmark. The best option among several candidates will be the one minimizing their consequences and the ratio of occurrence of such unsafe situations. Since our purpose is not to define a benchmarking solution for a particular engine control system, our interest will focus throughout this chapter only on the control loops that any automotive control application must provide, that is, those depicted in Figure 7.2.

7.3. BENCHMARK SPECIFICATION

Our dependability benchmark is built on top of the model defined in Section 7.2.2. In this section, we introduce the different components of our benchmark and we detail each component in a different section. A first draft of this specification was presented in [Ruiz et al. 2004].

7.3.1. Benchmark Overview

The system under benchmarking (from now on called the SUB) is the system on which the dependability benchmark experiments (BEs) are conducted. The benchmark target (the BT) is the benchmarking object, that is, the system or system component that is intended to be characterized by the benchmark. In our context, the SUB corresponds to the system depicted in Figure 7.2, and the BT is the software running inside the engine ECU.

The experimental dimension of our dependability benchmark is characterized by its input and output domains. The input domain corresponds to the stimuli (the workload) required to exercise the SUB and the set of injected faults (the faultload). The workload refers to the speed reference supplied by the car driver through the throttle and the state feedback provided by the sensors connected to the engine. On the other hand, the faultload is defined as the set of transient hardware faults that the ECU memory could suffer during its normal operation [Gracia et al. 2002]. The aggregation of these components defines the execution profile of our benchmark.

In general, the output domain is the set of observations (measurements) that are collected from the benchmark target during the experiments. These measurements are retrieved from the experiments following a so-called benchmark procedure. Their processing enables the computation of the benchmark dependability measures. As mentioned in Section 7.2.2, engine control applications are designed to be robust to external perturbations that may affect their inputs but they do not integrate any specific mechanism to recover from such type of faults. This is why the measures our benchmark provides basically characterise the robustness of the ECU control algorithms with respect to the faults affecting their inputs. In case of generating an incorrect control output (a failure), these measures also reflect the ability of the ECU to limit the impact of such failure on its controlled engine. This latter issue is of great importance since, as the next section explains, this impact may vary from the nonoptimal behavior of the engine to a situation in which the engine behavior becomes unpredictable. Accordingly, the best control system will be the one providing a safer behavior from the viewpoint of the controlled engine.

Before closing this overview, we want to underline the fact that the high integration scales used in today's electronic components are a major impairment for conducting benchmark experiments on the considered control applications. Although technical, this issue applies in general to any modern engine ECU and it has a deep impact on the definition of a suitable and realistic benchmark procedure for such automotive systems.

7.3.2. Dependability Measures

As stated in the previous section, the dependability measures of this benchmark evaluate the safety of an engine control system. This evaluation is not performed on the basis of a single measure but, rather, on the basis of a set of measures that estimates the impact of ECU control loop failures on the engine.

We consider that an engine ECU fails when it delivers incorrect control outputs or when it does not deliver any control output at all. Accordingly, one can identify the following different failure modes for an engine ECU:

- The *engine ECU reset* failure mode models the situation in which the ECU normal execution can only be restored through the (hardware) reset of the control unit.
- The *no new data* failure mode represents the case in which the engine control software hangs up without providing any new control output. It also models the case in which one or more control loops enter a computation cycle providing, despite the reads of the sensors, the same control outputs.
- The *close to nominal* and *far from nominal* failure modes characterize failure situations in which the control application provides outputs with incorrect values. One should notice that engines are typically able to absorb certain levels of discrepancies between the expected control values (the nominal values) and the ones actually provided by the ECU control software. The magnitude of these discrepancies cannot, however, be defined in general since it varies from one engine to another. Typically, discrepancies of more of the 30% of the nominal value represent failures of type far from nominal. It is thus obvious that the calibration of this discrepancy has a direct impact on the benchmark results.
- The *missed deadline time* failure mode represents a temporal failure that occurs when a deadline is violated by the control algorithms. This means that the control output is provided out of the temporal bounds fixed by the system specification.

In general, vehicle engines react to the different control failure modes defined above according to three different levels of criticality. The most critical level is the one in which the behavior of the engine becomes unpredictable, that is, we cannot determine the consequences of the control failure for the engine. This is why this situation is the most unsafe for both the engine and the vehicle passengers. The second level of criticality is noise and vibrations, in which the engine is noticeably not running according to its specification. Finally, the less critical impact is when the performance of the engine is nonoptimal. Typically, this is not perceived by the vehicle passengers while driving, but it has a deep impact on fuel consumption, the power delivered, and the pollution generated by the engine.

As Table 7.1 shows, the level of criticality of each control loop failure is different. The most critical failures, from the engine safety viewpoint, correspond to those affecting the control of the fuel injection process, and, more precisely, the moment at which the fuel is injected into the engine cylinder. In general, the engine behavior in that situation becomes unpredictable. However, when the fuel injection angle control loop suffers a time failure or a temporal value of the type close to nominal, the engine behaves in a nonoptimal mode. The table also shows that the reset of the engine ECU is critical. This is because

TABLE 7.1. Measures characterizing the impact of ECU control failures on the engine

	Engine ECU control outputs			
	Fuel injection		Air management	
Control failure modes	Angle	Timing	Volume	Flow shape
Engine ECU reset	Unpredictable			
Value Failures				
No new data	Unpredictable	Nonoptimal	Noise/Vibrations	Noise/Vibrations
Close to nominal	Nonoptimal	Noise/Vibrations	Nonoptimal	Nonoptimal
Far from nominal	Unpredictable	Nonoptimal	Noise/Vibrations	Noise/Vibrations
Miss deadline failure	Nonoptimal	Noise/Vibrations	Nonoptimal	Nonoptimal

▓ The vehicle engine behaves in an unpredictable way (most unsafe situation).
▒ The vehicle engine works, but not properly: it produces some noise and/or vibrations.
☐ The vehicle engine works properly but its performance is not optimal (least unsafe situation).

this failure prevents the engine ECU control loops from performing their computation. Hence, during the reset time, the engine behavior becomes unpredictable, since it is neither monitored nor controlled by the ECU. The rest of control failures lead the engine to produce noise and vibrations or to behave in a nonoptimal way.

The reader should notice that the impact of these control failures on each engine depends on the tolerance of its mechanical components and the dynamics desired for each particular engine. Thus, this impact varies from one engine to another.

The safety measures that one can deduce from Table 7.1 correspond to the percentage of failures falling in each table cell. The goal of presenting these measures in a tabulated form is to improve their readability. We also recommend coloring the cells of the table according to their criticality level. In that way, all the information can be perceived at a single glance.

7.3.3. Execution Profile

The computation of the benchmark measures specified in Table 7.1 requires the activation of the engine ECU with a particular execution profile. This profile has two main components: the workload and the faultload. The workload defines the type of stimuli needed for activating the engine ECU software during the benchmark experiments. The faultload characterize the faults that may perturb the normal execution of this software. The main challenge here is to define these benchmark components in a representative way, that is, according to the set of conditions that drive the execution of engine control applications in the real world.

7.3.3.1. Workload. Despite what happens in other benchmarks, the workload needed for exercising the control software of an engine ECU cannot be simply defined in terms of a set of programs. As Figure 7.2 showed, engine control applications execute according to two types of information. The former corresponds to the speed reference the driver imposes to the engine through the throttle. The latter is defined by the set of engine internal variables that the ECU monitors in order to feed back its control computation.

THROTTLE INPUTS. Defining the throttle inputs consists of modelling different ways of driving. For our purposes, we propose the use of the following driving cycles: the acceleration–deceleration driving cycle, the urban driving cycle, and the extraurban driving cycle. All these cycles are expressed in terms of engine speed, that is, in revolutions per minute, or rpm for short.

In the acceleration–deceleration driving cycle, the throttle is repeatedly pushed and released to test all possible regulation conditions of the engine system. At the beginning of the cycle, the engine is idle and it is progressively accelerated, without changing gears, by pushing the throttle from 0% to 100%. Then, the throttle remains pushed at 100% until the engine reaches a speed of 80% of the maximum engine rpm. The throttle is then progressively released from 100% to 0% and it is maintained completely released until the engine becomes idle once again. Then the cycle can be repeated again.

The urban and extraurban driving cycles are standard cycles specified for emission certification of light-duty vehicles in Europe [EEC Directive 90/C81/01 1999]. Figure 7.3 depicts their main features. As we can see, the standard is set in terms of vehicle speed— kilometers per hour (km/h for short). In order to transform this speed into engine speed (expressed in rpm), one must use the mathematical relation presented in Figure 7.4. Conversion from vehicle to engine speed requires the knowledge of the speed reduction factors applied by the transmission for each gear, the differential and the radius of the vehicle wheels. This information must be supplied by the benchmark user, since it varies from one vehicle to another.

The reader must understand that for the purposes of benchmarking, what is important is not to apply all the driving cycles described above each time the engine ECU is benchmarked, but to apply only those that make more sense according to the benchmark user purposes. It must be also noticed that the results obtained when considering different driving cycles are not comparable among them.

ENGINE INTERNAL VARIABLES. Although the benchmark experiments can be carried out using a real engine, it is evident that this solution is not suitable due to economic and safety reasons. This is easy to understand if one considers how unsafe the consequences of an engine ECU control failure can be (see Table 7.1).

In order to avoid the damage to the engine during the experiments, we propose to replace the real engine by a model. This model could have a mathematical or empirical nature. From a practical viewpoint, a mathematical model is only a good choice if it is available and ready to use at the moment of running the benchmark experiments. If this is not the case, it seems more reasonable to use an empirical model. This model can be easily defined; for instance, by tracing the activity of the real engine while running under the working conditions imposed by the throttle.

7.3.3.2. Faultload.

In general, benchmarking a system component prevents faults from being injected into this component. In other words, the faultload can only affect the execution environment of the benchmark target, but not the benchmark target itself. Our target is the software running inside the engine ECU. Consequently, faults cannot be introduced in this software, but they can be introduced in the hardware supporting its execution.

Some studies [Gil et al. 2002] point out that the likelihood of occurrence of hardware transient faults is increasing in integrated circuits (ICs). These results can be also applied to ECUs, since their manufacturing greatly benefits from improvements of integration scales in IC technologies. Moreover, some fault types that usually have been ne-

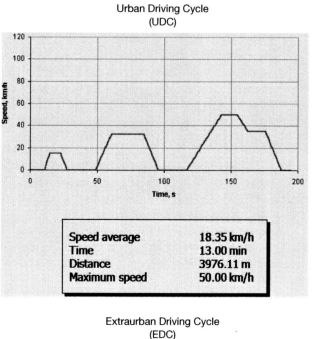

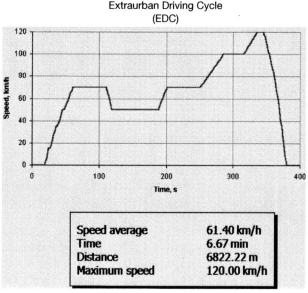

Figure 7.3. Urban and extraurban driving cycles.

glected for such type of systems will have an important impact. This is the case of faults in combinational logic (pulse fault model). At higher working frequencies, the likelihood of experiencing a combinational fault is going to rise considerably. Other unconsidered fault models like delay and indeterminism are going to increase their influence also, due to problems related to high-speed working. At high frequencies, skin and Miller effects will make delays in ICs nonconstant, causing time violations that can lead to indeterminate outputs. [Gracia et al. 2002] have shown that basic approaches toward

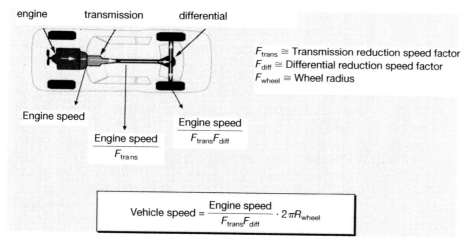

Figure 7.4. Parameters for converting the engine speed (rpm) to vehicle speed (km/h).

the consideration of the above fault models are single and multiple bit-flip fault models.

Accordingly, the faultload we propose is defined in terms of hardware transient faults emulated by bit flips that will affect the engine ECU memory during its normal use. As motivated above, the high scales of integration used for manufacturing modern engine ECUs make such electronic components very sensitive to the interferences produced by the different types of radiation existing in the environment. These interferences may provoke single event upsets (SEUs) that may impact the logic circuitry, in particular control signals, and may lead to single (or multiple) bit flip errors by the time the corrupted data reaches the memory. It must be remarked that current ECUs do not integrate error-correcting codes, which makes such units sensitive to bit flips. One can see memory bit flips as proxies for the emulation of many different types of errors, varying from simple SEUs to arithmetic logic unit (ALU) computational errors or software design errors. In fact, through the ECU memory content, one can have access to (i) the data used in the computation of the system operating system and the control software, (ii) the content of memory-mapped in-CPU registers, and (iii) the readings (and control actions) coming from (or going to) sensors (or actuators). Figure 7.6 provides a detailed view of the relationships existing between the different elements (sensors and actuators) connected to engine ECUs, the components [memory, processors, and analog/digital (A/D) and digital/analog (D/A) converters] integrated in such control units, and the different interfaces that must be identified for enabling the execution of the benchmark. Among these interfaces, the faultload interface is the one through which bit flips are injected in the ECU memory during the experimentation phase. As can be seen, by acting on the content of single (or multiple) ECU memory location(s) one can force single (or multiple) bit flip, which emulate the consequences of corruption in a control signal, an in-CPU register, or a computation variable. The description of this interface and the proposed fault-injection methodology are part of the benchmark procedure specification.

7.3.4. Benchmark Procedure

For a given engine control application, the dependability measures defined in Table 7.1 are deduced from measurements computed by comparing its behavior in absence of faults (golden run) with its behavior in presence of faults. In all the benchmark experiments, the same initial SUB configuration is required. From one experiment to another, the difference relies on the definition of the experiment execution profile and, more precisely, on the fault selected from the faultload.

7.3.4.1. Experimental Setup Components.

Figure 7.5 identifies the main components of the experimental setup required for running the benchmark experiments. This setup is built according to the model depicted in Figure 7.2. Within a single experiment, the experiment manager coordinates the activity of all the setup entities and sequences the execution of successive benchmark experiments.

The workload and faultload controllers are those entities devoted to the activation of the SUB according to the execution profile defined for each experiment. In order to do that, they use two different interfaces: the workload interface and the faultload interface. The former is defined in terms of the sensors that feed the control algorithms of the engine ECU. The latter is the interface through which the faultload is applied to the target system. It must be noted that the definition of this second interface is not as evident as the definition of the workload interface. Further insights on that issue are provided in Section 7.3.4.2.

The observation interface is used by the SUB monitor in order to obtain traces reflecting the target activity. We name these observations the benchmark measurements. These measurements are those from which the dependability measures specified in Table 7.1 are

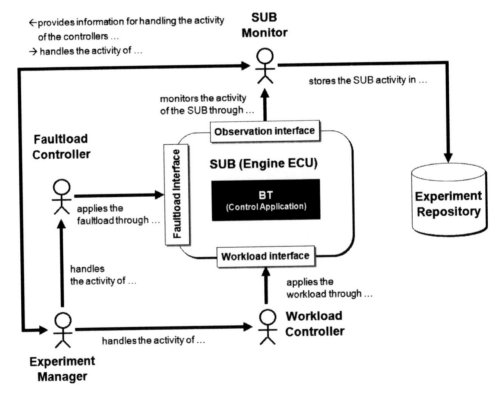

Figure 7.5. Experimental setup components.

later deduced. The place where the SUB monitor stores the benchmark measurements is called the experiment repository.

The reader must notice that the view of the experimental setup provided here is conceptual; the different entities depicted in Figure 7.5 can be mapped to a single entity or a set of different entities in the implementation. The experiment repository, for instance, can be implemented, despite its role in the experimental setup, as either a database or a file directory. These practical issues are, however, out of the scope of this specification and they will be commented on in Section 7.4.

7.3.4.2. Experimental Approach. The experiments with an execution profile containing one fault are carried out in three successive phases. In the first one, the experiment manager initializes the system under benchmarking, which leads to the initial conditions of the experiment. Then it asks to the setup controllers to run the execution profile. Finally, it supervises the activity of the SUB monitor, which stores in the experiment repository the information retrieved from the target internal activity. Golden runs are experiments with a simpler benchmark procedure that consists of running execution profiles with an empty faultload.

PHASE 1: SUB INITIALIZATION. First, the target application is reset. Then an initial start-up time must be devoted to the initialization of the system under benchmarking. During this time, the engine control software and the operating system are loaded in memory and their execution leads to a "ready-to-control" state. From a mechanical viewpoint, this initialization phase enables the engine to be started in order to warm up and reach the required initial speed. According to initial conditions of our workload (see Section 7.3.3.1), the initial speed that we need is 800 rpm, that is, the engine is idle at the beginning of the benchmark experiments. The internal temperature of the engine should be the one that the manufacturer considers as "normal".

The injection of faults during the experiments is triggered through a timer that must be programmed during this initialization phase. Although the fault injection time can be shorter than the experiment start-up time, this situation is only of interest when studying the start-up of the system in presence of faults, which is not our case. We consider that the fault injection time is always longer than the start-up time of the system under benchmarking (see Figure 7.8).

PHASE 2: EXECUTION PROFILE RUNNING. As Figure 7.6 shows, running the workload consists in feeding the sensors connected to the engine ECU with the adequate inputs. These inputs are those associated with the selected driving cycle and the feedback supplied by the engine. As discussed during the definition of the workload, both the throttle and the engine can be either real components or models. In the latter case, it must be noted that the sensor data is always digitized before being stored in a set of predefined memory locations. This issue can be exploited in order to write the sensor readings directly to these locations from another computer system (the workload controller). This is a technical issue that can simplify the design of the benchmark setup since it is not necessary to produce analogic signals for feeding the sensors if we are using neither real throttles nor real engines.

On the other hand, executing the faultload means injecting faults during the normal execution of the engine ECU. In our case, only one fault is injected per experiment. However, flipping bits in the memory of the engine ECU is more problematic than it may seem at a single glance. Ideally, the fault injection procedure should not interfere with the normal

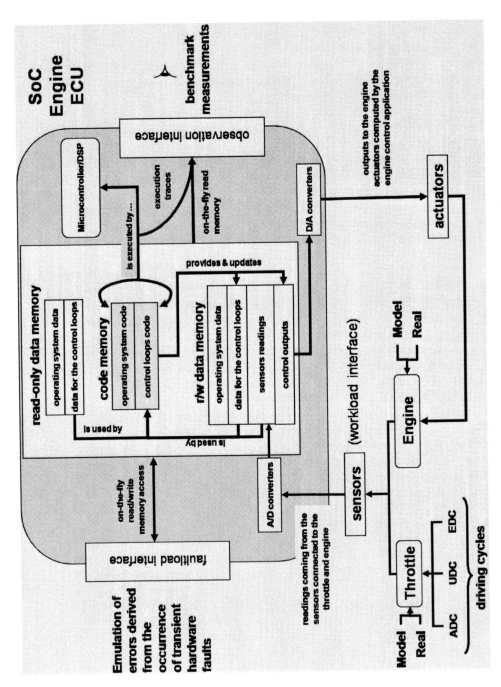

Figure 7.6. Role of the benchmarking interfaces in the experiments.

124

execution of the engine control software. In order to achieve that goal, this procedure must be defined taking into account that: (i) the benchmark target has a real-time behavior that should not be perturbed during the fault injection process, and (ii) if a real engine is used for the experiments, then its dynamics prevent the execution of the ECU software from being stopped. These issues are general and they concern all modern engine ECUs. Basically, a faultload interface suitable for our purposes must provide on-the-fly read/write memory access features. Using these features, the ECU memory content can be accessed and manipulated at runtime, minimizing the level of intrusion and without stopping the normal execution of the system. It is worth noting that on-the-fly memory access is nowadays increasingly present in automotive systems where it is exploited for calibration purposes.

Figure 7.7 describes how the on-the-fly memory access features of the faultload interface must be used in order to provoke the flip of a certain number of bits in a particular ECU memory position. First, the memory position content is read by the faultload controller. This controller defines a mask in which the bit or set of bits to be changed are set to the logical value 1; the rest become 0. In the case of a single bit flip, only one bit of the mask is set to 1; in case of a multiple bit flips, several bits in the mask take that logical value. The particular bit or set of bits to be set can be predefined or chosen randomly. Once the mask defined, it is applied to the memory content retrieved in step 1. The logical operation used is an XOR. Finally, the resulting word is written back to the memory, which concludes the fault injection process. The moment at which this fault injection process is triggered (the fault injection time) is randomly selected within the duration of a benchmark experiment. As stated before, this time must be greater than the SUB initialization time. It is important to notice that the memory position where the fault is injected can be selected randomly or predefined by the benchmark performed. More details about this issue will be provided in Section 7.4.2.2.

If all works well, the sequence of events depicted in Figure 7.8 must occur internally in the benchmark target. Once one fault is injected in the memory of the engine ECU, it remains dormant until the application exercises the location where it is stored. At this moment (the fault activation time), the fault is activated and it becomes an error, which can be detected or not. If it is detected, then the error recovery mechanisms execute and two new measurements can be defined: (i) the error detection latency, which is the difference between the error detection time and the fault activation time; and (ii) the recovery time, which can be defined as the execution time of the system error recovery mechanisms. If an error remains undetected, the activity of the target application must be monitored during the defined observation time. In our particular case, this time must be greater than the

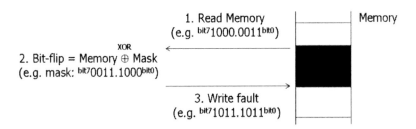

1. Read Memory
(e.g. $^{bit7}1000.0011^{bit0}$)

XOR
2. Bit-flip = Memory ⊕ Mask
(e.g. mask: $^{bit7}0011.1000^{bit0}$)

3. Write fault
(e.g. $^{bit7}1011.1011^{bit0}$)

Memory

Figure 7.7. Using the faultload interface features for flipping bits in the ECU memory.

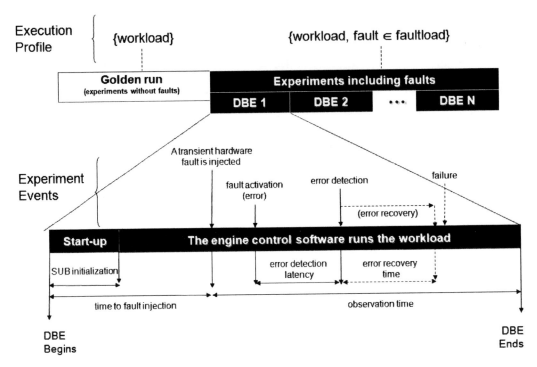

Figure 7.8. Main steps of the benchmarking experiment.

time required for running each loop of the engine control software. The observation of these events allow us to determine whether an error has been detected or not and, in the case of error detection, the type of the detected error. This issue is essential in order to determine when the engine ECU will be reset. As stated in Section 7.3.2, only certain errors cause the ECU to reset. Most of the time, this reset only affects the ECU internal hardware and it cannot be perceived from outside of this unit without being intrusive. If the error finally affects the outputs computed by the engine control algorithms, then a failure occurs in the system.

PHASE 3: RETRIEVING MEASUREMENTS FROM THE BENCHMARK TARGET. This phase executes in parallel with Phase 2. It starts once the system under benchmarking is running the execution profile.

Through the observation interface, the SUB monitor should have access to the control outputs computed by the ECU internal algorithms. These outputs can be captured internally (by reading their associated memory position) or externally (by reading the analog signals produced by the digital–analog converters of the ECU). It is worth noting that this second option requires the analogical signals produced by the ECU to be converted to digital signals by the SUB monitor. In addition, this solution is only viable when every computed control signal is externalized by the engine ECU. If this is not the case, then control outputs must be captured internally, which requires the engine ECU to provide on-the-fly read memory access facilities in order to minimize the level of intrusion in the target system.

Due to the real-time nature of the application under benchmarking, being able to obtain the instant of occurrence of a failure is also very important. This temporal information is required for deducing whether a deadline is missed or not. In order to understand how missing deadlines are detected, the reader should understand that in our context each control loop running inside the engine ECU is executed cyclically with a given frequency. The inverse of this frequency, typically expressed in milliseconds, is the computation period of each control loop. This period represents the amount of time each control loop has to compute new control outputs according to the current set of inputs. If this computation exceeds this amount of time, then the control loop violates its deadline, that is, the control output is not supplied within the bounds of the computation period. In order to detect such situations, it is essential to accurately know the times at which the engine control loops start, finish, resume, and stop their execution.

The reader should notice that the internal information depicted in Figure 7.8 is also of great interest from a validation viewpoint. One should not forget that once implemented the behavior of each benchmark prototype must be always verified according to its specification. This issue is extremely important for placing justified confidence on a particular implementation of the prototype and, by extension, on the dependability measures it provides. One of the objectives of this validation phase must be to check that the benchmark procedure is correctly conducted by the experiment manager. We want to emphasize that the importance of these measurements is not only limited to the validation of a particular implementation of our benchmark specification. The dependability measures that can be deduced from them, such as error detection latencies and error coverage, can be exploited for guiding the eventual design decisions that each engine ECU developer may adopt in order to improve the dependability measures of their implementations. These tuning decisions may be oriented, for instance, to the reduction of error detection latencies or to the improvement of error detection coverage.

As Figure 7.6 shows, retrieving all the observations defined here requires the SUB to provide interfaces with features for (i) tracing the internal activity of the engine control application and (ii) handling the ECU memory contents on the fly. It must be noted that these mechanisms refer to features existing in today's most sophisticated debugging standards for automotive embedded systems. This is why their existence is, from our viewpoint, an acceptable requirement for the considered SUB. The benchmark prototype section illustrates how to use one of these debugging interfaces, the one standardized as IEEE-ISTO 5001 [IEEE-ISTO 5001 1999], in order to cope with the observation requirements described here.

7.4. BENCHMARK PROTOTYPE

The prototype implementation presented here shows the feasibility of the dependability benchmark specified in the previous section. This prototype enables the comparison of different SoC-based diesel engine ECUs. In addition, it illustrates how the in-built debugging features of an SoC-based ECU can be exploited to facilitate the implementation of the benchmark experimental procedure.

Section 7.4.1 introduces the functional specification of the considered diesel engine ECUs. Then Section 7.4.2 describes the benchmark prototype in detail. Finally, Section 7.4.3 estimates the effort and cost required for its implementation.

7.4.1. Specification of the Case Study Benchmark Target

Figure 7.9 provides a view of the types of diesel engine ECUs that we consider. These ECUs work in three successive phases:

1. The ECU gets from the sensors six different types of information: (1) the pressure of the air in the engine intake; (2) the pressure of the fuel in the engine common rail; (3 and 4) the current angle of the crankshaft and the camshaft (see these components in Figure 7.1); (5) the current position of the throttle, which defines the engine speed reference; and (6) the current speed deployed by the engine, which is expressed in rpm. These analog values are then digitized and stored in the internal memory of the ECU (as shown in Figure 7.6).

2. According to the sensor readings, the ECU control loops compute: (i) the new pressure in the common rail, which impacts the diesel injection timing; (ii) the outputs required for controlling the swirl and waste gate valves that, respectively, regulate the shape flow and volume injected in the engine; and (iii) the duration and the angle of the fuel injection, which are control outputs directly applied to the engine diesel injectors. These control loops are executed cyclically with the following frequencies: the fuel timing control loop executes each 20 milliseconds, the fuel angle loop each 50 milliseconds, the air flow shape loop each 20 milliseconds, and the air volume loop each 500 milliseconds. Figure 7.9 details the set of inputs that each one of these control loops requires and the set of outputs it generates.

3. Once computed, the control outputs are stored in specific memory locations monitored by a set of D/A converters. These converters are those providing to the actuators the analog signals they need for regulating the engine behavior.

7.4.2. Prototype Description

Figure 7.10 provides a general view of the prototype benchmarking platform. An Athlon XP 2600 PC manages the execution of the experiments. The control algorithms for the

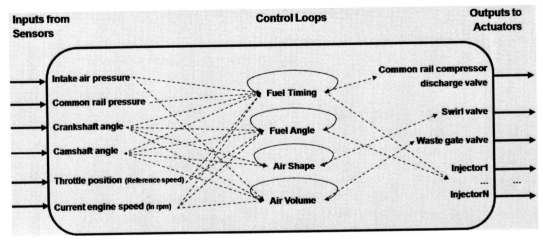

Figure 7.9. View of the case study diesel engine ECU.

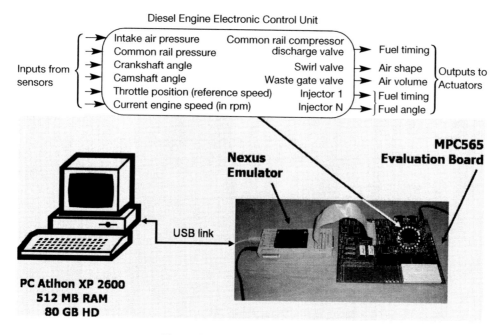

Figure 7.10. Experimental setup.

considered diesel ECUs run in a microcontroller-based MPC565 evaluation board. The MPC565 microcontroller embeds a built-in debugging circuitry offering a standard debugging interface, formally named IEEE-ISTO 5001 but typically called Nexus. The board provides a port to which a Nexus emulator can be connected. In our case, this emulator is commercial and is distributed by Lauterbach GmbH. The PC manages the Nexus interface of the microcontroller by means of this emulator.

The following sections detail the different elements of the prototype from the perspective of a reader interested in implementing the benchmark specified in the previous section.

7.4.2.1. Workload Implementation.

The prototype is designed to admit synthetic workloads. These workloads are defined using engine and throttle models. The definitions of engine models are supported by the tracing tool shown in Figure 7.11. Basically, this tool is able to monitor the behavior of any diesel engine providing the sensor data defined in Figure 7.9. The values showed in Figure 7.11 are, for instance, those supplied by the dynamics of a PSA DW12 engine, an engine with common-rail direct diesel injection, also known as HDI, when exercised using the acceleration–deceleration driving cycle. The information monitored by the tool is stored in tables that are also allocated in the memory of the ECU. These tables play the role of the memory locations in which the analogue–digital converters store the data coming from the sensors connected to the diesel engine (see Figure 7.6). In that way, the ECU is not aware of the absence of the real engine during the experiments.

The same approach is used in order to replace the real throttle with a model of its behavior. In this latter case, throttle models are directly deduced from the specification of the driving cycles introduced in Section 7.3.3.1.

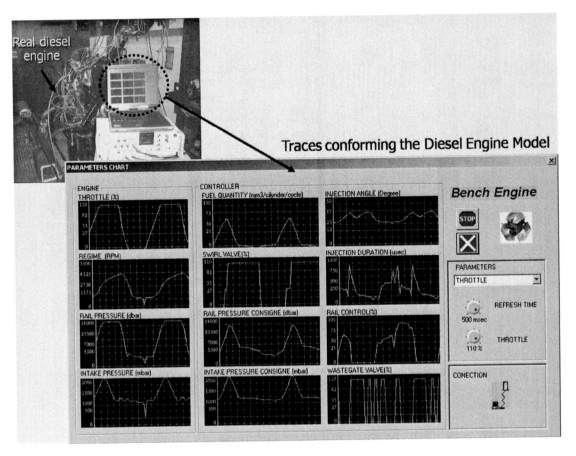

Figure 7.11. Diesel engine modeling tool.

7.4.2.2. Faultload Specification Tool.

In order to support the definition of the faultload, the benchmark prototype provides the tool depicted in Figure 7.12. Basically, it is a graphical tool that aims at the specification of (i) the total number of faults to be injected (one per experiment), (ii) the observation time, and (iii) the set of memory locations where the faultload is applied.

Each memory location corresponds to the set of bytes associated with each symbol of the program. This symbolic information is generated by the compiler when building the executable file of the engine ECU control algorithm. In Figure 7.12, the supplied file is called ECU.map. For the sake of clarity, the benchmark user can customize the view of the program symbols. Three possibilities are offered. In the *sort by sections* view, symbols are sorted according to the memory segment name in which they are allocated. In the *sort by file source* view, they are grouped according to the file in the source code in which they are defined. In the *sort by type* view, symbols are shown according to the type of memory segment (code, read-only data, and read/write data) in which they are allocated. Once a view is selected, the benchmark user can select one, several, or all the memory locations shown by the tool. It is also possible to provide a different weight to each memory location, or set of memory locations, according to its importance in the fault injection selection process. Those locations with a bigger weight will be those with a higher probabil-

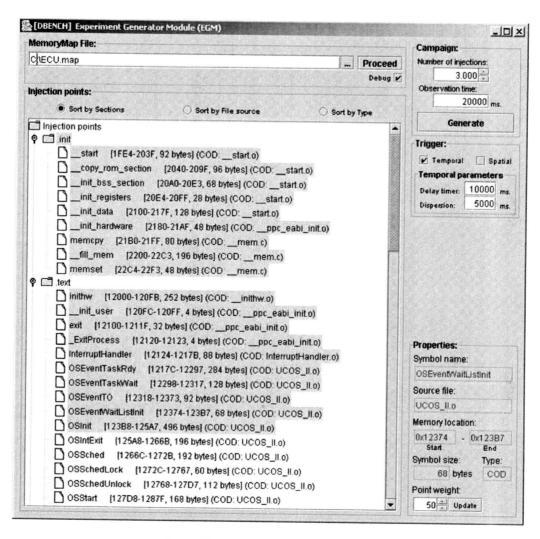

Figure 7.12. Faultload specification tool.

ity of being selected for fault injection during experimentation. By default, faults are randomly distributed in memory following a uniform probability distribution. The button *Proceed* launches the generation of the faultload.

7.4.2.3. Benchmark Procedure Implementation.
Nexus is the cornerstone of the implementation of our benchmark procedure. First, Nexus is a debug and calibration standard for real-time embedded systems. Second, the inspection and control features offered by this standard match the requirements identified in the Section 7.3.4.2. Third, Nexus is defined in a processor-independent way. Thus, solutions built according to its specification can potentially be ported and applied to any embedded platform supporting the interface.

In our case, the capabilities of Nexus are exploited in order to inject faults into the memory of the ECU while minimizing the interference with the execution algorithm. According to Figure 7.5, the faultload interface of our prototype corresponds to the compound formed by the Nexus emulator, the evaluation board, and the MPC565 microcontroller built-in Nexus debugging circuitry. First, a timer is programmed with the fault injection time at the beginning of each benchmark experiment. When the timer expires, a signal is sent, by the Nexus circuitry of the MPC565, to the PC through the Nexus emulator. The on-the-fly memory facilities of Nexus enable the PC to read, without stopping the execution of the ECU software, the contents of the memory position where the fault must be injected. Next, it flips the selected bit and, finally, it writes back the corrupted contents. The limitation of this approach is that it cannot guarantee that, in all the cases, the steps described before are executed without a simultaneous access of the ECU software to the considered memory location.

When programmed adequately, the Nexus circuitry can also generate messages that inform the emulator about the data and code memory locations accessed by the ECU software during its execution. These tracing capabilities and the ones providing on-the-fly read access to the engine ECU memory define the observation interface of our prototype. The reader must notice that the amount of trace memory of the emulator is limited (in our case to 16 mega-messages). This can become a limitation for the duration of the experiment in case of very long workloads, which is not the case in the driving cycles proposed here.

The interested reader can find in [Yuste et al. 2003a; Yuste et al. 2003b; Yuste et al. 2003c] more details about how to use the Nexus debugging capabilities for fault injection and observation purposes.

7.4.2.4. From Experimental Measurements to Dependability Measures.
Deducing the dependability measures from the measurements resulting from the experiments is far from trivial. First, the trace files of these experiments are difficult to handle due to their sizes. In our case, the size of some files exceeds 1 gigabyte. Second, the information stored in each file is a dump of the emulator tracing message memory. Thus, the format of this raw information is not directly exploitable for our benchmarking (comparison) purposes.

Figure 7.13 depicts the three-step process our data analyser follows in order to deduce the expected dependability measures from the measurements retrieved by the SUB monitor. These measurements are located in the experiment repository, in our case, a file directory. First, the measurements of each experiment are classified according to the type of probe through which they have been obtained. Then this probe-oriented representation is compared to another one deduced from the golden run. This comparison enables the identification of the relevant events happening during each experiment. Once this event-oriented representation is computed for all the experiments, the general measures defined in Table 7.1 are deduced. It is worth noting that, in addition to these general measures, the analysis tool also provides some specific measures regarding error latencies, error coverage, and error distribution. As noted in Section 7.3.4.2, these specific measures can be exploited for validation and tuning purposes.

7.4.3. Benchmark Experiments

The following sections describe the configuration considered for the experiments carried out with the aforementioned prototype. Then we present and discuss the results obtained from those experiments.

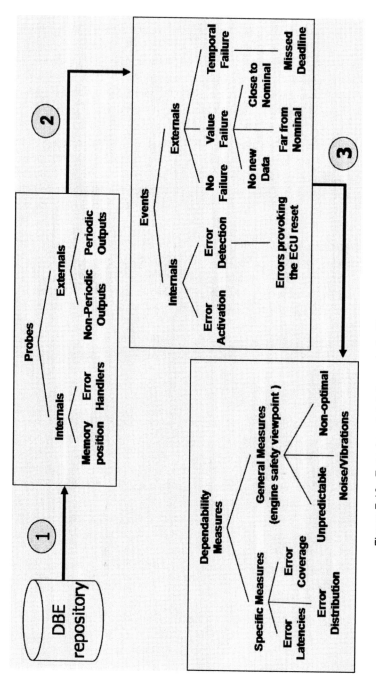

Figure 7.13. Experimental data analysis: From measurements to measures.

7.4.3.1. Benchmark Targets. Two different (prototype) versions of a diesel ECU (DECU for short) meeting the specification of the DBT described in Section 7.4.1 are considered in our experiments:

1. The first version runs on top of a real-time operating system, called μC/OS-II [Labrosse 2002]. In the following, this DECU will be referred as DECU with RTOS. Each control loop of this DECU is implemented as a different operating system task; the activity of each task is synchronized with the rest by means of semaphores and wait system calls. On the other hand, the operating system is configured in order to schedule the execution of the tasks following a rate-monotonic policy.

2. The second version of our case study DECU is directly implemented on top of the MPC565 microcontroller, so no operating system is available in that case. We will name this second DECU as DECU without RTOS. In its implementation, each control loop is deployed in a different program procedure and the main program schedules the execution of each procedure using a scheduling policy computed off-line.

7.4.3.2. Execution Profile. Both the urban and extraurban driving cycles have been considered in the workload. The throttle model for these cycles was deduced by taking into account the acceleration/deceleration information provided in Figure 7.3 and the dynamics imposed by the considered engine, which was a PSA DW12 engine. The model of this engine was obtained from measures performed using our engine modeling tool (see Figure 7.11).

As far as the faultload is concerned, transient hardware faults have been randomly injected into the memory of the ECU engine using a single bit flip fault model. These faults are selected using our faultload specification tool (see Figure 7.12) and the procedure followed for their injection was the one described in Section 7.4.2.3.

7.4.3.3. Results. We devoted one working week (5 days) to the execution of the benchmark experiments. During this time, 600 experiments were carried out; 300 with each driving cycle. Two hundred seconds were required for running each urban driving experiment, whereas double that (400 seconds) was required for the extraurban experiments. The analysis of the raw day obtained from the experiments, although automatically performed, took 16 hours. The entire process was performed automatically. The results included in Table 7.2 and Table 7.3 show the measures obtained from these experiments. It must be noted that these results have been computed according to the distribution of failure modes introduced in Table 7.1. For the sake of conciseness, only the percentage of experiments exhibiting unsafe engine behavior (unpredictable noise and vibrations or

Table 7.2. Results obtained using the urban driving cycle as workload*

ECU behavior	DECU with RTOS	DECU without RTOS
Unpredictable behavior	1.35%	0.34%
Noise and vibrations	2.48%	1.36%
Nonoptimal	1.93%	0.68%
Total observed failure ratio	**5.76%**	**2.38%**

*Total number of experiments is 300.

Table 7.3. Results obtained using the extraurban driving cycle as workload*

ECU behavior	DECU with RTOS	DECU without RTOS
Unpredictable behaviour	2.72%	1.28%
Noise and vibrations	2.00%	1.60%
Nonoptimal	2.38%	2.88%
Total observed failure ratio	**7.1%**	**5.76%**

*Total number of experiments is 300.

nonoptimal performance) is provided. This is the useful information that can be exploited by a system integrator who must make the choice between candidates.

Under urban conditions, we have observed that the DECU without RTOS exhibits safer behavior than the version integrating the operating system. First, the DECU with RTOS doubles the failure ratio of the version without RTOS. Second, the percentage of unpredictable failures that the former DECU has shown is four times greater than the one showed by the latter DECU. Following the same trend, the percentage of noise and vibrations and nonoptimal failure modes in the DECU with RTOS are twice the percentage without operating system.

Under extraurban driving conditions, both DECUs have shown similar failure ratios. The study of the failure distribution has shown that, in the case of the DECU version with RTOS, in 2.72% of the experiments the impact of engine faults was unpredictable. In the case of the DECU without RTOS, this percentage is 1.28%. However, we have observed that in 1.60% of the experiments, faults provoked noise and vibrations in the engine, whereas this failure mode was not observed in experiments with the operating system. As far as engine nonoptimal behaviour is concerned, both ECUs have shown similar failure ratios. The conclusion is that, according to the results of our experimentations, the DECU without RTOS seems also better for driving under extraurban driving conditions. In this case, it must be noted that this does not mean that it has a lower failure ratio than the version with RTOS; it means that the failures are distributed in such a way that their impact is safer from the viewpoint of the considered engine.

Accordingly, benchmark candidate one (DECU with RTOS) seems less safe than candidate two (DECU without RTOS) under both urban and extraurban conditions. However, these results should not be taken as an endorsement of, or an indictment of, a particular product. They must be only understood as a demonstration of the interest and feasibility of the proposed benchmark.

On the other hand, it is also important to note that, although a further detailed dependability analysis of results is possible (see [Yuste et al. 2003a, Yuste et al. 2003b, and Yuste et al. 2003c]), very detailed results are difficult to exploit by people with a limited dependability knowledge, like system integrators. We claim that conciseness must be a characteristic in dependability benchmarking results, as it is in performance benchmarking.

7.4.4. Implementation Cost and Effort

The economic cost related to the hardware depicted in Figure 7.10 was 18,000 €. The time required for developing our prototype was 120 man-days (6 man-months). Basically, 10 man-days has been spent in the development of the tools showed in Figure 7.11 and Figure 7.12; 50 more man-days were required to implement the benchmark procedure using the MPC565 Nexus capabilities; and, finally, the automation of the result analysis process required an additional effort of 60 man-days. It must be noted that this effort estimation includes both the time required for understanding the specification and the time devoted to getting skills needed for the programming of the selected hardware target platform. Our experience shows that programming languages selected for the implementation of the benchmark must be, if possible, functions of the programming skills of the developer. Otherwise, if the programming languages are imposed, for instance, due to enterprise practices, then an additional effort must be included in this temporal estimation.

We have also estimated the amount of time required for sequentially running 3000 experiments with each (urban and extraurban) driving cycle on the considered targets. The time needed for such experiments is of 1½ man-month. Although this time can be significantly reduced when running the experiments in parallel, this increases the economic investment for the benchmarking platform. Another solution is to reduce the number of experiments, bounding the experimental time to one man-week. This is what we have done in the experiments that we have performed. However, one must take into account the impact that this reduction in the number of experiments may have on the accuracy of the measures finally obtained. This interesting issue is a subject for future research.

7.5. BENCHMARK PROPERTIES AND THEIR VALIDATION

This section focuses on the verification of five properties of our dependability benchmark: portability, nonintrusiveness, scalability, repeatability of experiments, and representativeness of the dependability measures they provide.

7.5.1. Portability

The portability of a benchmark specification refers to its ability to apply to different benchmark targets. Our specification builds on a general engine model that abstracts the specifics associated with a particular type of engine. Thus, the control loops included in this model are those at the core of diesel and gasoline engine ECUs. From that viewpoint, the specification is applicable to both types of engines. However, one should not forget that each type of engine may have specific control features that have not been considered in our benchmark. In order to study the dependability of these control loops, the approach needs to be extended. This extension restricts the portability of the specification to engines of the same type if we consider, for instance, specific diesel or gasoline control features such as exhaust gas recirculation or spark control loops. The same applies if we consider control features of a particular (diesel or gasoline) engine model.

From the viewpoint of the deployed prototype, its implementation can be plugged into any engine ECU providing a Nexus debugging interface. The only requirement is that the interface must be Nexus Class 3 compliant. This issue has not been stressed before because it only influences the portability of the benchmark prototype. The fact is that engine ECUs with Nexus interfaces of Classes 1 and 2 supply neither on-the-fly memory access nor memory-tracing message facilities. Since these are the features sustaining the execution of our prototype, it cannot be ported to those SoC engine ECUs not providing Nexus Class 3 compliant ports. This is the only restriction on to the portability of our benchmark prototype.

7.5.2. Nonintrusiveness

As we have already emphasized in other sections, the strong encapsulation imposed by the SoC technologies on the manufacturing of today's engine ECUs makes difficult the benchmarking of the software running inside them without modifying the code of the SUB or affecting its temporal behavior.

As discussed in Section 7.3, we have chosen the solution of exploiting, for benchmarking purposes, the debugging features provided by most of today's automotive ECUs. These features are those described in Section 7.3.4. In order to assess the viability of this approach, we have developed a prototype, whose implementation relies on the Class 3 Nexus debugging interfaces. According to its specification, the built-in circuitry embedded in this interface must ensure, by construction, an absence of temporal intrusion when (i) accessing the engine ECU memory contents on the fly, and (ii) tracing the activity deployed by ECU software. Since these features are also enough from an observation viewpoint, no code instrumentation is required in order to adapt the code of the ECU software to the purposes of our benchmark; hence, neither is spatial intrusion required.

This practical work has shown that our specification can be implemented in a nonintrusive way from either a spatial and temporal viewpoint. It must be noted that Nexus has been chosen due to its increasing popularity in the automotive embedded systems domain. However, it is important to emphasize that our benchmark specification does not rely on Nexus, only our prototype does. Hence, any other debugging interface providing the features identified in the specification can also be used.

7.5.3. Scalability

What affects the scalability of our benchmark specification is the consideration of additional control loops. In that case, the benchmark must be revisited in order to enrich its specification, with the goal of covering also the characterization of the new features related to these control loops. It is obvious that the benchmark prototypes meeting the old specification must be updated according to the new requirements identified in the resulting benchmark. This is an exercise that has been left for future research.

7.5.4. Repeatability of the Experiments

Under identical initial conditions, and using the same execution profile, can the results obtained from experimentation be reproduced? This property must be guaranteed in the absence and in the presence of faults. In this latter case, the property must be verified despite the occurrence of errors and failures.

Basically, the idea is to run the same experiment several times in order to compare the resulting traces. In our experiments, two traces are said to be equal if they reflect the same ECU internal and external activity. The internal activity refers to the events depicted in Figure 7.8 and the external activity concerns the production of control outputs. This information is retrieved from the system using the tracing capabilities offered by the Nexus interface of the hardware platform. The goal is to check that the traced events are the same and they are ordered following the same temporal sequence. If a missed deadline failure does not occur, the exact time at which each event happens is not important for the verification of the repeatability property. The reader must notice at this point that the notion of statistical repeatability used by our partners does not apply in our case. This is mainly due to the fact that we do not consider in our benchmark the impact that faults have on the performance of the engine ECU, since this type of measure makes no sense in our context. Thus, the measures computed by our benchmark do not admit variations from one experiment to another; the set of events traced from one experiment must remain the same if the execution profile, the initial conditions, and the target system remains the same.

In the experiments, we have checked the repeatability of (i) the golden runs, (ii) the experiments with a faultload affecting an empty memory location, and (iii) the experiments with a faultload impacting occupied code/data memory locations that are used by the engine ECU software. In this latter type of experiment, we differentiate those leading to an internal error not leading to the failure of the target system and those causing the target system to fail. These experiments have been very fruitful in the first stages of the benchmark prototype development in order to fix some bugs in the implementation. As our benchmark prototype matures, it is harder to identify discrepancies between experiments executed on the same target using the same execution profile and the same initial conditions. For instance, the experiments depicted in Section 7.4.3 have been reproduced twice and no deviations have been found in the resulting dependability measures.

Further experiments are, however, required in order to check the difficulty of guaranteeing this level of repeatability when changing the hardware platform or when considering other benchmark targets.

7.5.5. Representativeness

The workload we have selected is representative for the automotive domain, as shown by the fact that it is used as a standard workload for emission certification of light-duty vehicles in Europe. It is well known that the combustion process of fuel inside the engine determines the level of contaminants that vehicles emit to the atmosphere. Thus, our choice makes sense if the workload is applied to the part of the engine ECU responsible for handling this combustion process. As discussed in Section 7.2.2, this is our case.

Concerning the faultload, recent publications [Gil et al. 2002; Gracia et al. 2002] have pointed out that the likelihood of finding hardware transient faults in integrated circuits will increase greatly. We have selected the (single and multiple) bit flip fault model for emulating the effects of such faults because it provides a good compromise between (i) the type of models widely accepted by the dependability community and (ii) the type of perturbations that can be injected in electronic components used in today's automotive systems.

7.6. CONCLUSIONS

The omnipresence of COTS in the automotive software industry together with the increasing need to minimizing costs and time to market justifies the interest in the benchmarking approach proposed in this chapter. This approach focuses on the study of the impact of engine control application failures on the most critical part of a vehicle: its engine.

The main contribution of this research is to (i) specify a set of dependability measures for comparing the dependability of fuel-based engine control systems and (ii) identify all the elements required for developing a benchmark prototype for obtaining those measures. The high scale of integration of today's engine ECUs is, without any doubt, the most important technological barrier to the development of such benchmarks. On the one hand, one must solve the problems regarding the application of the faultload to the engine control applications running inside the ECU. On the other hand, the control outputs and the internal ECU activity must be observed in order to compute the dependability results and validate the benchmarking platform. The prototype section of this chapter has illustrated how to solve, in a portable and nonintrusive manner, all these problems. The idea is to use the observability (tracing features) and controllability (on-the-fly memory access) features provided by modern automotive ECUs. In these units, these features are typically used for debugging and calibration purposes. Our proposal is to exploit them for running the faultload and tracing the engine ECU activity without inducing either temporal or spatial intrusion in the target system.

The feasibility of the approach has been illustrated through a real-life benchmark prototype, which requires the target system to provide a Class 3 Nexus debugging standard port. This standard has been chosen since it is, to the best of our knowledge, the only one having a processor-independent specification that guarantees, by definition, a sufficient degree of observation and control without interfering with the target system. These characteristics are essential for coping with the ambitious goals of our benchmark specification.

We are convinced that the technology discussed in this chapter constitutes a step forward to the provision of useful methodologies and tools for comparing the dependability of embedded automotive systems in general, and engine control applications in particular. The technology is currently mature enough to be migrated to industry, where it can enrich the existing engine control software development process. This is one of the directions of our current work. The other direction is more research oriented and focuses on extending our benchmark approach in order to characterize the dependability of more sophisticated (distributed) electronic control components that need to cooperate for managing mechanical elements that are delocalized in a vehicle. This is, for instance, the case of antilock braking control systems.

REFERENCES

[Donohoe et al. 1990] P. Donohoe, R. Shapiro, and N. Weiderman, "Hartstone Benchmark Results and Analysis," Carnegie Mellon Software Engineering Institute, Technical Report CMU/SEI-90-TR-007, 1990.

[EEC Directive 90/C81/01 1999] EEC-Directive:90/C81/01, Emission Test Cycles for the Certification of Light-Duty Vehicles in Europe, http://www.dieselnet.com/standards/cycles/ece_eudc.html, 1999.

[EEMC 2003] EEMC, "AutoMark Benchmark," EEMC (EDN Embedded Microprocessor Benchmark Consortium), available at http://www.eembc.hotdesk.com/.

[Fuchs et al. 1998] M. Fuchs, M. Eckrich, O. Müller, J. Philipps, and P. Scholz, "Advanced Design and Validation Techniques for Electronic Control Units," in *Proceedings of the International Congress of the Society of Automotive Engineers,* Technical Paper Series no. 980199, Detroit, MI, 1998.

[Gil et al. 2002] P. Gil, J. Arlat, H. Madeira, Y. Crouzet, T. Jaboui, K. Kanoun, T. Marteau, J. Durães, M. Vieira, D. Gil, J.-C. Baraza, and J. García, "Fault Repreentativeness," DBench Project, IST 2000-25425, Deliverable ETIE2, Available at http://www.laas.fr/DBench/Deliverables, 2002.

[Gracia et al. 2002] J. Gracia, D. Gil, L. Lemus, and P. Gil, "Studying Hardware Fault Representativeness with VHDL Models," in *Proceedings of the XVII International Conference on Design of Circuits and Integrated Systems (DCIS),* Santander, Spain, pp. 33–39, 2002.

[Heywood 1988] J. Heywood, *Internal Combustion Engine Fundamentals*, New York, McGraw-Hill, 1988.

[IEEE-ISTO 5001 1999] Nexus5001-Forum™, "IEEE-ISTO 5001™-1999, The Nexus 5001 Forum™ Standard for a Global Embedded Processor Debug Interface," available at http://www.nexus5001.org/standard/ieee_isto_5001_1999.pdf.

[Labrosse 2002] J. J. Labrosse, *MicroC OS II: The Real-Time Kernel*, CMP Books, CPM Media LLC, Lawrence, Kansas, 2002.

[Leaphart et al. 2006] E. G. Leaphart, S. E. Muldoon, and J. Irlbeck, "Application of Robust Engineering Methods to Improve ECU Software Testing," in *Proceedings of the International Congress of the Society of Automotive Engineers*, SAE Technical Paper Series, Paper no. 2006-01-1600, Detroit, MI, 2006.

[Leen and Heffernan 2002] G. Leen and D. Heffernan, "Expanding Automotive Electronic Systems," *Computer*, vol. 35, no. 1, pp. 88–93, 2002.

[Leveson 2000] N. G. Leveson, "System Safety in Computer-Controlled Automotive Systems," in *Proceedings of the International Congress of the Society of Automotive Engineers*, SP-1507, Paper no. 2000-01-1048, Detroit, MI, 2000.

[Miller et al. 1998] G. Miller, K. Hall, W. Willis, and W. Pless, "The Evolution of Powertrain Microcontrollers and its Impact on Development Processes and Tools," Motorola and Hewlett Packard Research Public Report, available at http://www.nexus5001.org, 1998.

[Pulkrabek 1997] W. W. Pulkrabek, *Engineering Fundamentals of the Internal Combustion Engine*, Prentice-Hall, Upper Saddle River, NJ, 1997.

[Ruiz et al. 2004] J.-C. Ruiz, P. Yuste, P. Gil, and L. Lemus, "On Benchmarking the Dependability of Automotive Engine Control Applications," in *Proceedings of the IEEE/IFIP International Conference on Dependable Systems and Networks (DSN)*, pp. 857–866, 2004.

[Spooner and Passino 1997] J. T. Spooner and K. M. Passino, "Fault-Tolerant Control for Automated Highway Systems," *IEEE Transaction on Vehicular Technology*, vol. 46, no. 3, pp. 770–785, 1997.

[Yuste et al. 2003a] P. Yuste, D. Andrés, L. Lemus, J. J. Serrano, and P. Gil, "INERTE: Integrated NExus-Based Real-Time Fault Injection Tool for Embedded Systems," in *Proceedings of the IEEE/IFIP International Conference on Dependable Systems and Networks (DSN)*, Tool Demonstrations Session, pp. 669–670, 2003.

[Yuste et al. 2003b] P. Yuste, L. Lemus, J. J. Serrano, and P. Gil, "A Methodology for Software Implemented Fault Injection Using Nexus," in *Proceedings of the IEEE/IFIP International Conference on Dependable Systems and Networks (DSN)*, Supplemental Volume, Fast Abstracts Session, pp. 14–15, 2003

[Yuste et al. 2003c] P. Yuste, J.-C. Ruiz, L. Lemus, and P. Gil, "Non-Intrusive Software Implemented Fault Injection in Embedded Systems," in *Proceedings of Latin-American Symposium, LADC 2003*, São Paulo, Brazil, 2003.

TOWARD EVALUATING THE DEPENDABILITY OF ANOMALY DETECTORS

Kymie M. C. Tan and Roy A. Maxion

8.1. INTRODUCTION

Over the years, intrusion detection has matured into a field replete with anomaly detectors of various types. These detectors are tasked with detecting computer-based attacks, insider threats, worms and other intrusive vermin. We are prompted to ask whether, apart from the increasing numbers of detectors, there is any evidence of progress in terms of the accuracy and reliability of anomaly detectors. Current evaluation strategies may provide such evidence; however, they suffer from a few problems, the most apparent of which is that they produce results of uncertain reliability. This means that the information provided by these results is not consistent, and it varies across different environments and systems. System defenders seeking to use these anomaly detectors are often left in a quandary because, despite the fact that a particular anomaly detector may have been shown to be effective in a given evaluation environment, the evaluation results typically provide no assurance that the detector will be effective in a defender's particular environment.

In an effort to improve evaluation mechanisms for anomaly-based intrusion detectors, this chapter seeks to identify and discuss the important issues regarding the core components of any evaluation strategy for benchmarking anomaly-based detectors for intrusion-detection systems. The term "core components" refers to such things as training data, test data, the characteristics of the signal, and the method of analyzing the results. Such components should be included in any evaluation of an anomaly detector.

We will step through these core components, describing the role of each of them in the overall assessment, the pertinent issues in each component, how these issues affect the final outcome of the assessment, and, finally, the measures that are required to provide some assurance regarding the effectiveness of the detector when deployed.

Dependability Benchmarking for Computer Systems. Edited by Karama Kanoun and Lisa Spainhower
Copyright © 2008 IEEE Computer Society

The chapter is laid out as follows: first a description of the background and related work; then a description of the issue of ground truth; and, finally, a series of sections each dedicated to a single stage in a typical anomaly-based intrusion-detector assessment process. These sections are:

- The composition of training data and its impacts on detector effectiveness
- The composition of test data and its impacts on detector effectiveness
- Injection issues
- Analyzing the results

The conclusion serves to summarize the lessons learned in the chapter.

8.2. BACKGROUND AND RELATED WORK

It can be argued that anomaly detection is the first step in the intrusion-detection process. Anomalous activities are the very first indicators that "something is wrong" on a system— that an attack or intrusion has occurred, or could still be occurring. Anomalous activity, such as atypical user behavior or complete system failure, serves to bring attention to a potential problem. Once attention has been drawn by the anomalous activity, an intrusion-detection process (or diagnostic process) may then proceed to determine what caused the anomalous activity and, perhaps, whether the anomalous activity can be used as a signature to detect future occurrences of the problem, thereby improving the intrusion-detection process.

Whether anomalous or not, manifestations of attacks that are found to be consistent and specific to the attack may be codified in automated intrusion-detection mechanisms such as signature-based intrusion detection systems like Cisco IDS (formerly NetRanger) [Cisco Systems, Inc., 2007], RealSecure [Internet Security Systems, Inc., 2007], and US-TAT [Ilgun 1993; Ilgun et al., 1995]. In the absence of any prior knowledge about an attack or intrusion, anomaly detection is the first, and probably only, mechanism by which the presence of attacks and intrusions may be detected. As a consequence, anomaly detection continues to occupy an important and central role in intrusion detection.

Anomaly detection is particularly significant in detecting novel or never-before-seen attacks that exploit unanticipated vulnerabilities on computer systems, and abuse-of-privileges-type attacks that do not actually involve exploiting any security vulnerability, for example, insider misuse or masquerading [Debar et al., 1999]. These two problems not only pose a significant threat to information systems, but are also notoriously difficult to detect and prevent. In both cases, the difficulty lies in the absence of any prior knowledge or signature of the attack or intrusion. It is impossible to analyze and extract signatures to facilitate the detection of attacks or behaviors that have never been seen before. For these kinds of security violations, detection via anomalous activity may be the only detection option available. There are currently no security systems that effectively detect and prevent the occurrences of these kinds of security violations.

In the intrusion detection literature, the most common method of evaluating the effectiveness of an anomaly detector can be summarized as follows [Anderson et al., 1993; Forrest et al., 1996; Ghosh et al., 1999, 1998; Jha et al., 2001; Warrender et al., 1999]: sets of *normal data* (obtained in the absence of intrusions or attacks) and *intrusive data* (obtained in the presence of attacks) are collected. The anomaly-based intrusion-detection system is trained on the normal data, referred to as *training data,* and then tested on *test data* that contains either intrusive data exclusively, or some mixture of normal and intrusive data. The success of the detection algorithm is typically measured in terms of hit (true positive), miss (false negative), and false alarm (false positive) rates, and charted on a receiver operating-characteristic (ROC) curve. The ideal result would be 100% hits and 0% misses and false alarms. The goal is to select a point at which the performance of the detector is most suitable to the defender (usually based on the relative cost of miss and false-alarm errors), or to observe performance trends over a range of values, and to compare those trends with trends of other detectors deployed on the same dataset.

In some cases, separate experiments are carried out to chart the false alarm rates by deploying the anomaly-based intrusion-detection system on purely normal data, for which both training and test data consist of different sets of normal behavior only. In this situation there should be, ideally, no false alarms. Since anomaly detectors are typically designed with various parameters (e.g., a window size for a sequence-based detector, or a learning constant for some neural-network-based detectors), this evaluation strategy may be repeated over a set of parameter values.

The evaluation procedure for anomaly-based intrusion-detection systems, summarized above, is based on three unsupported assumptions:

1. That an intrusion or attack will manifest in the data being analyzed by the anomaly-based intrusion detection system
2. That the manifestation is an anomalous event
3. That the anomaly detector is capable of detecting the specific kind of anomalous event that is manifested by an attack

The detected anomalies are related to the attacks by assumption alone. As a consequence, it is impossible to determine, given the described evaluation strategy, whether or not an anomaly detector was actually capable of detecting the real attack. No means are provided to determine the actual causal mechanism(s) of the detected anomalies. It is, therefore, very possible that the detected anomalies were the result of any number of possibly benign, "nonattack" events such as concept drift (nonstationarity) or system nondeterminism. This brings us to the issue of ground truth: if an anomaly is detected, how do we know that the anomaly was caused by a real attack? To answer such a question would require an evaluation dataset in which the causal mechanisms of every event are known (see [Killourhy et al., 2004] for an example of this). The next section examines the strategies and issues involved in obtaining ground-truth data.

8.3. THE ISSUE OF GROUND TRUTH

Ground truth is arguably the most critical issue in any strategy that seeks to evaluate the effectiveness of a detector. This section addresses three important questions regarding ground truth: what it is, why it is so important for evaluating the reliability of an anomaly detector, and why it must be clearly defined.

8.3.1 What is Ground Truth?

"Ground truth" is a term that is well understood in the earth sciences such as geophysics or cartography. It commonly refers to the data obtained from the field (that is, from the ground), to calibrate or verify the correctness of remote-sensing equipment [NASA, 2007a,b]. Ground truth data are obtained by means that are independent of the sensing equipment being evaluated. For example, ground truth for verifying the accuracy of a camera on a remote sensing satellite involves people actually visiting the location on the ground to measure and confirm that the features observed in the satellite image are in fact present on the earth. Ground truth, therefore, provides a statement of undisputed fact regarding each quantum of data in a test dataset. A quantum of data may refer to a collection of pixels in a picture or a single event such as the temperature at the core of the earth.

In the assessment of anomaly detectors, ground-truth data involves attributing a causal mechanism to each event about which an anomaly detector must make a decision. Its importance lies in providing a means by which an assessor is able to determine the detector's accuracy; the assessor must be able to verify that the alarms (particularly those that exceed a predetermined detection threshold) actually correspond to events caused by intrusions.

In establishing ground truth, two points are noteworthy:

1. Ground truth should be established by means that are independent of the system being evaluated.
2. Ground truth must be established in a way that is pertinent to the goal of the task at hand.

Each of these points will be addressed at length in the following two sections.

8.3.1.1. Establishing Ground Truth by Independent Means. Establishing ground truth by independent means is a point of common sense. To verify the accuracy of an instrument or system using ground truth established in nonindependent ways weakens the credibility of the verification results. However, if the independent means by which ground truth is established is in itself weak or incorrect, then the credibility of the verification results can still be weakened.

In a satellite image, for example, if a mountain range were obscured by bad weather and the process of establishing ground truth only required visual confirmation from several miles away, the ground truth established would be that no mountain range exists, because none was visible. This in turn would lead to the erroneous conclusion that the satellite camera is faulty as it reported something that does not exist. Errors in establishing ground truth will lead to erroneous results in the verification process, and this may promulgate erroneous knowledge about the capabilities of the sensing equipment being evaluated.

Similarly, if establishing ground truth only required knowledge that an attack was deployed, without requiring that the audit logs be checked to see if the attack actually showed up in them, an assessor could be led to make an erroneous conclusion. If the attack did not show up in the logs, then a detector may be deemed faulty because it did not detect an attack that was known to have been deployed on the system.

In anomaly-detection assessment, there are three main ways in which ground truth can be independently established:

1. By expert opinion—a system administrator's experience is used to establish the causal mechanisms for each event in the test corpus.
2. By assumption—assuming that a deployed attack manifested in the collected data, or by using the Denning hypothesis [Denning, 1987] to argue that anomalous events are highly correlated to intrusions.

3. By analysis—deploying an attack, tracking its effects, and collecting evidence to show how and where the attack manifests [Tan et al., 2002].

Unfortunately, establishing ground truth independently by each of the listed ways is problematic. Establishing ground truth by experts is prone to problems such as human error, expert disagreement, and, perhaps, even human limitations in comprehending the large amounts of data often logged on a system. Establishing ground truth by analysis, although desirable in that it can provide clear evidentiary links between event and attack, is often very difficult to accomplish. This method is currently an art, not a science, and more often than not has to be performed manually with a toolkit. This makes the method prone to scalability problems. The more complex the attack or the victim program, the more difficult it is to perform such an analysis.

Assumption is currently the dominant mechanism by which ground truth is established in anomaly detection evaluation methods. The assumption is typically made that the detected anomalies are, or are connected to, manifestations of the attacks, and that the deployment of an attack will result in its manifestation in the logged data. These assumptions bring with them very specific problems. The aim of this section is to clarify what these problems are, and to identify the subsequent limits of assessment results using ground truth established in this way.

8.3.1.2. Assumptions and Establishing Ground Truth to Support Evaluation Goals.
The question of what constitutes "good" or effective ground truth is one that bears discussion. Apart from establishing ground truth by independent means, ground truth must also be established in ways that actually support the goal of the evaluation. The following provides an example of the extent to which poorly established ground truth can undermine the goal of an evaluation.

The University of New Mexico (UNM) provided evaluation datasets for anomaly detectors [University of New Mexico, 2002]. These datasets were obtained by deploying exploits and collecting the data that were logged while these exploits were running. In addition, data for normal behavior were also collected for training purposes. Ground truth was established in terms of intrusions, specifically, the data that were collected while exploits were running were marked as "intrusive" data, and normal data were marked "normal."

The goal of the evaluation was to determine how effective the UNM anomaly detector was at detecting intrusions. Two things about the way ground truth was established in this case undermined the potency of the final results: first, it was not determined if the intrusions actually manifested in the data, and, second, there was no information that enabled the assessor to link the detected anomalies to the intrusions that were deployed.

The evaluation method, therefore, relied on the usual assumptions described above: that the detected anomalies are, or are connected to, manifestations of the attacks, and that the deployment of an intrusion will result in its manifestation in the logged data. In short, nothing was provided to show that the intrusions were actually manifested in the logged data. It is possible that some of the intrusions deployed did not appear at all in the logged data. As a consequence, despite claims of the detector's effectiveness, there really was no solid evidence to support those claims. All that can be concluded from the results is that the detector detected anomalies in the data.

Results from an evaluation using this type of ground truth can lead to erroneous conclusions about the capabilities of the detector. It may be concluded that the detector can detect intrusions because it did detect anomalies. However, since the causes of those anomalies were not unequivocally established, it was possible that the detector detected more innocuous events, perhaps due to concept drift or faulty sensors, and not intrusions. After the fact, it is hard to know.

8.4. COMPOSITION OF TRAINING DATA—IMPACTS ON EFFECTIVENESS

Training data is absolutely necessary in any deployment of an anomaly detector. Training data is expected to contain the "normal" behavior of the monitored subject. An anomaly detector extracts its internal model of normal behavior from training data. Such data will, therefore, set the baseline against which outliers can be identified.

In studying the impact of training data on detector effectiveness, it is important to observe that the data contains structure. The term "structure" is used intuitively to convey the idea that the elements within any stream of data may naturally form certain kinds of patterns (e.g., temporal clumps of events or sequential dependencies; a write system call will only occur after an open system call) that can serve to obscure or enhance the presence of an anomaly. It would be prudent to pay careful attention to how such structure will influence detector effectiveness, regardless of whether the data is synthetically constructed or is obtained from a real-world source.

To illustrate how structure in training data can influence the effectiveness of a detector, we describe an experiment that focuses on the effects of structure on two different sequence-based detectors: one that employs conditional probabilities (a Markov-based detector [Jha et al., 2001; Mehdi, 1998; Teng et al., 1990a,b]), and one that depends on the sequential ordering of categorical elements in its data stream (stide [Forrest et al., 1996; Warrender et al., 1999]). We show that a single type of structure in data will affect different detectors in different ways.

The Markov-based detector is not uncommon in the intrusion-detection literature [Jha et al., 2001; Mehdi, 1998; Teng et al., 1990a]. This detector acquires its model of normal behavior by computing the transition probabilities between each fixed-length sequence of size DW (detector window) and the DW + 1st element following that sequence. A transition probability is the probability that the DW + 1st element will follow the previous size–DW sequence. For example, given training data with an alphabet size of 2, the elements A and B, and a detector window of size 2 ($DW = 2$), then the transition probability, P, that the element A immediately follows the size-2 sequence BA can be computed as

$$P(A|BA) = F(BAA)/[F(BAB) + F(BAA)]$$

where $F(BAA)$ is the number of times that (or the frequency with which) the sequence BAA occurs in the training data stream and $F(BAB)$ is the number of times that (or the frequency with which) the sequence BAB occurs in the training data stream.

The stide detector acquires a model of normal behavior by segmenting training data into fixed-length sequences. This is done by sliding a detector window of length DW over the stream of training data. Each length DW sequence obtained from the data stream is stored in a "normal database" of sequences of length DW. A similarity metric is then used to establish the degree of similarity between the test data and the model of normal behavior obtained in the previous step. Sequences of length DW are obtained from the test data using a sliding window, and for each length DW sequence, the similarity metric simply establishes whether that sequence exists or does not exist in the normal database. A length

DW sequence from the test data that is found to exist in the normal database (where "existing" requires that a sequence be found in the normal database that is an identical match for the sequence obtained from the test data) is assigned the number 0. Sequences that do not exist in the normal database are assigned the number 1. The decision is binary; given a sequence from the test data, either there is an exact match in the normal database (0) or there isn't (1).

The Markov-based detector can be shown to be sensitive to structure in data, whereas the stide detector is not. This structure, referred to as data "regularity," can be measured by using conditional entropy [Lee and Xiang, 2001; Maxion and Tan, 2000; Shannon and Weaver, 1949]. To show the influence of regularity (or irregularity) on the effectiveness of the Markov detector, pairs of training and test data that differ *only* in terms of increasing irregularity (measured by conditional entropy) are generated. This means that the alphabet size, alphabet, and sample size are all kept constant, while regularity is calibrated to increase at fixed, steady intervals. Eleven streams of training and test data pairs that comply with these requirements were generated [Maxion and Tan, 2000]. The data generation process was designed to ensure that anomalous sequences or symbols were not introduced into the test-data stream. This is because the introduction of obviously anomalous phenomena into the data stream would confound the results of the experiment; it would be difficult to know whether the detector was responding to fluctuations in data regularity or to the presence of spurious anomalous sequences.

Each of the two detectors used in this experiment was deployed with a sequence length of 2, and a detection threshold set at 1; therefore, a hit was scored when the most anomalous response (i.e., the value 1) was issued by the detector. Figure 8.1 shows the results

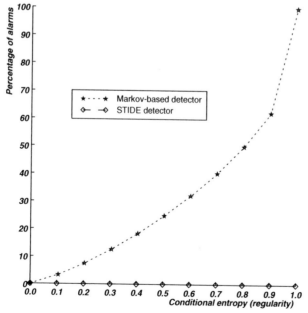

Figure 8.1. Comparison of the alarm rates between the Markov and stide anomaly detectors as irregularity (entropy) changes. Note the increasing alarm rate in the Markov detector, as irregularity increases in the data. Stide's "curve," showing no alarms, lies directly along the x-axis, unaffected by the change in the irregularity of the data.

of the experiments in terms of alarms. The behavior of the Markov detector is juxtaposed with the behavior of the stide detector [D'haeseleer et al., 1996; Forrest et al., 1996; Hofmeyr et al., 1998; Warrender et al., 1999], simply to show that the kind of structure that affects one detector may not necessarily affect another. The results show that in an experiment in which everything was kept constant except for data regularity, the Markov detector responded predictably to the changes in regularity, while stide remained unaffected. In the stream of the most irregular data (that is, random data), the Markov detector recorded close to 100% of anomalous events. Stide, however, was impervious to the regularity changes between the data streams; it produced no alarms, even in completely random data.

The lesson learned from this experiment is that the structure of the data within a training corpus can significantly affect a detector. The following points list some of the reasons why the effects of structure in data should be carefully considered in the final determination of detector efficacy:

- To improve the reliability of the final results, by identifying the kinds of environments that may elicit the type of detector behavior observed in the assessment. It is unreasonable to expect low false-alarm rates for the Markov-based detector when it is deployed in data environments that lie higher on the irregularity scale. In terms of a practical example, it is commonly known that a university environment exhibits less-regular behavior than a heavily regimented military environment in which almost all computer traffic is regulated.
- To understand and identify the phenomena that may obscure a detector's intrusion-detection capabilities. For example, in data environments where irregularity is high, even if the Markov-based detector consistently alarmed on legitimate intrusions, the abundance of alarms caused by the structure within "normal" training data may make it difficult to determine their origin.
- To facilitate a fair comparison of detector effectiveness. If the aim is to compare the intrusion-detection effectiveness of more than one detector, a more accurate reflection of relative effectiveness may be obtained if the playing field were "leveled" by ensuring that detectors that are sensitive to certain structural fluctuations in the training data are not compared directly with detectors that are immune to those same fluctuations.

The question that now arises is this: Does such regularity exist in real-world data? To determine this, we collected natural data from two systems at the University of Melbourne. In the first, system-call data were obtained from a Linux system used in a research environment in the University of Melbourne, using strace, a program that records system calls made by programs other than itself. (System calls are commonly used in studies of behavioral differences among users, programs, hosts, etc.; see [Forrest et al., 1994; Lane and Brodley, 1997a].) Figure 8.2(a) shows the regularities of system calls for 42 users, monitored over a 48-hour period.

In the second system, natural data (BSM audit data) were obtained from an undergraduate student computer running the Solaris operating system in the same university. System-call events were extracted for each user session in the 24-hour monitoring period. The regularities of the 58 user sessions active on one day are illustrated in Figure 8.2(b). The regularities in both cases do fluctuate, indicating that data from different environments do exhibit different degrees of structure (regularities).

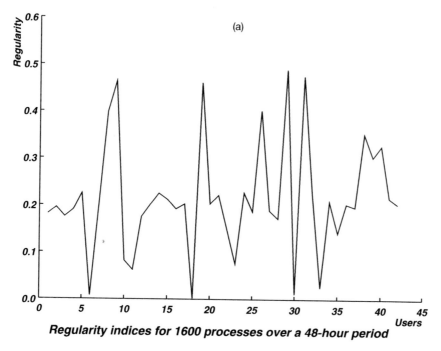

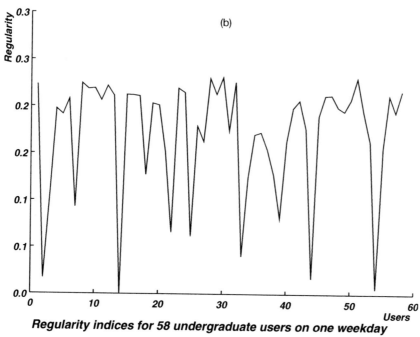

Figure 8.2. Regularities in real-world data for two different machines: (a) TAIFUN: a machine used by researchers. (b) LISTER: a machine used by undergraduate students.

8.5. COMPOSITION OF TEST DATA—IMPACTS ON EFFECTIVENESS

Test data can be described as the data that an anomaly detector responds to. Presented with test data, the anomaly detector produces an indication of how much each element under consideration deviates from the detector's internal model of normal behavior. Test data may contain intrusive data only, some mixture of normal and intrusive data, or normal data only. A stream of test data containing only normal data is often used by assessors to determine the baseline for false-alarm rates.

Test data can be seen as composed of background data and a signal. The signal refers to the event of interest that the detector is designed to detect, and the background data is the substrate in which the signal is embedded. The next two sections will address each of these components in detail.

8.5.1. Background Data

Background data can be viewed as the substrate into which the signal is embedded. Alarms on elements comprising the signal are hits, and alarms on elements comprising the background data are false alarms. Like training data, background data is essentially the "normal" behavior of the monitored subject and, like training data, background data also contains structure.

If a detector is sensitive to a particular kind of structure in the data (e.g., the Markov-based detector is sensitive to regularity), differences in structure between training data and background test data may produce false alarms. To illustrate this point, the following experiment was conducted. Using only the training data from the 11 pairs of training and test data used in the previous section, we observed the Markov-based detector's response to differences in structure between training and test data. The second most regular training data was used as training data (the choice of the second was arbitrary) and the rest of the training data were used as test data. The test data, therefore, had no embedded anomalies.

Figure 8.3 shows the effect of differences in regularity between training and test data. The alarms generated by the Markov-based detector were not caused by the presence of distinct anomalies in the test data, but only by the differences in structure between training and test data. It would, therefore, be prudent to pay careful attention to differences in such structure between training and background test data in any evaluation of detector effectiveness, regardless of whether the data is synthetically constructed or is obtained from a real-world source. The following lists some reasons arguing in favor of such prudence:

1. When real-world data is used, the resulting alarms may be caused by structural differences in training and test data, and not necessarily by the presence of attacks or intrusions. These structural differences may be the result of differing system environments, differing time cycles, differing program versions, and so forth.

2. Only detectors sensitive to the kind of structural differences present in the data will be affected. In the case above, if stide were to undergo the same experiments there would be no alarms registered, simply because stide is immune to regularity-based structural changes in the data.

3. When evaluating a detector's ability to detect a specific phenomenon, e.g., a partic-

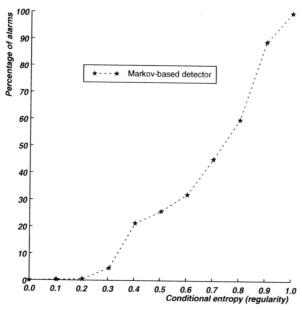

<u>Figure 8.3.</u> The alarm rates for the Markov-based detector trained on the second most regular training data and tested on the other training data of different regularities. Note that differences in structure (regularity) between test and training data produces alarms. No anomalies were embedded in the data.

ular kind of anomaly embedded in the test data, the structural differences between training and test data may obscure the detector's true capabilities by raising numerous false alarms. In such cases, care must be taken to construct training and test data with similar structural characteristics.

8.5.1.1. Signal Characteristics. The signal is the event or phenomenon the detector is designed to detect. The signals for signature-based intrusion-detection systems are the manifestations of attacks that align with the set of rules used to detect those attacks. The signals for anomaly-based intrusion-detection systems are outliers or anomalies.

One of most troubling aspects of applying anomaly detectors to intrusion detection is the fundamental assumption that anomalies are highly correlated to attacks or intrusions [Denning, 1987]. This is troubling because it is not at all clear that attacks always manifest as anomalies. In fact, mimicry attacks are examples of attacks whose manifestations are not anomalous [Wagner and Sotto, 2002]. However, allowing for the existence of such a class of attacks, for those attacks that do manifest as anomalies, what kinds of anomalies would these be? What are the characteristics of these anomalies, and would they be visible to *any* anomaly detector? These questions are often left unanswered by current evaluation strategies. These evaluation strategies often make the implicit assumption that the anomaly detector assessed is actually capable of detecting the specific kind of anomalous event that is the manifestation of the attack. Since the characteristics of the signal—the anomalous events—are very rarely identified and clearly defined in current strategies, it is extremely difficult to know what kind of anomalous event was effectively detected, how effectively, and under what circumstances.

The question, "What is an anomaly?" lies at the heart of the assessment strategy for anomaly detectors. It is important to clearly define the anomaly, because different detectors will see different phenomena as anomalies, depending upon their detection algorithm; for example, a probabilistic detector is able to detect anomalies in the form of rare sequences, but a sequence-based detector like stide [Forrest et al., 1994] is not. This is because stide has no notion of the frequency of events. Since Denning's seminal work, a wide range of anomaly detectors, based on a variety of anomaly-detection algorithms, has appeared in the intrusion detection literature. Some examples are neural networks [Debar et al., 1992; Fox et al., 1990; Ryan et al., 1997], hidden Markov models [Warrender et al., 1999], genetic algorithms [Mé, 1998], frequency-based algorithms [Javitz and Valdes, 1991], and algorithms that exploit differences in fixed-length categorical sequences [Forrest et al., 1996; Lane and Brodley, 1997b]. Each of these anomaly-detection algorithms has its own way of modeling normal behavior. Since an anomaly can only be defined with respect to an anomaly detector's own model of normal behavior, it follows that, at worst, there could exist an equally wide variety of definitions for the anomaly as there are anomaly-detection algorithms.

Another point to note is that the way in which an anomaly detector defines anomalies may not necessarily coincide with the way in which anomalies naturally occur in data. There are two factors that will influence the behavior of an anomaly detector: (1) how the anomaly detector itself perceives anomalies, and (2) how anomalous manifestations of attacks naturally exist in the data. If attacks manifest as anomalies that are invisible to the detector, then the detector will be ineffective at detecting those attacks. This argues in favor of clearly defining the kinds of anomalies that an anomaly detector is expected to detect. When a detector's capabilities are evaluated with respect to detecting those anomalies, we are able to determine, specifically, if there are anomalous events that the anomaly detector is incapable of detecting, and the conditions under which such blindness will manifest.

We will now present a case that underscores the importance of clearly characterizing the anomaly. This example illustrates the consequences to the evaluation results when the anomaly is not clearly defined. After assessing the capabilities of the stide anomaly detector, using the typical evaluation strategy (outlined in Section 8.2), it was observed that ". . . some unusual short sequences of system calls will be executed when a security hole in a program is exploited. If a program enters an unusual error state during an attempted break-in and if this error condition executes a sequence of system calls that is not already covered by our normal database, we are likely to notice the attack" [Forrest et al., 1994]. An unusual sequence of system calls, that is, a sequence that is "not already covered by our normal database," is what, in this chapter, we refer to as a foreign sequence.

It was perhaps erroneously concluded that the detector was fully capable of detecting foreign sequences. Although it is true that the detection algorithm is able to detect foreign sequences, it is also true that stide can sometimes be blind to such sequences. In short, stide cannot be relied upon to consistently detect foreign sequences despite what has been written in [Forrest et al., 1994].

This blindness was discovered only when anomalies such as "foreign sequences" were carefully characterized and defined. By doing so, it was found that [Tan and Maxion, 2002]:

1. Stide's detection capabilities were consistent toward certain types of foreign sequences, and variable toward others, depending on the values of the detector's window parameter.

2. There are foreign sequences that the anomaly detector is incapable of detecting (termed blindness).

3. The blindness manifests only when the detector window is *less than* the size of a particular kind of foreign-sequence anomaly.

Summarizing, the results of an evaluation that did not identify and characterize the anomaly (a foreign sequence) led to the erroneous conclusion that the detector will consistently detect all foreign sequences. The results of an evaluation that did identify and characterize the anomaly showed that the detector cannot be depended upon to consistently detect foreign sequences. Furthermore, these results were able to identify the kinds of foreign sequences to which the detector was blind, and the circumstances under which this blindness can occur.

8.6. INJECTION ISSUES

In constructing the test data for evaluating anomaly detectors, a fault-injection methodology may be used to embed the signal into the background data. Particular care is required when formulating the injection method, as a poorly considered injection methodology may introduce unintended artifacts that will undermine the accuracy of the final results.

The characteristics of the detector being evaluated will tend to influence the injection procedure. Some detectors, e.g., those that only process the frequencies of single elements, are more affected by the number of signal elements injected and less affected by the particular placement of those signal elements. In such a case, only signal quantity is an issue. It may, therefore, be sufficient to employ a simple process that only keeps track of the quantity of the signals (number of events) injected into the data stream. In this situation, such an injection process will not be required to employ complex positioning algorithms to locate suitable injection sites in the data stream.

On the other hand, detectors that process sequences of elements tend to be significantly affected by both the placement and the quantity of the signal. Under these circumstances, a more complex injection methodology would be required, taking into account the quantity and the placement of the signal to be embedded. As an example, consider the injection of an anomalous sequence into background data for an evaluation of a sequence-based detector, described below.

An anomalous sequence is to be embedded in a stream of background data. The sequence-based detector in question uses a fixed-size window that slides across the data stream, one adjacent element at a time. The first point to note is that the detector window will be "viewing" slices of the injected anomalous sequence as it slides across the anomaly. At each point of this "slide" across the anomaly, the detector will be comparing the sequence it sees in the test data with the model of normal behavior it obtained from the training data. This means that the presence of the anomalous sequence, as well as the sequences *within* the anomalous sequence, will affect the response of the detector. This is because the elements within the anomalous sequence will interact with adjacent elements in the background data when the sliding detector window straddles both anomaly and background data. If the interaction between the internal elements of the anomaly and the adjacent elements of the background data are not carefully controlled, the final results of the evaluation will contain the detector's response to the spurious, unintended interaction of such a mix. The true detection capability of the detector may be obscured, because the detector is not responding solely to the anomalous sequence, but also to the artifacts of a poorly controlled injection process. Depending upon the nature of these spurious "artifact sequences" the results could:

1. Report misleadingly high false-alarm rates (e.g., the detector's false-alarm rate is artificially elevated due to the presence of these artifactual sequences).

2. Report inaccurate hit rates (e.g., the detector may in fact be unable to detect an anomalous sequence, but may *appear* to do so because the presence of an artifactual sequence erroneously causes alarms. These alarms are incorrect because the detector is not responding to the anomalous sequence but, rather, to where the sequence happened to be placed in the data stream).

An example of how injection artifacts could lead to incorrect results is described using the Lane and Brodley detector. The Lane and Brodley (L&B) detector [Lane and Brodley, 1997b, 1998, 1999] is completely dependent on the sequential ordering of elements in the data stream. Given two fixed-length sequences of the same size, each element in one sequence and its counterpart in the same position in the other sequence is compared. Elements that do not match are given the value 0, and matching elements are given a score that incorporates a weight value. This weight value increases as more and more adjacent elements are found to match. The similarity metric produces a value between 0 and $DW(DW + 1)/2$, where 0 denotes the greatest degree of dissimilarity (anomaly) between the two sequences, and $DW(DW + 1)/2$ denotes the greatest degree of similarity (identical sequences). No probabilistic concepts, such as the calculation of frequencies or conditional probabilities, are used by this detector.

The L&B detector was evaluated on how well it detects foreign sequences. Two experiments were conducted. In the first, foreign sequences were carefully embedded in background data such that the "artifact sequences" (i.e., the sequences at the boundaries of the injected anomaly where some of the anomaly and some of the background data were processed by the detector) were not themselves foreign sequences. In the second experiment, foreign sequences were randomly embedded in the background data. The size of the detector window parameter and the size of the anomalous sequences were varied between 2 and 16, and 2 and 12, respectively (the limits 16 and 12 were arbitrary choices).

Figure 8.4(b) presents the results of the experiment that used a controlled injection process, and Figure 8.4(a) displays the results of the experiment that used an uncontrolled injection process. The x-axis marks the increasing length of the foreign sequence injected into the test-data stream, and the y-axis charts the length of the detector window required to detect a foreign sequence of a given length. Each star marks the length of the detector window required to detect a foreign sequence whose corresponding length is marked on the x-axis, where the term "detect" specifically means that a maximum anomalous response was registered. The areas without a star indicate that the foreign sequence whose corresponding length is marked on the x-axis was perceived as a completely normal sequence by the detector.

The most obvious aspect of the results for the controlled injection experiments is the inability of the L&B detector to detect the foreign sequence anomaly, even when the entire foreign sequence can be "seen" by the detector, i.e., when the detector window is equal to or larger than the size of the anomalous sequence. This blindness in the L&B detector can be attributed to the similarity metric that the detector employs. The similarity metric for the L&B detector is biased in favor of matching adjacent elements. It is possible for a foreign sequence to match every element of a normal sequence, except one. If the single, mismatching element is located at the very first or very last position of the for-

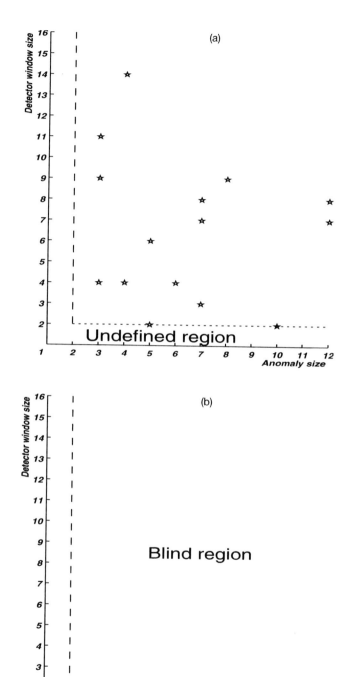

Figure 8.4. Detection-coverage maps for: (a) uncontrolled versus (b) controlled injections; both using the Lane & Brodley detector.

eign sequence, the detector returns a similarity value indicating that the foreign sequence is close to normal (a more detailed explanation of methodology behind this experiment can be found in [Tan and Maxion, 2005]).

Note, however, that if the injection process were not carefully controlled, and the anomalous events were randomly embedded in the background data, the blindness exhibited by the detector in the controlled experiments would have been masked. The spurious artifact sequences would have caused the detector to alarm [the stars in Figure 8.4(a) mark the detector's alarms], and the detector would appear to be "detecting" the injected anomalous foreign sequence, albeit sporadically. The conclusion that the detector is sometimes able to detect foreign sequences would be an erroneous one, and serves as an example underscoring the importance of carefully controlling injection artifacts in any detector-evaluation strategy.

8.7. ANALYZING THE RESULTS

The assessment results for anomaly-based intrusion detectors are usually reported in terms of hit, miss, false-alarm, and correct-rejection rates. These rates are typically presented on a receiver operating-characteristic (ROC) curve [Egan, 1975], and used to indicate the proportion of intrusive instances successfully or unsuccessfully detected by a given anomaly-based intrusion-detection system. It is important to understand precisely what information is being conveyed by the hit, miss, and false-alarm rates reported on an ROC curve.

Hit, miss, false-alarm, and correct-rejection rates are supposed to indicate the detector's ability to detect intrusions. Unlike signature-based systems, however (in which alarms are more directly related to the detection of the attack or aspects of the attack), an alarm in an anomaly-based system simply means that an anomaly was detected. It is often very misleading to report that an anomaly-based detector was successful at detecting attacks with an X% hit rate and a Y% false-alarm rate because it suggests that the detector directly and, by implication, consistently detected those attacks. This is not necessarily true. The only information conveyed by the results is that the detector detected a set of anomalies, some or none of which may have been the manifestation of an attack. It is also important to bear in mind that the characteristics of the detection algorithm must still be considered when analyzing the results of an assessment. If not, erroneous conclusions may be drawn from evaluation results. The following is an example of such a case.

It was noted in a study of stide that anomalous sequences appeared to "clump" in temporally local regions [Hofmeyr et al., 1998; Warrender et al., 1999]. From this observation, it was concluded that a characteristic of the intrusions present in the evaluation dataset for stide was a clumping of anomalies in temporally local regions. Furthermore, it was assumed from the observation of these clusters that the greater the number of anomalies in the test data, the more likely that the data are the result of an intrusion against the corresponding privileged program. It can be shown, however, that these "clusters" were not characteristics of intrusions at all; rather, they were artifacts of the detector itself. In other words, the clusters were due to the detector, and not the intrusion.

Stide uses a window as part of its detection mechanism, and it "slides" this window over the stream of data in which it is trying to detect anomalies. A window sliding over an anomaly amplifies the presence of that anomaly by producing an alarm at every instance at which the anomaly lies entirely within the sliding window. For example, take a foreign sequence of size 2. If the detector window is set to 2, a single mismatch (anomaly) is reported. When the detector window is set to 3, sliding the detector window over the size-2 foreign sequence will result in two mismatches (the first mismatch occurs when the size-2 foreign sequence takes up the first two places of the size-3 detector window, and the second mismatch will occur when the size-2 foreign sequence takes up the last two places in the size-3 detector window). Setting the detector window to 5 will result in 4 mismatches, and so on. Figure 8.5 illustrates the effect of increasing detector-window sizes on the mismatch (anomaly) count.

It can be seen from Figure 8.5 that "clumps" of temporally local mismatches become more prominent at larger window sizes. These clumps of anomalies can be misleading, as they suggest the presence of more anomalies than are actually there. In this case, there is only one, small anomalous sequence of size 2. Its presence, however, has been artificially amplified by the detector's sliding window, producing what appear to be clumps of "anomalies." This phenomenon may have led to the original, erroneous conclusion that anomalies clump, and that such clumping is a natural characteristic of the intrusion when, in fact, it is not.

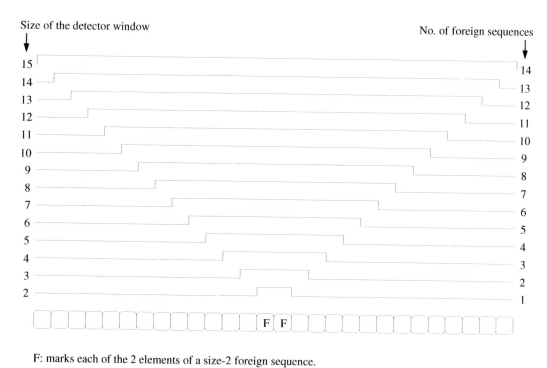

F: marks each of the 2 elements of a size-2 foreign sequence.

⌐_⌐ marks the sequences of size DW that are mismatches.

Figure 8.5. The effect of increasing the size of a detector window as it slides over a single minimal foreign sequence of size 2. The widening notch in the center depicts the number of mismatches (anomalies) detected as a detector window of a given size slides incrementally over a size-2 foreign sequence.

8.8. CONCLUSION

In this chapter, we focused on the problem of benchmarking the dependability of anomaly-based intrusion detection systems. We have observed from the intrusion-detection literature that the results from current assessment methodologies fluctuate significantly and unpredictability from dataset to dataset, suffering from issues of:

- Reliability—the knowledge gained from the evaluation results does not extend beyond the evaluation dataset to different data environments or systems.
- Accuracy—the results and conclusions do not necessarily reflect the native abilities of the evaluated detectors.

Statements such as, "It is not known what effect different training sets would have on the results presented in this paper" [Ghosh et al., 1998], only serve to erode confidence in deploying such detectors, despite the need for their services.

In order to understand the various factors that contribute to the lack of reliability and accuracy in anomaly detectors, we stepped through each stage of a typical evaluation for anomaly detectors to identify and discuss the pertinent issues that influence assessment results. We provided examples of the consequences that arise from ignoring some of these factors, and we showed that details such as the structure inherent in training and test data the composition of the signal (anomaly), and the injection methodology used to embed the signal into the test data, all contributed in varying degrees to the reliability and scope of the final evaluation results. We also examined the nature of ground truth, and showed that an evaluation dataset for which ground truth is simply the identification of data that were collected while intrusions were occurring on a system cannot effectively determine the efficacy of anomaly-based intrusion-detection systems.

We conclude this chapter by summarizing the issues that need to be addressed in the move toward attaining reliable and accurate assessment results for anomaly-based intrusion detectors:

- Training data (see Section 8.4):

  The intrinsic structure found in training data will influence detector effectiveness, and because different detectors respond to the same types of structure differently, the influence of that structure on detector effectiveness must be accounted for to obtain a true understanding of detector capability.

- Test data (see Section 8.5):

  The intrinsic structure found in test data will also influence detector effectiveness, and as in the case above (structure in training data), this influence must also be accounted for to obtain a true understanding of detector capability. The effect of structure on detector capability is particularly significant when structural differences exist between test and training data.

  When generating synthetic test data, it is necessary to carefully control the signal-injection process to avoid introducing unintended artifacts into the evaluation dataset. These unintended artifacts only serve to confound the final evaluation results by introducing anomalies that are not native to the data environment or that have anything to do with the intrusion signal.

- To avoid ambiguity regarding precisely what a detector can and cannot detect, it is necessary to understand the detection technology being evaluated, and to clearly characterize and define the signal being detected. In the case of anomaly detectors, since they do not directly detect attacks, obtaining hit, miss, and false-alarm rates based on anomalous alarms would be meaningless without a clear causal link between anomaly and attack manifestation.

- If real-world intrusion data is used, ensure that:

  The intrusions deployed actually manifest in the data being analyzed by the anomaly detector.

  The manifestation of the intrusion is an anomalous event (if the intrusion manifests as a normal event, then it would be questionable to conclude that the anomaly detector was ineffective if it failed to detect it).

  The anomaly detector is capable of detecting that specific kind of anomalous event.

ACKNOWLEDGMENTS

This work was supported by the National Science Foundation under grant number CNS-0430474. The views and conclusions contained in this document are those of the authors, and should not be interpreted as representing the official policies, either expressed or implied, of any sponsoring institution, of the U.S. government, or of any other entity.

REFERENCES

[Anderson et al., 1993] Anderson, D., Lunt, T., Javitz, H., Tamaru, A., and Valdes, A. "Safeguard Final Report: Detecting Unusual Program Behavior Using the NIDES Statistical Component." Technical Report SRI-CSL-95-06, Computer Science Laboratory, SRI International, Menlo Park, CA, 1993.

[Cisco Systems, Inc., 2007] Cisco Systems, Inc. NetRanger. Internet: http://www.cisco.com/en/US/products/ps6009/index.html, May 2007.

[Debar et al., 1992] Debar, H., Becker, M., and Siboni, D. "A Neural Network Component for an Intrusion Detection System," in *IEEE Computer Society Symposium on Research in Security and Privacy,* Oakland, CA, pp. 240–250, IEEE Computer Society Press, Los Alamitos, CA, 1992.

[Debar et al., 1999] Debar, H., Dacier, M., and Wespi, A. "Towards a Taxonomy of Intrusion-Detection Systems." *Computer Networks,* Vol. 31, no. 8, pp. 805–822, April 1999.

[Denning, 1987] Denning, D. "An Intrusion-Detection Model." *IEEE Transactions on Software Engineering,* vol. SE-13, no. 2, pp. 222–232, February 1987.

[D'haeseleer et al., 1996] D'haeseleer, P., Forrest, S., and Helman, P. "An Immunological Approach to Change Detection: Algorithms, Analysis and Implications," in *IEEE Symposium on Security and Privacy,* Oakland, CA, pp. 110–119, IEEE Computer Society Press, Los Alamitos, CA, 1996.

[Egan, 1975] Egan, J. P. *Signal Detection Theory and ROC-Analysis.* Academic Press, New York, 1975.

[Forrest et al., 1996] Forrest, S., Hofmeyr, S. A., Somayaji, A., and Longstaff, T. A. "A Sense of Self for Unix Processes," in *IEEE Symposium on Security and Privacy,* Oakland, CA, pp. 120–128, IEEE Computer Society Press, Los Alamitos, CA, 1996.

[Forrest et al., 1994] Forrest, S., Perelson, A. S., Allen, L., and Cherukuri, R. "Self-nonself Discrimination in a Computer," in *IEEE Computer Society Symposium on Research in Security and Privacy,* Oakland, CA, pp. 202–212, IEEE Computer Society Press, Los Alamitos, CA, 1994.

[Fox et al., 1990] Fox, K. L., Henning, R. R., Reed, J. H., and Simonian, R. "A Neural Network Approach Towards Intrusion Detection," in *Proceedings of the 13th National Computer Security Conference,* Washington, DC, National Institute of Standards and Technology, Gaithersburg, MD, pp. 125–134, October 1990.

[Ghosh et al., 1999] Ghosh, A. K., Schwartzbard, A., and Schatz, M. "Learning Program Behavior Profiles for Intrusion Detection," in *Proceedings of the 1st USENIX Workshop on Intrusion Detection and Network Monitoring,* Santa Clara, CA, USENIX Association, Berkeley, CA, pp. 51–62, 1999.

[Ghosh et al., 1998] Ghosh, A. K., Wanken, J., and Charron, F. "Detecting Anomalous and Unknown Intrusions Against Programs," in *Proceedings of the 14th Annual Computer Security Applications Conference,* Phoenix, IEEE Computer Society Press, Los Alamitos, CA, pp. 259–267, 1998.

[Hofmeyr et al., 1998] Hofmeyr, S. A., Forrest, S., and Somayaji, A. "Intrusion Detection Using Sequences of System Calls," *Journal of Computer Security,* vol. 6, no. 3, pp. 151–180, 1998.

[Ilgun, 1993] Ilgun, K. "USTAT: A Real-Time Intrusion Detection System for Unix," in *IEEE Computer Society Symposium on Research in Security and Privacy,* Oakland, CA, IEEE Computer Society Press, Los Alamitos, CA, pp. 16–28, 1993.

[Ilgun et al., 1995] Ilgun, K., Kemmerer, R. A., and Porras, P. A. "State Transition Analysis: A Rule-Based Intrusion Detection Approach," in *IEEE Transactions on Software Engineering,* vol. 21, no. 3, pp. 181–199, March 1995.

[Internet Security Systems, Inc., 2007] Internet Security Systems, Inc. RealSecure. Internet: www.iss.net./products/RealSecure_ServerSensor/product_main_page.html, Nov. 2007.

[Javitz and Valdes, 1991] Javitz, H. and Valdes, A. "The SRI IDES Statistical Anomaly Detector," in *IEEE Computer Society Symposium on Research in Security and Privacy,* Oakland, CA. IEEE Computer Society Press, Los Alamitos, CA, pp. 316–326, 1991

[Jha et al., 2001] Jha, S., Tan, K. M. C., and Maxion, R. A. "Markov Chains, Classifiers, and Intrusion Detection," in *Proceedings of the 14th IEEE Computer Security Foundations Workshop,* Cape Breton, Nova Scotia, Canada. IEEE Computer Society Press, Los Alamitos, CA, pp. 206–219, 2001.

[Killourhy et al., 2004] Killourhy, K. S., Maxion, R. A., and Tan, K. M. C. "A Defense-Centric Taxonomy Based on Attack Manifestations," in *International Conference on Dependable Systems and Networks (DSN-04),* Florence, Italy. IEEE Computer Society Press, Los Alamitos, CA, pp. 102–111, 2004.

[Lane and Brodley, 1997a] Lane, T. and Brodley, C. E. "An Application of Machine Learning to Anomaly Detection," in *Proceedings of the 20th Annual National Information Systems Security Conference,* Vol. 1, Baltimore, MD, National Institute of Standards and Technology, Gaithersburg, MD, pp. 366–380, 1997.

[Lane and Brodley, 1997b] Lane, T. and Brodley, C. E. "Sequence Matching and Learning in Anomaly Detection for Computer Security," in *Proceedings of AAAI-97 Workshop: AI Approaches to Fraud Detection and Risk Management,* Providence, RI, AAAI Press, Menlo Park, CA, pp. 43–49, 1997.

[Lane and Brodley, 1998] Lane, T. and Brodley, C. E. "Approaches to Online Learning and Concept Drift for User Identification in Computer Security," in *Proceedings of the Fourth International Conference on Knowledge Discovery and Data Mining,* New York, AAAI Press, Menlo Park, CA, pp. 259–263, 1998.

[Lane and Brodley, 1999] Lane, T. and Brodley, C. E. "Temporal Sequence Learning and Data Reduction for Anomaly Detection," *ACM Transactions on Information and System Security,* vol. 2, no. 3, pp. 295–331, August 1999.

[Lee and Xiang, 2001] Lee, W. and Xiang, D. "Information-Theoretic Measures for Anomaly Detection," in *IEEE Symposium on Security and Privacy,* Oakland, CA. IEEE Computer Society Press, Los Alamitos, CA, pp. 130–143, 2001.

[Maxion and Tan, 2000] Maxion, R. A. and Tan, K. M. C. "Benchmarking Anomaly-Based Detection Systems," in *International Conference on Dependable Systems and Networks,* New York, IEEE Computer Society Press, Los Alamitos, CA, pp. 623–630, 2000.

[Mé, 1998] Mé, L. "GASSATA, A Genetic Algorithm as an Alternative Tool for Security Audit Trails Analysis," in *First International Workshop on the Recent Advances in Intrusion Detection (RAID-98),* Louvain-la-Neuve, Belgium, September 1998.

[Mehdi, 1998] Mehdi, N. "Anomaly Detection for Markov Models," Technical Report RZ 3011 (#93057), IBM Research Division, Zurich Research Laboratory, Switzerland, March 1998.

[NASA, 2007a] NASA. JPL Physical Oceanography Distributed Active Archive Center. Internet: http://podaac.jpl.nasa.gov/WEB_INFO/glossary.html, November 2007.

[NASA, 2007b] NASA. Students' Cloud Observations On-Line. Internet: http://asd-www.larc.nasa.gov/SCOOL/groundtruth.html, November 2007.

[Ryan et al., 1997] Ryan, J., Lin, M.-J., and Miikkulainen, R. "Intrusion Detection with Neural Networks," in *Proceedings of the AAAI-97 Workshop on AI Approaches to Fraud Detection and Risk Management,* Providence, RI. AAAI Press, Menlo Park, CA, pp. 72–77, 1997.

[Shannon and Weaver, 1949] Shannon, C. E. and Weaver, W. *The Mathematical Theory of Communication.* University of Illinois Press, Champaign, IL, 1949.

[Tan et al., 2002] Tan, K. M. C., Killourhy, K. S., and Maxion, R. A. "Undermining an Anomaly-Based Intrusion Detection System Using Common Exploits," in *Fifth International Symposium on Recent Advances in Intrusion Detection (RAID-2002),* Zurich, Switzerland. Lecture Notes in Computer Science (LNCS) No. 2516, Andreas Wespi, Giovanni Vigna and Luca Deri (Eds.), Springer-Verlag, Berlin, pp. 54–73, 2002.

[Tan and Maxion, 2002] Tan, K. M. C. and Maxion, R. A. "Why 6? Defining the Operational Limits of Stide, an Anomaly-Based Intrusion Detector," in *IEEE Symposium on Security and Privacy,* Oakland, CA, IEEE Computer Society Press, Los Alamitos, CA, pp. 188–201, 2002.

[Tan and Maxion, 2005] Tan, K. M. C. and Maxion, R. A. "The Effects of Algorithmic Diversity on Anomaly Detector Performance," in *Proceedings of the International Conference on Dependable Systems and Networks (DSN-05),* Yokohama, Japan, IEEE Computer Society Press, Los Alamitos, CA, pp. 216–225, 2005.

[Teng et al., 1990a] Teng, H. S., Chen, K., and Lu, S. C.-Y. "Adaptive Real-Time Anomaly Detection Using Inductively Generated Sequential Patterns," in *IEEE Computer Society Symposium on Research in Security and Privacy,* Oakland, CA, IEEE Computer Society Press, Los Alamitos, CA, pp. 278–284, 1990.

[Teng et al., 1990b] Teng, H. S., Chen, K., and Lu, S. C.-Y. "Security Audit Trail Analysis Using Inductively Generated Predictive Rules," in *Proceedings of the Sixth Conference on Artificial Intelligence Applications,* Vol. 1, Santa Barbara, CA, IEEE Press, Piscataway, NJ, pp. 24–29, 1990.

[University of New Mexico, 2002] University of New Mexico Computer Immune Systems, Data Sets and Software: Sequence-Based Intrusion Detection. Internet: http://www.cs.unm.edu/immsec/ systemcalls.htm, November 2007.

[Wagner and Soto, 2002] Wagner, D. and Soto, P. "Mimicry Attacks on Host-Based Intrusion Detection Systems," in *Proceedings of the 9th ACM Conference on Computer and Communications Security,* Washington, DC, ACM Press, New York, pp. 255–264, 2002.

[Warrender et al., 1999] Warrender, C., Forrest, S., and Pearlmutter, B. "Detecting Intrusions Using System Calls: Alternative Data Models," in *IEEE Symposium on Security and Privacy,* Oakland, CA, IEEE Computer Society Press, Los Alamitos, CA, pp. 133–145, 1999.

9

VAJRA: EVALUATING BYZANTINE-FAULT-TOLERANT DISTRIBUTED SYSTEMS

Sonya J. Wierman and Priya Narasimhan

9.1. INTRODUCTION

Survivability, as defined in [Ellison et al. 1997], is the ability to continue operating correctly in the presence of accidental faults and malicious attacks. Some survivable systems are designed with only crash faults in mind, whereas others aim to survive Byzantine faults and attacks. The latter include ITDOS [26], Castro–Liskov BFT [Castro and Liskov 1999], Phalanx [Malkin and Reiter 1998], Immune [Narasimhan et al. 1999], and Secure-Spread [Stanton et al. 2000]. Although a great amount of work has gone into developing these Byzantine-fault-tolerant distributed systems, little is known of the effectiveness of their implementations besides the performance metrics that are widely reported. Because these systems are built using different underlying infrastructural mechanisms (e.g., RMI vs. CORBA middleware) and different programming languages (Java vs. C++), it becomes harder to compare the various systems against each other.

Our objective is to understand more of the actual behavior of these system implementations, not just their expected behavior based on the protocol specifications. Some of the questions that we seek to answer include:

- How does the real system react to faults?
- Does it actually tolerate the fault and, if so, how does the fault affect the system performance?
- Does it matter what phase of the protocol the system is in when a fault is injected?
- Are there threshold fault-arrival rates, beyond which the system breaks down?

Dependability Benchmarking for Computer Systems. Edited by Karama Kanoun and Lisa Spainhower
Copyright © 2008 IEEE Computer Society

- How does one system compare to another in how it reacts to faults?

To attempt to answer these questions, we developed the Vajra* framework to introduce both accidental and malicious faults into a number of running, survivable distributed systems with the aim of quantifying and comparing the results. Other important goals for Vajra that stemmed from this overall objective were transparency, nonintrusiveness, and meaningful metrics.

Transparency is a direct result of our primary objective of being able to benchmark survivable systems. To accomplish this, we need to be able to run Vajra identically on different target systems, to inject the same faults on each system in the same manner so as to determine that system's reaction to the fault. This means that we have to make Vajra target-agnostic, or transparent, so that its implementation will transcend the internal implementation details of each system.

Another objective is to make Vajra as *minimally intrusive* as possible. To get meaningful results about the system behavior, our fault injection should only incur a small performance overhead. If the act of injecting a fault has a significant impact on the latencies of the system's fault-tolerance mechanisms, no real insight into the system will be gained.

From an implementation standpoint, we aim for *distributed fault injection* so that different kinds of faults, at different rates, can be injected on processes running on different nodes at various times, as required. Vajra is not composed of only a single fault-injector that runs on a single node or that targets a single process; rather, it is an orchestrated framework of fault injectors that run simultaneously across the nodes of a distributed system. Thus, Vajra's fault injection campaign involves injecting faults into the many processes that constitute the distributed target system.

A final goal is our focus on *meaningful metrics* for evaluating survivability. There are many standard metrics, such as response time and throughput, for quantifying the performance of a system. Metrics such as error-detection time and recovery time are more indicative of a system's resilience, but have not generally been reported in the literature, as can be seen from our survey of current Byzantine-fault-tolerant systems in Section 9.2. These metrics can be difficult to measure without significant instrumentation that ultimately might skew the target system's performance. In our current initial study, we employ relatively simplistic metrics, such as a binary value of whether or not a fault is tolerated, to indicate the effectiveness of the target system. We expect to extend our focus to a wider range of metrics in the future.

In this chapter, we discuss the architecture of Vajra, its implementation to meet the objectives outlined above, and the empirical results of Vajra's fault-injection campaign in targeting the Castro–Liskov BFT system [Castro and Liskov 1999]. Our ultimate goal with Vajra is to provide a benchmarking tool for the community to compare various survivable distributed systems. The utility of Vajra would be (i) a standard way of reporting results about the survivability of different distributed systems, (ii) validation and testing of implementations of survivable systems, and (iii) generation of "faultloads" (analogous to workloads) based on the specific fault model of the target system.

9.2. BACKGROUND

A Byzantine fault is one in which a component may behave arbitrarily. A server may intentionally lie to the client or to other servers, send false responses, omit responses, or

---

*In Hindu mythology, Vajra is the powerful thunderbolt weapon wielded by Indra, king of the gods. In Buddhist mythology, Vajra symbolizes the power of good over evil, and represents the state of enlightenment.

purport to be someone else. A crash-fault-tolerant system that tolerates f faults employs a minimum of $f + 1$ replicas. On the other hand, because of its more demanding survivability guarantees, a Byzantine-fault-tolerant system typically employs a minimum of $3f + 1$ replicas to tolerate f arbitrary faults [Lamport et al. 1982].

In this section, we survey several notable Byzantine-fault-tolerant systems described in the literature. Table 9.1 contains a summary of our survey. As seen in this table, few of

TABLE 9.1. Various Byzantine-fault tolerant distributed systems and their evaluation practices

System	Technique	Application	Fault-free experiments and metrics	Faulty experiments and metrics
Practical BFT [Castro and Liskov 1999]	State machine replication	Null operations and Byzantine NFS (BFS)	Latency to perform null ops with and without replication. Andrew benchmark on BFS vs. NFS v2 and BFS with no replication.	None given
SecureRing [Kihlstrom et al. 2001]	Token ring for reliable delivery and group membership	Not given	Throughput for sending messages of varying sizes, various sizes of keys, and varying number of processors. Latency of message delivery for number of nodes and key size.	Time for membership change protocol- one group member is marked as suspicious
Immune [Narasimhan et al. 1999]	Replication and secure multicast for CORBA	Constant invocations by client	Throughput (invocations per second) for: unreplicated; active rep without voting or digests; active rep with voting and digests; active rep with voting, digests, and signatures.	None given
ITDOS [Sames et al. 2002, Tally et al. 2003]	Active replication over CORBA	Not given	None given	None given
BAR [Aiyer and Alvisi 2005]	State machine replication	BAR-B, a backup storage system	Latency of broadcast protocol	Latency of broadcast with 1 or max faults allowed. Faults not specified
Fleet (2-tier) [Malkhi and Reiter 2001]	Byzantine quorums	Method invocations	Response time for method invocation for single client for varying quorum size, and for multiple clients for a quorum of size 10	None given
Fleet (3-tier) [Fry and Reiter 2004]	Byzantine quorums	Method invocations	Response time for invocations of get and set from unreplicated clients with various digital signatures.	None given

the current survivable distributed systems report any survivability numbers or metrics, a deficiency that Vajra aims to address.

9.2.1. BFT

The Castro–Liskov Byzantine Fault Tolerance (BFT) toolkit [Castro and Liskov] is used to tolerate Byzantine faults in a client–server distributed application. BFT's algorithm totally orders messages within the system to guarantee safety and liveness properties. The safety property states that the replicated service is linearizable, so that operations can be placed in a global order. Liveness guarantees that clients will eventually receive responses to their requests.

BFT employs active replication, with which every server replica processes and responds to all requests from the client. One replica is designated as the primary for the purpose of ordering client requests. Upon receiving a request, the primary begins a three-phase commit process by sending a pre-prepare message to the other replicas. This message assigns a unique sequence number to the new request for the purpose of total ordering. A nonprimary replica accepts the pre-prepare message if it agrees on the ordering and is able to process the request. Each replica then sends a prepare message to each of the other replicas, letting them know that it is ready. On receiving $2f$ prepare messages, each replica knows that all correct replicas have agreed on a total order of requests. Each replica then sends a commit message and processes the request. Every replica then sends its response directly to the client, which determines the correct value from the received responses. This three-phase commit process guarantees that all requests are executed in the same order at all nonfaulty, or correct, replicas.

Each replica maintains its state checkpoints locally, and stores the pre-prepare, prepare, and commit messages for every response following the most recent checkpoint. This allows the replicas to "roll back" and guarantee that all of the replicas are in a consistent state if the primary fails and a new primary must be appointed.

As with other Byzantine-fault-tolerant systems, BFT uses a significant amount of resources to tolerate Byzantine faults. Not only are many $(3f + 1)$ replicas are needed to withstand a small number (f) of faults, but the number of messages required to execute a single client request is large. The algorithm uses cryptographic techniques such as digital signatures and message authentication codes (MACs) to authenticate messages.

9.2.2. SecureRing

SecureRing [Kihlstrom et al. 2001] is a group communication protocol that provides secure, reliable, totally ordered message delivery and group membership services in the presence of Byzantine faults. SecureRing implements a logical token ring to totally order messages and use message digests and digital signatures to authenticate messages. The group membership protocol detects Byzantine faulty processors and changes the membership to eject them from the group. Membership change times are reported for groups of various sizes when one node has been labeled suspicious.

9.2.3. Immune

The Immune system [Narasimhan et al. 1999] transparently provides survivability to CORBA applications through the use of a replication manager and secure multicast protocols. Immune tolerates communication, processor, and object replica faults. The replication manager provides resilience to object replica faults such as crashes, omissions, and value faults. It performs majority voting on all requests and responses from clients and servers. The replication manager also ensures that no replica will receive duplicate messages and that all replicas will receive the same message from a sender (a faulty replica cannot send different versions of the same message). The secure multicast protocols provide support for communication faults (message loss and corruption) and processor faults (crashes and Byzantine behavior). The message-delivery protocol provides secure, reliable, totally ordered messages by digitally signing each message and using the SecureRing protocol. The Byzantine-fault detector monitors replica behavior and inspects messages for faults. When it suspects a replica of being faulty, it alerts the processor membership protocol, which evicts the faulty processor from the group.

Immune allows for varying levels of survivability by selectively adding or removing security and voting mechanisms. The performance of the full system is significantly lower than the standard CORBA implementation. However, by removing digital signatures, the performance becomes closer to the standard.

9.2.4. ITDOS

The Intrusion Tolerant Distributed Object System (ITDOS) [Tally et al. 2003] is a layer that resides underneath middleware (specifically, CORBA) to provide intrusion tolerance transparently to applications. It groups replicas of clients and servers into replication domains, which are coordinated by group managers. The group managers establish connections between replication domain elements and produce symmetric keys for the connections. The members of the replication domains then use the keys for confidential exchange of messages. Each pair of replicas that communicate has a key, limiting the breach of confidentiality when a key is compromised. ITDOS employs the BFT protocol to ensure that each element of a replication domain receives totally ordered messages.

Like BFT, ITDOS requires $3f + 1$ replicas to withstand f failures. When a faulty replica is detected, it is removed from the system. New replicas are not able to be added to the group to replace faulty ones. ITDOS does support multitier configurations, where a group of servers can act as a client for another (server) tier.

ITDOS utilizes a voting mechanism to mask value faults. The application receives only one response from a group of replicas. The voter only waits for $f + 1$ identical messages, or $2f + 1$ total messages before voting. ITDOS uses the voter to detect faulty processes, but due to the fact that it only waits for $2f + 1$ replies, it does not always discover faults.

9.2.5. BAR

BAR [Aiyer and Alvisi 2005] introduces a new way of describing the behavior of nodes in a cooperative distributed system. Nodes in BAR can be Byzantine (act arbitrarily for no reason), altruistic (adhere to protocol, even if they would gain by deviating from it), or rational (act arbitrarily for personal gain). The BAR system aims to provide safety and liveness guarantees to non-Byzantine nodes. BAR uses a modified version of the Castro–Liskov protocol, adapted to meet their behavior model. Rational nodes are given an incentive to cooperate with the protocol, and may impose a penance on others for not responding in a timely manner. The modifications to BFT cause BAR to need $3f + 2$ nodes rather than BFT's $3f + 1$. A backup service, BAR-B, was developed to run on BAR, and the experimental results show data with faults being injected, but no detail is given on the faults or how they were injected.

9.2.6. Fleet

Fleet [Malkhi and Reiter 2001, Fry and Reiter 2004] is a middleware system designed to tolerate Byzantine faults. Fleet uses quorum replication, which requires operations on objects to be performed at a subset of the servers. This allows Fleet to scale better with the number of faults as compared to replicated state-machine approaches like BFT. Fleet is also able to support nested method invocations, in which the clients are replicated in addition to the servers. The Fleet papers report measurements of response time for method invocations, but do not include measurements in the presence of faults.

9.3. VAJRA'S ARCHITECTURE

The Vajra fault-injection framework, as shown in Figure 9.1., consists of a master fault injector (MFI), which coordinates the distributed fault injection, and individual fault injectors (IFIs), each of them performing the actual fault injection locally on its respective node. The fault-injection campaign is specified by configuration files fed into the MFI. The fault injection is accomplished through an interceptor that is transparently inserted into each target process' address space at run time. Each component of the Vajra framework is described below.

9.3.1. Interceptor

The interception of a process through library interpositioning allows us to examine and modify a process's behavior at the granularity of library routines and system calls. Library interpositioning exploits the operating system's run-time linker–loader facilities [Levine 2000] that allow shared libraries to be loaded into a process's address space at run time, as a part of the process's normal initialization. These additional shared libraries are mapped into a process's address space *after* the binary executable that the process represents is loaded into memory, and *before* any of the compile-time shared-library depen-

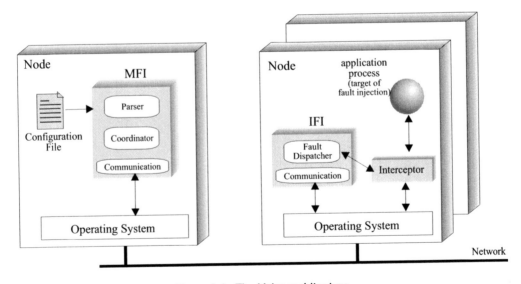

Figure 9.1. The Vajra architecture.

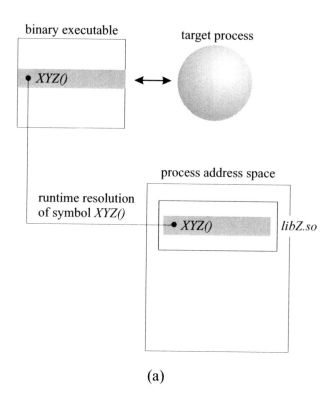

(a)

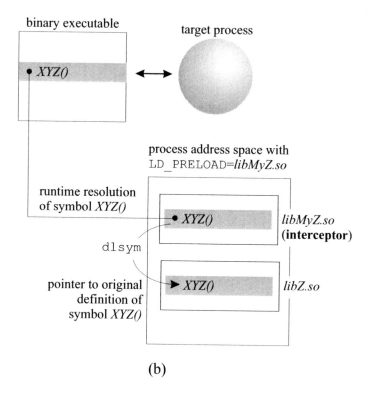

(b)

Figure 9.2. How interception works.

dencies can be mapped into the process space, as shown in Figure 9.2. The Unix linker–loader, `ld`, achieves this effect through the LD_PRELOAD environment variable in Unix-based operating systems. The dynamic linked libraries (DLLs) of the Windows NT operating system provide similar hooks that can be exploited. Our interception technique requires no modification, no relinking, and no recompilation of the target process's source code; it requires access merely to the binary executables (and not even access to the source code) of the intercepted target executable. Furthermore, our interceptor functions only at an executable's loading time, and its operation is language-agnostic, making it possible for us to intercept all target executables alike, regardless of whether their source code was originally written in Java, C, C++, and so on. Similarly, our interception technique is independent of any middleware (e.g., Java RMI vs. CORBA) that the target process uses. This makes the resulting interceptor transparent, with the target being completely unaware of its existence.

The underlying technique exploits the fact that a compiled binary that uses dynamic linking can have symbol definitions that remain intentionally unresolved until the binary actually executes. At run time, the first shared library in the process's address space that resolves a symbol, that is, provides a definition for the symbol, becomes the accepted source for that symbol's definition for the lifetime of that process's execution. If subsequent shared libraries within the same process's address space also provide definitions for the same symbol, the first accepted symbol definition "interposes" on, or hides, all of the definitions that follow for the same symbol. It is immaterial whether these definitions are identical or different.

Figure 9.2 shows a process and its executable that requires access to the symbol/function *XYZ()* in the normal course of events. As shown in Figure 9.2(a), the default definition for the symbol *XYZ* is resolved at run time from the standard library *libZ.so*. Figure 9.2(b) shows an interceptor, called *libMyZ.so*, that contains an alternative definition for the same symbol. When *libMyZ.so* is preloaded into the process's address space ahead of *libZ.so*, the Interceptor's definition of the symbol *XYZ* is accepted ahead of the default symbol definition. The latter can still be located and invoked, if needed by the interceptor, using the dynamic linking facilities (through APIs such as `dlsym`, `dlopen`, etc.) of the operating system. Thus, the definition of a symbol within the interceptor becomes that symbol's new default definition for the process during its execution. The trick, then, in overriding default symbols/functions of interest transparently, at run time, is to provide custom definitions of them within an interceptor, and to let the run-time linker–loader do its job.

9.3.2. Fault Injection

In our current implementation of Vajra, we have focused on six specific faults, which might be accidental or malicious: message loss, message corruption, message delay, crash, hang, and memory leak. These six faults are injected by intercepting one of only four system calls. To intercept the message passing among distributed nodes, we target the system calls involved in transmitting messages over sockets, namely, `send`, `sendto`, `recv`, and `recvfrom`. The faults are summarized in Table 9.2.

Message-loss faults are injected at the sender's side by overriding the `send` and `sendto` calls and causing them to return without sending the message. At the receiver's side, the message buffer is deleted before returning from `recv` or `recvfrom` calls in order to inject a message loss fault. Message-corruption and message-delay faults are injected in a similar manner. For message corruption, the interception code modifies the message buffer at the sender or receiver side. To inject message delay, the message is saved and scheduled to be sent at a later time, specified by the length of the delay.

TABLE 9.2. Faults injected by Vajra

Fault to inject	Parameter	System calls	Mechanism of injection
Message loss	Message type	send, sendto	Do not send message, return success so that process believes message was sent.
		recv, recvfrom	Wipe out receive buffer.
Message delay	Length of delay, message type	send, sendto	Save message for later send, but return success.
Message corruption	Type of corruption, message type	send, sendto, recv, recvfrom	Modify send/recv buffer
Crash		Any	Call kill(SIGKILL, myPID) inside interceptor.
Hang	Length of suspension	Any	Loop for time of suspension.
Memory leak	Size of leak	Any	Allocate memory of designated size and never release it.

The remaining three faults can be injected on any system call. As we are already intercepting the message-passing calls, we utilize these also for injecting crash, hang, and memory-leak faults. We inject hang faults by invoking kill() from within the intercepting code, causing a SIGKILL signal to be sent to the intercepted process. Hang faults are injected by waiting within the interceptor before returning control. To simulate resource-exhaustion faults, we inject memory leaks by periodically allocating memory that is never released.

9.3.3. Master Fault Injector (MFI)

The master fault injector (MFI) is the centralized component that coordinates the launching of target processes and the injection of faults into those processes. The MFI contains the communication, coordinator, and parser modules. The MFI parser module reads in data from configuration files or from user input, and passes it to the MFI coordination module. The information contained in the configuration files is discussed in Section 9.3.5.

The MFI communication module establishes connections for communication with the node-specific individual fault injectors (IFIs). Each IFI sends the MFI its unique node identifier, which the MFI's coordinator subsequently uses to identify the IFI's node and match it to the experimental setup specified in the configuration file. The MFI coordinator module decides which processes should be launched on the node and dispatches the launch command to the IFI.

The MFI coordinator also decides when fault commands should be sent to each node, and dispatches them at the appropriate time. A fault command contains the name of the fault to inject, the target process for injection, the system calls to intercept, the rate of injection, and any parameters (e.g., the length of delay) needed for the fault. The rate of injection can be specified as either the percentage of intercepted system calls in which a fault is injected, or the time between fault injections. The rate can also be set to zero, indicating a one-time fault. Example parameters include the size of the memory to be allocated for each memory leak and the type of message corruption. Parameters may also include protocol-specific information, such as the type of protocol message that should be dropped.

In addition to the fault commands that initiate faults, the MFI coordinator also dispatches fault-cancelation commands. These will cause the IFI to stop injecting recurring faults from a previous fault command.

9.3.4. Individual Fault Injector (IFI)

Each individual fault injector (IFI) contains the fault dispatcher and communication modules, and communicates with the interceptor that we have preloaded into every target process on the IFI's node. As previously mentioned, when each IFI is launched, its communication module connects to the MFI and transmits its unique node identifier. The IFI fault dispatcher then locally launches processes as dictated by the MFI, preloading them with the fault-injection interception code. As each target process is launched, its preloaded interceptor establishes a TCP connection with its local IFI's communication module. This connection will convey fault commands from the fault dispatcher and status information from the interceptor.

When a system call is intercepted, the interceptor invokes a CheckForUpdates function, which checks to see whether any fault commands have been received by its IFI's fault dispatcher. It also decides which faults, if any, should be injected into that system call. CheckForUpdates takes as parameters the type of system call and, optionally, a protocol-specific message type. If the indicated system call and message type match a fault command at the IFI, the flag for that fault is set by the IFI. The intercepting code will then proceed to inject the fault.

9.3.5. Configuration Setup

The configuration of a fault-injection campaign can be set up in one of two ways. The user can use a command-line menu to select the processes to launch and the faults to inject on each node. This option is useful for performing simple experiments with a few nodes, but can become tedious with multiple nodes, or when testing a range of fault options.

The second option is to specify a configuration file at the command line. The configuration file consists of three sections. Each section starts and ends with a designated keyword. The first section assigns each target process an identifier for future reference. The second section specifies which processes are to be launched on which nodes and command-line options for the launch command. The final section designates the faults to be injected.

A sample configuration file for fault injection on BFT is displayed in Figure 9.3. The file lists one process, whose executable is located at /users/sonyaj/run/server, to be launched on four nodes with respective identifiers 11, 12, 13, and 14. Two instances of message-loss faults are to be injected into intercepted sendto system calls. Each fault starts at time 0 and continues for 100 seconds thereafter, dropping 20% of the messages sent by the target process. The targets of the fault injection are process identifiers 100 on node 11 and on node 12. The last field is optional, indicating that the fault applies to all types of protocol messages.

9.3.6. Limitations

Although interception has its obvious advantages of transparency, language independence, and middleware independence, there are some limitations to its usage. These in-

```
// List of target processes
@BOL
100            /users/sonyaj/run/server
@EOL

// List of IFI node IDs and applications to be launched on each node
@BOL
11             100 -c con  g -f con  g_private/node1
12             100 -c con  g -f con  g_private/node2
13             100 -c con  g -f con  g_private/node3
14             100 -c con  g -f con  g_private/node4
@EOL

// List of faults to be injected
@BOL
msgLoss           sendto    0      100      0.2     11      100      all
msgLoss           sendto    0      100      0.2     12      100      all
@EOL
```

Figure 9.3. A sample Vajra configuration file.

clude the assumption of dynamic linking and the inability to fake cryptographic primitives of messages.

The only requirement for the use of library interpositioning is that the target process must be dynamically linked to the shared libraries containing the definitions of the system calls that we are intercepting. If the target process is statically linked, then we cannot override symbol definitions at loading time and preloading our interceptor library will fail to achieve its effect.

Many Byzantine-fault-tolerant systems employ cryptographic primitives, such as message authentication codes and digital signatures. These provide a guarantee to the recipient that the message has not been modified in transit. At the system-call level of interception, such cryptographic schemes have already been applied to the message. This means that the fact that we make changes to the message, such as in the message-corruption fault, will be visible to the recipient. This also prevents us from creating spurious messages and claiming that they were sent by a node unless we were to somehow be able to forge the digital signature or MAC from that node. If we were to inject faults within the target's source code (rather than at the system-call level), we would be able to modify messages before they were encrypted or authenticated. However, this would make our fault injection system-specific and would defeat our goal of creating a transparent, target-independent fault injector.

9.4. EXPERIMENTAL RESULTS

We used the Emulab test bed [White et al. 2002] to run our experiments, with each machine running a 3 GHz Zeon processor with 2 GB of memory. The machines communicate over a 100 Mbps LAN, and run Red Hat Linux 9.0.

Our fault-injection campaign involved all of the faults described in Section 9.3.2. Our target was the simple client–server test application provided with BFT. This application runs the agreement protocol, but causes no extra processing to be performed at either the client or the server. The client issues 10,000 requests, and normally completes in 12 seconds in the fault-free case. BFT requires $3f + 1$ servers to tolerate f faults. We experimented with BFT configurations that tolerate 1 (i.e., 4 servers) or 2 faults (i.e., 7 servers), respectively. We used separate machines for each BFT server, the BFT client, and the Vajra

MFI. Although we could also target the BFT client, we injected faults into the BFT servers alone, thereby focusing on the effect of faults on the agreement protocol.

9.4.1. Overhead of Vajra

To assess the overhead that Vajra imposes on the BFT system, we ran the simple client and server for ten runs of 10,000 iterations each. The total response time for BFT running with Vajra (under no faults) was 123.8452 seconds, as compared to 120.3952 seconds for BFT without Vajra. Thus, the use of Vajra imposes a 2.87% increase in response time due to the additional computational resources required to run the MFI and IFIs. This small overhead is reasonable for a tool that would be used primarily in the development stages of a system's life cycle.

9.4.2. Fault-Injection Results

Crash.   When we injected f crash faults into the BFT system, it continued operating normally with no noticeable effect on response time. If we crashed more than f servers, the entire protocol would halt. The remaining servers would send view-change messages repeatedly, but make no forward progress. This matches the expected behavior of the BFT specification.

Message Loss.   We injected varying levels of message loss based on several dimensions. We varied the percentage of messages dropped, the system call that was being intercepted, and the BFT message type that was being dropped.

Figure 9.4 shows a histogram graph of the response times for message losses. This experiment was run on a BFT setup with seven servers and $f = 2$. The first two plots show that message losses on fewer than f servers do not affect the response time. As the number of servers experiencing message losses increases beyond f, the peak of response times shifts to the right and other peaks start forming. The distance between the peaks corresponds to the time between message retransmissions.

To measure the effect of performing the same fault on different system calls, we performed message loss at both the sending and the receiving ends. Figure 9.5 shows the results of intercepting `sendto`, `recvfrom`, and both. As the graph shows, intercepting `sendto` calls has a larger impact than intercepting `recvfrom` calls, but not as large as both together.

We experimented with dropping only messages of a certain BFT-specific type, for example, preprepare, commit, or view-change, to investigate whether one phase of the protocol is more vulnerable than others. Figure 9.6 shows the results for dropping commit messages, compared with dropping total messages at the same loss probability. The results seen for commit messages are typical of all the BFT message types we tested. Thus, there is no difference in dropping specific kinds of BFT messages.

Message Corruption.   We injected message corruption into varying numbers of servers for a system configuration set up to tolerate one or two faults. The results were similar to that seen with crash faults. The types of corruption we used included modifying every character in the message buffer and rearranging characters in the buffer. For both types of corruption, the protocol halted when the messages of more than f servers were corrupted.

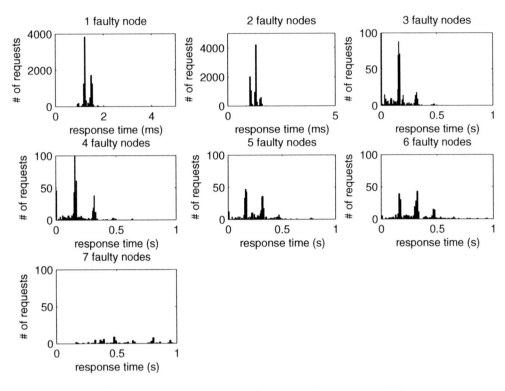

Figure 9.4. Message-loss faults; probability of loss = 20%.

Message Delay.   Figure 9.7 shows the effects of injected message delays of varying durations. The response time steadily increases with the number of nodes affected and the duration of the message delay.

Hang.   Figure 9.8 shows the results of injecting hang faults. It can be seen that the response time is affected for high rates of fault injection on more than one node. It is interesting to note that the effect does not depend on the number of faulty nodes once that number exceeds f.

Memory Leak.   We injected memory-leak faults onto varying numbers of servers by intercepting all system calls and all types of protocol messages. As Figure 9.9 shows, there was no impact on response time for any number of nodes, at any rate of injection, for any size of memory being `malloc`-ed at each fault. This is possibly due to the fact that the size of the memory being leaked here was not large enough to impact the available memory. Perhaps with longer experimental runs, the memory leak might have affected the performance more significantly.

9.4.3. Insights

The experimental results show that the BFT implementation does adhere to the behavior expected by its protocol specification for the most part. The target BFT-supported application tolerated f crash faults, and the response time was not affected when leq f machines

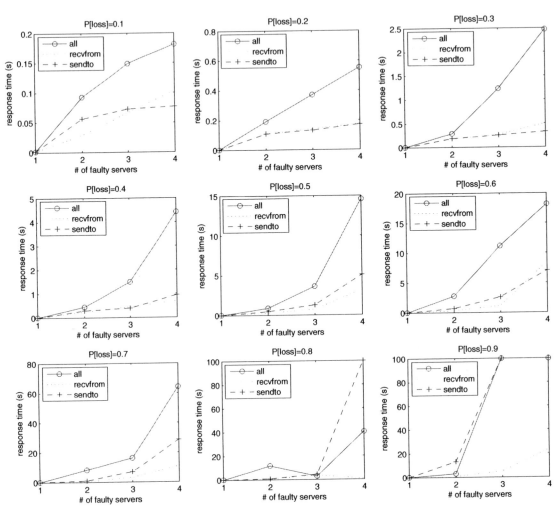

Figure 9.5. Message-loss faults on different system calls.

were injected with communication faults. When more machines experienced communication faults, they continued operating with increased response times. Depending on the user's performance requirements, significant rates (>10%) of message loss and delay can be tolerated, even when all machines are affected. The only fault for which BFT did not behave as expected was message corruption. This is likely due to implementation issues rather than any intrinsic problems in the protocol. By no means is our fault-injection campaign for BFT complete; we intend to examine the effect of increased fault rates and other forms of malicious and accidental faults.

9.5. RELATED WORK

There has been considerable work done in developing fault-injection systems [Alvarez and Christian 1997, Dawson et al. 1996, Han et al. 1995] and in analyzing the dependabil-

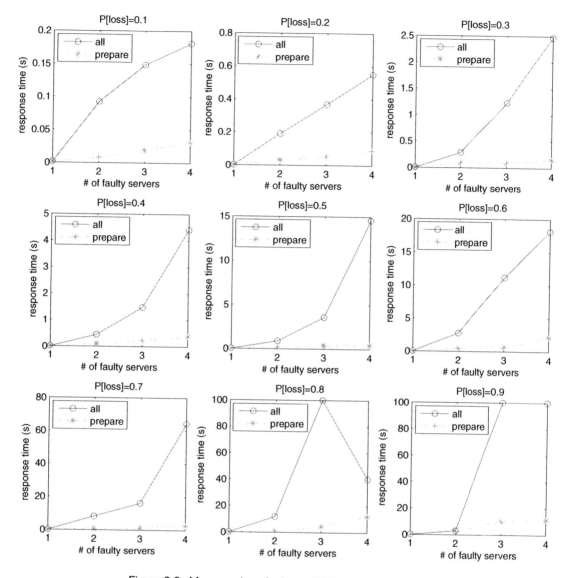

Figure 9.6. Message-loss faults on BFT commit messages.

ity of fault-tolerant systems [DBench 2004, Look and Xu 2003, Marsden and Fabre 2001]. In the following section, we describe three such efforts.

Loki [Chandra et al. 2000] is a fault injector for distributed systems that injects faults based on a partial view of the global system state. Loki allows the user to specify a state machine and a fault-injection campaign in which faults are triggered by state changes. Because each node only has a partial view of the global state, an offline analysis is done to determine whether faults were properly injected. Loki requires the user to develop the probe, the part of the run time architecture that detects state changes and injects faults, or to use the default-provided probe. Although Loki allows for complex fault-injection campaigns and provides a powerful mechanism for analyzing failure scenarios resulting from

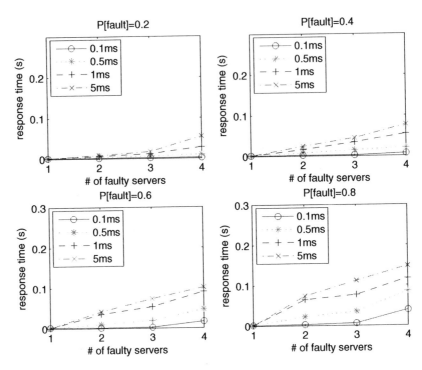

Figure 9.7. Message-delay faults.

correlated faults, the full functionality calls for modification to the application source code as well as system-specific information. This lack of generality makes it an unsuitable choice as a benchmark for comparing systems to each other.

The DBench Project [DBench 2004] aimed to develop standards for creating dependability benchmarks for computer systems. This joint cooperation characterized benchmarks as "represent[ing] an agreement that is widely accepted both by the computer industry and/or by the user community." The DBench framework defines dimensions along which to characterize benchmarks, as well as guidelines for development and usage. Several benchmarks for off-the-shelf components systems were developed in the areas of operating systems, embedded systems, and transaction processing systems. The dependability benchmark for operating systems [Kalakech 2004] measured the robustness of Windows NT4, 2000, and XP to faulty parameters in system calls. The systems were measured by the reaction of the operating system to faulty inputs (e.g., exception raised, panic state) and the effect on the application.

Orchestra [Dawson et al. 1996] is a fault injector that uses an interception approach similar to ours to inject communication faults into any layer in the protocol stack. The fault-injection core provides the ability to filter, manipulate, and inject new messages. The fault injection is controlled by scripts, written in *Tcl* or generated by their graphical user interface. Although Orchestra is designed to inject faults into distributed applications, the fault injector itself is not distributed. It does not have the ability to coordinate faults on one node based on the behavior of another node.

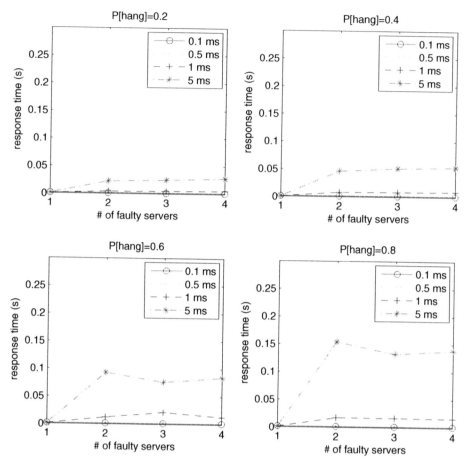

Figure 9.8. Hang faults.

9.6. FUTURE WORK

The next phase of the Vajra project is to evaluate other Byzantine-fault-tolerant systems and to determine whether we can, in fact, make dependability comparisons between systems. To this end, we are currently employing Vajra to inject faults into the PASIS [Goodson et al. 2004] and Query/Update [Abd-El-Malek et al. 2005] distributed survivable-storage protocols, both of which compare their fault-free performance to BFT.

PASIS is a survivable-storage system in which data is erasure-coded by clients and the data fragments are sent to a set of storage nodes. Erasure-coding requires less space than straightforward replication, but requires some subset of the fragments to recreate the original item. The storage nodes keep old versions of each data item to ensure that succeeding writes do not create an inconsistent view of the item. Several mechanisms, such as cryptographic hashes and storage-node verification, are used to prevent Byzantine clients from writing random data fragments and Byzantine storage nodes from corrupting the fragments they store. Much of the work of the protocol is performed by the clients, which allows the protocol to be more scalable than those, such as BFT, that use a state-machine approach.

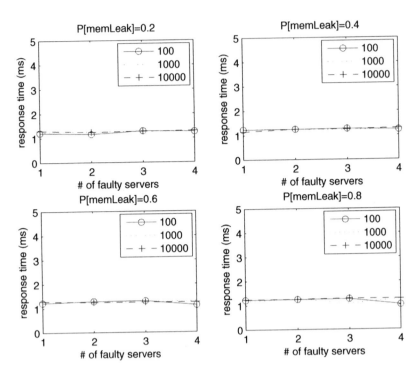

Figure 9.9. Memory-leak faults.

The Query/Update (Q/U) protocol is a quorum-based approach that allows clients to perform queries and updates on a set of objects located on the servers. Like the PASIS protocol, Q/U maintains old versions of the objects so that faulty updates can be repaired. This versioning allows for an optimistic approach to maintaining consistency for concurrent access to objects. The use of quorums places the onus on the client side to perform more work as the size of the quorums increases; thus, the system scales well as the size and, therefore, the number of faults tolerated, increases. For the same number f of faults tolerated, the use of quorums also requires more nodes (specifically, $5f + 1$), as compared with $3f + 1$ nodes for BFT's state-machine replication. We are interested in seeing how faulty behavior impacts the benefits and the scalability of using Q/U's optimistic approach.

We are interested in seeing how the three protocols—PASIS, Q/U, and BFT—compare in their resilience when faults are introduced. In addition to this ongoing benchmarking effort, we would also like to support more kinds of malicious and accidental faults to extend our fault-injection capabilities. Examples include creating the appearance that a node is malicious by sending its messages to unintended recipients or by spoofing the source of the message. We could also modify the source of a message at the receiving end for a similar effect. We are also interested in the effects of additional resource-exhaustion faults, e.g., creating bandwidth exhaustion by forcing one node to send large, meaningless messages.

Our long-term goal is to create a survivability benchmark. To make our benchmark realistic, we would like to incorporate real workloads and faultloads into Vajra. Prior studies have analyzed availability data from systems such as websites [Bakkalogh 2002], desktop PCs [Bolsky et al. 2002], and high-performance computers [Schroeder and Gibson 2006]. Incorporating real-world failure scenarios would increase the practical value of Vajra.

Our current results show the effect of faults on performance metrics such as latency. Although this provides some insight into the availability/responsiveness of a system under faults, other dependability metrics, for example, recovery time, might be more informative. However, we need to determine how we might be able to measure the values of these metrics in a generic and comparable way across different systems.

9.7. CONCLUSION

In this chapter, we have introduced Vajra, a distributed fault injector for evaluating the dependability of distributed survivable systems. We designed Vajra to be transparent and nonintrusive—it does not require any modifications to the target system under evaluation, and it is not specific to any one system. Vajra can be used to inject the same faults into a variety of different systems. The overhead of deploying Vajra is low—less than 3%. This low overhead shows that the performance effect that is seen when injecting faults into the system can be ascribed to the faults, rather than to the Vajra framework.

We demonstrated the use of Vajra to evaluate the fault tolerance of the Casto–Liskov BFT system. Our fault-injection campaign shows that the BFT implementation tolerated most of the faults (with the exception of message corruption) within the protocol's fault model. Our next steps include benchmarking the BFT against its peer protocols, in the context of distributed storage systems.

ACKNOWLEDGMENTS

This work has been partially supported by NSF CAREER grant CCR-0238381, and the Army Research Office through grant number DAAD19-02-1-0389 ("Perpetually Available and Secure Information Systems") to the Center for Computer and Communications Security at Carnegie Mellon University.

REFERENCES

[Abd-El-Malek et al. 2005] M. Abd-El-Malek, G. Ganger, G. Goodson, M. Reiter, and J. Wylie. "Fault-Scalable Byzantine fault-tolerant services," in *ACM Symposium on Operating Systems Principles,* Brighton, UK, pp. 59–74, October 2005.

[Aiyer and Alvisi, 2005] A. S. Aiyer, L. Alvisi, A. Clement, M. Dahlin, J.-P. Martin, and C. Porth. "BAR Fault Tolerance for Cooperative Services," in *ACM Symposium on Operating System Principles,* Brighton, UK, pp. 45–58, October 2005.

[Alvarez and Cristian 1997] G. A. Alvarez and F. Cristian. Centralized Failure Injection for Distributed, Fault-Tolerant Protocol Testing," in *International Conference on Distributed Computing Systems,* Baltimore, MD, May 1997.

[Bakkaloglu et al. 2002] M. Bakkaloglu, J. Wylie, C. Wang, and G. R. Ganger. "On Correlated Failures in Survivable Storage Systems," Technical Report CMU-CS-02-129, Carnegie Mellon University, Pittsburgh, May 2002.

[Bolosky et al 2000] W. J. Bolosky, J. R. Douceur, D. Ely, and M. Theimer. "Feasibility of a Serverless Distributed File System Deployed in an Existing Set of Desktop PCs," in *SIGMETRICS,* Santa Clara, CA, pp. 34–43, June 2000.

[Castro and Liskov 1999] M. Castro and B. Liskov. "Practical Byzantine Fault Tolerance," in *ACM Symposium on Operating Systems Design and Implementation,* New Orleans, LA, pp. 173–186, February 1999.

[Chandra et al. 2000] R. Chandra, R. M. Levefer, M. Cukier, and W. H. Sanders. "Loki: A State-Driven Fault Injector for Distributed Systems," in *International Conference on Dependable Systems and Networks,* New York, pp. 237–242, June 2000.

[Dawson et al. 1996] S. Dawson, F. Jahanian, T. Mitton, and T.-L. Tung. "Testing of Fault-Tolerant and Real-Time Distributed Systems via Protocol Fault Injection," in *Symposium on Fault Tolerant Computing,*Sendai, Japan, pp. 404–414, June 1996.

[DBench 2004] *DBench Project Final Report,* May 2004, http://www.laas.fr/dbench, project reports section.

[Ellison et al. 1997] R. J. Ellison, D. A. Fisher, R. C. Linger, H. F. Lipson, T. Longsta, and N. R. Mead. "Survivable Network Systems: An Emerging Discipline." Technical Report CMU/SEI-97-TR-013, Carnegie Mellon Software Engineering Institute, 1997.

[Fry and Reiter 2004] C. P. Fry and M. K. Reiter. "Nested Objects in a Byzantine Quorum-Replicated System," in *IEEE Symposium on Reliable Distributed Systems,* Florianopolis, Brazil, pp. 79–89, October 2004.

[Goodson et al. 2004] G. Goodson, J. Wylie, G. Ganger, and M. Reiter. "Efficient Byzantine-Tolerant Erasure-Coded Storage," in *International Conference on Dependable Systems and Networks,* Florence, Italy, pp. 135–144, June 2004.

[Han et al. 1995] S. Han, H. A. Rosenberg, and K. G. Shin. "Doctor: An IntegrateD SOftware Fault InjeCTiOn EnviRonment," in *International Computer Performance and Dependability Symposium,* Erlangen, Germany, pp. 204–213, April 1995.

[Kalakech et al. 2004] A. Kalakech, K. Kanoun, Y. Crouzet, and J. Arlat. "Benchmarking the Dependability of Windows NT4, 2000, and XP," in *International Conference on Dependable Systems and Networks,* Florence, Italy, pp. 681–686, June 2004.

[Kihlstrom et al. 2001] K. P. Kihlstrom, L. E. Moser, and P. M. Melliar-Smith. "The SecureRing Group Communication System," *ACM Transactions on Information and System Security,* vol. 4, no. 4, pp. 371–406, 2001.

[Lamport et al. 1982] L. Lamport, R. Shostak, and M. Pease. "The Byzantine Generals Problem," *ACM Transactions on Programming Languages and Systems,* vol. 4, no. 3, pp. 382–401, 1982.

[Levine 2000] J. R. Levine. *Linkers and Loaders.* Morgan Kaufmann Publishers, San Francisco, 2000.

[Looker and Xu 2003] N. Looker and J. Xu. "Assessing the Dependability of OGSA Middleware by Fault Injection," in *International Symposium on Reliable Distributed Systems,* Florence, Italy, pp. 293–302, October 2003.

[Malkhi and Reiter 1998] D. Malkhi and M. K. Reiter. "Secure and Scalable Replication in Phalanx," in *Symposium on Reliable Distributed Systems,* West Lafayette, IN, pp. 51–58, October 1998.

[20] D. Malkhi, M. K. Reiter, D. Tulone, and E. Ziskind. "Persistent Objects in the Fleet system," in *DARPA Information Survivability Conference and Exposition,* pp. 126–136, Anaheim, CA, 2001.

[Marsden and Fabre 2001] E. Marsden and J.-C. Fabre. "Failure Analysis of an ORB in Presence of Faults." Technical report, LAAS CNRS, Toulouse, France, October 2001.

[Narasimhan et al. 1999] P. Narasimhan, K. P. Kihlstrom, L. E. Moser, and P. M. Melliar-Smith. "Providing Support for Survivable Corba Applications with the Immune System," in *International Conference on Distributed Computing Systems,*Austin, TX, pp. 507–516, 1999.

[Sames et al. 2002] D. Sames, B. Matt, B. Niebuhr, G. Tally, B. Whitmore, and D. Bakken. "Developing a Heterogeneous Intrusion Tolerant CORBA System," in *International Conference on Dependable Systems and Networks,* Bethesda, MD, pp. 239–248, June 2002.

[Schroeder and Gibson 2006] B. Schroeder and G. Gibson. "A Large-Scale Study of Failures in High-Performance Computing Systems," in *International Conference on Dependable Systems and Networks,* Philadelphia, PA, pp. 249–258, June 2006.

[Stanton et al. 2000] J. R. Stanton, Y. Amir, G. Ateniese, D. Hasse, Y. Kim, C. Nita-Rotaru, T. Schlossnagle, J. Schultz, and G. Tsudik. "Secure Group Communication in Asynchronous Networks with Failures: Integration and Experiments," in *International Conference on Distributed Computing Systems,* pp. 330–343, Taipei, Taiwan, pp. 330–343, April 2000.

[Tally et al. 2003] G. Tally, B. Whitmore, D. Sames, B. Matt, and B. Niebuhr. "Intrusion Tolerant Distributed Object Systems: Project Summary," in *Proceedings of the DARPA Information Survivability Conference and Exposition,* Washington, DC, April 2003.

[White et al. 2002] B. White, J. Lepreau, L. Stoller, R. Ricci, S. Guruprasad, M. Newbold, M. Hibler, C. Barb, and A. Joglekar. "An Integrated Experimental Environment for Distributed Systems and Networks," in *USENIX Symposium on Operating Systems Design and Implementation,* Boston, pp. 255–270, December 2002.

USER-RELEVANT SOFTWARE RELIABILITY BENCHMARKING

Mario R. Garzia

10.1. INTRODUCTION

Software has become pervasive in our work and everyday life. Today it is virtually impossible to find a job that does not require interaction with software running on computers. At home, we use software to manage our schedules, plan our vacations, communicate with friends and family, play games, store and share our family photos and videos, and play our music. Whether at work, home, or on the road, basically all of the devices and transportation we use require increasing amounts of software to run properly and provide the necessary features and capabilities. The latest jetliners, for instance, have over five million lines of code to run their onboard computers. The software can guide the airplane through takeoff, navigating a prescribed route, and landing on a runway without pilot intervention.

Most of us are likely not even aware of how much we depend on software, and this dependency continues to grow. To deliver even greater (broader and more agile) access to the capabilities provided by software and at the same time reduce the need to maintain that software (e.g., applying fixes or updating to new versions with improved capabilities) a trend that began years ago, on-demand Software as a Service (SaaS), is now picking up great speed [Knorr 2006]. This software can be obtained directly over the Internet when needed, for however long it is needed, and users are assured that they are getting the latest and greatest version of that software each time they access it. This is in contrast to software the user purchases at a store, installs on a computer, and then takes on the responsibility for assuring that the latest fixes are applied and peruses newer versions to determine if the latest features are worth the effort of upgrading. SaaS provides clear advantages and, as a result, also greatly increases our dependency on software. Not only is the user now dependent on the software running in a computer but also on the software running private and public networks, and the software running on the servers used to deliver the service.

Given software's pervasiveness and its accelerating expansion to deliver ever growing service capabilities, software reliability has become central to assuring continued success. A recent newspaper article [Michaels and Pasztor 2006] points out that although onboard computing in airplanes has greatly lowered accident rates it has also resulted in airliner incidents in which software malfunctions required pilot overrides to keep the plane flying safely. Due to the criticality of this software, the article explains, identifying new ways to assure reliability has become a key area of focus for the Federal Aviation Administration.

The growing need to focus on software reliability is not unique to aviation but rather cuts across all industries, and is becoming even more critical as the complexity of software increases. The speed with which new software is released is also increasing. Web-based software distribution, and SaaS in particular, delivers software over the Internet, allowing for shorter software update cycles since distribution is no longer an issue. This increased update frequency can add to the difficulties in assuring software reliability as more updates come with ever shorter development cycles. There are many articles in trade publications highlighting both the growing popularity of this software delivery model and the resulting need to focus on software reliability, but the importance of software in everyday life makes this a media topic as well. Another recent newspaper article [Vara 2006] describes how service outages at leading SaaS providers seriously impacted customer's businesses when they were unable to access the service for a period of time. For SaaS to be fully successful, users have to be able to trust that the service will be available when needed. SaaS providers are now spending millions of dollars to assure the reliability of their services and using reliability as a competitive differentiator.

Although software reliability has become critical in today's world, assuring reliability is still a challenging endeavor [Littlewood and Strigini 2000]. There is work under way to develop benchmarks to assess software reliability [DBench] but there are still no broadly accepted industry benchmarks. This lack of accepted benchmarks makes it difficult for software development organizations and corporations to assure the reliability of their software and makes it virtually impossible for users to compare the reliability of competing software products. Our focus here is on how to assess software reliability from the user's perspective, expanding on previous work presented in [Garzia 2006]. Our main focus is mass-market software products for which there is a large and varied set of users, each with different usage scenarios and perspectives. In this chapter, we will use the term *reliability* as a general term to cover both the technical terms reliability and availability, where reliability is the probability of failure-free operation for a specified period of time, and availability is the probability of the software being functional at any point in time.

The benchmarks defined in this chapter arose from customer input on what they consider to be important characteristics of reliable software; however, these benchmarks are not meant to measure user perception but instead to measure actual software disruptions that will impact the user's perception of reliability. Although the benchmarks developed in this chapter are based on customer feedback collected by Microsoft® to assess user expectations of reliable software, the feedback is consistent with that gathered by other researchers (see Chapter 1 or [Brown and Shum 2005]) and, as such, these benchmarks should be broadly applicable. In the next section, we discuss how users evaluate the reliability of a software product and the resulting gap between standard reliability assessments and the user's perspective. We then present a set of five attributes that we believe characterize the user's perspective. In Section 10.3, we present the various components necessary for defining a reliability benchmark and how to associate the user reliability attributes with specific reliability events to build a benchmark. Section 10.4 provides a discussion of the applicability of these reliability attributes and benchmarks to software services. Section 10.5 presents a standard set of reliability metrics that can be used for the benchmarks, and Section 10.6 covers applications of these benchmarks at Microsoft. Section 10.7 includes the summary and areas for future work.

10.2. USER EXPECTATIONS FOR RELIABLE SOFTWARE

Although there are no established software reliability benchmarks that can be readily used today, there are standard approaches used by researchers and organizations to assess the reliability of software products. Most of these software reliability assessments result from the measurement of a limited set of failures that are then incorporated into an overall metric such as mean time to failure (MTTF) or availability [Musa 1999]. This is a well-established approach to reliability, with roots in hardware reliability, providing an important perspective on the functioning of the software system and its responsiveness to the user. However, this approach does not directly incorporate the user's experience with the software. For example, MTTF provides a measure of how often (on average) the user will encounter problems but does not capture the amount of effort required by the user to recover from the problem, and although availability takes recovery time into account it does not capture the impact to the user of having to apply frequent software patches to keep the software functioning at this level. Yet users take all of these types of considerations into account to determine their satisfaction with the reliability of the software.

This gap between the standard assessments and user's experiences results in reliability assessments that do not address the user's expectations and, therefore, are not good indicators of the software's ultimate success. All software implementations eventually interact with a user, whether directly or indirectly and whether in the role of end user or the role of system operator. As such, assessments that ignore the user's perspective or expectations are irrelevant for assessing the software's success. This situation is exacerbated when dealing with mass market software products, for which taking a user's perspective implies taking into account the needs and expectations of many different user groups. For example, an information technology professional (IT Pro) might want 24 × 7 stable operation with minimum disruptions, whereas an individual consumer or a user of software might want all their devices to work and their photos kept safe. Additionally, knowledge workers (office workers) do not want their applications to hang up.

For consumers, for example, MTTF calculated over a small set of failure types is not a relevant metric. A consumer running a PC application will not mentally tally up run times and failure counts to arrive at an MTTF on which to base their satisfaction with the reliability of the product. Instead, they focus on their experience with the product to determine their level of satisfaction with its reliability. User impact of a particular failure or event is also usually not considered in the standard metrics beyond their frequency of occurrence or impact on recovery time. Although a particular piece of software might be rated as providing high availability, this is of little satisfaction to the consumer if their application crashes frequently and they lose their input data (even if it the system quickly recovers). For an IT Pro in a corporate environment, although MTTF and availability are important, there are other measures that are important as well, such as the effort (for example, manual versus automated) required to recover from a failure or the impact on operations of applying frequent software patches. Our focus, therefore, is on establishing benchmarks that take the user's perspective into account.

To better understand the user's view of software reliability, we analyzed survey feedback collected by Microsoft from thousands of users covering a variety of user groups: knowledge (office) workers, IT professionals, software developers, and consumers. Most software products will have users in one or more of these segments and, as such, the insight gained here will apply to a broad cross section of software products. The feedback covered a variety of software products from desktop to server applications, allowing for free-format comments on their views of software products they have used—what went well and what did not go so well. This data was then used to understand how users view reliability and what things they take into account when they think of reliability that then leads to their satisfaction or dissatisfaction with the software product.

From this analysis, we learned that users take a broad perspective of reliability and that their expectations and level of satisfaction are based on their experiences, and these expectations vary across user groups and time. Yet there are common attributes for reliable software that can be defined and used to assess software reliability in a way that closely aligns with the user's expectations. With these attributes defined, it is then possible to develop a set of benchmarks that evaluate the software against these user-focused attributes.

A clear pattern of how users look at reliability emerged from our data, showing that the user's assessment is based on their experiences while using the software product, including failure situations, recovery experiences, and nonfailure maintenance activities such as updating their software. To them, reliability is more than just failure frequency and downtime duration, they take a very broad view of reliability. For example, is the behavior of the software consistent and responsive? They look at how much effort it takes to maintain the software and the amount of disruption caused by the maintenance—does it require an entire system shutdown to install an application patch? They look at their failure experience with the product, taking into account both the frequency of failures and the impact of those failures (e.g., a temporary slowdown versus an application crash resulting in data loss).

Users also take into account how easy it is to recover from a failure, where failures include the standard software bugs, crashes, hangs, unexpected interactions with other software, and data loss. For example, how much effort did it take to recover, was recovery automatic or did it require user interaction, was support or documentation easily available, and were fixes available from the software manufacturer in a timely manner?

Finally, they pay special attention to the quality of newly released software to determine if it is sufficiently mature to start using or whether they need to wait until the early bugs are worked out. Here, they take into account the frequency and size of software fixes that must be applied to the product. If these fixes need to come out very frequently or the patches are very big (many bug fixes packed into a single patch), then the product might be viewed as immature for widespread use. Given that users relate software reliability to their experiences during normal use, when recovering from a failure, or simply doing maintenance on the software, it is clear that the standard metrics for assessing software reliability (MTTF and availability) as an overall average by themselves are insufficient to capture the particular experiences users have with the software. Figure 10.1 highlights this mismatch between the current standard software reliability measures and the user's perspective.

One readily apparent discrepancy with the standard failure-based metrics is the user's attention to nonfailure (maintenance) events. Although nonfailure events are in general less impacting to the user than a failure that can result in lost work, maintenance activities

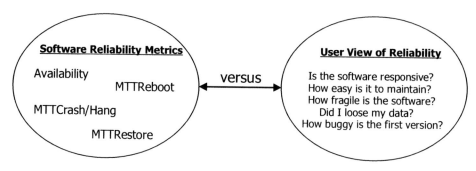

Figure 10.1. Comparison of common reliability metrics to user perspective.

such as installing a software update take time and effort and stop the user from doing their intended activities with the software. If these updates happen frequently to an end user, perhaps even requiring an entire system shutdown to complete the update, then the event can be very disruptive. If the software update needs to be applied to thousands of corporate systems by an IT professional, then this event will not only be time consuming and disruptive to the corporation's end users, but also very costly. It will require extensive testing prior to deployment to assure there is no adverse effect, scheduling the installation with operations and the end users, and human effort to deploy to all systems.

Maintenance work is often not included in reliability metrics calculations; for example, it is common practice to exclude scheduled maintenance periods from server availability assessments. However, it is clear that software users (from consumers to IT professionals) would prefer software that minimizes or even avoids the need for such disruptions. Not only do these events take time and effort, but the update frequency also gives an indication of the quality of the software in the first place. Although software updates will be required from time to time, especially for mass-market products for which the number of usage scenarios is very large and cannot all be covered in testing or beta deployment, these updates should be infrequent and have little user impact.

To capture this richer set of events impacting reliability, we need to expand beyond just considering failure events in our metrics and include all user disruptions, where a disruption is any event that interferes with the user's ability to carry out their intended activity with the software; this includes all failures and maintenance activities. Software reliability, then, is about providing the user with disruption-free operation.

Another readily apparent discrepancy is the way that different types of reliability disruptions need to be grouped in order to capture a particular user group experience. It is not sufficient to incorporate a set of failure events into a single overall metric; we need to group these failure (and nonfailure) events in specific ways to capture the experience. The discrepancy between the standard measures and how users think about reliability impairs our ability to assess ultimate user satisfaction with the software's reliability. To assure that our software meets user reliability expectations, it is necessary to evaluate the software from their perspective. To do this, we need to move beyond aggregating selected failures (e.g., software crashes and hangs) to cover all user disruptions grouped into common usage scenarios. Taking into account these user experiences is not only important for consumer products, but true in general. Although systems and software can be highly automated, users are always involved, to a greater or lesser extent, either as the users of the software activity (say, the passengers in a jetliner or users of a spreadsheet application) or responsible for setting up and running the software. It is these users that software must please and, thus, it is their experiences with the software that must be assessed to assure ultimate success, even when those impacted by the software are not aware of its existence or their dependence on its behavior.

From this user feedback emerged a clear set of attributes that users associate with software that they consider to be reliable. These attributes, shown in Table 10.1, form a set of usage scenario classes covering the most common user reliability experiences.

The first attribute, *predictable,* focuses on the software's ability to show consistency over time in terms of responsiveness and operation. For example, a memory leak in the software can cause responsiveness to go down over time and cause the software to become less predictable from the user's perspective. If the user purchases a new version of the software and it does not perform as before, say it is not backwards compatible with data or other software being used, then this also reduces the product's predictability. In essence, this attribute takes into account the consistency of the software's behavior.

Maintainable takes into account the degree to which performing standard maintenance operations, such as installing software upgrades or configuration changes, can be done with minimum or no user disruption. For example, installing a new application that requires a system shutdown is highly disruptive to the user. Not only does it take time to restart the system but also to restart and bring back all other software applications to their state prior to the shutdown. This can have a high impact on all users, and can be especially costly for datacenter servers providing production-level user services.

Resilient is a measure of how the system reacts to unexpected events. An example of resiliency is an application that saves input data frequently and automatically so that a sudden loss of power does not result in lost work. Another example of resiliency is a database server that is able to avoid crashing when going into overload and instead gracefully sustains near-maximum throughput by shedding the extra load based on specified policy. Although software may not be able to recover from all events, users expect that it can handle some of these and fail gracefully when it cannot; for example, with no loss of data.

Recoverable relates to a measure of how the software behaves when a failure has occurred, whether the software itself can quickly recover to a good known state or whether it requires user input. Software rejuvenation techniques [Castelli et al. 2001; IIS] are a good example of recoverability. When a worker process in Internet Information Services (IIS) starts to fail the IIS recycling feature quickly spawns a new worker process to take over new incoming traffic and lets the failing worker process finish handling its users before shutting it down. This is done without need for human intervention or without impacting user service.

The last attribute on the list, *proven,* is a measure of the software's readiness for use. Some users will not buy the first version of a software product because they believe it can be buggy (it is unproven). They will instead wait for the first set of fixes to be released or

TABLE 10.1. The five user-focused attributes of reliability

Reliability attributes	Attribute description
Predictable	Consistent, available service
Maintainable	Easy to manage and update without disruption
Resilient	Works despite changes in conditions
Recoverable	Easily restored without adverse impact
Proven	Ready to operate in a variety of environments

perhaps even the second version. Although users do not necessarily expect software to be bug free, they do expect it to have few problems. Software that requires several patches shortly after release fails to meet this criterion.

These five attributes encapsulate a generalized set of usage scenarios. In assessing the reliability of software, we need to measure the degree to which the software meets each of these criteria.

An approach similar to the one presented here is being followed by other researchers. In Chapter 2 (see also [Elling 2005]), the authors decompose reliability into three factors, R^3, and then develop several benchmarks to measure these. The three factors are rate, robustness and recovery. *Rate* looks at the frequency of faults, similar to the *proven* attribute. *Robustness* looks at whether faults cause service outages and the degree of error detection and correction built into the system, comparable to the *resilient* attribute above. The third R is for *recovery,* how quickly the system can be returned to operation after a fault or maintenance event, which is comparable to the *recoverable* attribute above but also includes some aspects of our *maintainable* attribute. One of their benchmarks, the Maintenance Robustness Benchmark (MRB-A), focuses on whether maintenance operations cause disruptions. In Chapter 6 the authors discuss reliability benchmarks being used for autonomic computing software; in this work their focus is on resiliency, which they arrive at based on user feedback. They then use this feedback to identify specific types of failures that detract from resiliency, which are then used to create their disruption load for the benchmark.

It is interesting to note that different studies have focused on varying numbers of attributes. For our case, it is certainly possible to break our five attributes down further into more specific scenario classes (subattributes). This results in more granular usage classes (more attributes), allowing us to better focus on specific experiences. But at some point it becomes impractical to track, with too many scenarios to consider. We could also aggregate the attributes and reduce their number to less than five, creating more general scenario classes, as was done with the recovery attribute in Chapter 2 (also see [Elling 2005]). Aggregating into too few attributes, however, reduces our ability to distinguish between user experiences, with the degenerate case being only one attribute for which we group all disruptions together as is normally done today. Although there is no number of attributes that is optimal, we have found that these five attributes present a good compromise between too much granularity and too little, and can be very effective in assessing product reliability.

10.3. DEVELOPING RELIABILITY BENCHMARKS FOR USER ATTRIBUTES

Our objective is to develop benchmarks for assessing software reliability for each of the five attributes. The benchmarks we define must satisfy the following properties [DBench]:

- Repeatable/Reproducible—benchmark results can be verified at different times and by different groups.
- Representative—benchmark results cover the set of scenarios to be experienced in normal and expected use.
- Nonintrusive—running the benchmark does not affect the results of the software's operation.

- Portable—the benchmark can be applied to different systems and setups.
- Cost-effective and scalable—the benchmark can be run in a cost-effective way and can scale to the needed systems and workloads.

The ability to repeat and reproduce the benchmark results is critical to being able to verify those results and to use the results in assessing improvement with future versions of the software product or comparing results to those of competing products. However, to properly evaluate a complex software product it is necessary to relax our definition of repeatable and reproducible to mean *statistically* repeatable and reproducible. The reason for this is that while many Bohrbugs (bugs in the software's response to inputs that always cause a failure when a particular operation is performed [Gray 1985, Shetti 2003]) can be captured in standard tests, the multiplicity of scenarios required for some software products cannot be properly covered in a limited set of test scenarios. In addition, Heisenbugs (errors in the software's assumptions about its environment, e.g., interactions with hardware or other software that do not always cause a fault when a particular operation is performed) are seldom caught in standard tests. Although the lab test approach can provide a completely repeatable/reproducible benchmark, it will not cover all the necessary scenarios. Instead, we need to also consider more varied and less controlled, real-use scenarios for which we say the benchmark results have been reproduced if they are statistically the same i.e., they fall within specified confidence bands. The *representative* property is important to assure that the benchmark captures the behavior of interest, which is completely in line with our discussion of user perspective. Although failures considered for some proposed reliability benchmarks are the result of random variations of input parameters, to be representative benchmarks need to be based on scenarios that actually occur in the real-world usage of that software and that are of importance to the target user base. Nonintrusiveness is necessary to make sure that the benchmark itself does not alter the observed results, and portability assures that the benchmarks can be applied to different systems by multiple groups. The last property assures that the benchmark can be implemented in a practical and useful way.

Benchmarks must include the following components (see Chapter 4, [DBench], and [Madeira 2005]):

- Environment
- Workload
- Disruption load
- Measures

All of these components are totally dependent on the user base and vary from product to product. For mass-market products such as the Windows operating system [Jalote et al. 2004], a high-level breakdown of the user base can be made into consumers, knowledge workers, and IT pros. Each of these groups can be further broken down into specific user areas; for example, IT pros can be broken down into small, medium, and large businesses, each having their own specific needs. The targeted use of the software under study determines the right level of user-base grouping.

The environment component includes the software under consideration, the user base, system (hardware and software it runs on), and other software/systems with which it interacts. For example, some applications might run on a PC and not interact with any other applications on the PC or with the network; for example, a simple PC calendar application.

Other applications, including e-mail and Web browsing, may have strong interactions with other programs and servers on the network. The fact that desktop/laptop (consumers and knowledge workers) software has different needs and applications than software running on a server is intuitively clear. However, whereas consumers and knowledge workers use similar hardware, their applications and usage can vary greatly. For example, a consumer will typically use their computer to store and play digital music, photos, and videos which themselves require attaching multiple devices through USB ports such as cameras and MP3 players. A knowledge worker environment, on the other hand, may consist of office software and business applications making very little use of devices. The hardware, software, and workload (usage) differ in these two user situations and, therefore, the reliability experience can be very different and needs to be assessed separately.

With the environment defined, we can then define the proper workload. For reliability benchmarks, there are currently no generally accepted workloads; there are, however, commonly used performance workloads such as TPC-C, which can be adapted to work for reliability (see Chapter 4 and [Kalakech et al. 2004]). Although these workloads might not be ideal, they are well established and their benefits and drawbacks generally well understood. In general however, we would need to define standard workloads based on a selected set of operational profiles for the user groups under consideration [Musa 1999]. The next element that must be defined is the disruption load (sometimes referred to as foreground workload). This is the set of disruptions (faults and other events such as required maintenance activities) that will be imposed on the system (environment + workload) to assess the response.

Since we are interested in assessing reliability based on the common usage scenarios, we need to define these disruptions based on their impact on each of the five reliability attributes. In our case, as mentioned earlier, this requires grouping the disruptions in a way that aligns with the user experiences represented by each attribute. Disruptions will vary from product to product as we adjust to the specific features of the software, the environment in which the software runs, and the needs of the specific user base. In addition, the importance assigned to each disruption by the product's users will vary from product to product and, in fact, will likely vary between user groups for a given product, as not all disruptions will detract from the product's reliability, nor will they have an equal impact on the user.

For the attributes defined, we need to determine which software disruptions (planned and unplanned) fall into each scenario; that is, which software disruptions, when they happen, detract from the user's perception of reliability under the specific usage class scenario (or attribute). The classification is dependent on the software product being considered and the types of disruptions that can take place; for example, if our usage scenario is an office worker then the unplanned and planned disruptions might be those that occur on a desktop or laptop using standard office productivity software as well as those resulting from interactions with servers.

A sample classification for a software product running on a PC is given in Table 10.2. This table does not represent a complete classification for a PC software product. It does, however, show how disruptions can be grouped based on their impact on each of the five user reliability attributes. Note that the same disruption may show up in more than one attribute, for example, software hangs. Although this might seem ambiguous, it is consistent with users' experience in the different scenarios. If a software application hangs while opening large files, then the user will get used to this behavior but will consider this application to lack resiliency. On the other hand, if the application sometimes hangs depending on system resource usage the user may not be aware of the reason for the hang

TABLE 10.2. A classification of user disruptions for the five reliability attributes

Predictable	Maintainable	Resilient	Recoverable	Proven
Performance degradation	Software/hardware installation/updates	Crashes	Incomplete error messages	Patch rate
Resource leaks	Software/hardware configuration changes	Hangs	Unhandled exceptions	Patch size
Hangs	BIOS/driver updates	Data corruption	State corruption	Bug rate
Installation failures		Data loss	Data corruption	Functionally incorrect response
Application/system incompatibility error		Race conditions	Transient errors	
Incorrect behavior		Hardware/ firmware failures	Restart failure	
Transient errors		Intersystem communication failure		

nor be able to predict when a hang might occur, detracting from the software's predictability. The important thing here is to focus on scenarios as experienced by the user instead of trying to identify a set of mutually exclusive causes for lack of reliability.

As will be seen later, once the set of disruptions is defined for a particular attribute, we can use standard reliability metrics calculated over the set of disruptions to characterize the attribute. This is the last component for our benchmark and is covered in Section 10.5.

10.4. RELIABILITY ATTRIBUTES FOR SOFTWARE SERVICES

The reliability attributes presented here, although developed specifically for products and based on user feedback about products, also apply to services. From a service user's perspective, the predictable, resilient, recoverable, and proven attributes still apply, and the events in Table 10.2 still have meaning for the attributes. For IT personnel running the software, the events in Table 10.2 apply directly. For the user of a software service, only the impact of the events on the service rendered matter. However, when considering services we also need to add events resulting from the interaction with the network and other computers/servers.

For example, *predictable* may also include events such as the load on the network that can lead to long delays or time-outs. *Resilient* might include disruptions resulting from connectivity loss to the serving site. *Recoverable* might include some end-user events such as the ability to recover data entered online following a server or network glitch. For SaaS, *proven* may require special scrutiny due to increased speed to market and ease of distribution of the new bits resulting in higher software update frequency. This increased delivery speed can tax existing processes and theory on how to assure sufficiently reliable software at the time of release. Maturity of the software at the time of release is an area of user focus; many users will wait for revisions before upgrading to the new software. On the other hand, the speed with which updated versions can be made available with SaaS also assures that problems that are quickly identified can also be quickly corrected. As such, implementation of a strong failure feedback and resolution process can greatly help improve the reliability of these services. Maintainable, on the other hand, is not important for an end user since a distinct benefit of SaaS is the ability to forgo maintenance issues when using the service, since the bits used at any specific time are always the latest version of the software.

However, to the IT professional responsible for delivering the service, maintainability still plays a central role. The degree to which software needs to be updated and, in general, maintained can greatly impact the software's cost of ownership and service availability. In order to maintain high service availability for users, IT professionals must spend extra time and resources to schedule tests and assure proper operation of the updated software, schedule around service peak times, and purchase and maintain additional hardware to allow updates to occur offline while service capacity is maintained by rotating systems in and out of production during upgrades. These variations again highlight the need to identify the target user base for the software and to consider the disruptions critical to a given user base.

Although these attributes clearly apply to the software as a service case because of similarities in many of the experiences, the feedback used to arrive at the above attributes was focused mainly on the user's experience with software products and not software services. The comparable user feedback research for SaaS still needs to be carried out and given the broader set of possible experiences (accessing and using software on-demand over a public network), it is not unreasonable to expect that we will have to include additional events (as already mentioned) and perhaps even additional attributes.

10.5. USER-FOCUSED SOFTWARE RELIABILITY BENCHMARK MEASURES

With attributes defined and disruptions assigned to each attribute, one can define measures that can be used to assess software reliability. This is the last of the components necessary for our benchmark. As we have discussed earlier, the issue is not that we need a different set of metrics or formulas, but what faults and what events we use to calculate/evaluate our metrics. A common approach for running a reliability benchmark is to apply the disruption load to the system under benchmarking (SUB) composed of the environment and workload, and then use standard metrics such as mean time to disruption, mean time to restore, and availability to assess software reliability (see Chapter 4 and [Madeira 2005]). Since we are interested in assessing reliability for each of the five user attributes, the disruption load is carried out on a per-attribute basis (using disruption mapping as in Table 10.2) and then applied to the SUB. For example, for the set of disruptions $\{d_1, d_2, \ldots, d_n\}$ corresponding to Attribute A, where $\{u_i^{j_i} \mid j_i = 1, 2, \ldots, k_i\}$ are the set of k_i software uptimes ending in disruption d_i, we can calculate $MTTD_A$ (mean time to disruption for attribute A) as

$$MTTD_A = \frac{\sum_{i=1}^{n} \sum_{j_i=1}^{k_i} u_i^{j_i}}{\sum_{i=1}^{n} k_i}$$

where n is the number of observed disruptions for attribute A. Similarly, we can define $MTTR_A$ (mean time to restore for attribute A), with $\{r_i^{j_i} \mid j_i = 1, 2, \ldots, k_i\}$ denoting the restoration times for disruption d_i, and availability as

$$MTTR_A = \frac{\sum_{i=1}^{n} \sum_{j_i=1}^{k_i} r_i^{j_i}}{\sum_{i=1}^{n} k_i}$$

$$\text{Availability} = \frac{MTTD_A}{MTTD_A + MTTR_A}$$

One can, of course, also specify other types of metrics; for example, Chapter 6 uses throughput under disruption load to assess resiliency. In addition, it is also often necessary to use qualitative measures to capture some of the qualities important to users, such as the degree of recovery automation. For example we can use a scale, say 1 to 10, and then rate the system based on how it performs under the specific disruption load. In Chapter 2, the maintenance robustness benchmark is evaluated by rating the system behavior on a scale of 1 to 100, where 1 means that all maintenance actions result in a system outage and 100 means all components can be replaced without an outage. A drawback of this approach is that without specific criteria for rating components, the rating will be highly subjective, and without an industry-established standard the results will vary from one rater to another, impacting the repeatability characteristic needed for a benchmark. In this case we could use MTTR or availability as measures, but these would not directly capture the "quality" of the recovery that is of importance to the user, such as whether it required manual interaction or was fully automated. Another example of this type of qualitative metric is given in Chapter 6, where a maturity index is used to assess resiliency using a scale from 0 to 8, where 0 means that the user had to refer to manuals to recover the system after a disturbance and 8 means that the software automatically self-managed through the disturbance according to business policy. Although both types of metrics, quantitative and qualitative, have benefits and drawbacks in our experience both are necessary to properly capture reliability from the user's perspective. However, even in the qualitative case, care must be taken to specify clear and objective criteria for the ratings so that the resulting values do not depend on the individual or group rating the component. That is, the rating will support the repeatability and portability properties and, thus, will be (essentially) the same regardless of who rates the component.

10.6. APPLYING THE RELIABILITY BENCHMARKS

For the past several years, there have been efforts at Microsoft aimed at addressing aspects of these benchmarks to assess and drive product reliability. Over the past two years, as part of Microsoft's Trustworthy Computing effort, we have worked to expand the existing work to arrive at a set of benchmarks that capture the user's perspective based on the five reliability attributes.

One attribute that has received extensive focus over the past several years across Microsoft is *resilient,* particularly focused on product crashes, hangs, and data corruption. For this case, data on crashes and hangs is collected from beta systems through our Windows Error Reporting feedback mechanism during the development process [WER]. This data includes reports on crashes and hangs with the information necessary to debug and fix the problem. The metric used here is reported failure frequency.

These failure reports are automatically analyzed in the back end and classified into buckets, with each bucket representing a bug. Bugs are then prioritized and filed. These failure reports come from test systems and Microsoft employees running the software, and from beta users in the field. This allows us to drive product improvement during development and assure that we are meeting our objectives for addressing failures based on the failure frequency distribution. Once the product is released in the field, users have the option of sharing failure data with Microsoft. This results in a strong feedback mechanism that allows us to continue to improve the product after release to adjust to new usage scenarios.

The reported failure-frequency metric mentioned above can and has been also used for the *proven* attribute by allowing us to characterize, for example, the incoming rate for hard failures (i.e., crashes and hangs). To capture a set of user disruptions, including other failures (that do not result in a hang or crash) and nonfailure situations such as shutdowns due to software upgrades (Table 10.2), we also use MTTD and availability metrics based on a broad set of disruptions. This data is collected for servers using the Microsoft Reliability Analysis Service (MRAS) [Garzia 2003a, MRAS 2004] which includes information on a broad variety of system/software disruptions.

Starting with Windows Server® 2000, we assure that the Operating System meets the *proven* objective for each major milestone build (Betas, RCs, and the final RTM) by carrying out a study of software reliability in a production environment, representing all major server roles in deployment, as part of our product release criteria. Since this is an actual production environment, there is no disruption load applied other than normal operation of the product in a field situation. Figure 10.2 shows the results of our Windows Server® 2003 *proven* attribute production study [Garzia 2003b]. In the study, disruptions that occur during the assessment period are diagnosed to determine if they were caused by the operating system and if so they are included in the disruption count. Disruptions that are not caused by the operating system, say hardware failures, are not counted

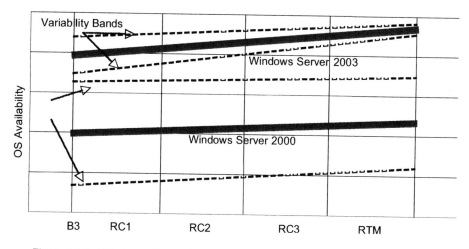

Figure 10.2. Windows Server 2003 reliability release study for *proven* attribute.

against the metric since they are not reflective of OS reliability (planned disruptions such as software updates were not included in this study). The upper solid line shows the change in Windows Server 2003 availability between the Beta 3 and RTM milestones. The second, lower, solid line shows the comparable results for Windows Server 2000. The two dashed lines surrounding each of the solid lines represent the interquartile variability range based on the server population size and runtime. As can be seen from this figure, Windows Server 2003 had much higher availability for *proven* than the comparable study for Windows Server 2000 at the time of release. We also assess this attribute during our long-haul test environment where we apply disruption loads as part of our normal testing and assess the results. This type of analysis for the *proven* attribute is now being used for Windows Vista™, and is also being used on other software products across Microsoft.

The *resilient* and *proven* attribute implementations discussed here meet our benchmark criteria. They are (statistically) repeatable; given a sufficiently large sample of users with a given workload and environment, we have seen this repeatability during development of our operating system where the metrics that we evaluate for these attributes on internal builds are corroborated with the results from a broader set of comparable beta users once the beta is released.

The workload and environment however are very important variables that can lead to significant differences in results when they differ from one case to another, the challenge here is to identify the proper operational profile [Musa 1999] for the target user base and then apply that profile in the study. The studies are also representative for sufficiently large populations with common operational profiles since they are based on real-world usage, and they are nonintrusive as they depend on system reports after the disruption has occurred.

These implementations have been shown to be scalable and able to work for a few to millions of deployed systems. They are being used extensively at Microsoft, including playing a key role in current development efforts such as the Windows Vista operating system and the next version of Microsoft's Office software. Although they are inherently portable, portability and cost can be an issue given that they require the use of sophisticated tools [WER, MRAS 2004] and sufficiently large samples. An example of portability, however, is a crash/hang-type analysis that has been done in academic research [Ganapathi and Patterson 2005] to analyze failures using data collected from departmental machines at Berkeley.

Most of the implementations described in this section are based on measuring actual usage during the various stages of software development and once the software is released. As such, no workloads or fault loads need to be defined, we simply measure the software's reliability under normal operational conditions for the target user group. However, these benchmarks can also be applied in a laboratory environment by using an appropriate workload and fault load representing the target user group's operational profile, as is the case with our long-haul tests. Both of these approaches, actual usage and laboratory tests, are important and each provides its own benefits and insights.

10.7. SUMMARY AND FUTURE WORK

In this chapter, we have discussed the need to assess reliability from the user's perspective. We propose that the standard way of assessing reliability, aggregating a limited set of failures into a single overall average such as MTTF, will not capture reliability based on the user's experience with the product and thus miss user-critical characteristics in the assessment. Instead, we need to consider how the different disruptions impact the user's experience. Based on extensive user feedback, we have defined a set of five reliability attributes representing user experiences that capture the user's perspective. These attributes, together with an appropriate workload and disruption load, can then be used to develop a user-focused set of benchmarks. Although the focus of this work was on software products, we also showed that the five attributes can be used for software-based services. However more work is still needed in this area, potentially resulting in some new additional attributes. Examples were presented of attribute-based studies being done at Microsoft to assess the reliability of its products, including the new Windows Vista operating system.

There are several areas for further investigation and expansion of this work. Once we have measures for each of the five attributes, it would be advantageous to combine these into a single reliability index for the product. This would make it easier to rate one product against another; for example, a prior version or a competitive product. However, doing this is not trivial, especially when considering both quantitative and qualitative measures. Furthermore, this index would have to be such that it does not hide the impact of any of the five attributes so that it provides a complete user perspective.

Another area that requires further investigation is the use of weights for disruptions. In the above discussion, it was suggested that for each disruption we determine if it was important for the specific user group under consideration before using it in the benchmark, in essence assigning a weight of 1 if it was important or a weight of 0 if it was not. However we can relax this constraint by assigning weights between 0 and 1, based on the level of importance. For example, a datacenter manager might assign high importance to an occasional software crash that translates into a high cost for the service offered by that software. For a home user, an occasional software crash may be simply an annoyance and, therefore, merit a low weight (though not necessarily 0) but they might assign a very high weight (say 1) to losing their hard drive with their family photos. The weights would be assigned based on user input; for example, by starting with disruptions that the user agrees are the worst (e.g., application crash) and therefore have a weight of 1, and then arriving at weights for the lesser disruptions based on their impact in comparison to the worst disruptions. These disruptions and weights would then be used to calculate reliability metrics for each of the five attributes. Finally, as mentioned earlier, additional work is needed to validate and, if necessary, expand the attributes to properly cover software as a service.

REFERENCES

[Brown and Shum 2005] A. B. Brown and P. Shum. "Measuring Resiliency of IT Systems," in *Proceedings of International Symposium on Software Reliability Engineering (ISSRE)*, SIGDeb Workshop, Chicago, 2005.

[Castelli et al. 2001] V. Castelli, R. E. Harper, P. Heidelberger, S. W. Hunter, K. S. Trivedi, K. Vaidyanathan and W. Zeggert. "Proactive Management of Software Aging," *IBM Journal of Research & Development*, vol. 45, no. 2, March 2001.

[DBench] "Dependability Benchmarking Project." http://www2.laas.fr/DBench.

[Elling 2005] R. Elling. "RAS Benchmarking at Sun: Four Views of Mount Fuji," in *Proceedings of International Symposium on Software Reliability Engineering (ISSRE)*, SIGDeb Workshop, Chicago, 2005.

[Ganapathi and Patterson 2005] A. Ganapathi and D. Patterson. "Crash Data Collection: A Windows Case Study," in *Proceedings of International Conference on Dependable Systems and Networks (DSN)*, Yokohama, Japan, pp. 280–285, 2005.

[Garzia 2003a] M. R. Garzia. "Assessing the Reliability of Windows Servers," in *Proceedings of International Conference on Dependable Systems and Networks (DSN)*, San Francisco, 2003.

[Garzia 2003b] M. R. Garzia and B. Levidow. "A Customer Focused Approach to Architecting for Software Reliability," Microsoft Research (MSR) Faculty Summit. Redmond, WA, July 2003.

[Garzia 2006] M. R. Garzia. "Assessing Software Reliability from the Customer's Perspective," in *Proceedings of International Service Availability Symposium (ISAAS)*, Helsinki, Finland, 2006.

[Gray 1985] J. Gray. "Why Computers Stop and What Can be Done About Them?" http://www.cs.berkeley.edu/~yelick/294-f00/papers/Gray85.txt, 1985.

[IIS] "How Worker Process Recycling Works (IIS 6.0)." http://www.microsoft.com/technet/prodtechnol/WindowsServer2003/Library/IIS.

[Jalote et al. 2004] P. Jalote, B. Murphy, M. Garzia, and B. Errez. "Measuring Reliability of Software Products," in *Proceedings of International Symposium on Software Reliability Engineering (ISSRE)*, Saint-Malo, Bretagne, France, pp. 269–276, 2004.

[Kalakech et al. 2004] A. Kalakech, K. Kanoun, Y. Crouzet, and J. Arlat. "Benchmarking the Dependability of Windows NT 4, 2000 and XP," in *Proceedings of International Conference on Dependable Systems and Networks (DSN)*, Florence, Italy, pp. 681–686, 2004.

[Knorr 2006] E. Knorr. "Software as a service: The next big thing." http://www.infoworld.com/article/06/03/20/76103_12FEsaas_1.html, 2006.

[Littlewood and Strigini 2000] B. Littlewood and L. Strigini. "Software Reliability and Dependability: A Roadmap," in *The Future of Software Engineering*, A. Finkelstein Ed., ACM Press, New York, pp. 177–183, 2000.

[Madeira 2005] H. Madeira. "Dependability Benchmarking for Transactional and Web Systems," in *Proceedings of International Symposium on Software Reliability Engineering (ISSRE)*, SIGDeb Workshop, Chicago, 2005.

[Michaels and Pasztor 2006] D. Michaels and A. Pasztor. "Incidents Prompt New Scrutiny of Airplane Software Glitches." *The Wall Street Journal*, Vol. CCXLVII, No. 125, p. A1, May 30, 2006.

[MRAS 2004] Improving Availability and Reliability with Microsoft Reliability Analysis Service. http://www.microsoft.com/windowsserver2003/mras/mrasavail.mspx, 2004.

[Musa 1999] J. Musa. *Software Reliability Engineering.* McGraw-Hill, New York, 1999.

[Shetti 2003] N. M. Shetti. "Heisenbugs and Bohrbugs: Why are They Different?" http://www.cs.rutgers.edu/~rmartin/teaching/spring03/cs553/papers01/06.pdf, 2003.

[Vara 2006] V. Vara. "Web Services Face Reliability Challenges." *The Wall Street Journal*, p. B3, February 23, 2006.

[WER] Windows Error Reporting. http://msdn2.microsoft.com/en-us/library/ms681662.aspx.

INTERFACE ROBUSTNESS TESTING: EXPERIENCES AND LESSONS LEARNED FROM THE BALLISTA PROJECT

Philip Koopman, Kobey DeVale, and John DeVale

11.1. INTRODUCTION

When the Ballista project started in 1996 as a 3-year DARPA-funded research project, the original goal was to create a Web-based testing service to identify robustness faults in software running on client computers via the Internet. Previous experience suggested that such tests would find interesting problems but it was unclear how to make robustness testing scalable to large interfaces. A major challenge was finding a way to test something as large and complex as an operating system (OS) application programming interface (API) without having to resort to labor-intensive manual test construction for each API function to be tested. In the end, a scalable approach was found and was successfully applied not only to operating system APIs but several other nonoperating system APIs as well.

The robustness testing methodology Ballista is based upon using combinational tests of valid and invalid parameter values for system calls and functions. In each test case, a single software module under test (or MuT) is called once. An MuT can be a stand-alone program, function, system call, method, or any other software that can be invoked with a procedure call. (The term MuT is similar in meaning to the more recent term dependability benchmark target [DBench 2004].) In most cases, MuTs are calling points into an API. Each invocation of a test case determines whether a particular MuT provides robust exception handling when called with a particular set of parameter values. These parameter values, or *test values,* are drawn from a pool of normal and exceptional values based on the data type of each argument passed to the MuT. Each test value has an associated *test object,* which holds code to create and clean up the related system state for a test (for example, a file handle test object has code to create a file, return a file handle test value, and subsequently delete the file after the test case has been executed). A test case, therefore, consists of the name of the MuT and a tuple of test values that are passed as parameters [i.e., a test case would be a procedure call of the form: returntype MuT_name(test_value1, test_value2, . . . , test_valueN)]. Thus, the general Ballista approach is to test the robustness of a single call to an MuT for a single tuple of test values, and then iterate this process for multiple test cases that each have different combinations of valid and invalid test values.

The Ballista testing method is highly scalable with respect to the amount of effort required per MuT, needing only 20 data types to test 233 POSIX functions and system calls [Kropp 1998]. An average data type for testing the POSIX API has 10 test cases, each having 10 lines of C code, meaning that the entire test suite required only 2000 lines of C code for test cases (in addition, of course, to the general testing harness code used for all test cases and various analysis scripts). Robustness testing of other APIs was similarly scalable in most cases.

This chapter describes the key design tradeoffs made during the creation and evolution of the Ballista robustness testing approach and associated toolset. It summarizes some previous results to draw together high-level lessons learned. It also contains previously unpublished robustness testing results, and key intermediate results that influenced the course of the project.

11.2. PREVIOUS ROBUSTNESS TESTING WORK

Although the Ballista robustness testing method described here is a form of software testing, its heritage traces back not only to the software testing community but also to the fault tolerance community as a form of software-based fault injection. Ballista builds upon more than 15 years of fault injection work at Carnegie Mellon University, including [Schuette 1986, Czeck 1986, Barton 1990, Siewiorek 1993, Dingman 1995, and Dingman 1997], and makes the contribution of attaining scalability for cost-effective application to a reasonably large API. In software testing terms, Ballista tests responses to exceptional input conditions; they are sometimes called "dirty" tests, which involve exceptional situations, as opposed to "clean" tests of correct functionality in normal situations. The Ballista approach can be thought of as a "black box," or functional testing technique [Bezier 1995] in which only functionality is of concern, not the actual structure of the source code. Among other things, this permits Ballista to be used on already-compiled software for which no source code is available. However, unlike the usual testing approaches, Ballista is concerned with determining how well a software module handles exceptions rather than with functional correctness.

Some people only use the term robustness to refer to the time between operating system crashes under some usage profile. However, the authoritative definition of robustness is "the degree to which a system or component can function correctly in the presence of invalid inputs or stressful environmental conditions [IEEE 1990]." This expands the notion of robustness to be more than just catastrophic system crashes, and encompasses situations in which small, recoverable failures might occur. Although robustness under stressful environmental conditions is indeed an important issue, a desire to attain highly repeatable results has led the Ballista project to consider only robustness issues dealing with invalid inputs for a single invocation of a software module from a single execution thread. It can be conjectured, based on anecdotal evidence, that improving exception handling will reduce stress-related system failures, but that remains an open area of research.

Robustness testing in general has, of course, existed for many years, including manual testing to overload systems, but most software product development efforts have very limited time and budget for testing, often leading to testing focused on correct functionality rather than robustness. An automated robustness testing approach could make it practical to obtain much better robustness information within a limited testing budget.

An early method for automatically testing operating systems for robustness was the development of the Crashme program [Carrette 1996]. Crashme operates by writing random data values to memory, then spawning large numbers of tasks that attempt to execute those random bytes as concurrent programs. Although many tasks terminate almost immediately due to illegal instruction exceptions, on occasion a single task or a confluence of multiple tasks can cause an operating system to fail. The effectiveness of the Crashme approach relies upon serendipity; in other words, if run long enough Crashme may eventually get lucky and find some way to crash the system.

Similarly, the Fuzz project at the University of Wisconsin has used random noise (or "fuzz") injection to discover robustness problems in operating systems. That work documented the source of several problems [Miller 1990], and then discovered that the problems were still present in operating systems several years later [Miller 1998]. The Fuzz approach tested specific OS elements and interfaces (as opposed to the completely random approach of Crashme), although it still relied on random data injection.

Other work in the fault-injection area has also tested limited aspects of robustness. The FIAT system [Barton 1990] uses probes placed by the programmer to alter the binary process image in memory during execution. The FERRARI system [Kanawati 1992] is similar in intent to FIAT, but uses software traps in a manner similar to debugger break points to permit emulation of specific system-level hardware faults (e.g., data address lines, condition codes). Xception [Carreira 1998] similarly performs software injection of faults to emulate transient hardware faults. The FTAPE system [Tsai 1995] injects faults into a system being exercised with a random workload generator by using a platform-specific device driver to inject the faults. MALFADA-RT [Rodriguez 2002] uses software to perform bit flips on memory values and run-time parameters. Although all of these systems have produced interesting results, none was intended to quantify robustness on the scale of an entire OS API.

While the hardware fault tolerance community has been investigating robustness mechanisms, the software engineering community has been working on ways to implement robust interfaces. As early as the 1970s, it was known that there are multiple ways to handle an exception [Hill 1971, Goodenough 1975]. The two methods that have become widely used are the signal-based model (also known as the termination model) and the error-return-code model (also known as the resumption model).

In an error-return-code model, function calls return an out-of-band value to indicate that an exceptional situation has occurred (for example, a NULL pointer might be returned upon failure to create a data structure in the C programming language). This approach is the supported mechanism for creating portable, robust systems in the POSIX API [IEEE 1993, lines 2368–2377].

On the other hand, in a signal-based model, the flow of control for a program does not address exceptional situations, but instead describes what will happen in the normal case. Exceptions cause signals to be "thrown" when they occur, and redirect the flow of control to separately written exception handlers. It has been argued that a signal-based approach is superior to an error-return-code approach based, in part, on performance concerns, and because of ease of programming [Gehani 1992, Cristian 1995]. Some APIs, such as CORBA, [OMG 1995] standardize this approach, whereas other APIs, such as POSIX, do not standardize it to a degree that is useful in creating robust systems.

11.2.1. Previous Ballista Publications

Work on Ballista has previously been reported in several publications. Koopman and coworkers [Koopman 1997] described portable, although not scalable, robustness testing applied to six POSIX functions and the idea of using data types for scalability. They also introduced the CRASH severity scale, discussed later. Kropp and coworkers [Kropp 1998] later demonstrated that the ideas proposed in the previous paper actually could be scaled up to test a full-size API in the form of POSIX operating systems. Koopman and coworkers [Koop 1998] described the overall Ballista approach being developed, emphasizing the approaches to scalability and ability to quantify robustness results. The paper by DeVale and coworkers [DeVale 1999] was the initial description of the Ballista test harness approach, involving a testing server connected via the Internet to a testing client. (Ballista later evolved into a stand-alone test platform.) Koopman and DeVale [Koopman 1999] then presented refined testing results for POSIX, including subtracting the effects of nonexceptional tests and "silent" test faults. This paper also found that even independently developed versions of operating systems and C libraries frequently contain identical robustness defects. A subsequent paper by Koopman and DeVale [Koopman 2000] was a more thorough treatment of POSIX operating system robustness results. Pan and coworkers [Pan 1999] studied early Ballista testing results and concluded that most robustness failures observed were the result of either a single parameter value or a tuple of related parameter values rather than the result of complex interactions among parameter values. Fernsler and Koopman [Fernsler 1999] reported robustness testing results of the HLA distributed simulation backplane. Shelton and Koopman [Shelton 2000] reported Ballista testing results on several versions of the Microsoft Windows operating system. Pan and coworkers [Pan 2001] reported results of testing and hardening CORBA ORB implementations. DeVale and Koopman [DeVale 2001] described the exception handling performance of the STDIO library in the POSIX operating system, and additionally examined the robustness and performance of the SFIO library, which was designed to provide a more robust interface. They later [DeVale 2002] described techniques to reduce run-time overhead of robustness checks to a few percent, even for quite fine-grained checking, and additionally described a case study in which it was shown that some programmers wrote code that diverged significantly from their expectations of robustness.

11.3. EVOLUTION OF BALLISTA

The Ballista approach to robustness testing was built upon many years of precursor work on fault injection and software testing. It evolved and was further refined by many contributors over a number of years. Its refinement was very much a product of evolution and learning, as are many other research efforts.

A note on terminology is in order. We use the historical terminology developed as Ballista evolved rather than attempting a mapping of the rather imprecise understanding we had at the time to more precise current terminology. Our understanding of the problem space evolved only after many years of work, as did the terminology used by researchers in this area.

11.3.1. Early Results

The seeds of Ballista were sown by a combination of fault injection into parameter values using sentries [Russinovich 1993], and a switch from run-time fault injection to designing test cases for APIs. The initial work using sentries injected faults into procedure calls on the fly, inverting bits in data values. The general assumption was that software would display robustness vulnerabilities only in complex situations, and those vulnerabilities would depend on system state as well as, perhaps, timing situations. This corresponded with the collective wisdom from researchers in industry and universities that mature, commercial software would only be vulnerable to complex, subtle problems. Nobody really expected single-line tests to be able to crash mature, stable systems, so looking for such vulnerabilities systematically was not a primary objective at first. Even so, researchers at Carnegie Mellon were finding system-killer problems in high-integrity avionics systems [Dingman 1995] (the Advanced Spaceborne Computer module in this case).

11.3.2. Scalability Via Generic Functions

The detection of a system-killer call in deployed high-integrity software gave rise to the question as to whether such vulnerabilities were common in other software. Finding out whether software robustness was a significant issue in deployed code bases required testing significant APIs. The problem in doing that was one of scalability. The approach used to that point was essentially a type of software testing, and software testing effort is generally proportional to the number and complexity of functions being tested. Thus, robustness testing of large, complex APIs was impractical unless some scalable approach could be found.

Mukherjee and Siewiorek [Mukherjee 1997] tried to attain scalability by creating generic templates based on operations commonly performed by functions (e.g., reference an object before it is created, delete an active object, allocate objects until resources are exhausted). The approach was successful in creating 252 tests for Unix file operations by exercising combinations of test values, but did not fundamentally solve the scaling problem because effort was still required to map each function being tested to a generic hierarchy.

11.3.3. The Start of Ballista

The Ballista project per se was started under a DARPA research contract in the fall of 1996. This project proposed setting up a testing server that would connect to clients anywhere on the Internet and direct robustness tests. Although Ballista was always intended to be a generic API robustness testing technique, the first experimental results were obtained for POSIX operating systems because of the ready availability of a large number of implementations available for comparison purposes throughout the Carnegie Mellon campus.

Initial work on Ballista involved hand-creating tests based on the code used in [Dingman 1995] to see which test values would be most effective in exposing robustness failures. Within a few months, the team had confirmed (as reported in [Mukherjee 1997]) that machine crashes were not the only robustness failures that might matter. There were some failures that caused task hangs, some tests that should have failed but did not (e.g., a request to allocate 3 GB of memory on a system with fewer than 32 MB, but the return values indicated that memory was allocated as requested), and many tests that resulted in a task abnormal termination. One incident in particular that pointed out the need for broadening the measurement of robustness was a microkernel function in the QNX operating system (send/receive) that abnormally terminated the calling task by generating a signal, even though the user manual for that function unambiguously stated that an error code (EFAULT) should be returned to avoid incurring a segment violation signal.

Although initial results suggested that robustness failures seemed to be possible in a variety of commercial-grade software implementations, scalability remained a problem. Scalability was finally obtained through a combination of two approaches: creating a scalable oracle, and automated, scalable test-case generation.

11.3.4. The CRASH Scale

Normally, testing is the execution of software with a particular workload and comparison of the results of execution with an "oracle" to determine if the test matches the expected outputs (a "pass") or differs from the expected outputs (a "fail"). Generating random inputs to a function to test it could always be done for scalability. Unfortunately, generating detailed results for what should happen when executing a function did not scale well. (This problem with random testing is well known and discussed, for example, in [Duran 1984] and [Thevenod-Fosse 1991].)

The solution to this dilemma was constraining the properties that the oracle predicted to narrowly reflect robustness properties, rather than attempting to represent functionality in a broader sense. In particular, the Ballista approach to testing used the following fixed properties for every function being tested:

1. **A test should never crash the system.** Violation of this property is a "catastrophic" failure. System-killer tests had to be manually detected, but in most cases they were infrequent and readily detected by the person administering the tests. (For example, HP-UX machines had a "heartbeat" LED. System crashes amounted to "cardiac arrest" when that LED went dead.) Not many system killers were found, but for most systems they were treated by vendors as a high-priority problem.

2. **A test should never hang.** This is a "restart" failure, requiring a restart of the task that failed so as to recover the system. Monitoring for restart failures was automated by using a time-out in the test harness, and killing tasks that took more than several seconds to execute (normally, each test executed within a few hundred milliseconds, depending on disk drive usage). Task hangs were uncommon except in VxWorks testing, where they were almost as common as task crashes.

3. **A test should never crash the testing task.** This is an "abort" failure. Monitoring for abort failures was automated by catching signals generated by tasks via the test harness. Task crashes were common in most systems tested.

4. **A test should report exceptional situations.** Lack of reporting an exception when one should be reported is a "silent" failure. Some systems accepted exceptional inputs with no indication of error—neither a signal nor an error code. Automating detection of silent failures would involve creating an oracle that could predict whether a test case was an exception or not, which is impractical, so this was not done in the run-time test harness. Multiversion comparison techniques did allow us to deduce how frequent this situation was for POSIX operating systems [Koopman99]. Estimated silent failure rates ranged from 6% to 19% across POSIX operating systems tested. (This is a concept distinct from an injected fault that is not activated; in the case of a silent failure, an exceptional value was acted upon and failure to report it is clearly erroneous.)

5. **A test should not report incorrect error codes.** This is a "hindering" failure. Manual analysis of small-scale tests indicated that even when error codes were generated, they were often incorrect or misleading in some operating systems, but usu-

ally correct in others [Koopman 1997]. However, as with Silent failures, no practical way has yet been found to automate the analysis of this type of failure.

The names of the above five failure categories form the acronym for the "CRASH" severity scale [Koopman 1997], although Ballista is only able to automatically detect the "C," "R," and "A" type failures without additional data analysis. However, those three types of failures alone provide valuable robustness measurement results, and make Ballista scalable via use of a simple, automated oracle function of "doesn't crash, doesn't hang."

There are two additional possible outcomes of executing a test case. It is possible that a test case returns an error code that is appropriate for invalid parameters forming the test case. This is a case in which the test case passes; in other words, generating an error code is the correct response. Additionally, in some tests the MuT legitimately returns no error code and successfully completes the requested operation. This happens when the parameters in the test case happen to be all valid, or when it is unreasonable to expect the OS to detect an exceptional situation (such as pointing to an address past the end of a buffer, but not so far past as to go beyond a virtual memory page or other protection boundary). For operating systems, approximately 12% of all executed test cases were nonexceptional tests [Koopman 1999].

It is important to note that the concepts of "silent" failures and "nonexceptional" tests differ significantly from the notion of a "nonsignificant test" (e.g., as discussed in [Arlat 1990]). Nonsignificant tests are a result of an injection of a fault that is not activated during test execution (for example, inverting a bit in a memory variable that is never read by a program, or corrupting an instruction that is never executed). In contrast, a silent failure is one in which the test program did in fact involve the corrupted or exceptional value in a computation but failed to detect that a problem occurred. A nonexceptional test is one in which a fault or exception was not actually injected at all, meaning the MuT's failure to detect that nonexistent error is correct operation.

11.3.5. Test Cases Based on Data Types

Beyond classifying results, it was important to have a scalable way to generate test cases. This was done by organizing tests by *data types* of parameters rather than the functionality of the MuT itself. Many APIs use far fewer types than functions (for example, POSIX requires only 20 data types as arguments for 233 functions and system calls). Thus, Ballista completely ignores the purpose of a function, and instead builds test cases exclusively from data type information. This is done by creating a set of test values for each data type that is likely to contain exceptional values for functions. For example, an integer data type would contain –1, 0, 1, the maximum permitted integer value and the minimum permitted integer value. Although some of these values are likely to be nonexceptional for many MuTs, it was also likely that some of these values would be exceptional.

Given a dictionary of "interesting" test values for each data type, tests are composed by using all combinations of test values across all the parameters of the function (shown in Figure 11.1). Ballista thus ends up using an idea similar to category-partition testing [Ostrand 1988].

Although Ballista evolved into a general-purpose API robustness testing tool, the initial application of Ballista was for a set of 233 POSIX functions and calls defined in the IEEE 1003.1b standard [IEEE 1993] ("POSIX.1b" or "POSIX with real-time extensions with C language binding"). All standard calls and functions supported by each OS implementation were tested except for calls that take no arguments, such as getpid(); calls that do not return, such as exit(); and calls that intentionally send signals, such as kill().

For each POSIX function tested, an interface description was created with the function name and type information for each argument. In some cases, a more specific type was created to result in better testing (for example, a file descriptor might be of type int, but was described to Ballista as a more specific file descriptor data type).

As an example, Figure 11.1 shows test values used to test write(int filedes, const void *buffer, size_t nbytes), which takes parameters specifying a file descriptor, a memory buffer, and a number of bytes to be written. Because write() takes three parameters of three different data types, Ballista draws test values from separate test objects established for each of the three data types. In Figure 11.1, the arrows indicate that the particular test case being constructed will test a file descriptor for a file that has been opened with only read access, a NULL pointer to the buffer, and a size of 16 bytes. Other combinations of test values are assembled to create other test cases. In the usual case, all combinations of test values are generated to create a combinatorial number of test cases. For a half-dozen POSIX calls, the number of parameters is large enough to yield too many test cases for exhaustive coverage within a reasonable execution time. In these cases, pseudorandom sampling is used. (Based on a comparison to a run with exhaustive searching on one OS, sampling 5000 test cases gives results accurate to within 1 percentage point for each function [Kropp 1998].)

11.3.6. Test Case Construction: Parameter Constructors and Destructors

Even with a dictionary of test values, there were still difficulties in sequencing the operations associated with some tests. For example, tests requiring access to files might rely

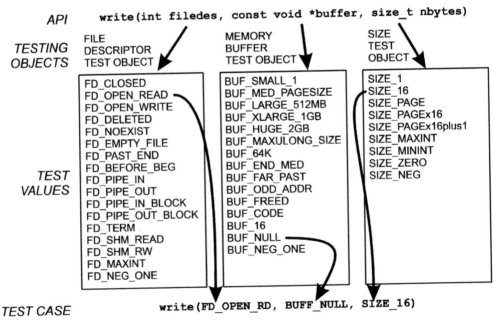

Figure 11.1. Ballista test case generation for the write() function. The arrows show a single test case being generated from three particular test values; in general, all combinations of test values are tried in the course of testing.

upon a set of files with various properties precreated by the test harness. However, such an approach was inefficient because, typically, only one or two files out of the pool were needed for any particular test. Moreover, sometimes multiple copies of a particular preinitialized data structure or file were needed to execute a test when a MuT's parameter list contained more than one instance of a particular data type. An additional issue was ensuring that any data structures or files that were created for a test were properly cleaned up, to avoid unintentionally running out of memory or filling up a disk as tests were executed. This was solved by associating constructors and destructors with test values.

Each test value (such as FD_OPEN_READ in Figure 11.1) is associated with a triplet of test object code fragments that are kept in a simple database in the form of a specially formatted text file, comprising a test object associated with each test value. The first fragment for each test object, the *create* fragment, is a constructor that is called before the test case is executed (it is not literally a C++ constructor but, rather, a code fragment identified to the test harness as constructing the instance of a test value). The create code may simply return a value (such as a NULL), but may also do something more complicated that initializes system state. For example, the create code for FD_OPEN_READ creates a file, puts a predetermined set of bytes into the file, opens the file for reading, then returns a file descriptor for that file.

Create code fragments are not permitted to release resources. As an example, a create code fragment to set up system state for a "file created, closed, and then deleted" test value would create a file, but not delete it. This prevents situations in which successive invocations of create code fragments reclaim and reuse resources. Consider an example situation in which a first file handle points to a closed, deleted file, while a second file handle points to a file open for reading. If the first file handle is released by closing the file while setting up the first test object, it is possible that the second test object will reuse system resources for the first file handle when preparing the second file handle. The result could be the first file handle referring to a file open for reading (i.e., pointing to the same file state as the second file handle). To avoid unintentional sharing via recycling of resources, no system resources are released until after all system resources required have been obtained.

The second fragment in each test object performs a commit function. This modifies the system state to release resources before a test case is executed. All create code fragments are executed for a test case before any commit code fragments are executed. This avoids unintended sharing of reclaimed resources within a single test case. Examples in which this commit code are required include releasing allocated memory, closing file handles, deleting files, and releasing federation members in a distributed system.

The third code fragment for each test value is a destructor that deletes any data structures or files created by the corresponding constructor (for example, the destructor for FD_OPEN_READ closes and deletes the file created by its matching constructor). Tests are executed from within a test harness by having a parent task fork a fresh child process for every test case. The child process first executes create code fragments for all test values used in a selected test case, then executes all commit code fragments, then executes a call to the MuT with those test values, then calls destructors for all the test values used. Special care is taken to ensure that any robustness failure is a result of the MuT, and not attributable to the constructors or destructors themselves. Functions implemented as macros are tested using the same technique, and require no special treatment.

The test values used in the experiments were a combination of values suggested in the testing literature (e.g., [Marick 1995]), values that found problems in precursor research, and values selected based on personal experience. For example, consider file descriptor test values. File descriptor test values include descriptors to existing files, negative one, the maximum integer number (MAXINT), and zero. Situations that are likely to be exceptional in only some contexts are tested, including file open only for read and file open only for write. File descriptors are also tested for inherently exceptional situations such as file created and opened for read, but then deleted from the file system without the program's knowledge.

The guideline for test value selection for all data types were to include, as appropriate: zero, negative one, maximum/minimum representable values, null pointers, pointers to nonexistent memory, lengths near virtual memory page size, pointers to heap-allocated memory, files open for combinations of read/write with and without exceptional permission settings, and files/data structures that had been released before the test itself was executed. While creating generically applicable rules for thorough test value selection remains an open subject, this experience-driven approach was sufficient to produce useful results and uncover common robustness vulnerabilities across many different systems.

It is important that both valid as well as invalid parameters be used for each parameter of a MuT. This is partly to help in identifying which bad parameter is actually responsible for a robustness failure. If a particular MuT has a large number of failures, those failures often are insensitive to the value of most parameters. The easiest way to pin down which parameters really matter is to find individual test cases in which all parameters but one or two are valid. A more subtle reason for including valid parameters is that many MuTs have partial robustness checking. For example, a module that takes two pointers as inputs might check the first pointer for validity but not the second pointer. If the first pointer is invalid for all tests, then the module will catch that and mask the fact that the MuT is vulnerable to invalid second parameter values. To more fully test this MuT, at least some test cases must include a valid first pointer (the one that the MuT checks) and an invalid second pointer (the one that the MuT does not check).

An important benefit derived from the Ballista testing implementation is the ability to automatically generate the source code for any single test case the suite is capable of running. In many cases that are only a dozen lines or fewer of executable code in size, these short programs contain the constructors (create code fragments and commit code fragments) for each parameter, the actual function call, and destructors. These single-test-case programs have been used to reproduce robustness failures in isolation for use by OS developers and to verify test result data.

11.3.7. Repeatability

One concern with early Ballista results was the repeatability of individual tests. For example, an early implementation included pseudorandom values for some data types, including pointers. To alleviate concerns that random pointers were valid but incorrect (e.g., pointing to inappropriate locations in the heap or stack, which could be difficult to check for correctness at run time in any software system), those tests were eliminated in favor of deterministic test values. The general characteristics of the test results were unchanged by the elimination of pseudorandom variables.

An additional issue arose because Ballista ran tests in large batches rather than one at a time for reasons of efficiency. It was possible that problems created by one test might carry over to another test, meaning that it was possible that problems being seen were not the result of a test being run but, rather, the result of activating a fault created dozens or even thousands of tests earlier. This concern was initially addressed by adding a capability to the Ballista test harness of generating a stand-alone single-test program for any desired test. An experiment involving generating and executing every single stand-alone test compared to batch testing for Digital Unix revealed that almost all cases (well above

99%) created programs that correctly reproduced robustness problems seen in large test runs. (What happened in the few other cases is unclear, but the difference was attributed to the fact that the large test harness had a much different execution environment than the small single-test programs.) The main benefit of this approach was the availability of automatically generated bug-report programs to help vendors identify and correct robustness defects. The biggest problem was that it was very time-consuming to generate, compile, and execute more than 100,000 individual test programs to confirm results. And even if individual test programs were executed, it still might be the case that there was residual system damage from one stand-alone test to the next that caused carryover of problems. This batch approach worked well for systems with hardware memory protection, but repeatability was an issue revisited for each set of tests conducted.

A better approach for ensuring repeatability than executing tests one at a time was found in the form of reordering tests. Two complete sets of tests can be executed on an identical platform, but in reverse testing order. If the result of each and every test matches from run to run regardless of order, then it is unlikely that the results are being affected by carryover from one test to the next identically in both forward and reverse order. The results of reordering tests (as well as one experiment in which tests were conducted in randomized order) indicated that carryover effects were exceedingly rare for all operating systems except VxWorks (discussed later). Indeed, test reordering first detected that VxWorks had significant carryover problems that were an issue for both batch tests and tests executed one at a time.

The only other significant order-dependent problem that was noted was for Digital Unix 3.2 when running an external swap partition, which caused a system crash when three test cases in a row executed mq_receive() with very large buffer sizes.

11.3.8. Concurrency

It came as a surprise that the vast majority of OS robustness vulnerabilities, including system killers, could be reproduced via simple test programs involving a single function call. The community's consensus at the time was that the only system killers to be found in mature commercial operating systems would be caused by concurrency, timing problems, or "wearout" problems. To see if Ballista was missing even more problems, some experiments were performed trying to extend Ballista to explore concurrency issues.

One attempt to explore concurrent testing was performed as a graduate course project [Pientka 1999]. The approach was to launch multiple concurrent copies of Ballista tests on Red Hat Linux 5.2 (kernel 2.0.36). Some resource depletion problems were found when executing repeated calls to memory management functions, but the only true concurrency-based problem found was when some threads executing munmap with exceptional values got stuck in the kernel and could not be terminated without rebooting the system. The problem was traced to a nonreentrant exception handler. Once the failure mode was understood, the effect was highly reproducible by launching multiple parallel copies of exceptional calls to that function.

Other follow-on research had some initial success by systematically attempting to deplete resources such as memory. It is clear that vulnerabilities to such system stresses exist, but unmodified methods used by Ballista have not been very effective in revealing them. The more important result from Ballista, however, is that there appear to be substantive problems that are *not* a result of timing or concurrency problems, even though system designers and researchers alike initially thought such problems were unlikely to exist.

11.3.9. Dimensionality

Related to the notion that robustness problems would be found only in complex timing situations was the notion that problems would also involve subtle interactions of parameter values. This lead to exploring the response regions of faults [Koopman 1997] to determine what patterns of test values appeared in robustness failures. The expectation was that robustness problems would emerge only when test cases had particular values for each parameter (such as, for example, a file that happens to be open for reading, *and* a null pointer used as a buffer, *and* a string count greater than 64KB, *and* all zero data values, or some similar complex situation).

Instead, in the vast majority of cases, only one or two data values in a single system call were necessary to cause an abort failure. This lead us to analyze the *dimensionality* of faults in terms of number of parameters that affected whether a particular test result was robust or nonrobust [Pan 1999]. The result was that the vast majority of robustness failures were due to one or two parameter values. Moreover, the common two-parameter sensitivities were based on related values, such as a buffer pointer and associated buffer length.

The result that only single calls of low dimensionality (a single or two related exceptional parameter values) rather than high dimensionality (multiple unrelated parameters having a specific set of coincident values) could expose significant robustness defects was counter to initial expectations and feedback from others in the field, but the general rule for the results of almost all Ballista work is that robustness defects tend to have low dimensionality and are in general the result of fairly simple problems such as omitting a check for null pointer values.

11.3.10. Fine-Grain Data Structures

One of the aspects of the initial Ballista approach that had to be improved over time was the way in which parameter tests were created. Some parameter values were relatively simple, such as integers, whereas some were much more complex, such as files. The initial Ballista implementation picked selected values of complex data structures such as files (e.g., a file to which the test program has both read and write access permissions is buffered and is currently opened for reading). The combinations inherent in such complex data structures were a small impediment to scalability but were still viable.

As APIs beyond operating systems were tested, it became clear that more sophisticated notions of complex data structures were needed to deal with data structures defined by those other APIs. As an example, the SFIO library [Korn 1991] defines a file parameter that has a file state, a buffer type, and a flag value. To handle this case, Ballista was expanded to include a concept of tupled test values. Tupled test values are independently selected for testing by the test harness but combine to create a single parameter value passed to the MuT.

An example is different aspects of a file state being combined to create a single file handle value for testing purposes (Figure 11.2). Testing Sfseek requires test values for two data types: Sfio_t* and integer. The integer parameter is the position within the file for the seek operation and is tested with various integer test values used for all Ballista integer tests. In Figure 11.2, it so happens that the integer value of ZERO is selected for a particular test case but, in general, any of the IntValues might be selected for a test case. The first parameter is a complex test data type that includes values for file state (open, closed, etc.), buffer type (mapped, buffered, or nonbuffered), and various combinations of flag values. One test value from each of the subtypes (File State, Buffer Type, and Flags)

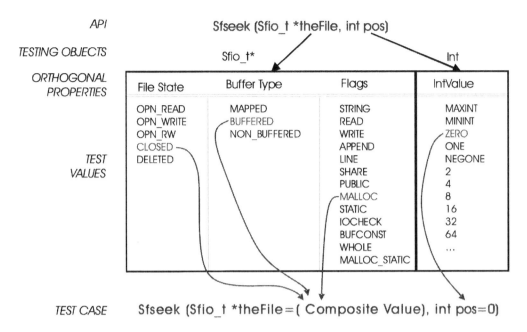

Figure 11.2. Example of fine-grain tupled test values for an SFIO function test.

is selected for a particular test case to form a composite test value. In Figure 11.2, the selection happens to be CLOSED, BUFFERED, and MALLOC. It would have also been possible to further make Flags a composite test type, but the developers of the tests thought that there were few enough interesting Flag test values that simply enumerating them all was manageable.

11.3.11. Initialization of System State

An additional challenge that became apparent as successive API implementations were tested was creating a simple approach to initialize the state behind the API interface. As a simple example, the POSIX random number generator rand(void) returns a random number based on a seed set with the call srand(unsigned seed). Attempting to test rand for robustness is only really meaningful if it is paired with a call to srand to set an exceptional seed value.

The initial solution to system state initialization was to have a per-function initialization code (for example, call srand before testing the rand function). Although this worked for POSIX and a few other APIs, it was in general an unsatisfactory solution because it required an additional mechanism beyond the central parameter-based approach of the rest of Ballista.

Eventually, a cleaner way of initializing system state was discovered by permitting some parameters specified in a Ballista test to be declared as *phantom* parameters. Phantom parameters are processed as regular parameters for Ballista test harness purposes, having their constructor and destructor code called in normal sequence. However, phantom parameters are omitted from the parameter list of the MuT. So, for example, the Ballista test signature for a random-number generator might be rand (+phantom_seed), where

"+" means that the parameter is a phantom parameter, and is thus omitted when calling rand() for test. However, the test values associated with phantom_seed are still executed, and in particular the constructor for phantom_seed can call srand to set an appropriate exceptional value for testing to be used by rand.

The need for system state initialization increased as the amount of inherent state in APIs being tested increased. CORBA, the HLA simulation backplane, and especially the industrial process automation software made extensive use of system state initialization, with five different general initialization states sufficing for all HLA tests executed. That experience lead to the idea of using phantom parameters as a generic state initialization technique. (The HLA testing itself [Fernsler 1999] did not use phantom parameters in this manner; that idea came from the HLA work, but only near the end of that work, as a retrospective lesson about how it could have been done better.)

11.3.12. Quantifying the Results

Because Ballista testing often produces as many as 100,000 individual test results for an API implementation, a summary metric for the robustness of an API is essential. Based on experience testing several APIs, and a number of intermediate techniques, two elements emerged as useful robustness metrics:

1. Number of functions tested that had a least one catastrophic result. Attempting to report the number of catastrophic results encountered is difficult because of the manual intervention needed to restore operation after a system crash. Additionally, many crashes could be due to a single exceptional value problem that appears in multiple tests. Since system crashes affect few functions in most APIs, a simple report of the number of functions that have crashed (regardless of how many times they crash) suffices.

2. The normalized mean abort failure rate across functions. The percent of abort failures is equally weighted across all functions tested, then averaged to give a general representation of the API. Although in practice some functions are used more than others [Musa96], workloads make such different use of each API that no single weighting would give an accurate picture. (We recognize that each percentage is in fact a ratio involving test failures compared to tests conducted, and that taking an arithmetic mean across such ratios is problematic in a pure mathematical sense. However, in terms of benchmarking, the approach is that each individual function's failure ratio is a robustness "score." Averaging scores across tested functions gives an average score that, in our experience, corresponds quite closely with our informal observations about the overall robustness of tested systems. Until a useful methodology is found to map these scores onto the frequency of function executions in application programs, there does not seem to be much point digging deeper into mathematical analysis of the ratios.)

Restart failures are usually so rare (except for VxWorks) that they do not really affect results and can either be combined with abort failure rates as an aggregate failure rate or simply omitted.

As a practical matter, most APIs also have a few functions that have much higher than average abort failure rates. It is useful to report which functions those are so they can either be repaired by vendors or avoided (to the degree possible) by application programs. To permit identification of functions with very high abort failure rates and enable application-specific weighting of failure rates, Ballista testing records the failure rate of each call in the API. More sophisticated methods of quantifying robustness testing results are evolving over time (e.g., [Duraes 2002]), but the above robustness metrics sufficed for the customers of the Ballista project.

11.3.13. System Killer Vulnerabilities

Some of the Ballista robustness-testing results, particularly those that deal with tasks abnormally terminating via throwing a signal, are controversial, as discussed in subsequent sections. However, the one set of results that is generally accepted as important is when Ballista finds "system killer" robustness vulnerabilities. A *system killer* is a single robustness test case that causes a complete system crash or hang, necessitating a system reset to recover. Depending on the operating system being used, a system crash might manifest as a "kernel panic" for Unix systems, a "blue screen of death" for Windows systems, or simply a system so locked up that only a hardware reset or power-cycle operation will recover the system.

System killer defects are surprisingly tedious to isolate, because test logs tend to be lost or corrupted by such crashes despite concerted efforts to flush writes to file systems and otherwise capture system state just before the test that caused a crash. Nonetheless, a tedious search through sets of tests usually revealed an exact, single system call that caused a crash. Perhaps surprisingly, crashes can often be caused by very simple user programs such as these examples:

- Irix 6.2: munmap(malloc((1<<30)+1), ((1<<31)-1)))
- Digital UNIX (OSF 1) 4.0D: mprotect(malloc((1 << 29)+1), 65537, 0)
- Windows 98: GetThreadContext(GetCurrentThread(), NULL)
- Windows 98: MsgWaitForMultipleObjects(INT_MAX, (LPHANDLE)((void*) -1), 0, 129, 64)

Table 11.1 summarizes the systems tested within the Ballista project, including how many distinct functions had system killer vulnerabilities and an overall normalized abort robustness failure rate (discussed later). In some cases, precise data is not available, so the best available data is presented.

It is recognized that software versions tested significantly predate the writing of this chapter. During the course of our research, system developers uniformly said that a more recent version of software (which was not available to the Ballista team at the time of testing) would be dramatically better. But the new version usually looked pretty much like the old version, and sometimes was worse unless the developers incorporated Ballista-style testing results into their own testing process or specifically fixed system killers previously identified for correction. Since the point of this chapter is to relate lessons learned from Ballista, there has been no attempt to perform the extensive work required to remeasure systems.

11.4. LESSONS LEARNED

Some of the technical lessons learned in developing Ballista have already been discussed. But beyond the lessons learned in engineering the Ballista test tools are the technical and nontechnical lessons revealed by the results of the tests.

TABLE 11.1. System killer vulnerabilities found by Ballista testing

API and implementation	Functions tested	System killer functions	System killer function names	Normalized robustness failure rate, %
AIX 4.1	186	0	n/a	10.0%
FreeBSD 2.2.5	175	0	n/a	20.3
HPUX 9.05	186	0	n/a	11.4
HPUX 10.20	185	1	mmap	13.1
Irix 5.3	189	0	n/a	14.5
Irix 6.2	225	1	munmap	12.6
Linux 2.0.18	190	0	n/a	12.5
Red Hat Linux 2.2.5	183	0	n/a	21.9
LynxOS 2.4.0	222	1	setpgid	11.9
NetBSD 1.3	182	0	n/a	16.4
OSF-1 3.2	232	1	mqreceive	15.6
OSF-1 4.0B	233	0	mprotect (4.0D only, not 4.0B)	15.1
QNX 4.22	203	2	munmap, mprotect	21.0
QNX 4.24	206	0	n/a	22.7
SunOS 4.13	189	0	n/a	15.8
SunOS 5.5	233	0	n/a	14.6
Windows NT SP 5	237	0	n/a	23.9
Window 2000 Pro Beta Build 2031	237	0	n/a	23.3
Windows XP RC 1	235	0	n/a	23.1
Windows 95 rev B	227	8	DuplicateHandle, FileTimeToSystemTime, GetFileInformationByHandle, GetThreadContext, HeapCreate, MsgWaitForMultipleObjectsEx, ReadProcessMemory, fwrite	17.2
Windows 98 SP 1	237	7	DuplicateHandle, GetFileInformationByHandle, GetThreadContext, MsgWaitForMultipleObjects, MsgWaitForMultipleObjectsEx, fwrite, strncpy	17.8
Windows 98 SE SP 1	237	7	CreateThread, DuplicateHandle, GetFileInformationByHandle, GetThreadContext, MsgWaitForMultipleObjects, MsgWaitForMultipleObjectsEx, strncpy	17.8
Windows CE 2.11	179	28	See [Shelton00]	13.7
Sun JVM 1.3.1-04 (Red Hat Linux 2.4.18-3)	226	0	n/a	4.7
Timesys J2ME Foundation 1.0 (Linux 2.4.7; Timesys GPL 3.1.214)	226	Unknown (JVM crashes)	"Process received signal 11, suspending" message causing JVM crashes.	Approx. 5%

TABLE 11.1. *Continued*

API and implementation	Functions tested	System killer functions	System killer function names	Normalized robustness failure rate, %
VxWorks (without memory protection)	75	2	bzero; gmtime_r	13.0
RTI-HLA 1.3.5 (Digital Unix 4.0)	86	0	(found a server crash in a pre-1.3.5 version)	10.2
RTI-HLA 1.3.5 (Sun OS 5.6)	86	0	n/a	10.0
SFIO	36	0	n/a	5.6
Industrial Process Automation Object Manager (COM/DCOM)	52	0	n/a	5 methods had abort failures

11.4.1. Mature Commercial Software Has Robustness Vulnerabilities

A key result of the Ballista robustness testing project is that even mature commercial software such as operating systems can and often does have catastrophic responses to even very simple exceptional parameter values sent to an API. Moreover, it is common to have a significant fraction of robustness tests generate abort failures, although abort failure robustness varies significantly depending on the API and implementation.

The version of an implementation of an API has little effect on the overall abort failure robustness level. It is just as common for abort failures to increase as decrease in a later version of a piece of software. It is also just as common for system killers to appear and disappear between software versions, even with seemingly minor changes. For example, the system killer reported in Table 11.1 for OSF-1 4.0D was not present in OSF-1 4.0B.

Other evidence suggests that system killer robustness defects can come and go depending on small changes to software, lurking until a chance set of circumstances in a system build exposes them to being activated by the API. The most striking example was a vulnerability to system crashes in Windows 95 via the system call FileTimeToSystemTime. While Microsoft fixed all the system crashes the Ballista team reported for Windows 98, they did not search for the cause of the FileTimeToSystemTime problem in Windows 95, because it did not cause a crash in Windows 98. Unfortunately, in a beta version for Windows ME, that same system killer had reappeared, causing system crashes. From this experience and other observations discussed in the next section, it seems important to track down and fix any system killers revealed via robustness testing, regardless of whether they go into remission in any particular release. One can reasonably expect that a system killer that mysteriously goes away on its own will reappear in some future release if not specifically corrected.

Most APIs studied have a few functions with highly elevated abort failure rates. In other words, usually it is only a handful of functions that are severely nonrobust. For example, in the Timesys Linux-RT GPL + RT-Java testing, three methods out of 266 methods tested had elevated robustness failure rates. String(), convValueOf(), and append() all had had robustness failure rates above 70%, whereas all other methods tested had robustness failure rates below 25%. Moreover, the three methods with elevated failure rates were the most interesting to the spacecraft system designers requesting the tests, because they were the only methods having failures due to problems other than missing null pointer checks.

11.4.2. Robustness Soft Spots Sometimes Contain System Killers

Based on several anecdotal observations, there appears to be some truth to the notion that modules with high rates of abort robustness failures can harbor system killer defects. In general, functions that had system killers tended to have high abort failure rates, but exact data is not available because machines suffering catastrophic failures usually corrupt test data during the crash. The following incidents, while somewhat circumstantial, support this notion.

The difference between abort failure rates in QNX 4.22 and QNX 4.24 is in large part due to a near-100% abort failure rate for the functions munmap and mprotect in version 4.24. These are the two functions that had system killer defects in version 4.22. Although the system killers were eliminated in version 4.24 (after the Ballista team had reported them to QNX), it is clear that they came from functions that were overall nonrobust.

HPUX 10.20 had a higher abort failure rate than HPUX 9.05 and, in particular, the abort failure rate for memory management functions went from 0% to essentially 100%. A discussion with the system designers revealed that the memory management functions had been rewritten for HPUX version 10. It so happened that the one system killer found in that operating system was mmap, one of the functions with a high abort failure rate.

It is not always the case that system killers lurk in areas of high abort failure rates (for example, the munmap system killer in Irix 6.2 was in a set of functions with near-0% abort failure rates). Nonetheless, looking for system killers in otherwise nonrobust software seems like a productive strategy.

11.4.3. Dynamic Tension between Fault Masking and Fault Detection

During discussions with various developers, it became clear that there were two opposing perspectives on the notion of whether signals and other exceptions that normally cause task termination were acceptable responses to exceptional conditions. The division hinged upon whether or not the primary goal was fault-detection or fault tolerant operation.

Organizations that primarily exist for the purpose of software development tended to say that generating unrecoverable exceptions was desirable. In that way, developers cannot miss a defect, and have incentive to fix it so as to avoid embarrassing code crashes. Some developers went so far as to say that abort failures were the right thing to do in all cases, and asserted that their code intentionally threw signals in any situation in which an exceptional parameter value was encountered. (This claim was not borne out by Ballista test results.) They also claimed that code with low abort failure rates probably had high silent failure rates. (This claim was true in a sense, but FreeBSD 2.2.5, which was said to be designed to intentionally generate abort failures, had even more silent failure rates than AIX 4.1, which had the lowest abort failure rate of POSIX systems tested.)

Organizations that primarily survive by supporting fielded equipment tended to say that generating unrecoverable exceptions was never desirable. In fact, one had gone to some lengths to intentionally generate silent failures in preference to abort failures for some legacy applications. The developers stated that this was to ensure no field failures of software, which would result in a situation in which customers were unequipped to diagnose, repair, recompile, and reinstall software that crashed. (However, they still had significant abort failure rates in their code.)

The results of these observations are twofold. First, there is truth to both sides of the division as to whether abort failures are good or bad. Developers want to know that something is wrong in their code. Maintainers do not want software crashing in the field. A challenge is to somehow help both sets of stakeholders in real systems. Second, most software has both abort and silent robustness failures, even in cases in which developers stated that they intended to eliminate one of those categories of exception responses.

11.4.4. Programmers Do Not Necessarily Understand the Trade-offs They Are Making

During the course of the Ballista project, developers repeatedly stated that making software robust would cause it to be too inefficient to be practicable. However, it appears that this perception may be incorrect. For one thing, it seems that at least some developers overstate the true execution cost of increasing robustness. [DeVale 2001a] reports an experiment in manually hardening the math libraries of FreeBSD 3.0. In that experiment, hardening the code against all robustness failures identified by Ballista reduced abort failure rates from 12.5% to zero. Attaining this robustness improvement cost only a 1% slowdown compared to the unmodified library code, but developers had already incurred a 13% speed penalty to reduce abort failure rates from 15.3% (with all checks manually removed) to 12.5% (for released code). Thus the developers were paying almost all the necessary speed penalty without actually gaining much robustness in return compared to what they could have had.

In addition to overstating performance penalties for improving robustness, developers who intended to implement all-abort or all-silent robustness responses did not succeed at doing so. This gave rise to the question as to whether developers in general are making well-informed and effectively executed engineering decisions when they design an intended level of robustness into their software.

A case study tested the hypothesis that developers put the intended level of robustness into their software, reported in [DeVale 2001a]. That study examined three sets of industry code modules from a large corporation and found that none of the developers achieved exactly the robustness they set out to. One of the three development teams came very close, but the other two teams had many more abort failures in their Java code than they expected.

An additional data point on this topic was obtained by testing the robustness of the SFIO (Safe, Fast I/O) library. An interview with the developers, who are very experienced industry professionals, established that they believed they had incorporated all the robustness that was practical into SFIO, and that any remaining nonrobust behaviors would either be impractical to resolve (e.g., situations too complex to reasonably test for) or would take an unacceptable run-time overhead to resolve. DeVale and Koopman [DeVale01] report the results of selecting eight functions from the SFIO library for hand improvement of robustness. Abort failure rates for those eight functions were reduced from 2.86% to 0.44%–0.78% (depending on the underlying operating system), with an average speed penalty of only 2%.

The lesson learned from these experiences is that even highly experienced industry practitioners probably cannot implement the level of robustness they intend to without gaps in the absence of a robustness measurement tool such as Ballista. Moreover, intuition as to the likely speed penalty of robustness checking is often incorrect. A measurement tool helps provide feedback as to whether a desired level of robustness quality has been reached. Beyond that, actual speed measurement is required to determine whether checking for exceptional parameters incurs too much overhead, and in every case we have seen, it doesn't.

11.4.5. Programmers Often Make the Same Robustness Mistakes

Some approaches to software fault tolerance rely on the use of diverse sets of software to help provide independent software failures (e.g., [Avizienis 1985]). The topic of how diversity can be measured and ensured is a difficult one and has been discussed in many previous publications (e.g., [Eckhardt 1991] and [Avizienis 1988]). Contemporaneous with Ballista work, Littlewood and Strigini [Littlewood 2000] introduced the concept of "robustness diversity" to describe the concept of two different implementations of a function producing different responses when subject to exceptional values. The ability to measure the robustness of many different implementations of the same operating operating system API with Ballista provided an excellent chance to gather information about robustness diversity on commercially available software.

Koopman and DeVale [Koopman 1999] examined the question of whether independently developed software was likely to have similar robustness vulnerabilities, especially to abort failures. The result was that 3.8% of robustness failures occurred in all thirteen POSIX operating systems examined. The two most diverse (from this point of view) operating systems (AIX and FreeBSD) had 9.7% of the same system call robustness failures and 25.4% overall common-mode robustness failures for the entire POSIX API, including C library calls. Based on this, it is clear that independently developed software cannot, without further qualification, be considered perfectly diverse with respect to robustness vulnerabilities. (Whether or not this lack of perfect diversity matters in practice, of course, depends on the intended application.)

An additional data point is that Windows CE had many of the same system killer vulnerabilities as Windows 95 and Windows 98, despite the fact that they were said to be developed by different teams within Microsoft and have different code bases.

The evidence to date indicates that one must assume that independent programmers will leave similar robustness vulnerabilities in their code unless some specific and effective countermeasure is in place to prevent it.

11.4.6. Memory Protection Really Works

As has been mentioned in previous sections, Ballista testing of the VxWorks operating system produced some anomalous behaviors. The version of VxWorks tested did not have memory protection. (Historically, VxWorks was designed for resource-constrained systems and did not include memory protection as a supported feature, although newer versions of VxWorks are said to do so.) Testing results included 9944 tests on 37 functions and caused 2920 abort and restart failures (in approximately equal proportions). The results included 360 system crashes. (An additional 38 functions were tested by an industry partner, with similar results.)

VxWorks testing was made very difficult by the fact that test results were highly sensitive to the order in which they were run. Changing the order of test execution significantly changed which tests suffered abort and restart failures, indicating a high carryover of faults from one test to another. Given a lack of memory protection, this was not really a surprise. The carryover was so pervasive that the only way repeatable results could be obtained was to install an automated reset box that completely reset the test hardware between each and every single Ballista test run. The fact that other systems had minimal carryover suggests that the memory protection in place in other systems is a valuable fault containment mechanism.

The startling (to us, at the time) result was not that there was carryover with VxWorks but, rather, that complete crashes were so rare in the tests run. Eliciting and isolating tests that caused clean system crashes was quite difficult. Most often, the system would degrade in some way and keep working to some degree for an extended period of time after tests rather than failing quickly. Failing "fast" was a rare outcome. This suggests that a lack of memory protection reduces the validity of "fail-fast" assumptions in the absence of any specifically designed fail-fast enforcement mechanism.

11.4.7. Ballista Scaled Well, Within Some Practical Limits

In the end, the parameter-based testing approach used with Ballista scaled well across several APIs of varying characteristics. The use of fine-grain data types and phantom parameters solidified a single mechanism (a parameter list with data-type-based test values) for addressing a wide variety of situations. The main limitations to Ballista testing are scalability with respect to internal system state behind the API and difficulty in exercising "software aging" phenomena.

Ballista-style testing scales best with APIs having little state, such as operating system calls and programming libraries. It scales less well as the system requires more state behind the API. CORBA client testing and HLA RTI simulation backplane testing worked moderately well, because the number of different types of system start-up operations necessary to perform testing were much smaller than the number of functions to be tested, and could readily be represented as phantom parameters that performed operations such as initializing the system, forming a federation (an HLA operation [DoD 1998]), and so on. However, testing the industrial process control automation object manager became difficult because of the significant amount of work needed to set up a clean copy of a database before every test. In general, Ballista-style testing is not suitable for APIs that access a database.

A second significant limitation to Ballista-style testing is that it is not designed to stress system vulnerabilities related to concurrency or resource leaks (especially "software aging" phenomena). Some concurrency problems can be searched for in a straight-forward manner by looking for nonreentrant exception handlers. And some aging problems can be revealed simply by running Ballista test sequences many times over. But, it remains unclear how to effectively test for other such problems. Such problems do exist, but Ballista is not really designed to find them.

A third limitation to Ballista testing is nontechnical. Some people believe that the abort failures it finds are important, especially as an indicator of general system robustness, and some people do not. This remains partly an issue of culture (see also Section 11.4.3), and partly an issue of whether anyone can demonstrate with certainty that code suffering high levels of Abort failures really is prone to catastrophic failures as well. Fortunately, most people believe that finding system killers is useful, and Ballista is effective enough at finding them to be worth using on many systems, regardless of opinion on the importance of abort failures.

11.4.8. Parameter Checking Need Not Be Slow

A commonly cited technical impediment to improving system robustness is the execution cost of performing parameter-value checks to permit so-called wrappers to detect and reject calls having exceptional values (for example, using the techniques in Xept [Vo 1997]). As has already been discussed, usually parameter checking is fast enough to not be a problem (see Section 11.4.4), but one can do even better.

More advanced CPU hardware could tend to further reduce the cost of performing exceptional parameter-value checking. If compiler hints help the CPU speculate that values are nonexceptional, then the critical path of the computation can proceed, and checking can take place as hardware resources permit before the critical path instruction results are retired. This has the potential to effectively eliminate parameter-value checking execution costs on superscalar, speculative, out-of-order execution hardware.

DeVale and Koopman [DeVale 2002] addressed this problem further by developing a novel scheme to cache checks and reuse them to reduce the overhead of performing parameter checks. The insight is that many parameter values are used multiple times (e.g., a file handle for character I/O operations). Rather than check the validity of such a parameter every time an API function is called, the API can remember that it has checked the value once, and simply reuse the results of that check, stored in a software cache, until the value is altered. Using this technique reduced parameter checking overhead to less than 5%, even for the worst case of very short functions being called, and to 2% for most other cases studied.

11.5. CONCLUSIONS

In the past decade, robustness testing and related areas have grown into a thriving area within the dependability research community. Researchers involved in extending, adapting, augmenting, and creating alternative ideas to Ballista-style testing are too numerous to mention individually.

Two collaborative efforts are, however, worth specific mention. The first is the Special Interest Group on Dependability Benchmarking, which is the sponsoring organization of this book. The second is the DBench Consortium [DBench 2004], which performed a thorough exploration of the subject of dependability benchmarking in Europe, looking at it as a combination of many related techniques, including fault injection and API robustness testing.

With the hindsight of 10 years of experience, the early decisions of Ballista worked out well. Especially fortuitous was the choice of basing test values on parameter data types, which extended to a number of APIs well beyond the originally envisioned operating systems tests. In the end, system killer robustness vulnerabilities lurk in even the most mature commercial software. Nonrobust behavior in the form of abort failures is prevalent, with anything less than a 10% abort failure rate being achieved only by developers who take special care. From a technical point of view, exploring concurrency-related problems and wear-out phenomena requires a significant step beyond Ballista.

Perhaps the biggest open challenges are nontechnical. Developers vary widely in their belief that software robustness beyond absence of system killer vulnerabilities matters, and the research community has yet to produce compelling evidence that they are wrong to think so. For developers who do strive to reduce noncatastrophic robustness vulnerabilities, it appears that a tool such as Ballista is essential to double check their efforts and help prevent missing vulnerabilities.

A copy of the Ballista toolset remains available from the authors and, for the indefinite future, at http://ballista.org.

ACKNOWLEDGMENTS

Many people have contributed to Ballista over the years. Dan Siewiorek has been very active in advising and supporting the project throughout. The late Asad Zaidi created the first Ballista testing Web-based server, and others ran tests on various APIs, contributed ideas, coauthored publications, and otherwise helped this project succeed: Roy Maxion, Charles Shelton, Jintao Pan, Kim Fernsler, Nathan Kropp, Geoff Hendrey, David Guttendorf, Chris Dingman, John Sung, Michael Abowd, Keith Arner, Bemina Atanacio, Dave Hanekamp, Mark Hsu, Ying Shi, Scott Wen, Kanda Runapongsa, Orna Raz, Brigette Pientka, Meredith Beveridge, and Ted Marz.

Ballista has also benefited from the collaboration with and sponsorship from many organizations, the most significant of which was DARPA (contract DABT63-96-C-0064). Other sponsors include ABB, Emerson, Microsoft, AT&T, Cisco, Office of Naval Research, Lucent, IBM, and in-kind support from DRC. We also received equipment donations from Intel, Digital Equipment Corporation/Compaq, the U.S. Navy, and QNX.

REFERENCES

[Arlat 1990] Arlat, J., Aguera, M., Amat, L., Crouzet, Y, Fabre, J.-C., Laprie, J.-C., Martins, E., and Powell, D., "Fault Injection for Dependability Validation—A Methodology and Some Applications," *IEEE Transactions on Software Engineering,* vol. 16, no. 2, pp. 166–182, February 1990.

[Avizienis 1985] Avizienis, A., "The N-version Approach to Fault-tolerant Software," *IEEE Transactions on Software Engineering,* vol. SE-11, no.12, pp. 1491–1501, 1985.

[Avizienis 1988] Avizienis, A., Lyu, M. R., and Schutz, W., In Search of Effective Diversity: A Six-Language Study of Fault-Tolerant Flight Control Software, *Eighteenth International Symposium on Fault-Tolerant Computing,* Tokyo, Japan, pp. 15–22, 1988.

[Barton 1990] Barton, J., Czeck, E., Segall, Z., and Siewiorek, D., "Fault Injection Experiments Using FIAT," *IEEE Transactions on Computers,* vol. 39, no. 4, pp. 575–582.

[Beizer 1995] Beizer, B., *Black Box Testing,* Wiley, New York, 1995.

[Carreira 1998] Carreira, J., Madeira H., and Silva J., "Xception: A Technique for the Experimental Evaluation of Dependability in Modern Computers," *IEEE Transactions on Software Engineering,* vol. 24, no. 2, pp. 125–136, February 1998.

[Carrette 1996] Carrette, G., "CRASHME: Random Input Testing," http://people.delphi.com/gjc/crashme.html, accessed July 6, 1998.

[Cristian 1995] Cristian, F., "Exception Handling and Tolerance of Software Faults," in *Software Fault Tolerance,* Michael R. Lyu (Ed.), pp. 81–107, Wiley, Chichester, UK, 1995.

[Czeck 1986] Czeck, E., Feather, F., Grizzaffi, A., Finelli, G., Segall, Z., and Siewiorek, D., "Fault-free Performance Validation of Avionic Multiprocessors," in *Proceedings of the IEEE/AIAA 7th Digital Avionics Systems Conference,* Fort Worth, TX, 13–16 Oct. 1986, pp. 803, 670–677.

[DBench 2004] *DBench Project Final Report,* IST-2000-25425, LAAS-CNRS, May 2004, http://www.laas.fr/Dbench.

[DeVale 1999] DeVale, J., Koopman, P., and Guttendorf, D., "The Ballista Software Robustness

Testing Service," in *16th International Conference on Testing Computer Software*, pp. 33–42, 1999.

[DeVale 2001] DeVale, J., and Koopman, P., "Performance Evaluation of Exception Handling in I/O Libraries," in *International Conference on Dependable Systems and Networks (DSN)*, Göteborg, Sweden, July 2001.

[DeVale 2001a] DeVale, J., *High Performance Robust Computer Systems*, Ph.D. dissertation, Carnegie Mellon University ECE Dept., Pittsburgh, PA, December 2001.

[DeVale 2002] DeVale, J., and Koopman, P., "Robust Software—No more excuses," in *International Conference on Dependable Systems and Networks (DSN)*, Washington DC, July 2002.

[Dingman 1995] Dingman, C., "Measuring Robustness of a Fault Tolerant Aerospace System," in *25th International Symposium on Fault-Tolerant Computing*, June 1995. pp. 522–527.

[Dingman 1997] Dingman, C., *Portable Robustness Benchmarks*, Ph.D. thesis, Dept. of Electrical and Computer Engineering, Carnegie Mellon University, Pittsburgh, PA, May 1997.

[DoD 1998] U.S. Department of Defense, *High Level Architecture Run Time Infrastructure Programmer's Guide, RTI 1.3 Version 5*, Dec. 16, 1998, DMSO/SAIC/Virtual Technology Corp.

[Duran 1984] Duran, J., and Ntafos, S., "An Evaluation of Random Testing," *IEEE Trans. On Software Engineering*, Vol. SE-10, No. 4, pp. 438–443, July 1984.

[Duraes 2002] Durães J., and Madeira, H. "Multidimensional Characterization of the Impact of Faulty Drivers on the Operating Systems Behavior," *IEICE Transactions on Information and Systems*, vol. E86-D, no. 12, pp. 2563–2570, December 2002.

[Eckhardt 1991] Eckhardt, D. E., Caglayan, A. K., Knight, J. C., Lee, L. D., McAllister, D. F., Vouk, M. A., and Kelly, J. P. J.; "An Experimental Evaluation of Software Redundancy as a Strategy for Improving Reliability," *IEEE Transactions on Software Engineering*, vol. 17, no. 7, pp. 692–702, July 1991.

[Fernsler 1999] Fernsler, K., and Koopman, P., "Robustness Testing of a Distributed Simulation Backplane," in *ISSRE 99*, Boca Raton, FL, pp. 189–198, 1999.

[Gehani 1992] Gehani, N., "Exceptional C or C with Exceptions," *Software—Practice and Experience*, vol. 22, no. 10, pp. 827–848, 1992.

[Goodenough 1975] Goodenough, J., "Exception Handling: Issues and a Proposed Notation," *Communications of the ACM*, vol. 18, no. 12, pp. 683–696, December 1975.

[Hill 1971] Hill, I., "Faults in Functions, in ALGOL and FORTRAN," *The Computer Journal*, vol. 14, no. 3, pp. 315–316, August 1971.

[IEEE 1990] *IEEE Standard Glossary of Software Engineering Terminology*, IEEE Std 610.12-1990, IEEE Computer Society, Los Alamitos, CA, 1990.

[IEEE 1993] *IEEE Standard for Information Technology—Portable Operating System Interface (POSIX) Part 1: System Application Program Interface (API) Amendment 1: Realtime Extension [C Language]*, IEEE Std 1003.1b-1993, IEEE Computer Society, Los Alamitos, CA, 1994.

[Kanawati 1992] Kanawati, G., Kanawati, N., and Abraham, J., "FERRARI: A Tool for the Validation of System Dependability Properties," in *1992 IEEE Workshop on Fault-Tolerant Parallel and Distributed Systems*. Amherst, MA, pp. 336–344, 1992.

[Koopman 1997] Koopman, P., Sung, J., Dingman, C., Siewiorek, D., and Marz, T., "Comparing Operating Systems Using Robustness Benchmarks," in *Proceedings of Symposium on Reliable and Distributed Systems*, Durham, NC, pp. 72–79, 1997.

[Koopman 1998] Koopman, P., "Toward a Scalable Method for Quantifying Aspects of Fault Tolerance, Software Assurance, and Computer Security," in *Post proceedings of the Computer Security, Dependability, and Assurance: From Needs to Solutions (CSDA'98)*, Washington, DC, pp. 103–131, November 1998.

[Koopman 1999] Koopman, P., and DeVale, J., "Comparing the Robustness of POSIX Operating Systems," in *28th Fault Tolerant Computing Symposium*, pp. 30–37, 1999.

[Koopman00] Koopman, P., and DeVale, J., "The Exception Handling Effectiveness of POSIX

Operating Systems," *IEEE Transactions on Software Engineering*, vol. 26, no. 9, pp. 837–848, September 2000.

[Korn 1991] Korn, D., and Vo, K.-P., "SFIO: Safe/Fast String/File IO," in *Proceedings of the Summer 1991 USENIX Conference*, pp. 235–256, 1991.

[Kropp 1998] Kropp, N., Koopman, P., and Siewiorek, D., "Automated Robustness Testing of Off-the-Shelf Software Components," in *28th Fault Tolerant Computing Symposium*, pp. 230–239, 1998.

[Littlewood 2000] Littlewood, B., and Strigini, L., *A Discussion of Practices for Enhancing Diversity in Software Designs*, DISPO LS-DI-TR-04_v1_1d, 2000.

[Marick 1995] Marick, B., *The Craft of Software Testing*, Prentice-Hall, Upper Saddle River, NJ, 1995.

[Miller 1990] Miller, B., Fredriksen, L., and So, B., "An Empirical Study of the Reliability of Operating System Utilities," *Communication of the ACM*, vol. 33, pp. 32–44, December 1990.

[Miller 1998] Miller, B., Koski, D., Lee, C., Maganty, V., Murthy, R., Natarajan, A., and Steidl, J., *Fuzz Revisited: A Re-examination of the Reliability of UNIX Utilities and Services*, Computer Science Technical Report 1268, University of Wisconsin–Madison, May 1998.

[Mukherjee 1997] Mukherjee, A., and Siewiorek, D. P., "Measuring Software Dependability by Robustness Benchmarking," *IEEE Transactions on Software Engineering*, vol. 23, no. 6, pp. 366–378, June 1997.

[Musa 1996] Musa, J., Fuoco, G., Irving, N., Kropfl, D., and Juhlin, B., "The Operational Profile," in Lyu, M. (Ed.), *Handbook of Software Reliability Engineering*, pp. 167–216, McGraw-Hill/IEEE Computer Society Press, Los Alamitos, CA, 1996.

[OMG95] Object Management Group, *The Common Object Request Broker: Architecture and Specification*, Revision 2.0, July 1995.

[Ostrand 1988] Ostrand, T. J., and Balcer, M. J., "The Category-Partition Method for Specifying and Generating Functional Tests," *Communications of the ACM*, vol. 31, no. 6, pp. 676–686, 1988.

[Pan 1999] Pan, J., Koopman, P., and Siewiorek, D., "A Dimensionality Model Approach to Testing and Improving Software Robustness," in *Autotestcon99*, San Antonio, TX, 1999.

[Pan 2001] Pan, J., Koopman, P., Siewiorek, D., Huang, Y., Gruber, R., and Jiang, M., "Robustness Testing and Hardening of CORBA ORB Implementations," in *International Conference on Dependable Systems and Networks (DSN)*, Göteborg, Sweden, pp. 141–150, 2001.

[Pientka 1999] Pientka, B., and Raz, O., *Robustness in Concurrent Testing*, Project Report, Carnegie Mellon University, Pittsburgh, PA, May 23, 1999.

[Rodriguez 2002] Rodríguez, M., Albinet, A., and Arlat, J., "MAFALDA-RT: A Tool for Dependability Assessment of Real Time Systems," in *Proceedings of IEEE/IFIP International Conference on Dependable Systems and Networks (DSN-2002)*, Washington, DC, pp. 267–272, 2002.

[Russinovich 1993] Russinovich, M., Segall, Z., and Siewiorek, D., "Application Transparent Fault Management in Fault Tolerant Mach," in *The Twenty-Third International Symposium on Fault-Tolerant Computing*, pp. 10–19, Toulouse, France, June 22–24 1993.

[Schuette 1986] Schuette, M., Shen, J., Siewiorek, D., and Zhu, Y., "Experimental Evaluation of Two Concurrent Error Detection Schemes," in *16th Annual International Symposium on Fault-Tolerant Computing Systems*, Vienna, Austria, pp. 138–43, 1986.

[Shelton 2000] Shelton, C., and Koopman, P., "Robustness Testing of the Microsoft Win32 API," in *International Conference on Dependable Systems and Networks (DSN)*, New York, 2000.

[Siewiorek 1993] Siewiorek, D., Hudak, J., Suh, B., and Segal, Z., "Development of a Benchmark to Measure System Robustness," in *23rd International Symposium on Fault-Tolerant Computing*, June 1993, Toulouse, France, pp. 88–97.

[Thevenod-Fosse91] Thévenod-Fosse, P., Waeselynck H., and Crouzet, Y., "An Experimental Study of Software Structural Testing: Deterministic versus Random Input Generation," in *Pro-*

ceedings of 21st IEEE International Symposium on Fault-Tolerant Computing (FTCS-21), Montréal, Québec, Canada, pp. 410–417, 1991.

[Tsai 1995] Tsai, T., and Iyer, R., "Measuring Fault Tolerance with the FTAPE Fault Injection Tool," in *Proceedings of Eighth International Conference on Modeling Techniques and Tools for Computer Performance Evaluation,* pp. 26–40, Heidelberg, Germany, Springer-Verlag, London, 1995.

[Vo 1997] Vo, K-P., Wang, Y-M., Chung, P., and Huang, Y., "Xept: A Software Instrumentation Method for Exception Handling," in *The Eighth International Symposium on Software Reliability Engineering,* Albuquerque, NM, pp. 60–69, 1997.

12

WINDOWS AND LINUX ROBUSTNESS BENCHMARKS WITH RESPECT TO APPLICATION ERRONEOUS BEHAVIOR

Karama Kanoun, Yves Crouzet, Ali Kalakech, and Ana-Elena Rugina

12.1. INTRODUCTION

Software is playing an increasingly important role in our day-to-day life. In particular, operating systems (OSs) are more and more used even in critical application domains. Choosing the operating system that is best adapted to one's needs is becoming a necessity. For a long time, performance was the main selection criterion for most users and several performance benchmarks were developed and are widely used. However, an OS should not only have good performance but also a high dependability level. Dependability benchmarks emerged as a consequence. Their role is to provide useful information regarding the dependability of software systems. This chapter is devoted to the specification, application, and validation of two dependability benchmarks of OSs using two different workloads: PostMark, a file system performance benchmark; and JVM (Java Virtual Machine), a software layer on top of the OS allowing applications in Java language to be platform independent.

Benchmarking the dependability of a system consists of evaluating dependability or performance-related measures, experimentally or based on experimentation and modeling, in order to characterize objectively the system behavior in the presence of faults. Such an evaluation should allow nonambiguous comparison of alternative solutions. Nonambiguity, confidence in results, and meaningfulness are ensured by a set of properties a benchmark should satisfy. For example, a benchmark must be representative, reproducible, repeatable, portable, and cost-effective. These properties should be taken into consideration from the earliest phases of the benchmark specification as they have a deep impact on almost all benchmark components. Verification of the benchmark key properties constitutes a large part of the benchmark validation.

Our dependability benchmark is a robustness benchmark. The robustness of an OS can be viewed as its capacity to resist/react to external faults, induced by the applications running on top of it, or originating from the hardware layer, or from device drivers. In this chapter, we address OS robustness as regards possible erroneous inputs provided by the application software to the OS via the application programming interface (API). More explicitly, we consider corrupted parameters in system calls. For the sake of conciseness, such erroneous inputs are referred to as *faults*.

The work reported in [Shelton et al. 2000] is the most similar to ours; it addressed the "nonrobustness" of the POSIX and Win32 APIs (while we are interested in robust and nonrobust behavior). Pioneer work on robustness benchmarking is published in [Mukherjee and Siewiorek 1997]. Since then, a few studies have addressed OS dependability benchmarks, considering real-time microkernels [Arlat et al. 2002] or general-purpose OSs [Koopman and DeVale 1999; see also Chapter 11 of this book]. Robustness with respect to faults in device drivers is addressed in [Chou et al. 2001, Durães and Madeira 2002, Albinet et al. 2004; see also Chapter 14 of this book].

The work reported in this chapter is a follow-up of the European Project on Dependability Benchmarking, DBench [DBench, Kanoun et al. 2002, Kanoun et al. 2005]. Our previously published work on OS dependability benchmarks was based on (i) TPC-C Client-performance benchmark for transactional systems [Kalakech et al. 2004b], (ii) PostMark [Kanoun et al. 2005a], and (iii) JVM workload [Kanoun and Crouzet 2006].

The remainder of the chapter is organized as follows. Section 12.2 gives the specification of the OS benchmarks. Section 12.3 presents benchmark implementation and results related to PostMark workload for Windows and Linux families. Section 12.4 presents benchmark implementation and results related to JVM workload. Section 12.5 refines the benchmark results for PostMark and JVM. Section 12.6 outlines the main benchmark properties that are meaningful to OS benchmarks, and briefly shows what has been achieved to ensure and check them. Section 12.7 concludes the chapter.

12.2. SPECIFICATION OF THE BENCHMARK

In order to provide dependability benchmark results that are meaningful, useful, and interpretable, it is essential to define clearly the following benchmark components:

1. The benchmarking context
2. The benchmark measures to be evaluated and the measurements to be performed on the system to provide the information required for obtaining the measures
3. The benchmark execution profile to be used to exercise the operating system.
4. Guidelines for conducting benchmark experiments and implementing benchmark prototypes

These components are discussed below.

12.2.1. Benchmarking Context

An OS can be seen as a generic software layer that manages all aspects of the underlying hardware. The OS provides (i) basic services to the applications through the API, and (ii) communication with peripheral devices via device drivers. From the viewpoint of dependability benchmarking, the *benchmark target* corresponds to the OS with the minimum set of device drivers necessary to run the OS under the benchmark execution profile.

However, for the benchmark target to be assessed, it is necessary to run it on top of a hardware platform and to use a set of libraries. Thus, the benchmark target along with the hardware platform and libraries form the *system under benchmarking*. Although, in practice, the benchmark measures characterize the system under benchmarking (e.g., the OS reaction and restart times are strongly dependent on the underlying hardware), for clarity purposes we will state that the benchmark results characterize the OS.

The benchmark addresses the user perspective; that is, it is primarily intended to be performed by (and to be useful for) someone or an entity who has no in-depth knowledge about the OS and whose aim is to significantly improve her/his knowledge about its behavior in the presence of faults. In practice, the user may well be the developer or the integrator of a system including the OS.

The OS is considered to be a "black box" and the source code does not need to be available. The only required information is the description of the OS in terms of system calls (in addition, of course, to the description of the services provided by the OS).

12.2.2. Benchmark Measures

After execution of a corrupted system call, the OS is in one of the states summarized in Table 12.1. These are:

SEr—corresponds to the case in which the OS generates an error code that is delivered to the application.

SXp—corresponds to the case in which the OS issues an exception. Two kinds of exceptions can be distinguished depending on whether it is issued during the application software execution (user mode) or during execution of the kernel software (kernel mode). In the user mode, the OS processes the exception and notifies the application (the application may or may not explicitly take into account this information). However, for some critical situations, the OS aborts the application. An exception in the kernel mode is automatically followed by a *panic state* (e.g., blue screen for Windows and "oops" messages for Linux). Hence, thereafter, the latter exceptions are included in the panic state and the term "exception" refers only to user mode exceptions.

SPc—In the panic state, the OS is still "alive" but it is not servicing the application. In some cases, a soft reboot is sufficient to restart the system.

SHg—In this state, a hard reboot of the OS is required.

SNS—In the no-signaling state, the OS does not detect the presence of the corrupted parameter. As a consequence, it accepts the erroneous system call and executes it. It may thus abort, hang, or complete its execution. However, the response might be erroneous or correct. For some system calls, the application may not require any ex-

TABLE 12.1. OS outcomes

SEr	An *error code* is returned
SXp	An *exception* is raised, processed and notified
SPc	*Panic* state
SHg	*Hang* state
SNS	No-signaling state

plicit response, so it simply continues execution after sending the system call. SNS is presumed when none of the previous outcomes (SEr, SXp, SPc, or SHg) is observed.*

Panic and *hang* outcomes are actual states in which the OS can stay for a while. They characterize the OS's nonrobustness. Conversely, SEr and SXp characterize only events. They are easily identified when the OS provides an error code or notifies an exception. These events characterize the OS's robustness.

The benchmark measures include a robustness measure and two temporal measures:

OS Robustness (POS) is defined as the percentage of experiments leading to any of the outcomes listed in Table 12.1. POS is thus a vector composed of five elements.

Reaction Time (Treac) corresponds to the average time necessary for the OS to respond to a system call in the presence of faults, either by notifying an exception, returning an error code, or executing the system call.

Restart Time (Tres) corresponds to the average time necessary for the OS to restart after the execution of the workload in the presence of one fault in one of its system calls. Although under nominal operation the OS restart time is almost deterministic, it may be impacted by the corrupted system call. The OS might need additional time to make the necessary checks and recovery actions, depending on the impact of the fault applied.

The OS reaction time and restart time are also observed in absence of faults for comparison purposes. They are respectively denoted $\pi reac$ and πres.

Note that our set of measures is different from the one used in [Shelton et al. 2000], where only nonrobust behavior of the OS is taken into account. They use the CRASH scale to measure the OS nonrobustness (**C**atastrophic, **R**estart, **A**bort, **S**ilent, and **H**indering failures). Our aim is to distinguish as clearly as possible the proportions of robust versus nonrobust behavior of the OS. Also, we completed the set of measures by adding to it the two temporal measures (Texec and Tres) presented in the list above.

12.2.3. Benchmark Execution Profile

For performance benchmarks, the benchmark execution profile is a workload that is as realistic and representative as possible for the system under benchmarking. For a dependability benchmark, the execution profile includes, in addition, corrupted parameters in system calls. The set of corrupted parameters is referred to as the faultload.

The benchmark is defined so that the workload could be any performance benchmark workload (and, more generally, any user-specific application) intended to run on top of the target OS. In [Kalakech et al. 2004b] we have used the workload of TPC-C Client [TPC-C 2002], and in this work we use two workloads: PostMark [Katcher 1997] and JVM [Lindholm and Yellin 1999]. The two workloads will be discussed further in Sections 12.3 and 12.4.

The faultload consists of corrupted parameters of system calls. For Windows, system calls are provided to the OS through the Win32 environment subsystem. For Linux OSs,

---

*In our work, we do not address "hindering" errors (e.g., incorrect error codes being returned) as in [Shelton et al. 2000]. This is extremely difficult to deal with, and it is almost impossible to automate their identification.

these system calls are provided to the OS via the POSIX API. During runtime, the workload system calls are intercepted, corrupted, and reinserted.

We use a parameter corruption technique relying on thorough analysis of system call parameters to define *selective substitutions* to be applied to these parameters (similar to the one used in [Koopman et al. 1997]). A parameter is either data or an address. The value of data can be substituted either by an *out-of-range* value or by an *incorrect* (but not out-of-range) value, whereas an address is substituted by an *incorrect* (but existing) address (containing usually incorrect or out-of-range data). We use a mix of these three corruption techniques.* Note that nonexisting addresses are always detected. Hence, they are not considered to be interesting substitution values.

To reduce the number of experiments, the parameter data types are grouped into classes. A set of substitution values is defined for each class. They depend on the definition of the class. Some values require a *pre* and a *post* processing such as the creation and the destruction of temporary files. For example, for Windows we group the data types into 13 classes. Among these classes, nine are pointer classes. Apart from *pvoid* (a pointer that points to anything), all other pointers point to a particular data type. Substitution values for these pointers are combinations of pointer substitution values and the corresponding data type substitution values. Similarly, for Linux we group the data types into 13 classes among which five are pointer classes. We use the same substitution values for basic data types (i.e., integer) for both Windows and Linux. Nevertheless, some data types are system dependent. Consequently, they have specific substitution values. In Linux, for example, we define a class corresponding to the type *mode*. A mode is an integer with a particular meaning: read/write modes or permission flags. As the validity domain of this data type can be identified precisely, pertinent substitution values are defined for it. Table 12.2 reviews the substitution values associated with the basic data type classes.

TABLE 12.2. Parameter substitution values

Data type class	Substitution values					
Pvoid	NULL	0xFFFFFFFF	1	0xFFFF	−1	Random
Integer	0	1	MAX INT	MIN INT	0.5	
Unsigned integer	0	1	0xFFFFFFFF	−1	0.5	
Boolean	0	0xFF (Max)	1	−1	0.5	
String	Empty	Large (> 200)	Far (+ 1000)			

12.2.4. Benchmark Conduct and Implementation

Since perturbing the operating system may lead the OS to hang, a remote machine, referred to as the benchmark controller, is required to reliably control the benchmark experiments, mainly in case of OS hang or panic states or workload hang or abort states (that cannot be reported by the machine hosting the benchmark target). Accordingly, for running an OS dependability benchmark we need at least two computers: (i) the *target machine* for hosting the benchmarked OS and the workload, and (ii) the *benchmark controller* that is in charge of diagnosing and collecting part or all benchmark data. The two machines perform the following functions:

---

*A discussion about the adequacy of this choice is given in Section 12.6.1.3.

1. Restart of the system before each experiment and launch of the workload
2. Interception of system calls with parameters
3. Corruption of system call parameters
4. Reinsertion of corrupted system calls
5. Observation and collection of OS outcomes

The experiment steps in case of workload completion are illustrated in Figure 12.1. In case of the workload noncompletion state (i.e., the workload is in the abort or hang state), the end of the experiment is provided by a watchdog timeout as illustrated in Figure 12.2. The timeout duration is fixed to a value that is three times greater than the largest workload execution time without faults.

To intercept Win32 functions, we use the Detours tool [Hunt and Brubaher 1999], a library for intercepting Win32 binary functions on X86 machines. The part of Detours in charge of system call interception is composed of 30 kilolines of code (KLOC). The modifications we carried out on this tool concern (i) the replacement of system call parameters by corrupted values (this module is 3 KLOC) and (ii) the addition of modules to observe the reactions of the OS after parameter corruption, and to collect the required measurements (this module is 15 KLOC). To intercept POSIX system calls, we used another interception tool, Strace [McGrath and Akkerman 2004]. Strace is composed of 26 KLOC. Also, we added two modules to this tool to allow (i) substitution of the parameters and (ii) observation of Linux behavior after parameter corruption (these modules correspond to 4 KLOC together). The reaction time is counted from the time the corrupted system call is

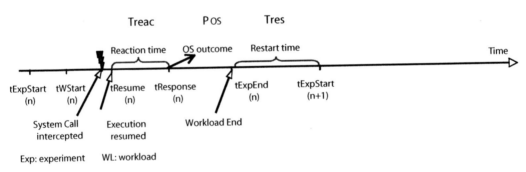

Figure 12.1. Benchmark execution sequence in the case of workload completion.

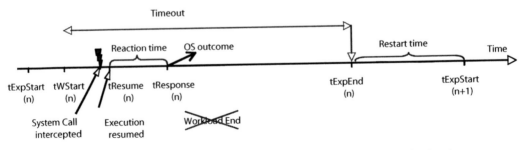

Figure 12.2. Benchmark execution sequence in the case of workload abort or hang.

reinserted. Hence the time to intercept and substitute system calls is not included in the system reaction time, as shown in Figures 12.1 and 12.2.

Figure 12.3 summarizes the various components of the benchmark environment. All the experiments have been run on the same target machine, composed of an Intel Pentium III Processor (800 MHz) and a memory of 512 Megabytes. The hard disk is 18 Gigabytes, ULTRA 160 SCSI. The benchmark controller in both prototypes for Windows and Linux is a Sun Microsystems workstation.

Before each benchmark run (i.e., before execution of the series of experiments related to a given OS), the target kernel is installed, and the interceptor is compiled for the current kernel (interceptors are kernel dependent both for Windows and Linux because they depend on kernel headers that are different from one version to another). Once the benchmarking tool is compiled, it is used to identify the set of system calls activated by the workload. All parameters of all these system calls are then analyzed and placed into the corresponding class. A database of substitution values is then generated accordingly.

Following the benchmark execution sequence presented in Figures 12.1 and 12.2, at the beginning of each experiment, the target machine (TM) records the experiment start instant $t_{ExpStart}$ and sends it to the benchmark controller (BC) along with a notification of experiment start-up. The workload starts its execution. The observer module records, in the experiment execution trace, the start-up instant of the workload, the activated system calls, and their responses. This trace also collects the relevant data concerning states SEr, SXp, and SNS. The recorded trace is sent to the BC at the beginning of the next experiment.

The parameter substitution module checks whether the current system call has parameters. If it does not, the execution is simply resumed; otherwise, the execution is interrupted, a parameter value is substituted, and the execution is resumed with the corrupted parameter value (t_{Resume} is saved in the experiment execution trace). The state of the OS is monitored so as to diagnose SEr, SXp, and SNS. The corresponding OS response time ($t_{Response}$) is recorded in the experiment execution trace. For each run, the OS reaction time is calculated as the difference between $t_{Response}$ and t_{Resume}.

At the end of the execution of the workload, the OS notifies the BC of the end of the experiment by sending an end signal along with the experiment end instant, t_{ExpEnd}, and then it restarts so that the current experiment does not have any effects on the following

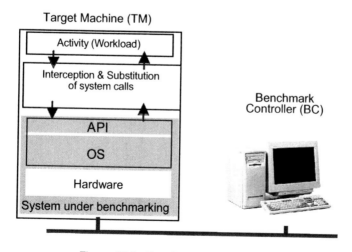

Figure 12.3. Benchmark environment.

experiment. If the workload does not complete, then t_{ExpEnd} is governed by the value of a watchdog timer. The BC collects the SHg state and the workload abort/hang states. It is in charge of restarting the system in such cases. When no faultload is applied, the average time necessary for the OS to execute PostMark or JVM is less than 1 minute for Windows and for Linux. We considered that three times the normal execution time is enough to obtain the experiment's result. Thus, we have fixed the watchdog timer to 3 minutes. If, at the end of this watchdog timer, the BC has not received the end signal from the OS, it attempts to ping the OS. If the OS responds (ping successful), the BC attempts to connect to it. If the connection is successful, then a workload abort or hang state is diagnosed. If the connection is unsuccessful, then a panic state, SPc, is deduced. Otherwise, SHg is assumed. If workload abort/hang or SPc or SHg are observed, $t_{Response}$ does not take any value for the current experiment. Thus, the measure Treac is not skewed by the watchdog timer value.

At the end of a benchmark execution, all files containing raw results corresponding to all experiments are on the BC. A processing module extracts automatically the relevant information from these files (two specific modules are required for Windows and Linux families). The relevant information is then used to evaluate automatically the benchmark measures (the same module is used for Windows and Linux).

12.3. POSTMARK DEPENDABILITY BENCHMARK IMPLEMENTATION AND RESULTS

PostMark creates a large pool of continually changing files and measures the transaction rates for a workload emulating Internet applications such as e-mail or netnews. It generates an initial pool of random text files ranging in size from a configurable low bound to a configurable high bound. The file pool is of configurable size and can be located on any accessible file system. The workload of this benchmark, referred to as PostMark for simplicity, is responsible for realizing a number of transactions. Each transaction consists of a pair of smaller transactions: (i) create file or delete file and (ii) read file or append file. PostMark is written in the C language. From a practical point of view, PostMark needs to be compiled separately for each OS.

Six versions of Windows OSs were targeted: Windows NT4 Workstation with SP6, Windows 2000 Professional with SP4, Windows XP Professional with SP1, Windows NT4 Server with SP6, Windows 2000 Server with SP4, and Windows 2003 Server. In the rest of this chapter, Windows 2000 Professional and Windows NT4 Workstation will be referred to as Windows 2000 and Windows NT4, respectively. Four Linux OSs (Debian distribution) are targeted: Linux 2.2.26, Linux 2.4.5, Linux 2.4.26, and Linux 2.6.6. Each of them is a revision of one of the stable versions of Linux (2.2, 2.4, 2.6). Table 12.3 summarizes the number of system calls targeted by the benchmark experiments carried out along with the number of corresponding parameters and the number of experiments for each OS.

OS robustness is shown in Figure 12.4. It shows that all OSs of the same family are equivalent, which is in conformance with our previous results, related to Windows using TPC-C Client [Kalakech et al. 2004b]. It also shows that none of the catastrophic outcomes (panic or hang OS states) occurred for all Windows and Linux OSs. Linux OSs returned more error codes (59–67%) than Windows (23–27%), whereas more exceptions were raised with Windows (17–22%) than with Linux (8–10%). More no-signaling cases have been observed for Windows (55–56%) than for Linux (25–32%). In [Shelton et al. 2000], it was observed that, on the one hand, Windows 95, 98, 98SE, and CE had a few

TABLE 12.3. Number of system calls, corrupted parameters, and experiments for each OS, using PostMark

	Windows family						Linux family			
	W-NT4	W-2000	W-XP	W-NT4S	W-2000S	W-2003S	L-2.2.26	L-2.4.5	L-2.4.26	L-2.6.6
No. of system calls	25	27	26	25	27	27	16	16	16	17
No. of parameters	53	64	64	53	64	64	38	38	38	44
No. of experiments	418	433	424	418	433	433	206	206	206	228

catastrophic failures and, on the other hand, Windows NT, Windows 2000, and Linux are more robust and did not have any catastrophic failures, as in our case.

The reaction time is given in Figure 12.5. Globally, Windows OSs have shorter response times than Linux OSs. The standard deviation is significantly larger than the average for all OSs. Except for the two revisions of Linux 2.4, τreac is always larger than Treac, the reaction time in the presence of faults. This can be explained by the fact that after parameter corruption, the OS detects the anomaly in almost 45% of cases for Windows and 75% of cases for Linux, stops system call execution, and returns an error code or notifies an exception.

Note that for the Windows family, Windows XP has the lowest reaction time in the presence of faults and for the Linux family, Linux 2.6.6 has the lowest reaction time. For Linux 2.6.6, we notice that τreac is almost two times larger than for the other revisions. A detailed analysis of the results showed that this is due to one system call, execve, for which the execution time is 15,000 μs for Linux 2.6.6 and 6000 μs for other versions. These values may be considered as outliers. Removing them and reevaluating the average lead to more representative results. Another measure of interest in this case could be the median, since it is not sensitive to extreme values.

The restart times are shown in Figure 12.6. The average restart time without faults, τres, is always lower than the average restart time with faults (Tres), but the difference is not significant. Linux seems to be globally faster (71–83 s) than Windows (74–112 s). However, if we consider only OS versions introduced in the market after 2001, the other

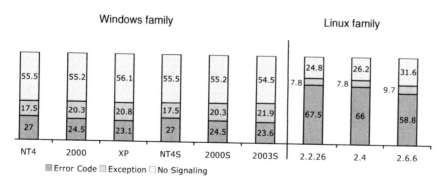

Figure 12.4. Robustness (%), using PostMark.

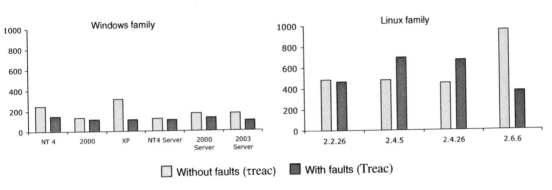

Figure 12.5. Reaction time (in microseconds), using Postmark.

OSs rank as follows: Linux 2.2.26 (71 s), Windows XP (74 s), Windows 2003 server (77 s), Linux 2.4.5 (79 s), Linux 2.6.6 (82 s), Linux 2.4.26 (83 s).

Concerning the Linux family, we note that the restart time increases with new versions or revisions, except for Linux 2.6.6. This progression is due to the increasing size of kernels with the version evolution. The exception of Linux 2.6.6 is justified by the fact that the Linux kernel was restructured in its version 2.6.

12.4. JVM DEPENDABILITY BENCHMARK IMPLEMENTATION AND RESULTS

Java Virtual Machine (JVM) is a software layer between the OS and Java applications, allowing applications in Java language to be platform independent. The specifications of the virtual machine [Lindholm and Yellin 1999] are independent from the hardware platform but each platform requires a specific implementation. The benchmark based on JVM has been applied to three Windows versions (NT, 2000, and XP) and to the four Linux versions considered in the previous section. In this benchmark, JVM is solicited through a small program allowing it to activate 76 system calls with parameters for the Windows family and 31 to 37 system calls with parameters for the Linux Family, as indicated in Table 12.4. These system calls are intercepted and corrupted using the corruption tech-

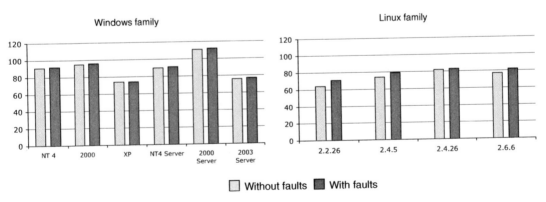

Figure 12.6. Restart time (in seconds), using Postmark.

TABLE 12.4. Number of system calls, corrupted parameters, and experiments for each OS, using JVM

	Windows family			Linux family			
	W-NT4	W-2000	W-XP	L-2.2.26	L-2.4.5	L-2.4.26	L-2.6.6
No. of system calls	76	76	76	37	32	32	31
No. of parameters	216	214	213	86	77	77	77
No. of experiments	1285	1294	1282	457	408	408	409

nique presented in Section 12.2.3, which leads to the number of experiments indicated in the last line for each OS.

Robustness is given in Figure 12.7. As for the PostMark workload, no hang or panic states have been observed. It can be seen that the three Windows versions are roughly equivalent, as are the Linux versions.

Comparison with Figure 12.4 shows that the robustness of each family is the same using PostMark or JVM workloads (within 5% discrepancy). Furthermore, we have observed the same robustness for Windows versions using TPC-C as workload in our previous work [Kalakech et al. 2004a]. The three workloads solicit different numbers of system calls and only some of them are the same. Nevertheless, they lead to the same robustness.

The reaction times in the presence of faults (and without fault) are given in Figure 12.8. Note that for the Windows family, XP has the lowest reaction time, and for the Linux family, 2.6.6 has the lowest one. However, the reaction times of Windows NT and 2000 are very high.

A detailed analysis showed that the large response times for Windows NT and 2000 are mainly due to system calls LoadLibraryA, LoadLibraryExA, and LoadLibraryEXW. Not including these system calls when evaluating the average of the reaction time in the presence of faults leads, respectively, to 388 μs, 182 μs, and 205 μs for NT4, 2000, and XP. For Linux, the extremely high values of the reaction times without faults are due to two system calls (sched_getparam and sched_getscheduler). Their execution times are significantly larger without faults than in the presence of faults. A detailed analysis of the results showed that for these two system calls most of the corruption experiments ended with an error code (SEr). Thus, we assume that the system calls were abandoned after an early anomaly detection by the OS. Also for Linux, the reaction times in the presence of faults are relatively high. This is due to three system calls (execve, getdents64, and nanosleep). Not including

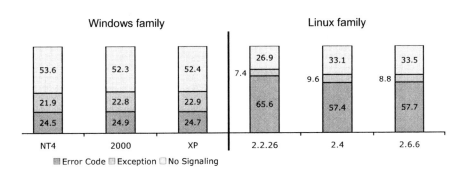

Figure 12.7. Robustness measures with JVM.

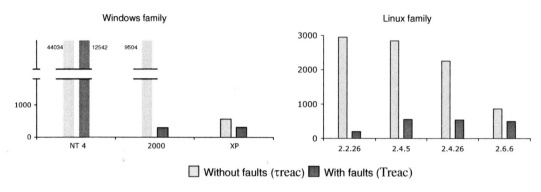

Figure 12.8. OS reaction time (in microseconds), using JVM.

the reaction times associated with these system calls leads, respectively, to a Treac of 88 μs, 241 μs, 227 μs, and 88 μs for the 2.2.26, 2.4.5, 2.4.26, and 2.6.6 versions.

The restart times are given in Figure 12.9. As for the PostMark workload, the average restart time without faults, τres, is always lower than the benchmark restart time (in the presence of faults), Tres, but the difference is not significant. The standard deviation is very large for all OSs. Linux 2.2.26 and Windows XP have the lowest restart time (71 seconds in the absence of faults) whereas Windows NT and 2000 restart times are around 90 seconds and those of Linux versions 2.4.5, 2.4.26, and 2.6.6 are around 80 seconds.

It is interesting to note that the order of the OSs considered is the same for PostMark and for JVM, except for Windows NT and 2000 (which have the highest restart times). Indeed, the only change concerns Windows 2000, whose restart time is slightly decreased for JVM, making it better than Windows NT.

12.5. RESULTS REFINEMENT

The benchmark temporal measures are refined to provide more insights into those presented in Sections 12.3 and 12.4. We first consider PostMark, then JVM. For each of them, we mainly detail the temporal measures.

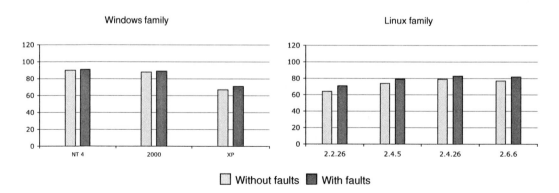

Figure 12.9. OS restart time (in seconds), using JVM.

12.5.1. PostMark

12.5.1.1. Reaction Time. Table 12.5 presents the detailed reaction times with respect to OS outcomes after execution of corrupted system calls (error code, exception, and no signaling). Thus, three average times are added to detail Treac: TSEr, TSXp (the times necessary to return, respectively, an error code or an exception), and TSNS (the execution time of the corrupted system call, in case of the no-signaling state).

For the Windows family, it can be seen that for versions 2000, 2000 Server, XP, and 2003 Server, returning an error code takes less time than raising an exception. This can be explained by the fact that when returning an error code, tests are carried out on the parameter values at the beginning of the system call code and the system call is abandoned, whereas the exceptions are raised from a lower level of the system under benchmarking. Nevertheless, in the cases of Windows NT4 and NT4 Server, TSEr is higher than TSXp. The cause of this anomaly lies in the long time necessary for the GetCPInfo system call to return an error code when its first parameter is corrupted.

Concerning the Linux family, the averages presented in this table do not take into account execve system call execution time. Numbers in bold correspond to high values of the standard deviation and are commented on in the following text. We notice the high values of TSNS corresponding to the two revisions of version 2.4, compared to the two other versions. The very high standard deviation suggests a large variation around the average, which is confirmed in Figure 12.10, which gives the OS reaction time for all system calls leading to the no-signaling state for all Linux OSs. We can clearly see that for Linux 2.4, the average time necessary for executing mkdir is more than 10 times larger than for all other system calls. We have noticed that mkdir has an extremely long execution time when its second parameter (which corresponds to the permissions to apply on the newly created folder) is corrupted.

TABLE 12.5. Detailed reaction time, using PostMark

	Windows Family					
	NT4		2000		XP	
	Avg.	Std. Dev.	Avg.	Std. Dev.	Avg.	Std. Dev.
Treac	148 μs	219 μs	118 μs	289 μs	114 μs	218 μs
TSEr	45 μs	107 μs	34 μs	61 μs	45 μs	118 μs
TSXp	40 μs	15 μs	37 μs	15 μs	50 μs	96 μs
TSNS	234 μs	437 μs	186 μs	375 μs	168 μs	265 μs
	NT4 Server		2000 Server		2003 Server	
Treac	110 μs	221 μs	131 μs	289 μs	102 μs	198 μs
TSEr	41 μs	66 μs	29 μs	33 μs	25 μs	61 μs
TSXp	35 μs	15 μs	37 μs	15 μs	48 μs	20 μs
TSNS	166 μs	280 μs	210 μs	396 μs	156 μs	252 μs
	Linux Family					
	2.2.26		2.4.5		2.4.26		2.6.6
Treac	167 μs	300 μs	**466 μs**	**2276 μs**	**425 μs**	**2055 μs**	93 μs	12 μs
TSEr	**208 μs**	**361 μs**	92 μs	105 μs	84 μs	6 μs	91 μs	10 μs
TSXp	88 μs	5 μs	91 μs	8 μs	91 μs	8 μs	106 μs	13 μs
TSNS	85 μs	5 μs	**1545 μs**	**4332 μs**	**1405 μs**	**3912 μs**	91 μs	11 μs

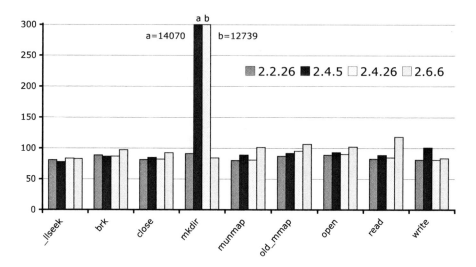

Figure 12.10. Linux reaction time in case of SNS (in microseconds), using PostMark.

Also, a very large average time to return an error code is observed for Linux 2.2.26, with a high standard deviation. Figure 12.11 details the times necessary to return error codes for Linux system calls. It is clear that these times are very similar except for the un-link system call in Linux 2.2.26, which explains the high TSEr of Linux 2.2.26 compared to the other versions. After discarding the exceptional values corresponding to execve, mkdir, and unlink system calls, the average reaction times Treac of the four targeted Linux OSs become very close. The largest difference is 8 μs. Also, the average reaction times with respect to OS outcomes after execution of corrupted system calls (TSEr, TSXp, and TSNS) become very close. The largest difference is 18 μs. Furthermore, τreac and Treac become very close.

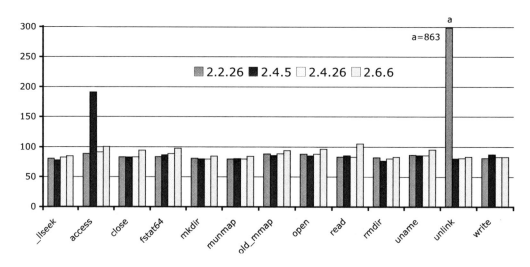

Figure 12.11. Linux reaction time in case of SER (in microseconds), using PostMark.

12.5.1.2. Restart Time. Detailed analyses show that all OSs of the same family have similar behavior and that the two families exhibit very different behaviors. For Windows, there is a correlation between the restart time and the state of the workload at the end of the experiment. When the workload is completed, the average restart time is statistically equal to the restart time without parameter substitution. On the other hand, the restart time is larger and statistically equal for all experiments with a workload abort or hang. This is illustrated in Figure 12.12 for the case of Windows NT, 2000, and NT. For example, the average restart time in case of workload completion is 73 s and 80 s in case of a workload abort or hang for Windows XP.

Linux restart time is not affected by the workload final state. Detailing Linux restart times shows high values appearing periodically. These values correspond to a "check-disk" performed by the Linux kernel every 26 target machine restarts. This is illustrated for Linux 2.2.26 and 2.6.6 in Figure 12.13, and induces an important standard deviation on this measure. Also, it is interesting to note that the check-disk duration decreases with the version evolution, whereas the regular restart time increases. It seems natural for the time needed to complete a check-disk to decrease while the Linux kernel evolves. The increase of the regular restart time may be due to the increasing size of Linux kernels.

12.5.2. JVM

12.5.2.1. Reaction Time. Similarly to Table 12.5, Table 12.6 presents the detailed reaction times with respect to OS outcomes after execution of corrupted system calls (error code, exception and no signaling).

For the Windows family, the averages presented in this table do not take into account LoadLibraryA, LoadLibraryExA, and LoadLibraryExW system call execution times. As in the case of the use of the PostMark workload, we notice that, for Windows 2000 and Windows XP, TSEr is higher than TSXp, which is higher than TSNS. The standard devi-

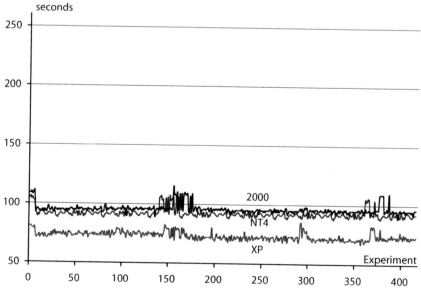

Figure 12.12. Detailed Windows restart time, using PostMark.

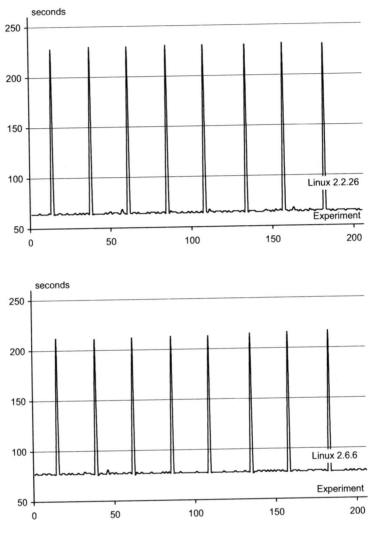

Figure 12.13. Detailed Linux restart time, using PostMark.

ations for these measures are rather small. On the other hand, for Windows NT4 TSEr is lower than TSXp. Figure 12.14 details the times necessary to raise exceptions for Windows system calls. It is clear that these times are similar except for the system call Find-NextFileW. The execution time of this system call is greater than 13,400 µs for Windows NT4, whereas for the other Windows OSs it is smaller than 75 µs. It is noteworthy that the execution time of this system call is also the cause for the large values for TSE and TSXp in the case of NT4.

Concerning the Linux family, the averages presented in this table do not take into account execve, getdents64, and nanosleep system call execution times. As in the case of the use of the PostMark workload, we notice the high values of TSNS corresponding to the two revisions of version 2.4, compared to the two other versions. The very high standard deviation suggests a large variation around the average, which is confirmed in Figure

Table 12.6. Detailed reaction time, using JVM

	Windows Family					
	NT4		2000		XP	
	Avg.	Std. Dev.	Avg.	Std. Dev.	Avg.	Std. Dev.
Treac	388 μs	3142 μs	190 μs	451 μs	214 μs	483 μs
TSEr	298 μs	3006 μs	47 μs	110 μs	51 μs	103 μs
TSXp	424 μs	3862 μs	84 μs	168 μs	98 μs	209 μs
TSNS	417 μs	2858 μs	307 μs	588 μs	344 μs	625 μs

	Linux Family						
	2.2.26		2.4.5		2.4.26		2.6.6	
Treac	88 μs	85 μs	241 μs	1479 μs	227 μs	1438 μs	88 μs	26 μs
TSEr	90 μs	101 μs	79 μs	6 μs	84 μs	30 μs	86 μs	8 μs
TSXp	87 μs	7 μs	85 μs	8 μs	87 μs	8 μs	98 μs	15 μs
TSNS	84 μs	6 μs	572 μs	2545 μs	523 μs	2545 μs	89 μs	43 μs

12.15, which gives the OS reaction time for all system calls leading to the no-signaling state for all Linux OSs. As in the case of the use of the PostMark workload, for Linux 2.4 the average time necessary for executing mkdir is more than 10 times larger than for all other system calls.

After discarding the exceptional values corresponding to execve, getdents64, nanosleep, and mkdir system calls, the average reaction times Treac of the four targeted Linux OSs become very close. The largest difference is 15 μs. Also, the average reaction times with respect to OS outcomes after execution of corrupted system calls (TSEr,

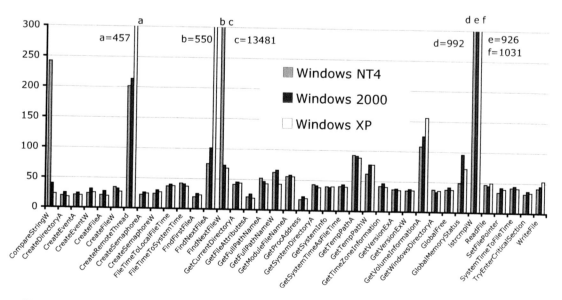

Figure 12.14. Windows reaction time in case of SXp (in microseconds), using JVM.

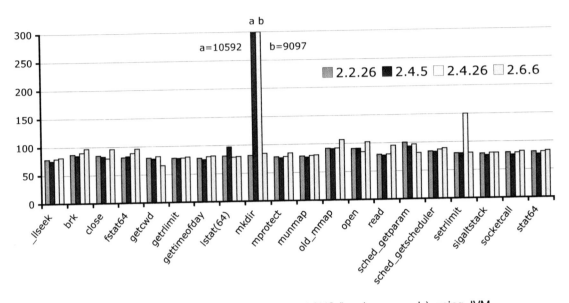

Figure 12.15. Linux reaction time in case of SNS (in microseconds), using JVM.

TSXp, and TSNS) become very close. The largest difference is 28 μs. Furthermore, πreac and Treac become very close (if we discard the executions times for sched_getparam and sched_getscheduler system calls).

12.5.2.2. Restart Time. As in the case of the PostMark workload, for Windows there is a correlation between the restart time and the state of the workload at the end of the experiment. When the workload is completed, the average restart time is statistically equal to the restart time without parameter substitution. On the other hand, the restart time is larger and statistically equal for all experiments with a workload abort or hang. This is illustrated in Figure 12.16. For example, for Windows XP, the average restart time in case of workload completion is 68 s and 82 s in case of a workload abort or hang.

As in the case of the PostMark workload, Linux restart time is not affected by the workload final state. Detailing the restart times shows high values appearing periodically, due to a "check-disk" performed by the kernel every 26 target machine restarts. This is illustrated for Linux 2.2.26 and 2.6.6 in Figure 12.17. Also, it is noteworthy that the check-disk duration decreases with the version evolution, whereas the regular restart time increases.

12.5.3. PostMark and JVM

OS robustness of all OSs with respect to PostMark and JVM workloads is shown in Table 12.7. It shows that none of the catastrophic outcomes (panic or hang OS states) occurred for all Windows and Linux OSs. It also shows that Linux OSs reported more error codes (57%–67%) than Windows (23%–27%), whereas more exceptions were raised with Windows (17%–25%) than with Linux (7%–10%). More no-signaling cases have been observed for Windows (52%–56%) than for Linux (25%–33%). For the Linux family, Linux 2.2.26 seems to have the most robust behavior (the smallest proportion of no-signaling), whereas for Windows family, the differences between OSs are too small to differentiate them clearly.

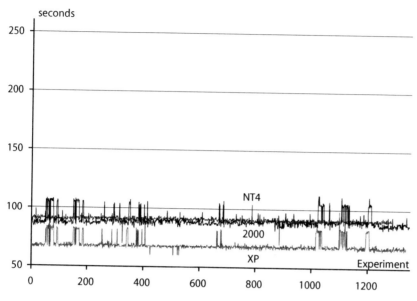

<u>Figure 12.16.</u> Detailed Windows restart time, using JVM.

The reaction times in the presence of faults are globally smaller for Windows family OSs than for Linux family OSs (if we exclude a few systems calls for which the reaction time is exceptionally very long). We have noticed that the execution times of a minority of system calls can have important consequences on the mean reaction time values. For instance, the execution time of a mkdir system call for Linux 2.4 biases the Treac measure. High standard deviations on this measure are due to a minority of system calls with very large reaction time compared to the majority. If we discard these exceptional values, Treac and τreac become very close. Moreover, Treac for Windows and Linux families become close.

The restart times in the presence of faults (Tres) are always higher than the restart times without faults (τres). The lowest Tres was observed for Linux 2.2.26 and Windows XP (71 s). For the Windows family, the restart time is higher in the case of a workload abort/hang both when using PostMark and JVM as workloads. For the Linux family, the standard deviation on this measure is high because of check-disks performed every 26 target machine restarts. We have noticed that check-disks take a longer time to perform when using JVM as workload than when using PostMark. The regular restart time is the same when using PostMark and JVM.

The ordering of the OSs with respect to the restart time is the same for Postmark and JVM except for Windows 2000, for which the restart time is better than for Windows NT using JVM, whereas it is worse when using PostMark.

12.6. BENCHMARK PROPERTIES

In order to gain confidence in dependability benchmark results, one has to check that the key properties are fulfilled. These properties are addressed successively in the rest of this section. We first define the property, then we show what has been achieved to satisfy and check it.

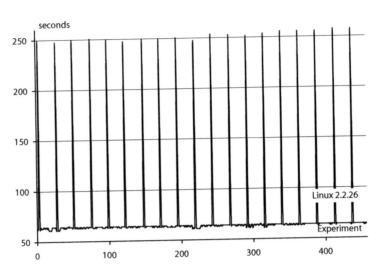

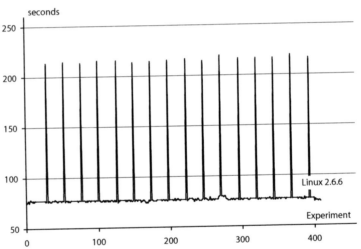

Figure 12.17. Detailed Linux restart time, using JVM.

TABLE 12.7. Linux and Windows robustness using PostMark and JVM

| | PostMark | | | JVM | | |
	SEr	SXp	SNS	SEr	SXp	SNS
Linux 2.2.26	67.5%	7.8%	24.8%	65.6%	7.4%	26.9%
Linux 2.4.x	66.0%	7.8%	26.2%	57.1%	9.8%	33.1%
Linux 2.6.6	58.8%	9.7%	31.6%	57.7%	8.8%	33.5%
Windows NT4	27.0%	17.5%	55.5%	24.5%	21.8%	53.6%
Windows 2000	24.5%	20.3%	55.2%	24.8%	22.8%	52.3%
Windows XP	23.1%	20.7%	56.1%	24.7%	22.8%	52.4%

12.6.1. Representativeness

Representativeness concerns the benchmark measures, the workload, and the faultload.

12.6.1.1. Measures. The measures evaluated provide information on the OS state and temporal behavior after execution of corrupted system calls. We emphasize that these measures are of interest to a system developer (or integrator) for selecting the most appropriate OS for his/her own application. Of course, other measures would help.

12.6.1.2. Workload. We have selected two benchmark workloads whose characteristics, in terms of system calls activated, are detailed below. Nevertheless, the selection of any other workload does not affect the concept and specification of our benchmark.

The PostMark workload activates system calls belonging to functional components: file management, thread management, memory management, and system information. Most of system calls belong to the file management functional component (62% for Linux, 48% for Windows). However, a significant amount of system calls belong to the thread management (12% for Linux, 32% for Windows) and to the memory management (19% for Linux, 8% for Windows) functional components. In total, 93% of the system calls for Linux and 88% for Windows are in these functional components. The PostMark workload is representative if the OS is used as a file server.

Let us stress that we chose the workload to be the JVM and not a particular Java application to focus on system calls activated by the JVM, regardless of the Java application running on top of it. The JVM is solicited through a very small program. The JVM workload activates system calls fairly distributed with respect to functional components (file management, thread management, memory management, user interface, debugging and handling, and interprocess communication). Similarly to the PostMark workload, most of the activated system calls (88% for Linux, 73% for Windows) belong to the file management (40% for Linux, 26% for Windows), the thread management (24% for Linux, 36% for Windows), and to the memory management (24% for Linux, 11% for Windows) functional components.

12.6.1.3. Faultload. The faultload is without any doubt the most critical component of the OS benchmark and more generally of any dependability benchmark. Faultload representativeness concerns (i) the parameter corruption technique used and (ii) the set of corrupted parameters.

PARAMETER CORRUPTION TECHNIQUE. In our previous work [Jarboui et al. 2002], performed for Linux, we have used two techniques for system call parameter corruption: the *systematic bit-flip* technique consisting in flipping systematically all bits of the target parameters (i.e., flipping the 32 bits of each considered parameter) and the *selective substitution technique* described in Section 12.2. This work showed the equivalence of the errors induced by the two techniques. In [Kalakech et al. 2004b], we obtained the same robustness for Windows 2000 using the systematic bit-flip technique and the selective-substitution technique.

The application of the bit-flip technique requires much more experimentation time compared to the application of the selective-substitution technique. Indeed, in the latter case, the set of values to be substituted is simply determined by the data type of the parameter (see Section 12.2), which leads to a more focused set of experiments. We have thus preferred the selective substitution technique for pragmatic reasons: it allows derivation of results that are similar to those obtained using the well-known and accepted bit-flip fault-injection technique, with much fewer experiments. Our benchmark is based on selective substitutions of system call parameters to be corrupted.

PARAMETERS TO BE CORRUPTED. The selective-substitution technique used is composed of a mix of three corruption techniques as mentioned in Section 12.2: out-of-range data (OORD), incorrect data (ID), and incorrect addresses (IA). Let us denote the fault-load used in our benchmarks by FL0. To analyze the impact of the faultload, we consider two subsets, including, respectively, (i) IA and OORD only (denoted FL1) and (ii) OORD only (denoted FL2). For each workload (PostMark and JVM), we ran the benchmarks of all OSs considered using successively FL0, FL1, and FL2. The results obtained confirm the equivalence between Linux family OSs as well as the equivalence between Windows family OSs, using the same faultload (FL0, FL1, or FL2). Note that for each OS, its robustness with respect to FL0, FL1, or FL2 is different, but the robustness of all OSs of the same family with respect to the same faultload is equivalent. The same results have been obtained in [Kalakech et al. 2004b], using TPC-C Client as workload.

The number of substitutions (hence the number of experiments) decreases significantly when considering FL1 and F2. By way of examples, Table 12.8 gives the number of experiments for Windows NT4 and Linux 2.4 for PostMark, and Figure 12.18 shows the robustness of Windows NT4, 2000, and XP with respect to FL1 and FL2, for PostMark. (Robustness with respect to FL0 is given in Figure 12.3).

FURTHER VALIDATION CONCERNING SELECTIVE SUBSTITUTION. For each parameter-type class, we performed a sensitivity analysis regarding specific values of parameter substitution. This analysis revealed that different random values chosen to substitute for the original parameter lead to the same outcome of benchmark experiments. Hence, the benchmark results are not sensitive to the specific random values given to the corrupted parameters as substitution values.

Moreover, we checked the representativeness of incorrect data faults. One could argue that the OS is not assumed to detect this kind of fault as the substitution values are inside the validity domain of the parameter type. The analysis of the execution traces corresponding to experiments with incorrect data substitution that led to notification of error codes in the case of Linux revealed that 88.6% of the faults correspond to out-of-range data in the very particular context of the workload execution. Consequently, the notification of error codes was a normal outcome in these cases. Incorrect data are thus very useful; they can provide a practical way for generating out-of-range data in the execution context. Note that an enormous effort would be needed to analyze all execution contexts for all system calls to define pertinent substitution values for each execution context.

TABLE 12.8. Faultloads considered

	ID	IA	OORD	No. of experiments, PostMark (Windows NT4)	No. of experiments, PostMark (Linux 2.4)
FL0	x	x	x	418	206
FL1		x	x	331	135
FL2			x	77	55

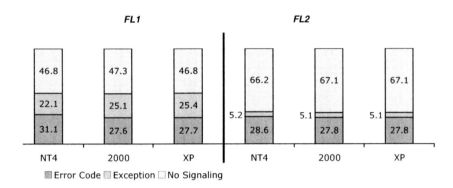

Figure 12.18. OS Robustness using FL1 and FL2 (%) and PostMark

12.6.2. Repeatability and Reproducibility

The benchmarking of a given system can be based either on an existing benchmark implementation (an existing prototype) or on an existing specification only. Repeatability concerns the benchmark prototype whereas reproducibility is related to the benchmark specification.

Repeatability is the property that guarantees *statistically equivalent results* when the benchmark is run more than once in the *same environment* (i.e., using the same system under benchmark and the same prototype). This property is central to benchmarking. Our OS dependability benchmark is composed of a series of experiments. Each experiment is run after system restart. The experiments are independent from each other and the order in which the experiments are run is not important at all. Hence, once the system calls to be corrupted are selected and the substitution values defined, the benchmark is fully repeatable. We have repeated all the benchmarks presented three times to check for repeatability.

Reproducibility is the property that guarantees that *another party* obtains statistically equivalent results when the benchmark is implemented from the *same specification* and is used to benchmark the same system. Reproducibility is strongly related to the amount of details given in the specification. The specification should be at the same time (i) *general enough* to be applied to the class of systems addressed by the benchmark and (ii) *specific enough* to be implemented without distorting the original specification. We managed to satisfy such a trade-off. Unfortunately, we have not checked explicitly the reproducibility of the benchmark results by developing several prototypes by different people. On the other hand, the results seem to be independent from the technique used to corrupt system call parameters. This makes us confident about reproducibility. However, more verification is still required.

12.6.3. Portability

Portability concerns essentially the faultload (i.e., its applicability to different OS families). At the specification level, in order to ensure portability of the faultload, the system calls to be corrupted are not identified individually. We decided to corrupt all system calls of the workloads. This is because OSs from different families do not necessarily comprise the very same system calls as they may have different APIs. However, most OSs feature comparable functional components.

At the implementation level, portability can only be ensured for OSs from the same family because different OS families have different API sets.

Let us consider the case of PostMark as an example, for which the first prototype developed was for Windows 2000. It proved to be portable without modification for Windows 2000 Server and Windows 2003 Server (PostMark activates the same 27 system calls with parameters), and with minor adaptations for the others. One system call (FreeEnvironmentStringA) is not activated under Windows NT4, NT4 Server, and XP, and another system call (LockResource) is not activated under NT4 and NT4 Server. In these cases, the system calls that are not activated are dropped from the substitution values database.

For Linux, the prototype was found to be portable across all OSs except the interceptor Strace, which is kernel dependent. Consequently, we used one version of Strace for Linux 2.2 and 2.4 and another version for Linux 2.6. Also, PostMark activates the same system calls for Linux 2.2.26 and 2.4, but it activates a supplementary system call (mmap2) for Linux 2.6.6. Consequently, we added this system call to the set of activated system calls and an entry in the substitution values database.

12.6.4. Cost

Cost is expressed in terms of effort required to develop the benchmark, run it, and obtain results. These steps require some effort that is, from our point of view, relatively affordable. In our case, most of the effort was spent in defining the concepts, characterizing the faultload, and studying its representativeness. The implementation of the benchmark itself was not too time-consuming.

Let us first consider PostMark, then JVM (which benefited a lot from the PostMark benchmarks as all benchmark components existed and we had only to adapt them).

For PostMark, the benchmark implementation and running took us less than one month for each OS family, spread as follows:

- The installation of PostMark took one day both for Windows and Linux.
- The implementation of the different components of the controller took about two weeks for each OS family, including the customization of the respective interceptors (Detours and Strace).
- The implementation of the faultload took one week for each OS family, during which we (i) defined the set of substitution values related to each data type and (ii) created the database of substitution values. Both databases are portable on OSs belonging to their family (one database for the Windows family and one database for the Linux family). However, small adaptations were necessary (see Section 12.6.3).
- The benchmark execution time for each OS is less than two days.

The duration of an experiment with workload completion is less than 3 minutes (including the time to workload completion and the restart time), whereas it is less than 6 minutes without workload completion (including the watchdog timeout and the restart time). Thus, on average, an experiment lasts less than 5 minutes. The series of experiments of a benchmark is fully automated. Hence, the benchmark execution duration ranges from one day for Linux to less than two days for Windows (25–27 system calls are activated by PostMark on Windows, whereas only 16–17 system calls are activated on Linux).

For JVM, the first step consisted in executing JVM for each OS to be benchmarked, to identify system calls activated. The second step was devoted to defining, for each system call, the parameters to be corrupted and the exact substitution values, to prepare the database to be used in the interception/substitution/observation modules. This step took a couple of days for the Linux family (activating 31–37 system calls depending on the version considered) and the double that for Windows because it activates 76 system calls. Adaptation of the benchmark controller and of the interception/substitution/observation modules required about one day for each family. The benchmark duration ranges from one day for each Linux OS to less than three days for each Windows OS.

12.7. CONCLUSION

We have presented the specification of a dependability benchmark for OSs with respect to erroneous parameters in system calls, along with prototypes for two families of OSs, Windows and Linux, and for two workloads. These prototypes allowed us to obtain the benchmark measures defined in the specification. We stress that the measures obtained for the different OSs are comparable as (i) the same workloads (PostMark and JVM) were used to activate all OSs, (ii) the faultload corresponds to similar selective substitution techniques applied to all system calls activated by the workload, and (iii) the benchmark conduct was the same for all OSs.

Concerning the robustness measure, the benchmark results show that all OSs of the same family are nearly equivalent. They also show that none of the catastrophic states of the OS (panic or hang) occurred for any of the Windows and Linux OSs considered. Linux OSs reported more error codes than Windows, whereas more exceptions were raised with Windows than with Linux. More no-signaling cases have been observed for Windows than for Linux.

Concerning the OS reaction time, results show that, globally, Linux reaction time, related to system calls activated by the workload, is longer than Windows reaction time. Refinement of this measure revealed a great variation around the average and that a minority of system calls with large execution times skewed the average. When these system calls are not considered, the reaction times of all the OSs of the same family become equivalent.

With respect to the restart time measure, Windows XP and Linux 2.2.26 have the shortest restart times in the presence of faults (71 s). Detailed analysis showed (i) a correlation between Windows restart time and the workload final state (in case of workload hang or abort, the restart time is 10% higher than in case of workload completion) and (ii) that Linux performs a check-disk after each 26 restarts. A restart with a check-disk is three to four times longer than the average.

We validated our benchmark, paying particular attention to representativeness of faultload and to the properties of repeatability, reproducibility, portability, and cost-effectiveness of the benchmark.

ACKNOWLEDGMENT

This work was partly supported by the European Commission (Project IST-2000-25425: Dbench, and Network of Excellence IST-026764: ReSIST). We would like to thank all the DBench colleagues who, through the numerous discussions throughout the project, helped us in defining the OS benchmark as is presented in this chapter. In particular, we are grateful to Jean Arlat, who contributed to the OS benchmark based on TPC-C Client.

REFERENCES

[Albinet et al. 2004] A. Albinet, J. Arlat, and J.-C. Fabre, "Characterization of the Impact of Faulty Drivers on the Robustness of the Linux Kernel," in *International Conference on Dependable Systems and Networks* (Florence, Italy), pp. 867–876, 2004.

[Arlat et al. 2002] J. Arlat, J.-C. Fabre, M. Rodríguez, and F. Salles, "Dependability of COTS Microkernel-Based Systems," *IEEE Transactions on Computers,* vol. 51, no. 2, pp. 138–163, February 2002.

[Chou et al. 2001] A. Chou, J. Yang, B. Chelf, S. Hallem, and D. Engler, "An Empirical Study of Operating Systems Errors," in *Proceedings of 18th ACM Symposium on Operating Systems Principles (SOSP-2001),* Banff, AL, Canada, pp. 73–88, ACM Press, New York, 2001.

[DBench] http://www.laas.fr/DBench, Project Reports section, project short final report.

[Durães and Madeira 2002] J. Durães and H. Madeira, "Characterization of Operating Systems Behavior in the Presence of Faulty Drivers through Software Fault Emulation," in *Proceedings of 2002 Pacific Rim International Symposium on Dependable Computing (PRDC-2002),* Tsukuba City, Ibaraki, Japan, pp. 201–209, 2002.

[Hunt and Brubaher 1999] G. Hunt and D. Brubaher, "Detours: Binary Interception of Win32 Functions," in *Third USENIX Windows NT Symposium,* Seattle, Washington, pp. 135–144, 1999.

[Jarboui et al. 2002] T. Jarboui, J. Arlat, Y. Crouzet, K. Kanoun, and T. Marteau, "Analysis of the Effects of Real and Injected Software Faults: Linux as a Case Study," in *Proceedings of 2002 Pacific Rim International Symposium on Dependable Computing (PRDC-2002),* Tsukuba City, Ibaraki, Japan, pp. 51–58, IEEE Computer Society Press, Los Alamitos, CA, 2002.

[Kalakech et al. 2004a] A. Kalakech, T. Jarboui, J. Arlat, Y. Crouzet, and K. Kanoun, "Benchmarking Operating System Dependability: Windows 2000 as a Case Study," in *Proceedings of 2004 Pacific Rim International Symposium on Dependable Computing (PRDC-2004),* Papeete, Tahiti, pp. 261–270, 2004.

[Kalakech et al. 2004b] A. Kalakech, K. Kanoun, Y. Crouzet, and J. Arlat, "Benchmarking the Dependability of Windows NT, 2000 and XP," in *Proceedings of International Conference on Dependable Systems and Networks (DSN-2004),* Florence, Italy, pp. 681–686, 2004.

[Kanoun et al. 2002] K. Kanoun, H. Madeira, and J. Arlat, "A Framework for Dependability Benchmarking," in *Supplemental Volume of the 2002 International Conference on Dependable Systems and Networks (DSN-2002)—Workshop on Dependability Benchmarking,* Washington, DC, pp. F.7–F.8, 2002; see also http://www.laas.fr/DBench.

[Kanoun et al. 2005] K. Kanoun, H. Madeira, M. Dal Cin, F. Moreira, and J. C. Ruiz Garcia, "DBench (Dependability Benchmarking)," in *Fifth European Dependable Computing Conference (EDCC-5)—Project Track,* Budapest, Hungary, 2005; see http://www.laas.fr/DBench.

[Kanoun et al. 2005a] K. Kanoun, Y. Crouzet, A. Kalakech, A.-E. Rugina, and P. Rumeau, "Benchmarking the Dependability of Windows and Linux Using Postmark Workloads," in *Proceedings of 16th International Symposium on Software Reliability Engineering (ISSRE-2005),* Chicago, 2005.

[Kanoun and Crouzet 2006] K. Kanoun and Y. Crouret, "Dependability Benchmarking for Operating Systems," *International Journal of Performance Engineering,* vol. 2, no. 3, pp. 275–287, 2006.

[Katcher 1997] J. Katcher, PostMark: A New File System Benchmark, Network Appliance, www.netapp.com/tech_library/3022.html, no. 3022, 1997.

[Koopman and DeVale 1999] P. Koopman and J. DeVale, "Comparing the Robustness of POSIX Operating Systems," in *Proceedings of 29th International Symposium on Fault-Tolerant Computing (FTCS-29)*, Madison, WI, pp. 30–37, IEEE Computer Science Press, Los Alamitos, CA, 1999.

[Koopman et al. 1997] P. J. Koopman, J. Sung, C. Dingman, D. P. Siewiorek, and T. Marz, "Comparing Operating Systems Using Robustness Benchmarks," in *Proceedings of 16th International Symposium on Reliable Distributed Systems (SRDS-16)*, Durham, NC, pp. 72–79, IEEE Computer Science Press, Los Alamitos, CA, 1997.

[Lindholm and Yellin 1999] T. Lindholm and F. Yellin, *The Java Virtual Machine Specification*, Addison-Wesley Professional, Reading, MA, 1999.

[McGrath and Akkerman 2004] R. McGrath and W. Akkerman, Source Forge Strace Project, http://sourceforge.net/projects/strace/, 2004.

[Mukherjee and Siewiorek 1997] A. Mukherjee and D. P. Siewiorek, "Measuring Software Dependability by Robustness Benchmarking," *IEEE Transactions of Software Engineering,* vol. 23 no. 6, pp. 366–376, 1997.

[Shelton et al. 2000] C. Shelton, P. Koopman and K. D. Vale, "Robustness Testing of the Microsoft Win32 API," in *Proceedings of the International Conference on Dependable Systems and Networks (DSN-2000)*, New York, pp. 261–270, IEEE Computer Science Press, Los Alamitos, CA, 2000.

[TPC-C 2002] TPC-C, TPC Benchmark C, Standard Specification 5.1, available at http://www.tpc.org/tpcc/. 2002.

DeBERT—DEPENDABILITY BENCHMARKING OF EMBEDDED REAL-TIME OFF-THE-SHELF COMPONENTS FOR SPACE APPLICATIONS

Diamantino Costa, Ricardo Barbosa,
Ricardo Maia, and Francisco Moreira

13.1. INTRODUCTION AND PREVIOUS WORK

In real-time systems, correctness of operation depends not only on the accuracy of the results provided but also on the results being produced within certain time constraints imposed by the system specification [Laplante 1997].

Real-time embedded applications in general, and particularly embedded applications in the aeronautics and space domains, have a significant number of requirements regarding the predictability of their response times. These system requirements are then passed down to real-time kernels (RTKs) and real-time operating systems (RTOS). RTKs/RTOS must exhibit predictable timing (and value) behavior despite the occurrence of unpredictable external events. Known and predictable interrupt latencies, task switch latencies, and device driver latencies are examples of requirements put on RTKs/RTOSs selected for safety-driven application designs [DOT/FAA 2002].

Adding to the picture, there is recently a trend to propose the usage of RTKs built on top of widespread commercial off-the-shelf (COTS) operating systems for avionics and space environments. Proper assessment of their behavior is needed, taking into account that they were developed without considering the dependability requirements in place on those domains.

Malfunctioning RTKs may have a strong impact on the dependability of an embedded system. Considering that embedded systems are difficult, and often impossible, to change or correct once deployed, assessing their predictability is of paramount importance. Recent standards and research papers [ISO/IEC-25051 2006] [DOT/FAA 2002] advise on quality requirements and pinpoint potential failure areas on such COTS products used in the scope of avionics and space. Still, those recommendations miss a straightforward methodology for assessing the timeliness related to safety and dependability of a COTS product. There is an increasing trend in using dependability benchmarks [Brown et al. 2002, Zhu et al. 2002], particularly on the subject of failure modes and robustness of real-time kernels [Chevochot and Puaut 2001, Koopman 1997, Arlat et al. 2002]. However, specific benchmarks targeted at dependability attributes of embedded real-time systems were not known so far to the best of our knowledge. A seminal work in the scope of benchmarking embedded real-time systems was the Hartstone synthetic benchmark [Weiderman 1989], which introduced a set of timing requirements for testing a system's ability to handle hard real-time applications. Hartstone workload is based on a variant of the well-known Whetstone benchmark [Wichmann 88].

The benchmark discussed here was developed in the scope of DBench [DBench 2001], and shares a common taxonomy and framework with other benchmarks targeted at other application domains in the DBench project.

The work presented here is the specification and validation of a benchmark for assessing the predictability of response time of a real-time kernel. This benchmark allows integrators and developers to assess and compare the determinism of response time of the service calls of different real-time kernels. Although this specific benchmark is targeted at space domain systems, the fundamentals of the work is applicable to any real-time system. The faultload used in this benchmark is composed by robustness faults at the real-time kernel interface with surrounding software components (typically an application using the real-time services). The measurements collected are combined into one single metric—predictability of response time.

Robustness is one key dependability attribute that impacts on the system property we are accessing—determinism of response time. Robustness testing has been widely used to assess COTS systems, especially when its internal structure is unknown, revealing deficiencies [Laplante 1997, Rodriguez et al. 2002, Moreira et al. 2003, DOT/FAA 2002]. Robustness testing usually considers the system as a "black box," applying a set of test values to its interface.

The rest of the chapter is organized as follows. Section 13.2 presents the benchmark specification, whereas Section 13.3 describes a specific implementation on the RTEMS real-time kernel. Section 13.4 describes the validation approach and Section 13.5 presents some concluding remarks. A list of acronyms used in this chapter is provided in Appendix 13.A.

13.2. BENCHMARK SPECIFICATION

This benchmark aims to evaluate the behavior of a real-time kernel in an onboard space system in the presence of faults, allowing for the quantification of one dependability attribute—the predictability of its response time.

The benchmark specification is composed of a set of measures (combined into one final metric), procedures, rules, configurations, methods, workload, and faultload. The benchmark target (BT) is the real-time kernel component of the system.

The following subsections present the benchmark characteristics: the benchmark objectives and description, its setup, procedures and measures, the workload, and the definition of the faultload model.

13.2.1. Objectives of the Benchmark

The objective of the proposed benchmark, DeBERT, is to allow integrators and developers to compare the predictability of a real-time kernel with respect to system calls response time.

13.2.2. System Under Benchmarking

The system under benchmarking (SUB) is an onboard space data system composed by several modules defined herein as the application or workload, a set of basic services (API) exposed by a real-time kernel (RTK), and the hardware computing platform. The workload application exercises a subset of control and data handling functionalities used in common onboard satellite space systems. Figure 13.1 depicts the layout of a complete space mission system, highlighting the system under benchmarking.

The benchmark target (BT) is a RTK that is a small-sized software component composed of a set of core functions common to the RTOS. Typically, a RTK is a library or unit used to link an application program to the processor. It offers a number of functions and procedures to manage, for instance, tasks, semaphores, system memory, interrupts, and signals, via its application programming interface (API).

13.2.3. Benchmark Conduct, Procedures, and Rules

The benchmark configuration must implement the conditions and steps described in the next subsections.

Benchmark Setup. Three main elements compose the setup required to run the DeBERT benchmark (see Figure 13.2):

1. The system under benchmarking running the benchmark target together with the defined workload.
2. The benchmark management system (BMS) responsible for (i) uploading the workload and the faultload into the SUB, (ii) controlling the benchmark execution, and (iii) storing the results in a database.

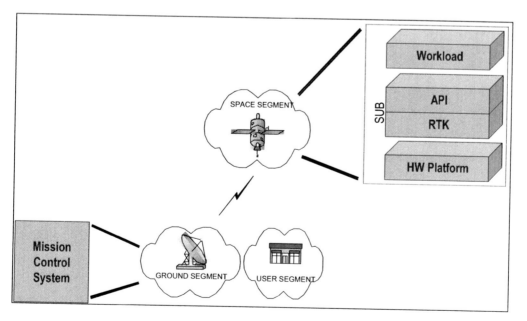

Figure 13.1. System under benchmarking definition.

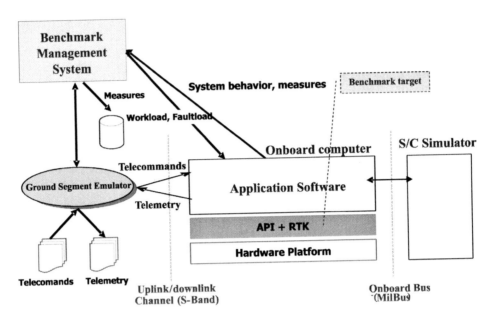

Figure 13.2. DeBERT benchmark setup.

3. The ground segment emulator (GSE). The GSE is not part of the SUB but is needed to provide the workload running on it with the necessary telecommands to be processed and to receive the associated telemetry.

The benchmark management system must perform the following functions:

1. Control the benchmarking process supervising the execution of all experiments.
2. Manage the workload uploading and start the workload in the SUB.
3. Manage the generation of the faultload and its application to the target system.
4. Collect results of experiments—execution times of API functions of the real-time kernel—from the SUB and store them in a nonvolatile memory format (file, database, etc.). The stored information should consist at least of the function names and the execution times.
5. Calculate the final benchmark results based on the collected data measurements.

The ground segment emulator (GSE) interacts with the workload sending the set of telecommands, at a predefined time, to be processed. When the telecommands are later executed, the GSE receives any telemetry sent by the system under benchmarking.

General Features. The generic features to take in consideration on the use of the DeBERT benchmark are presented next:

1. Every execution (nominal or with faults) of the workload shall include the reading of time stamps before and after the execution of each API function. The time interval calculated from time stamps (difference between end and start) is the execution

time of the function and must be sent to the benchmark management system just after its calculation.

2. The measurement of the execution time shall cancel out any possible preemption between the two time stamps. It is a feature of the proposed benchmark to measure uniquely the API response time. In terms of the implementation of the measurement procedure, this can be done by avoiding preemption or measuring any preemption time and subtract it from the overall measured execution time.

3. Two sequential readings of time stamps must be performed at the beginning of the workload execution. The time interval between them is sent to the benchmark management system as the time-measurement overhead. This execution time is used to cancel out the overhead to perform the measurements. For more details on this topic, see Appendix 13A, Section A.2.

4. The resolution of the clock/timer used in the system under benchmarking must be enough to "read" the time measurement overhead (TOverhead in Appendix 13A Section A.2).

5. The system under benchmarking is reset before executing the workload (both nominal execution and with faults).

6. During the benchmark execution, there should not be any interaction with the system under benchmarking apart from the benchmark management system and the ground segment emulator to reduce possible influences in the measured execution times.

7. There is no function under test for which the execution time would be dependent on the input parameters passed to it (e.g., functions like *sleep*) since a change on the execution time of such a function caused by a fault in the parameter is a correct behavior.*

8. There is also no function/parameter under test that can cause the currently executed task to be suspended or change the application scheduling process (e.g., functions like obtain_semaphore) since it can also influence the time of execution of some functions but it would be a correct behavior.

Benchmark Execution Steps. A two-step procedure should be performed when applying the DeBERT benchmark. This procedure ensures that the best performance of the benchmark is achieved and the trustworthiness on the measurements is increased.

STEP 1. EXECUTE THE NOMINAL WORKLOAD (E.G., WITHOUT FAULTS). Execute the workload the number of times necessary to achieve a level of confidence of 95% that the standard error of the results collected is lower (or equal to) than 10% of the average of the total workload execution time. The upper bound of the resulting confidence interval is denoted as TWorkLoad.

There is an obvious trade-off between confidence level and number of benchmark runs. The more time you let the benchmark run, more samples you will have.

STEP 2. EXECUTE THE WORKLOAD WITH FAULTS. Only one fault is injected per workload execution. The benchmark is not set up to deal with multiple faults per "download" of the

---

*For example, *sleep* (*time_interval*), where *time_interval* is faulted from its nominal value, for example 50, to another one, for example, 5, and will impact correctly the execution time of the *sleep* function from 50 to 5 units of time.

code; the idea is that each benchmark run begins with the run time system in the same initial state.

During this step, each parameter of every API function used in the workload is exercised with all test values. The number of possible combinations defines the number of times that the workload is executed in this step. The test values for each parameter type are defined in Section 13.3.6.

If the workload is not finished after 2*TworkLoad, its execution is aborted, speeding up the benchmark execution. The value of 2*TWorkLoad was chosen empirically from observation that it was enough to capture delays in execution but not too long to delay overall benchmark execution time.

13.2.4. Measurements and Metrics

In order to perform correct measurements, a set of metrics and measurement techniques are defined. This section defines the measures collected and the final benchmark metric used to assess experimental results.

Notation and Definitions. All definitions in this subsection concern the data collected during the execution of the benchmark.

Time durations are represented in time units (seconds, milliseconds, microseconds, or nanoseconds as deemed necessary for the particular benchmark target). The number of measurements for each function depends exclusively on the execution profile of the workload.

Divergence Metric (Dx). The divergence of each function X is denoted as D_X. Divergence is expressed as a percentage and represents the difference between longest measured time duration of function X in presence of faults and the upper bound of nominal execution of the function. Thus, it is calculated as

$$D_X = \frac{F_{max} - N_{max}}{N_{max}}$$

where F_{max} = maximum execution time with the faulty workload for function x, and N_{max} = maximum execution time with the nominal workload for function x. The divergence variation is from 0% (best) to ∞% (worst).

Both F_{max} and N_{max} time durations are calculated cancelling out time overheads as discussed previously.* The ground segment emulator (GSE) interacts with the workload sending the set of telecommands, at a predefined time, to be processed. When the telecommands are later executed, the GSE receives any telemetry sent by the system under benchmarking.

SPECIAL CASES WITH THE DIVERGENCE METRIC. If D_X is less than zero after the calculation, then D_X is assigned 0 (zero value). Indeed, there are cases where the execution time of a function with a faulty parameter may be lower than its nominal execution time. It happens mostly due to validity-checks code on the input parameters that return early when an error is detected. This causes, from a pure measurement perspective, D_X to be

---

*In order to reduce the impact of possible imprecision in the overhead measurement, the minimum measured overhead is subtracted from the nominal execution time and the maximum measured overhead is subtracted from the execution time with faults.

lower than zero. The option to floor these cases to zero was taken to reward RTOS designs that do this kind of assertion checking (e.g., defensive programming). Since divergence (D_X) being zero represents a response time with faults that "equals" the baseline execution, the authors have decided to pick it.

Whenever the workload execution is aborted and it can be proved that a specific function caused the system to hang, this function is assigned an execution time of TWorkLoad (upper bound of the observed nominal workload execution time).

Frequency of Out of Boundaries Execution (B_X). The frequency of out of boundaries execution of each function X is denoted as B_X. It is expressed as a percentage and represents the percentage of cases that the execution of a function in the presence of faults is longer than the upper bound of nominal execution of the function:

$$B_X = \frac{\text{number of cases where } F_{max} > N_{max}}{\text{total number of cases}}$$

The rationale for this metric is to expose the cases in which the impact of the faults causes execution times to extend well beyond variations that occurred during nominal runs. The lower the B_X, the better the RTK is. B_X varies from 0% (best) to 100% (worst)).

Predictability Metric (P_X). The Predictability P_X, used as a single summary result for each function X, is defined as

$$P_X = \frac{(1 - B_X)}{(1 + D_X)}$$

The value of P_X is in the range $[0 \dots 1]$ and the more near 1 P_X is, the more predictable a function X is.

Figure 13.3 illustrates the predictability figure vis-à-vis execution time. The predictability is then the ratio between the area of predictable executions (shaded area) and

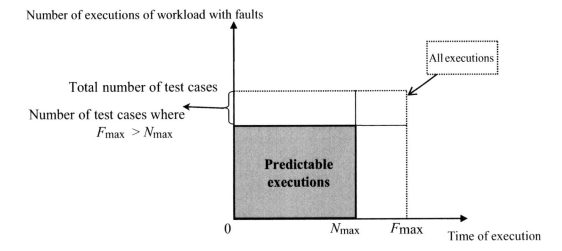

Figure 13.3. Predictability Model Definition

the area of all executions with faults. These areas are depicted as rectangles, with the time of execution shown as width and the number of executions shown as height.

RESULTS COMPUTATION FOR LOGICAL GROUPS OF FUNCTIONS. The individual function results may be grouped by some logical relationship between them. It is considered that task-related functions, for instance, have a logical relationship between them. Signal and memory-management-related functions are examples of two other logical groups of functions.

The divergence and frequency of each group is calculated as the average of the divergence and frequency, respectively, of every function in the group. Finally, predictability is calculated for group G:

$$D_G = \text{Average}_{\text{for all } X \in G}(D_X)$$

$$B_G = \text{Average}_{\text{for all } X \in G}(B_X)$$

$$P_G = \frac{(1 - B_G)}{(1 + D_G)}$$

The DeBERT Benchmark Metric. The summary DeBERT benchmark metric is computed as:

- **Divergence,** a measure of how *much* response times diverge from nominal ones in the presence of faults.
- **Frequency of out-of-boundaries execution,** a measure of how *often* that divergence occurs in presence of faults.
- **Predictability,** a combination of the both previous measures that measures *how much* and *how often* real-time kernel functions execution times diverge from nominal values in presence of faults.

The divergence D is calculated as the average of the computed divergence of every group of functions:

$$D = \text{Average}_{\text{for all } G}(D_G)$$

The frequency of out-of-boundaries execution (B) is calculated as the average of the computed frequency of every group of functions:

$$B = \text{Average}_{\text{for all } G}(B_G)$$

The Predictability P evaluates the determinism in response time, combining both the divergence in response time and the number of times it happens. It is calculated as

$$P = \frac{(1 - B)}{(1 + D)}$$

13.2.5. Workload

The workload proposed in this benchmark was developed with the requirement of being illustrative of applications, algorithms, and functionalities used and required in onboard space systems, but with a lot of simplification. The workload mimics a satellite function to schedule telecommands for later execution. The workload defined in this benchmark is then a telecommand onboard scheduler (OBS) process based on a functional model derived from the European Packet Utilization Standard [PUS 2003]. The purpose is to simulate the reception of telecommands, store them, and dispatch them in accordance to their activation time.

The onboard scheduler (OBS) receives telecommands that are recorded and will be executed at a specified later time. Figure 13.4 shows the general architecture of an onboard scheduler. The workload is divided in three major modules that are defined in the following subsections.

The OBS exercises several kernel functionalities such as task handling, task synchronisation, message passing, and timing. It receives telecommands from the input channel that are kept in the telecommand storage area until their release time when they are dispatched through the output channel.

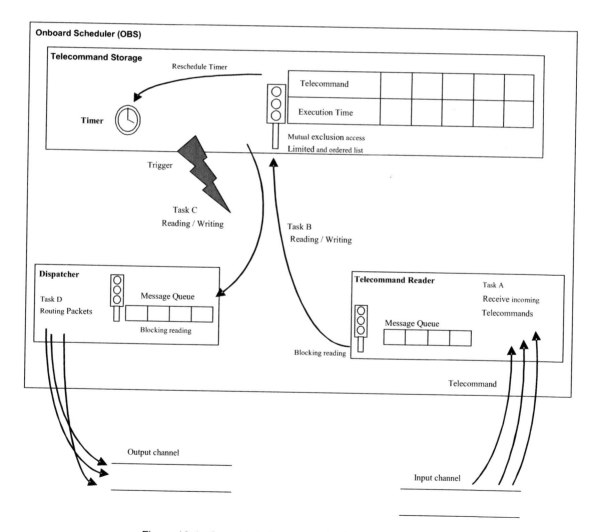

Figure 13.4. Onboard telecommand scheduler architecture.

TELECOMMAND READER. The telecommand reader is responsible for receiving the telecommands to be scheduled. As shown in Figure 13.4, one or more Tasks A is/are responsible for receiving the telecommands through the input channel and storing them in a message queue. More than one reader task ensures a higher throughput in the input channel. The access to this queue is synchronized with a semaphore. If the message queue is full, the task(s) will wait until a message is removed from the queue. Figure 13.5 presents an activity diagram for the telecommand reader task.

TELECOMMAND STORAGE. Telecommand storage is responsible for storing the telecommands in a way that allows a quick access to the release time of each telecommand to be executed. The access to the storage structure is synchronized and protected with a local binary semaphore.

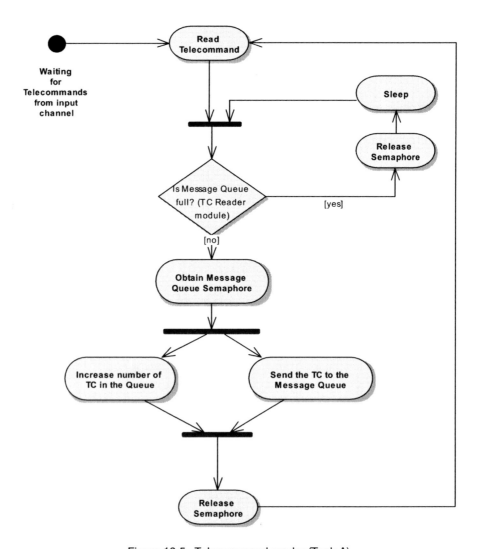

Figure 13.5. Telecommand reader (Task A).

Task B remains suspended until a new TC is inserted in the message queue. The total number of TCs in the system is protected by binary semaphores. They are obtained in each update, insertion, or removal of TCs in the telecommand storage. Whenever a telecommand is inserted or retrieved from the storage, a timer resets to the time of execution of the next telecommand to be released. Whenever a change occurs in the telecommand storage, the workload will keep track of the availability of each slot. Telecommands may be sent to the OBS in an out-of-order way. If a TC arrives and its execution time has already passed, it is released at once and the timer reset after its execution.

Finally, the timer is in charge of triggering Task C (see Figure 13.4), which retrieves the telecommands that are ready for execution and sends them to the dispatcher.

Figure 13.6 presents the activity diagram for the Task B in the telecommand storage module. The activity diagram of Task C is presented in Figure 13.7.

DISPATCHER. The dispatcher is responsible for sending the telecommands through the output channel to a specific instrument of the spacecraft (e.g., a camera, rover drill, etc.). It includes a message queue in which access is both synchronised and protected. The dispatcher may have one or more tasks that retrieve telecommands from the queue and send them through the output channel. This assures that the telecommands are dispatched even if an instrument is taking longer to respond.

Task D (Figure 13.4) retrieves telecommands from the queue and sends them through the output channel.

SYSTEM LOAD. The system load is defined by the set of telecommands sent by the ground segment emulator to the SUB (see setup in Figure 13.2).

Table 13.1 shows the times when the telecommands should be sent to the system under benchmarking and their associated release times.

The last telecommand sent is a special ending telecommand that forces the OBS to clean up the system, deleting all objects used and returning the used memory, and to terminate its execution.

13.2.6. Fault Model and Faultload

The fault model is based on robustness testing, which usually considers the system as a "black box," applying a set of test values to its interface.

The target of this benchmark is a RTK. The faults are injected into kernel function calls at the parameter level, corrupting a parameter value (Figure 13.8). The RTK code is never touched or changed. Only a single fault is inserted at a time. All system calls having parameters and used in the workload are to be corrupted during the benchmark process. The parameter corruption consists in replacing one parameter of one of the function calls in the workload with one test value from the set of values defined below. Only one parameter is corrupted at a time. Figure 13.9 shows an example of the corruption process.

Ideally, all possible values should be used as test values. Since this would have a huge impact on the total benchmark execution time and many of the values would have a similar impact, only a set of representative test values is considered from the entire possible range. The set of test values to use for each basic type include, typically, the values 0, 1, −1 and the boundaries (minimum and maximum) defined for the type plus $N*$ other val-

---

*It is assumed that $N = 100$ is statistically significant. Changing the number of test values used for each basic data type impacts on the total benchmark execution time.

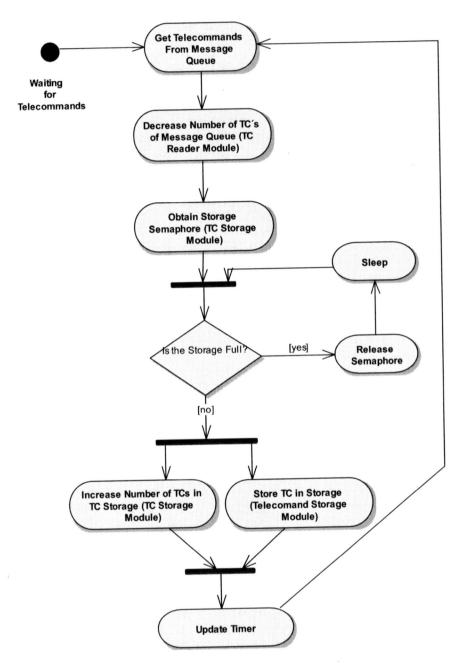

Figure 13.6. Telecommand storage (Task B).

ues from the range of the basic type. For unsigned data types, of the memory size of M bits, with range such as $[0; 2^M - 1]$, these values V_i for $i = 1 \ldots N$, are generated according to the formula

$$V_i = 2^{\left(i \times \frac{M}{(N+1)}\right)} \tag{13.1}$$

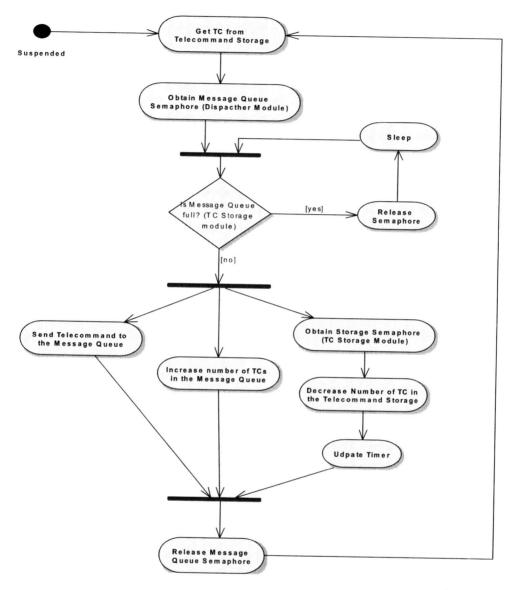

Figure 13.7. Activity diagram of Task C.

The test values generated by the formula are evenly spread among the range, in a logarithmic scale that diversifies the generated population. The values obtained are representative of each data type and repeatable. In order to have noninteger values, the expression $i \times [M/(N + 1)]$ shall be treated as real value in computation.

For signed data types with range such as $[-2^M; 2^M - 1]$, half of test values are calculated with the above formula for two times smaller N, and another half of values are the opposite numbers. The generated test values should be rounded to the integer type if necessary. Table 13.2 shows the set of test values defined for each basic data type.

TABLE 13.1. Schedule of telecommands sent to the system under benchmarking

Delay between the telecommands sent (measured in milliseconds in the GSE)	Release time (measured in microseconds from boot in SUB)	Delay between the telecommands sent (measured in milliseconds in the GSE)	Release time (measured in microseconds from boot in SUB)
1000	100	1000	730
500	150	1000	830
200	170	100	840
100	180	100	850
100	190	100	860
100	200	100	870
100	210	1000	970
200	230	1000	1070
1000	330	1000	1170
1000	430	1000	1270
1000	530	1000	1370
1000	630	1000	1470

13.3. BENCHMARK TRIAL WITH RTEMS REAL-TIME KERNEL

This section presents a trial of the DeBERT benchmark. It includes descriptions of the implementation of the workload, the faultload, and the set of procedures deployed to execute the Benchmark. Disclosure is given on the measurements and result analysis performed to achieve the benchmark metric, predictability.

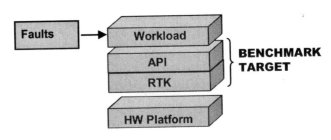

Figure 13.8. Fault load location in a system under benchmarking.

Normal code	Corrupted code
(…) TIMESTAMP1; Function_X (a, b); TIMESTAMP2; (…)	(…) TIMESTAMP1; Function_X (0, b); /* Parameter 'a' is corrupted */ TIMESTAMP2; (…)

Figure 13.9. Snippet of code with examples before and after fault Insertion.

TABLE 13.2. Test values used for each basic data type

Type name	Typical and boundaries values used for each basic data type	Other values
Char	0, 1, 255	V_I for $I = 1 \ldots N$ according
Signed char	0, −1, 1, −128, 127	to the Eq. (13.1)
Int	0, −1, 1, −2147483648, 2147483647	
Unsigned int	0, 1, 4294967295	
Short int	0, −1, 1, −32768, 32767	
Unsigned short int	0, 1, 65535	
Long	0, −1, 1, −9223372036854775808, 9223372036854775807	
Unsigned long	0, 1, 18446744073709551615	
Pointers	NULL*	

*The only typical test value used for pointers is the NULL pointer. Other test values will also be generated according to Eq. 13.1.

13.3.1. Experiment Setup

Benchmark Configuration. Figure 13.10 presents the benchmark configuration used.

The benchmark management system was implemented using the Xception™ tool [XCEPTION]. Xception™ was used to automate the execution of the experiments and to control the process of fault insertion.

Xception™ requires three scripts to automate the experiments:

1. *Build.* This script compiles the workload and builds it together with the RTK into an image file that is executed in the target system.
2. *Input Generator.* This script is used to notify the ground segment emulator that the workload is running and that the telecommands can be sent.
3. *Output Collector.* This script extracts the relevant workload output to be stored in the database.

The ground segment emulator is the process that interacts with the SUB sending the predefined set of telecommands and receiving the telemetry provided by it.

The system under benchmarking is composed by the workload compiled together with the benchmark target running on a Sparc-ERC32 simulator.* All processes were running on a single machine whose characteristics are summarized in Table 13.3.

Features concerning the implementation of the workload (OBS) are:

- The measurement of the execution time of functions was done using timer functions as defined in specification, where the time was read just before and just after the execution of the functions. The execution time is immediately sent to the standard output after its calculation.
- The workload does not send anything to the standard output, apart from the execution times of the analyzed functions.

*The simulator used is embedded in sparc-rtems-gdb, a flavored version of the GNU Debugger.

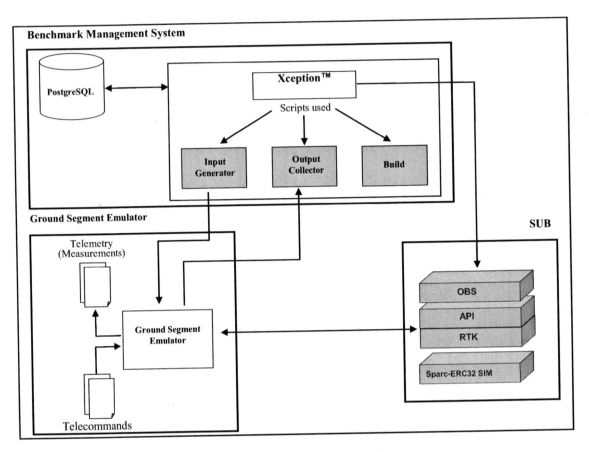

Figure 13.10. Benchmark configuration.

TABLE 13.3. Test machine configuration

vendor_id	GenuineIntel
cpu family	6
Model	5
model name	Pentium II (Deschutes)
cpu MHz	400.915
cache size	512 KB
RAM Mem	256 MB
OS running	Linux kernel 2.4.19-4GB SuSe 8.1
Database	PostgreSQL 7.2.2
Compiler	cross-compiler sparc-ERC32-rtems v2.95.2 19991024 (release)
ERC32 Sim.	4.18 (configured for SPARC-ERC32 target)
Injection tool	Xception™ 2.0 (with ERC32-RTEMS Software plug-in)

- To avoid other running tasks influencing the results, preemption is not considered in the workload during the measurement of the execution time of the examined functions.

BENCHMARK TARGET (BT) DESCRIPTION—RTEMS. The real-time executive for multi-processor systems (RTEMS) is a real-time kernel that provides a high performance environment for embedded critical and military applications with the following features:

- Multitasking capabilities
- Homogeneous and heterogeneous multiprocessor systems support
- Event-driven, priority-based, preemptive scheduling
- Optional rate monotonic scheduling
- Intertask communication and synchronization
- Priority inheritance mechanisms
- Responsive interrupt management
- Dynamic memory allocation
- High level of user configurability

The internal architecture for RTEMS can be viewed as a set of layers that work closely with each other to provide the set of services to the real-time applications. The executive interface presented to the application is formed by directives (RTEMS API Calls) grouped into logical sets called resource managers, as presented in Figure 13.11.

RTEMS 4.5.0 provides several APIs for real-time application programming. The Classic API was selected and used by the workload. The Classic API is the native and older RTEMS API. Each manager is responsible for a specific feature:

- The initialization manager is responsible for initiating and shutting down RTEMS.
- The task manager provides a comprehensive set of directives to manage and administer tasks.
- The clock manager provides support for time-of-day-related capabilities.
- The timer manager provides support for timer facilities.

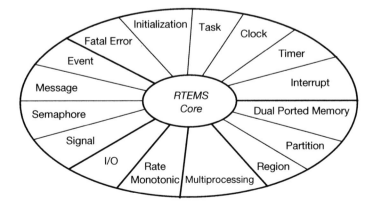

Figure 13.11. RTEMS Classic API internal architecture.

- The semaphore manager provides support for synchronization and mutual exclusion capabilities.
- The message manager provides communication and synchronization facilities using RTEMS message queues.
- The interrupt manager allows the application to connect a function to a hardware interrupt vector.
- The event manager provides a high-performance method for intertask communication and synchronization.
- The signal manager provides the features required for asynchronous communication.
- The partition manager provides facilities to dynamically allocate memory in fixed-size units.
- The region manager provides facilities to dynamically allocate memory in variable sized units.
- The dual ported memory manager provides facilities for converting addresses between internal and external representations for multiple dual-ported memory areas (DPMA).
- The I/O manager provides a well-defined mechanism for accessing device drivers and a structured methodology for organizing device drivers.
- The fatal error manager provides facilities to process all fatal and irrecoverable errors.
- The rate monotonic manager provides facilities to manage the execution of periodic tasks.
- The user extensions manager provides the applications developer facilities to augment the executive by allowing them to supply extension routines that are invoked at critical system events.
- The multiprocessing manager provides facilities for implementing multiprocessor environments.

The RTEMS version 4.5.0 is distributed via anonymous ftp. This release can be found in ftp://ftp.oarcorp.com/pub/rtems/releases/4.5.0. The complete source code and documentation can be found in www.rtems.com. The list of API functions used in this workload implementation is presented in the next section.

WORKLOAD. The workload implements the onboard system scheduler as defined in the specification. It is divided in several modules coded in the C language that are described in the following subsections.

MODULES DESCRIPTION. The workload consists of a set of six concurrent tasks that exercise a set of specific RTEMS functions calls. As defined in the specification, it does define a set of three distinct modules: telecommand reader, telecommand storage, and dispatcher modules. Each module exercises a set of functions from several RTEMS managers such as task manager, clock manager, timer manager, semaphore manager, message manager, and partition manager. The initialization procedures and each module are defined in the following subsections.

INITIALIZATION PROCEDURES. The *main* and *init* tasks are responsible for the initialization of all other tasks, system memory, structures, objects, and variables used in the workload. Table 13.4 lists the kernel functions used by the initialization tasks.

TABLE 13.4. RTEMS function calls used in the initialization process

API Name	Manager
rtems_task_create	Task
rtems_task_start	Task
rtems_task_set_priority	Task
rtems_task_mode	Task
rtems_clock_set	Clock
rtems_timer_create	Timer
rtems_partition_create	Partition
rtems_partition_get_buffer	Partition
rtems_semaphore_create	Semaphore
rtems_semaphore_obtain*	Semaphore
rtems_semaphore_release	Semaphore
rtems_message_queue_create	Message

*This function call, used by the workload, was not measured since its response time depends on other system variables.

TELECOMMAND READER MODULE. Telecommand reader receives telecommands sent by the GSE, temporally stores them in a queue and then sends them to the telecommand storage. A single task for receiving telecommands from the input channel was implemented. This module uses several RTEMS functions as shown in Table 13.5.

TELECOMMAND STORAGE MODULE. The telecommand storage module is responsible for storing the telecommands in a defined structure. The storage was implemented using RTEMS partitions. A local binary semaphore was used to synchronize and protect the accesses to the storage. The counting of the number of TCs in the system is protected by binary semaphores, which are obtained in each update, insertion, or removal of TCs. Whenever a telecommand is inserted or retrieved from storage, the system timer is reset to the time of execution of the next telecommand to be launched. The TC may be sent to the OBS in an out-of-order way. If a TC arrives and its execution time has already passed, it is executed at once and the timer is rescheduled after its execution. The RTEMS functions exercised in this module are listed in Table 13.6.

TABLE 13.5. RTEMS function calls used by the telecommand reader module

API Name	Manager
rtems_task_set_priority	Task
rtems_task_mode	Task
rtems_task_set_priority	Task
rtems_timer_fire_after	Timer
rtems_timer_cancel	Timer
rtems_semaphore_obtain	Semaphore
rtems_semaphore_release	Semaphore
rtems_message_queue_send	Message
rtems_message_queue_get_message_pending	Message

TABLE 13.6. RTEMS functions call used by TC storage module

API Name	Manager
rtems_task_resume	Task
rtems_task_set_priority	Task
rtems_task_mode	Task
rtems_clock_get_time	Clock
rtems_timer_fire_after	Timer
rtems_timer_cancel	Timer
rtems_semaphore_release	Semaphore
rtems_message_queue_send	Message
rtems_message_queue_receive	Message
rtems_message_queue_get_message_pending	Message

DISPATCHER MODULE. The dispatcher module includes a message queue by which access is both synchronised and protected. A special ending telecommand (with the command "END") is used (i) to force the OBS to clean up the system, deleting all objects used and returning the used memory, and (ii) to terminate its execution. The RTEMS functions exercised in this module are described below in Table 13.7.

TIME MEASUREMENT. The execution time of the API function calls was measured by collecting a time stamp just before and after calling the API function. The associated timer was initialized just before collecting the first time stamp. In order to eliminate influences on the results by other running tasks, preemption was avoided during the measurement process. This was accomplished by taking into account three actions that assure that only a single task is inside the measuring block at a time and that this task will not be preempted:

- A semaphore is used.
- The task's priority is raised.
- The task's execution mode is changed to avoid preemption,* to avoid asynchronous signals and to avoid time for slicing between tasks.

13.3.2. Faultload

The typical test values for each data type were used as specified. One hundred test values for each data type were computed by applying the formula provided in the benchmark

*Refer to Appendix 13.B on the rationale behind this benchmark requirement.

TABLE 13.7. RTEMS functions call used by dispatcher module

API Name	Manager
rtems_task_set_priority	Task
rtems_task_mode	Task
rtems_semaphore_release	Semaphore
rtems_message_queue_receive	Message
rtems_message_queue_get_message_pending	Message

specification. The test values were inserted, changing the workload source code, and then the workload was compiled, built, and executed.

13.3.3. Experiments and Results

The test values defined (in Section 13.2.6) applied to the workload implementation generated a total of 5300 different faults. Each fault was applied in the workload one by one in independent executions of the workload. The average execution time was approximately 26 seconds and the maximum execution time obtained was about 43 seconds. Faults with direct influence on the response time of a specific function were not considered in the experiments. Furthermore, any fault that may have caused preemption during the measurement process was not taken into account as well.

The results should be read understanding that:

- The **divergence** represents the averaged difference between the longest measured execution time of all APIs in presence of faults and the upper bound of nominal execution execution time. It ranges from 0% (best) to $\propto$% (worst).
- The **frequency** is the number of executions where the response time was bigger than the nominal. Ranges from 0% (best) to 100% (worst).
- The **predictability,** $P_x = [(1 - F_x)/(1 + D_x)]$, is used as single summary result and is proportional to the number of faulty executions, where the response time is equal or lower than the nominal time, and inversely proportional to the divergence. It ranges from 0.0 (worst) to 1.0 (best).

FINAL RESULTS. The final benchmark value is obtained according to the specification. As presented in Table 13.8, the predictability value suggests that the RTK under analysis has a high degree of determinism.

Figure 13.12 depicts the predictability of the response time for the groups of functions ("managers" in RTEMS parlance) of RTEMS. It is clearly an heterogeneous distribution with Semaphore calls response time being fairly unpredictable and the Partition Manager calls highly predictable.

Table 13.9 gives a summary per API call for the semaphore management set of functions on RTEMS. Response time of the semaphore release operations is quite unpredictable in the presence of faults ($\sim$0.46) when compared with create or delete operations.

More detailed information including the raw measurements and intermediate results leading to these final results can be found in the DBench project reports.

EFFORT NEEDED. The effort needed to execute the proposed benchmark depends on the know-how available. The effort described considers that the person/team implementing it has some knowledge and is familiarized with embedded systems, real-time processing, cross-compilation, onboard scheduling, and testing.

TABLE 13.8. Final benchmark results

	Divergence	Frequency	Predictability
Target System	16.7 %	0.9 %	0.8492

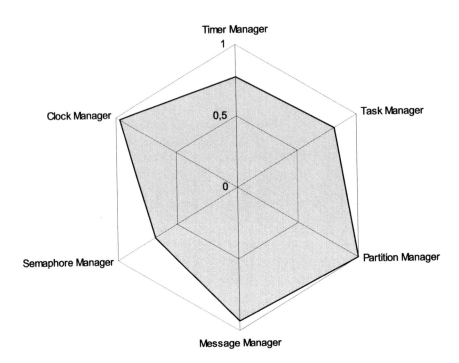

<u>Figure 13.12.</u> Predictability of RTEMS managers response time.

Starting from the specification, to acquire some know-how, implementing the work-load specified, the fault model, and the scripts to perform a brief result analysis took us 3 man-months. Furthermore, automating the benchmark execution process, executing the benchmark, and analyzing the results took one additional man-month.

Benchmarking a new system but reusing data from an available trial is a much simpler and less time-consuming process. It includes porting the workload, configuring the auto-mated fault generation tool (Xception™), and adapting the automation process. This process is estimated to take 1 man-month.

BENCHMARK EXECUTION DURATION. The benchmark is composed of a set of execu-tions, where the workload is executed without applying any faults, and a second set of ex-ecutions applying the faultload.

For practical reasons, the second set of executions was divided into five different sub-sets. The total execution time was about 2 days ($\approx$ 46.24 hours) executing continuously. This was calculated taking the average execution time per gold run multiplied by the

<u>TABLE 13.9.</u> Benchmark evaluation for the RTEMS semaphore manager

	Number of measurements	Divergence	Frequency	Predictability
Semaphore Manager Function call	197636	44.57 %	0.74 %	0.6866
rtems_semaphore_release	187843	116.67 %	7.5e-3 %	0.4615
rtems_semaphore_delete	3302	13.33 %	0.3 %	0.8797
rtems_semaphore_create	6491	3.7 %	1.91 %	0.9459

number of gold runs plus the average execution time with faults multiplied by the total number of faults injected (5300).

The total benchmark execution time can be customized to the requirements and/or limitations of the benchmark user. This customization is done by changing the number of test values for each data type and/or by changing the number of nominal workload executions. Decreasing the number of nominal executions impacts on the confidence level of the results. Decreasing the number of test values for each data type (reducing the number N in Eq. 13.1 impacts directly on the time required to execute the benchmark. It also impacts on the representativeness of the faultload and on the confidence level.

13.4. BENCHMARK VALIDATION

A methodology for the validation of a proposed benchmark was set up in the DBench project. It basically consists of ensuring that a set of properties defined are verified by the benchmark specification and its implementation(s). The properties defined are the representativeness, repeatability and reproducibility, portability, nonintrusiveness, and scalability. This section discusses these properties in the scope of the DeBERT benchmark.

13.4.1. Representativeness

Measures. Real-time applications in general and in the space domain in particular have (hard) deadlines to meet. Since their functionality is dependent on the services provided by the underlying real-time kernel, the role played by it is of paramount importance. Proving statistically that a hard real-time application will always meet its deadlines often requires some kind of worst-case execution analysis. In a similar way, forecasting missed deadlines on a soft real-time application is not trivial. Knowing the degree of determinism of the response time of an RTK helps to assure the correctness of such analysis and assure that the hard real-time application will (statistically) meet its deadlines.

Workload. The workload selected implements the functionality standard for the space domain that is present in almost all spacecraft. Although not exhaustive on the use of the RTK API calls, it provides a realistic distribution of the services that space data handling applications require on a RTOS.

Faultload. Critical embedded systems are usually thoroughly verified and tested before deployment but even in this type of system around 10 software defects per 1000 lines still remain after deployment [Regan 2004]. The faultload defined emulates software defects whose consequences are to call an RTK service with values that are valid in the parameter definition domain but are semantically erroneous.

13.4.2. Reproducibility and Repeatability

This dependability benchmark is composed of a set of experiments. In each experiment, the system is reset and the application is uploaded to it. This makes the experiments independent from each other.

Portability. A dependability benchmark is portable if it can be easily applied to different benchmark targets. The workload is defined in a general way without referring to any peculiarities of any RTK, thus being able to be implemented for different RTKs. The faultload definition is also generic and portable. Every parameter of every system call (whatever it is) used in the workload implementation is to be corrupted using a set of test values. The test values are defined referring to the basic data type with counterparts in every system and programming language.

Nonintrusiveness. It is a characteristic of these types of embedded systems that the workload and the kernel are combined together into one single image file that is burned in an EPROM and placed in (or uploaded to) the target system. The faults are inserted at the workload when calling a RTK service call. The benchmark target (the RTK) is never modified.

Scalability. The benchmark specification has several characteristics that allow scaling. The size of the queues in the workload components can vary according to the number of tasks interacting with the input/output channels. Also, the number and frequency of telecommands sent to the target system can be adapted for systems with different sizes. The number of test values for each basic data type can also be adapted depending on the system size and restrictions. The number of test values for each basic data type impacts directly on the number of faults to insert and on the total time required to execute the benchmark.

13.5. CONCLUSIONS

COTS real-time kernels are increasingly used in embedded systems and in particular in the aeronautic, space, and powertrain domains. The applications running on these systems depend on the services being provided correctly and within the time constraints. This chapter presented the specification of DeBERT, a dependability benchmark for assessing the predictability of response time of real-time kernel service calls.
The summary DeBERT benchmark metric is computed as:

- **Divergence,** a measure of how *much* response time diverge from nominal ones in presence of faults.
- **Frequency of out-of-boundaries execution,** a measure of *how* often that divergence occurs in presence of faults.
- **Predictability,** a combination of the both previous metrics that measures *how much and how often* real-time-kernel function execution times diverge from nominal values in presence of faults.

A portable and simple fault model based on robustness testing was defined to be applied in the parameters of the benchmark target service calls. Robustness is indeed one key dependability attribute that impacts on the property we were accessing—determinism of response time.
Description of a benchmark trial, applied to the widely used RTEMS real-time kernel, was made, along with analysis of the results obtained. The trial showed that the benchmark specification can be implemented in short time and effort—roughly 3 man-months.
The outcomes of the DeBERT trial on RTEMS 4.5.0 highlighted that:

- Divergence is 16.7% (zero % being the best value possible)
- Frequency of "out-of-boundaries" is 0.1% (only 1 time in 1000 is a function response time beyond the upper bound due to the presence of faults)
- The Predictability is 0.8492, a very good score (1 being the best and zero the worst)

Furthermore, the data made available enables us to conclude that predictability is not homogenous for the entire product; specific types of functions show different behavior. The semaphore release function, for instance, is quite unpredictable (predictability of 0.46, mainly driven by a very high divergence figure of 116%). This kind of insight is a powerful demonstrator that the benchmark can provide feedback to enhance product score, thus effectively contributing to a better product.

So far, and to the best of our knowledge, the work herein described is the first attempt to combine performance and dependability properties for a real-time system on a single benchmark. Despite picking a space domain application, the fundamentals of the work presented here are applicable to any real-time system, making DeBERT easily portable to other application domains such as aeronautics, powertrain, or industrial automation.

Ongoing and future work comprises two main directions:

- Trials of the benchmark on RTLinux, VxWorks, and RTAI on top of single-board computers and simulators of PowerPC and SPARC-based processors.
- Introducing a simple set of metrics aimed at quick feedback for practitioners: average response time in the presence of faults and worst-case response time.

APPENDIX 13.A

A.1. Acronyms and Definitions

Acronyms	Description
API	Application Programming Interface
BMS	Benchmark Management System
BT	Benchmark Target
COTS	Commercial-Off-The-Shelf
DBS	Dependability Benchmark Specification
DeBERT	**De**pendability **B**enchmarking of **E**mbedded **R**eal-**T**ime Off-the-Shelf Components for Space Applications
ERC32	Radiation-tolerant SPARC V7 processor developed for space applications
GSE	Ground Segment Emulator
OS	Operating System
PUS	ESA Packet Utilization Standard
RTEMS	Real-Time Executive for Multiprocessor Systems
RTK	Real-Time Kernel
RTOS	Real-Time Operating System
SUB	System Under Benchmarking
TWorkLoad	Upper bound for the observed execution time of the nominal workload, i.e., execution without faults.

A.2. Reasoning for the Calculation of the Time Measurement Overhead

Measuring the execution time of any function by wrapping it with calls to a time stamp function imposes some overhead on the measured time. Getting two consecutive time stamps allows measuring this overhead ($T_{Overhead}$ in Figure 13.13) in order to remove it from the execution time of the measured function.

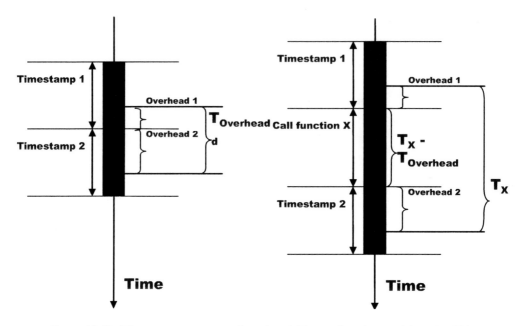

Figure 13.13. Time measurements of overhead ($T_{Overhead}$) and normal function (T_x).

The time returned by the time stamp function corresponds to a point in time during its execution. The execution time measured for a function (T_x in Figure 13.13) includes the overhead that comes from time stamping before and after calling the function. Subtracting the overhead ($T_{Overhead}$) from the measured time (T_x) adds more precision to the measured execution time.

Removal of this overhead is crucial to compare different systems using different hardware platforms. Indeed, bear in mind that in our case the benchmark target does not include the hardware platform. Subtracting the overhead from the measured time makes the calculations and comparisons fair since only the contribution of the real-time kernel is being taken into account. Otherwise, the comparison may not be fair, as the overheads of time stamping can be different in different implementations and on different platforms.

APPENDIX 13.B AVOIDING PREEMPTION IN TIME MEASUREMENTS

In a multitasking environment, the RTOS/RTK scheduler is responsible for task scheduling. Several algorithms may be implemented (rate monotonic, deadline monotonic, etc.), or a basic time-slicing management can be provided. Since its creation, a task is activated and can be suspended or blocked before its termination (see Figure 13.14). A task can get out of an "execution" state due to the execution of a higher-priority task (preemption), because its time slice (or period) on the processor has elapsed or blocks itself .

In order to measure the execution time of an API function call, it is important to assure that we are only measuring the execution time of the task that is in charge to execute the API call. In this sense, it is possible to measure the total time of execution allowing preemption (sum of all execution times on Task A; see Figure 13.15) or just measure the execution time, avoiding preemption althogether. Since the measurement of the execution

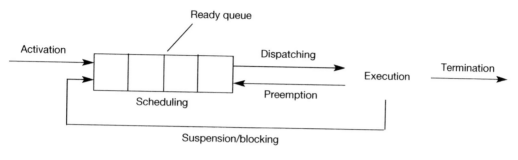

Figure 13.14. Task life cycle.

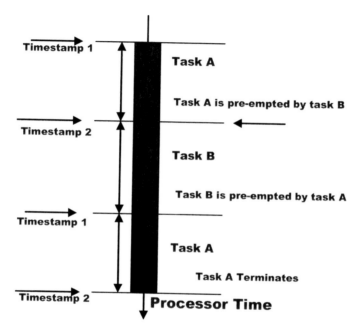

Figure 13.15. Measurements of execution time of Task A, preempted by Task B, in response to some API function call.

times does not change the pattern of execution of the workload, the process of avoiding preemption is nonintrusive. It was chosen to be used within this implementation.

REFERENCES

[Arlat et al. 2002] J. Arlat, J.-C. Fabre, M. Rodríguez, and F. Salles, "Dependability of COTS Microkernel-Based Systems," *IEEE Transactions on Computers,* vol. 51, no. 2, pp. 138–163, 2002.

[Brown et al. 2002] A. Brown, L. C. Chung and D. A. Patterson, "Including the Human Factor in Dependability Benchmarks," in *Proceedings of the 2002 DSN Workshop on Dependability Benchmarking,* Washington, DC, 2002.

[CCSDS 2003] Space Packet Protocol. Blue Book. Issue 1. September 2003.

[Chevochot and Puaut 2001] P. Chevochot and I. Puaut, "Experimental Evaluation of the Fail-Silent Behavior of a Distributed Real-Time Run-Time Support Built from COTS Components," in *Proceedings of the International Conference on Dependable Systems and Networks (DSN-2001)*, pp. 304–313, Göteborg, Sweden, IEEE Computer Science Press, Los Alamitos, CA, 2001.

[DBench 2001 CF1] CF1—State of the Art, August 2001, DBench (http://www.laas.fr/DBench/Deliverables/CF1.pdf).

[DBench 2001 CF2] CF2—Preliminary Dependability Benchmark Framework, August 2001, DBench (http://www.laas.fr/DBench/Deliverables/CF2.pdf).

[DBench 2002 ETIE1] ETIE1—Measurements, June 2002, DBench (http://www.laas.fr/DBench/Deliverables/ETIE1.pdf).

[DBench 2002 ETIE2] ETIE2—Fault Representative, June 2002, DBench (http://www.laas.fr/DBench/Deliverables/ETIE2.pdf).

[DBench 2002 ETIE3] ETIE3—Workload and Faultload, June 2002, DBench (http://www.laas.fr/DBench/Deliverables/ETIE3.pdf).

[Donohoe 1990] P. Donohoe, R. Shapiro, and N. Weiderman, "Hartstone Benchmark User's Guide," CMU/SEI-90-UG-1, ESD-90-TR-5, 1990.

[DOT/FAA 2002] Study of Commercial Off-The-Shelf (COTS) Real-Time Operating Systems (RTOS) in Aviation Applications, Technical Report DOT/FAA/AR-02/118, December 2002.

[ISO/IEC-25051 2006] ISO/IEC 25051 Software Engineering—Requirements for quality of Commercial Off-The-Shelf (COTS) Software Product and Instructions for Testing, Final Draft International Standard, 2006.

[Koopman 1997] P. J. Koopman, J. Sung, C. Dingman, D. P. Siewiorek, and T. Marz, "Comparing Operating Systems Using Robustness Benchmarks," in *Proceedings of 16th International Symposium on Reliable Distributed Systems (SRDS-16)*, Durham, NC, pp. 72–79, 1997.

[Kropp et al. 1998] N. Kropp, P. Koopman, and D. Siewiorek, "Automated Robustness Testing of Off-the-Shelf Software Components," in *28th Fault Tolerant Computing Symposium*, June 1998.

[Laplante 1997] P. A. Laplante, *Real-time Systems Design and Analysis: An Engineer's Handbook*, 2nd ed., IEEE Press, New York, 1997.

[Moreira et al. 2003] F. Moreira, R. Maia, D. Costa, N. Duro, P. Rodríguez-Dapena, and K. Hjortnaes., "Static and Dynamic Verification of Critical Software for Space Applications," in *Proceedings of the Data Systems In Aerospace (DASIA 2003)*, 25 June 2003 (http://www.eurospace.org/presentations_dasia_2003.htm).

[OAR 2000] OAR, RTEMS C User's Guide, September 2000, www.rtems.com.

[PUS 2003] Space Engineering—Ground Systems and Operations—Telemetry and Telecommand Packet Utilization, ECSS-E-70-41A, 30 January 2003.

[Regan 2004] P. Regan and S. Hamilton, "NASA's Mission Reliable," *IEEE Computer,* vol. 37, no 1, pp. 59–68, January 2004.

[Rodriguez et al. 2002] M. Rodríguez, J.-C. Fabre, and J. Arlat, "Assessment of Real-Time Systems by Fault Injection," in *ESREL 2002 European Conference,* pp. 101–108, Lyon, France, 2002.

[RTLinux 2005] http://www.rtlinuxfree.com/.

[Shames 2004] P. Shames, T. Yamada, and N. Lindman, "Tools for the Reference Architecture for Space Data Systems," in *Ground Systems Architectures Workshop*, March 30–April 1, Manhattan Beach, CA, 2004.

[Wang 2002] A. Wang, "Using Java Hartstone Benchmark In A Real-Time Systems Course," in *32nd ASEE/IEEE Frontiers in Education Conference,* Boston, 2002.

[Weiderman 1989] N. Weiderman, "Hartstone: Synthetic Benchmark Requirements for Hard Real-Time Applications," CMU/SEI-89-TR-23, June 1989.

[Wichmann 88] B. A. Wichmann,"Validation Code for the Whetstone Benchmark," Technical Report DITC 107/88, National Physical Laboratory, Teddington, Middlesex, UK, March, 1988.

[XCEPTION] Critical Software, Xception™ Tool—Automated Fault-injection Environment, White Paper, http://www.xception.org/.

[Zhu et al. 2002] J. Zhu, J. Mauro, and I. Pramanick, "R-Cubed (R3): Rate, Robustness, and Recovery—An Availability Benchmark Framework," TR-2002-109, Sun Microsystems Laboratories, 2002.

14

BENCHMARKING THE IMPACT OF FAULTY DRIVERS: APPLICATION TO THE LINUX KERNEL

Arnaud Albinet, Jean Arlat, and Jean-Charles Fabre

14.1. INTRODUCTION

Dependability concerns, encompassing robustness assessment, are essential questions to answer before a developer can make the decision whether to integrate off-the-shelf (OTS) components into a dependable system. Here, and in what follows, robustness is understood as the degree to which a system operates correctly in the presence of exceptional inputs or stressful environmental conditions, in compliance with the generic definition (dependability with respect to external faults) given in [Avižienis et al. 2004].

From a cost-effectiveness viewpoint, operating systems and kernels are privileged OTS components as candidates for integration into a system. However, integrators are often reluctant to make such a move without obtaining a deeper knowledge and understanding about such a component beyond functional issues, in particular with respect to its failure modes and its behavior in the presence of faults. Due to the opacity that is often attached to the commercial offer and to the difficulty and significant cost associated with the availability of the source code, the Open Source option, for which access to the source code is granted, is progressively making its way as an attractive and promising alternative. Also, results of many studies have shown that Open Source solutions did not exhibit significantly more critical failure modes and in some cases they were even found to demonstrate behaviors superior to commercial options [Koopman and DeVale 1999, Arlat et al. 2002, Marsden et al. 2002, Vieira and Madeira 2003]; see also Chapter 5 for the latter. In this chapter, we will simply denote such components (either commercial or Open Source) as OTS components.

In the past years, several experimental studies have addressed this important issue from different perspectives [Koopman and DeVale 1999 (see also Chapter 11), Arlat et al. 2002, Madeira et al. 2002]. This has also led to the proposal of tentative dependability benchmarking approaches, aimed at characterizing the robustness of computer systems and OTS [Tsai et al. 1996, Mukherjee and Siewiorek 1997, Brown and Patterson 2000]. However, such proposals were still preliminary and did not reach the level of recognition attached to performance benchmarks. As pointed out earlier (e.g., in the Preface and several chapters), the DBench project, in which this work was included, was another major contribution aimed at promoting such an approach by defining a comprehensive framework for the definition and implementation of dependability benchmarks, see also [Kanoun et al. 2002, Kanoun et al. 2005a].

A large part of the code that makes up an operating system consists of device driver programs and the OS configuration may change not only at installation time, but also in operation. For example, in the case of Linux, drivers have consistently represented more than half of the source code [Godfrey and Tu 2000]. This ratio is smoothly increasing; recent releases have accounted for almost 60% of the code [Gu et al. 2003]. More importantly, as the whole size of the kernel is rapidly growing, this results in an exponential increase in the number of lines of code of the driver programs. Such programs are commonly developed by third-party hardware device experts and integrated by kernel developers. This process is not always well mastered and erroneous behavior of such programs that are intimately connected to the kernel may have dramatic effects. As pointed out in [Murphy and Levidow 2000] for Windows and as shown by the analysis of the Linux source code carried out in [Chou et al. 2001], a significant proportion of operating system failures can be traced to faulty drivers. Things are not improving much; indeed, as quoted in [Swift et al. 2004], in Windows XP, driver programs are reported to account for 85% of recently reported crash failures.

It is thus necessary to investigate and propose new methods, beyond the collection of field data, for specifically analyzing the impact of faulty drivers on operating systems. Fault injection techniques, whereby faulty behaviors are deliberately provoked to simulate the activation of faults, provide a pragmatic and well-suited approach to support such an analysis. Among the fault injection techniques, the software-implemented fault injection (SWIFI) technique (e.g., see [Carreira et al. 1998]) provides the proper level of flexibility and low intrusiveness to address this task. Based on these principles, we have developed an experimental environment for the evaluation of the robustness of the Linux kernel when faced to abnormal behaviors of its driver programs.

To our knowledge, very few research studies have been reported on this topic. The work reported in [Edwards and Matassa 2002] also concerns the Linux kernel but focuses, rather, on the dual problem of characterizing the robustness of driver programs when subjected to hardware failures. The authors have devised a sophisticated approach to inject faults in the driver under test that relies on the appealing notion of the common driver interface (CDI) that specifies the driver interactions within the kernel space. In [Gu et al. 2003], the authors have conducted a comprehensive dependability analysis of the Linux kernel. However, in this study fault injection has been related to the execution stream of the kernel code; more precisely, a selected set of functions of the kernel has been targeted, namely, the processor dependent code, the file system support code, the core kernel code, and the memory management code.

Our goal is instead to benchmark the robustness of an operating system kernel in the presence of faulty drivers. In line with this objective, but considering several instances of the Windows series, in [Durães and Madeira 2003] the authors have used mutations of the executable code of the driver to simulate a faulty driver. The work reported in this chapter is rather complementary, in the sense that we investigate an alternative approach: fault injection is targeting the parameters of the kernel core functions at the specific interface between the driver programs and the kernel. To support this approach, we revisit and adapt the notion of the common driver interface of [Edwards and Matassa 2002] by focusing the injection on the service/system calls made by the drivers to the kernel via the core functions. This way, the definition of the fault injection experiments more thoroughly impact the interactions between the drivers and the kernel. Also, the errors provoked can simulate both the consequences of design faults or hardware-induced faults. It is worth noting that a subsequent and complementary work has been reported recently that adopts the same system model (explicit separation between the kernel and the drivers) and a similar fault model to study the impact of faulty drivers on a Windows CE-based system [Johansson and Suri 2005]. The main goal was to study the error propagation process to support the placement of protection wrappers (e.g., see [Fraser et al. 2003]), as was already carried out in [Arlat et al. 2002].

The material reported herein elaborates on the work published in [Albinet et al. 2004]. The organization of the chapter is as follows. Section 14.2 describes the specific issues addressed by the approach we propose, in particular in the light of other works dealing with the characterization of operating system robustness. In Section 14.3, we briefly describe the various types of driver programs and introduce the specific interface considered to simulate faulty drivers for the Linux kernel, the *driver programming interface*. Section 14.4 presents the benchmarking attributes, namely, the faultload, the workload, the measurements, and the measures that allow for performing analyses accounting for several end-user viewpoints. Section 14.5 describes the main features of the RoCADE (Robustness Characterization Against Driver Errors) platform that supports the conduct of the experiments. Section 14.6 presents a sample of results and illustrates how the proposed benchmarking framework can support the analysis of the results. Finally, Section 14.7 concludes the chapter.

14.2. CONTEXT AND DEFINITION OF THE APPROACH

Due to their central role in the functioning of a computer system, operating systems are the primary targets for developing dependability benchmarks. Figure 14.1 depicts the

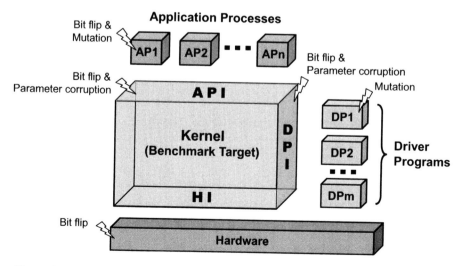

Figure 14.1. Interactions between an operating system kernel and its environment.

software architecture of a computer system. In this chapter, due to the emphasis put on the analysis of the impact of the driver programs, the benchmark target (BT), according to the terminology put forward by the DBench project (e.g., see [Kalakech et al. 2004], as well as Chapters 5 and 6), is the operating system kernel. Drawing further on that terminology, the whole figure describes the system under benchmark (SUB), that is, the supporting environment and context within which the analyses are conducted. As shown on the figure, the kernel features three main interfaces with its environment. The first one is basically concerned with hardware interactions, whereas the other two are software related.

The "lightning" symbols in Figure 14.1 identify possible locations where faults can be applied. The interfaces and related faults are briefly described as follows:

1. The hardware interface (HI) is primarily related to the hardware layer. The main interactions are made via the raising of exceptions. At this level, several studies have been reported in which faults were injected by means of bit flips into the memory of the SUB; for example, see [Arlat et al. 2002, Gu et al. 2003]; see also Chapter 15 for what concerns the latter reference.

2. The interface with the applications processes corresponds to the application programming interface (API). The main interactions are made by means of system calls. A significant number of studies were reported that target the API to assess the robustness of the operating systems (e.g., in the form of code mutations [Durães and Madeira 2006]; see also Chapter 6), by means of bit flips [Jarboui et al. 2003] or by corrupting the system calls [Koopman and DeVale 1999, Kanoun et al. 2005b]; see also Chapters 11 and 12 for what concerns these respective references.

3. The interactions with drivers are made through the driver programming interface (DPI), which is the programming interface for the development of the drivers. The detailed definition of this interface is presented in Section 14.3.

Concerning the third item, the form of fault injection we are advocating is carried out by way of corruption of the calls to the functions of the kernel made by the drivers. Such an approach has been motivated by the work carried out in [Jarboui et al. 2003]. In this work, assertions issued from traces characterizing the actual erroneous behavior induced by faulty drivers were used to assess whether similar error patterns could be obtained by using several fault injection techniques (either bit flip or parameter corruption) at the API level. This study showed that API-level fault injection was not able to produce errors that matched the error patterns provoked by real faults in drivers. This result further substantiates the need to conduct investigations specifically aimed at closely simulating the impact of faulty drivers. To this end, we have concentrated our efforts on intercepting and corrupting the parameters of the system calls issued by the drivers at the DPI [Edwards and Matassa 2002]. Compared with the mutation of the code of the drivers used in [Durães and Madeira 2003], this approach allows for carrying out a more focused and efficient set of experiments that are suitable to thoroughly test the various kinds of interactions between the drivers and the kernel. The price to pay for this is a precise identification of the DPI upon which the faults are specified. However, it is worth noting that (as for the approaches targeting the API), such a preliminary analysis has to be carried out only once for each kernel family and can be reused for analyzing most drivers. More details on the types of faults considered are given in Section 14.4.1.

The interfaces depicted in Figure 14.1 (especially the API and the DPI) also provide suitable locations to observe the consequences of the injected faults. At the API level, the typical relevant behaviors include error codes returned to the calling application process-es and kernel hangs. In practice, although a lot of exceptions are raised by the SUB at the hardware layer, for the sake of efficiency they are often caught at the API when reported via the kernel. The DPI provides a favorable level of observation for the detailed charac-terization of the reactions of the kernel to the corrupted service calls issued by the drivers. The related measurements include error codes returned to the driver. Comprehensive measurements can also be made at the application level, for example, workload abort and completion. Although time measurements can be collected to evaluate the workload exe-cution in the presence of faults [Kalakech et al. 2004], the reported results only consider nontimed robustness measures expressed as frequencies of occurrence of each considered outcome.

As a general comment, it is important to stress that the founding of the benchmarking attributes proposed in this chapter (especially the faultload and measurements) on explicit interfaces (namely the DPI and API) that can be easily shared by several candidate BTs is fundamental for guaranteeing a fair assessment. Indeed, this is an essential and favorable feature for sustaining the development and dissemination of relevant dependability benchmarks, elaborating on the approach proposed in this chapter.

14.3. THE DRIVER PROGRAMMING INTERFACE

In this section, we briefly recall the functional interactions that characterize the communi-cation between the drivers and the kernel. This allows for the kernel functions and para-meters involved in these interactions to be identified and, thus, the DPI on which we de-fine the types of faults to be injected.

14.3.1. Application Processes, Kernel, and Drivers

Classically, the application processes execute in a restricted address space (user space). This is meant to reduce the risk for an application process to corrupt the kernel addressing space. This way, it is likely that the errors caused by a faulty application process mainly impact its own address space and, thus, are limited to its execution. Conversely, mainly for performance reasons, the kernel and the drivers are executed in privileged mode (ker-nel mode) and thus share the same address space. This means that the risk for a defective driver to impact the behavior of the kernel cannot be neglected. Due to the fact that it is not always possible to associate a "pedigree" to the whole set of drivers that can potential-ly be integrated, drivers are a potential threat for the kernel. This is further exacerbated by the programming languages (such as C language) that use pointer arithmetic without IMM (integrated memory management). This applies to several popular general-purpose operating systems (e.g., Linux and Windows9x). The drivers can also access the whole set of functions of the kernels, not only those that are used to carry out operations on the kernel space, but also on the application space.

14.3.2. The Various Drivers

An interesting comparative study of driver interfaces for several popular operating sys-tems is presented in [Zaatar and Ouaiss 2002] as an initial step toward the standardiza-tion of the Linux driver interface. Irrespective of the different solutions adopted for a specific operating system family, in practice two main categories of drivers can be distinguished:

1. Software drivers—they have no direct access to the hardware layer of the devices, but rather to an abstraction (e.g., tcp/ip stack, file system).
2. Hardware drivers—they are concerned with hardware devices, either peripheral (network card, disk, printer, keyboard, mouse, screen, etc.) or not (bus, RAM, etc.).

In both cases, the role of a driver is to provide an abstract interface for the operating system to interact with the hardware and the environment:

- More specifically, a driver is meant to implement a set of basic functions (read, write, etc.) that will activate peripheral devices.
- On top of drivers, the input–output instructions no longer depend on the hardware architecture.
- Drivers define when and how the peripheral devices interact with the kernel.

For example, in the case of a driver relying on polling, an application process issues a request, via a system call (`open, read or ioctl`) to access a peripheral device (network card, disk, printer, keyboard, mouse, screen, etc.). The processor enters the supervisor mode, via a stub in the case of Linux, and executes the code of the driver corresponding to the proper operation. After completion of the operation, the driver frees the processor and the processor then resumes the execution of the application process in user mode.

Although device drivers may induce a strong influence on the kernel (as most of them are run in kernel mode), they are often developed by third parties and then integrated into the kernel after its distribution. This explains why it has been found that they significantly contributed to the failure of the operating system [Chou et al. 2001].

14.3.3. Specification of the DPI

The drivers make use of specific system calls (denoted symbols for dynamic module drivers in the case of Linux) in order to perform tasks. The most salient categories are depicted in Table 14.1.

Each of these categories gathers a set of functions that are devoted to the programming of the kernel and drivers using execution privileges within the kernel address space. For example, in the case of Linux, functions allow for acquiring and releasing of an interrupt channel (`request_irq, free_irq`) and for retrieving the status of such a channel (`irq_stat`). These symbols form the basis for the development of drivers for managing the interrupt channels. All such symbols feature a calling protocol that is similar to the system calls of the Linux API.

This is illustrated by the *signature* of the `request_irq`:

```
int request_irq(unsigned int irq,
        void (*handler)(),
        unsigned long irqflags,
        const char * devname,
        void *dev_id)
```

TABLE 14.1. Outline of the categories of symbols for Linux

Categories	Examples of typical symbols
Memory Management	Kmalloc, kfree, free_pages, exit_mm, . . .
Interrupt Management	add_timer, del_timer, request_irq, free_irq, irq_stat, add_wait_queue, _wait_queue, finish_wait, . . .
File System Management	fput, fget, iput, follow_up, follow_down, filemap_fdatawrite, filemap_fdatawait, lock_page, . . .
Control Block Management	blkdev_open, blkdev_get, blkdev_put, ioctl_by_bdev, . . .
Registration	register_sysctl_table, unregister_sysctl_table, sysctl_string, sysctl_intvec, . . .
Others: Software interrupts, dma management, buffering management, resource handling, process management, interfaces, debug, miscellaneous "tools"	raise_softirq, open_softirq, cpu_raise_softirq, dump_stack, ptrace_notify, current_kernel_time, sprintf, snprintf, sscanf, vsprintf, kdevname

The `request_irq` function allocates a peripheral device to an interrupt channel. The function returns a success (error) code (an integer value) to inform the calling driver program of the proper (or not) handling of the reservation of the channel. The first argument, `irq`, is an unsigned integer that designates the channel to allocate. The second one, handler, is a pointer to the interrupt manager. The third one is an unsigned long integer that represents the flags that define the type of the reservation (exclusive or not, etc.). The parameter devname is the name of the peripheral device that is reserving the channel. The last parameter is a pointer to a "cookie" for the interrupt manager.

From more than a thousand symbols (including functions, constants, and variables), Linux release 2.4.18 includes about 700 kernel functions. Some are more used than others. The kernel functions devoted to memory reservation are definitely much more solicited than the ones attached to the handling of a pcmcia device. The types of the parameters being used in kernel programming are voluntarily restricted to integers (`short` or `long`, `signed` or `unsigned`) and `pointers`. We have referenced all these functions along with their signature, which allows for the number of parameters and their types to be specified for each symbol. These types are defined over a validity space (see extreme values in Section 14.4.1)

In the same way that the API gathers all the available system calls issued by the application processes, the DPI gathers all the functions of the kernel that are available to be used by the drivers. These kernel symbols constitute the features offered to the developers in kernel mode.

14.4. THE BENCHMARKING ATTRIBUTES

This section briefly describes the *execution profile* and the *measures* that are considered for the benchmarking analysis [Arlat et al. 1990]. The execution profile includes both the *workload* (the processes that are executed to activate the drivers and the kernel) and the *faultload* (the set of faults that are applied during the fault injection experiments via the DPI). The experimental *measures,* which are meant to characterize the reaction and/or behavior of the kernel in presence of a faulty driver, are elaborated from a set of observations (*readouts* and *measurements*) that are collected during each experiment.

In order to illustrate how measurements can be used to derive useful measures, we will consider several dependability viewpoints according to the perceptions that different users can have of the observed behaviors. In the sequel to this section, we consider in turn the faultload, the workload, the measurements, and the measures that build up on these measurements with the objective of dependability benchmarking.

14.4.1. The Faultload

For corrupting the parameters of the symbols of the DPI, we have used the SWIFI technique because of its flexibility and ease of implementation. More precisely, in order to generate more efficient test conditions, we have focused the corruption of function parameters on a set of specific values. In particular, this provides a better control of the types of corruptions that are made, which significantly facilitates the interpretation of the results obtained. Faults are injected into each parameter of each relevant function of the DPI, as shown in Figure 14.2.

The principle of the method is to intercept a function when it is called, to substitute the value of its parameters with a corrupted value, and then to resume the execution of the function with this faulted value. The value that is substituted to the original value of the faulted parameter depends upon the type of the parameter. Table 14.2 shows the values considered for each relevant type. For the first three types, bounding and mid values are considered. For pointers, the set of corrupted values are: NULL, a max bounding value, and a random value.

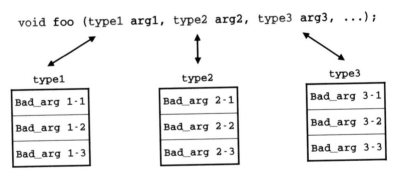

Figure 14.2. Principle of corruption of the parameters of a function.

TABLE 14.2. The faulty parameters for each type

Type	Bad_Arg 1	Bad_Arg 2	Bad_Arg 3
int	INT_MIN	0	INT_MAX (0x7FFFFFFF)
uint	0	INT_MIN (0x80000000)	ULONG_MAX (0xFFFFFFFF)
ushort	0	SHRT_MIN (0x8000)	USHRT_MAX (0xFFFF)
pointer	NULL	random( )	All bits = 1 (0xFFFFFFFF)

14.4.2. The Workload

In order to provoke the activation of the DPI by the driver programs, so as to mimic the nominal behavior, we rely on an indirect activation procedure by means of a workload applied at the level of the API. We consider a synthetic and modular workload combining several activation processes, each targeting one (or several) of the drivers evaluated. Each application process carries out a set of elementary operations concerning a specific hardware or software driver component:

1. Deinstallation of the target component that permits (only if the driver is currently used by the system) starting the test later on by registering the component.
2. (Re-)installation of the component allowing for testing component registration.
3. Series of requests meant to test the driver's operation.
4. Deinstallation, by which the unregistration of the component is tested.
5. Reinstallation, whenever needed, in particular if the driver is mandatory for the SUB's operation (e.g., network card or file system).

For example, in the case of a network card, the application process disables the network, unloads the network driver, reloads it, enables the network, runs a test on a private Ethernet network (intranet), disables the network, unloads the driver, reloads it, and, finally, enables the network.

The main differences between the application processes that form the workload concern the specific requests to be applied to stimulate the driver.

In order to better assess the impact of the fault on the whole SUB, a subsequent workload execution is carried out after the fault has been withdrawn; this is particularly useful to improve the diagnosis in the cases when no outcome is observed as the result of the run when a fault is injected (the so-called "silent" behavior as reported in the CRASH scale proposed in [Koopman and DeVale 1999, see also Chapter 11]. In the reported experiments the workload that is executed for improving the diagnosis is the same as the workload used for the fault injection experiments. Accordingly, hereafter we will refer to it as the "replay" workload.

14.4.3. The Measurements

The goal of the set of experiments reported here is to determine the set of relevant observations to be incorporated into a prototype dependability benchmark, focusing on robustness with respect to faulty drivers. Accordingly, to get relevant insights from the conducted experiments, it is necessary to obtain a good variety of results. To that end, we have specified two levels of observation: (i) *external or user-oriented,* meant to characterize the faulty behavior, as perceived at the level of the API, (ii) *internal or peripheral device oriented,* which detail the impact of the faults on the kernel, as perceived at the level of the DPI.

The *external* level includes the observation of the errors reported by the kernel to the application processes in the workload (exceptions, error codes, etc.). These observations can be augmented by a more *user-oriented* perception by means of observations directly related to the application processes (e.g., the *execution time* of the workload or the *restart time*). The *internal* level focuses on the exchanges between the kernel and the faulted driver. The specific observations made at each level as well as the related appraisals are depicted in Table 14.3.

TABLE 14.3. Observation levels, events, and appraisals

Level	Event	Appraisal good/bad	Abbreviated name
Internal	DPI Error Code: Code returned by the kernel at the level of the DPI	good	EC
External	Exception: Processor's exceptions observed at the API level	good	XC
	Kernel Hang: The kernel no longer replies to a request issued via the API	bad	KH
	Workload Abort: The workload has been abruptly interrupted (some API service requests could not be made).	bad	WA
	Workload Incorrect: The workload completes, but not all the return codes are "success."	bad	WI
	Workload Completion: This event allows for the execution time of the workload programs to be measured.	good	WC

The *error code* returned by a function of the kernel provides an essential insight into the impact of the fault on the intimate behavior of the kernel. Indeed, from a robustness viewpoint, the kernel symbol should be able to react to a service call including an argument with a corrupted value by returning an error code that matches the type of fault being injected. When a hardware *exception* is raised while a process executes in the kernel address space, the kernel tries to abort the process or enters the "panic" mode. The consideration of *workload*-related events (WA or WI) allows for additional insights to be obtained, especially in cases when no error is reported by the kernel. In that respect, the "replay" workload that is executed after each run during which a parameter is corrupted allows for the damage caused by the application of faulty call to be assessed by identifying whether the SUB was able to recover a stable state on its own or if a specific restart is necessary.

A *hang* of the kernel is diagnosed when the kernel is no longer replying to requests. The main reasons for such blocking are either because it executes an infinite loop or it is waiting for an event while interrupts are masked. Such outcomes cannot be observed by the system and, thus, require external monitoring.

Measuring the execution time of the workload programs provides useful information on the capacity of the kernel to handle the applications processes in presence of faults and is thus a desirable feature from the benchmarking point of view. Due to the specific nature of the workload (synthetic workload), such a measurement was not carried out in the study described here. The interested reader can refer to the work reported in [Kanoun et al. 2005b]; see also Chapter 12. The technique used therein can be applied to obtain the corresponding measurements.

14.4.4. Interpretation of Measurements to Yield Benchmarking Measures

The observations described in the previous section offer a basis upon which various types of analyses can be carried out, depending on how one interprets the impact of the combined behaviors observed for various dependability concerns. In practice, different interpretations of the measurements are possible depending on the specific context in which the kernel is to be integrated. In particular, when one is favoring safe behavior of the workload, then error notification via error code return or even kernel hangs might be proper or acceptable behaviors. Conversely, returned error codes or selective application process aborts are much more suited for cases in which availability of the kernel is the desired property. This is further exacerbated in cases in which several outcomes (e.g., error code returns and hangs) are observed simultaneously within the same experiment run. So as to reliably account for various points of view, one has to carefully analyze such cases. It is worth pointing out that the types of analyses that we are proposing here are in line with and elaborate on the related study reported in [Rodríguez et al. 2002] and on the assessment framework used in [Durães and Madeira 2003].

14.4.4.1. Outcomes and Diagnoses. Table 14.4 identifies the outcomes and several criteria that can be considered for exploiting the outcomes. The first set of columns shows the possible outcomes (i.e., combinations of the events defined in Table 14.3). Two categories are distinguished: error notification (explicit error reporting) and failure modes. The second part of the table illustrates how the outcomes of several event collections per experiment can be diagnosed according to a set of simple criteria (order of occurrence of observed events and priority given either to error notification or failure modes).

First, it is worth noting that all events considered are not fully independent; accordingly, not all combinations are valid. In particular, this is the case for workload abort (WA) and workload incorrect (WI); indeed, WA dominates WI, that is, no WI can be observed when a WA has been diagnosed. This is identified by "X" in Table 14.4. This explains

TABLE 14.4. Possible outcomes and diagnoses

	Outcomes					Priority to		
	Notification			Failure modes		First event	Error notification	Failure modes
#	EC	XC	WA	WI	KH			
O1	0	0	0	0	0	No Obs.	No Obs.	No Obs.
O2	1	0	0	0	0	EC	EC	EC
O3	1	1	0	0	0	EC	EC+XC	EC+XC
O4	0	1	0	0	0	XC	XC	XC
O5	1	1	0	0	1	EC	EC+XC	KH
O6	1	0	0	0	1	EC	EC	KH
O7	0	1	0	0	1	XC	XC	KH
O8	0	0	0	0	1	KH	KH	KH
O9	1	1	1	X	1	EC	EC+XC	KH+WA
O10	1	0	1	X	1	EC	EC	KH+WA
O11	0	1	1	X	1	XC	XC	KH+WA
O12	0	0	1	X	1	KH	KH+WA	KH+WA
O13	1	1	1	X	0	EC	EC+XC	WA
O14	1	0	1	X	0	EC	EC	WA
O15	0	1	1	X	0	XC	XC	WA
O16	0	0	1	X	0	WA	WA	WA
O17	1	1	0	1	0	EC	EC+XC	WI
O18	1	0	0	1	0	EC	EC	WI
O19	0	1	0	1	0	XC	XC	WI
O20	0	0	0	1	0	WI	WI	WI
O21	1	1	0	1	1	EC	EC+XC	WI+KH
O22	1	0	0	1	1	EC	EC	WI+KH
O23	0	1	0	1	1	XC	XC	WI+KH
O24	0	0	0	1	1	WI	WI+KH	WI+KH

Legend—EC: error code, XC: exception, KH: kernel hang, WA: workload abort, WI: workload incorrect.

why the table has only 24 rows. Among these, row O1 designates cases in which none of the events has been observed. This is a classical issue in testing and experimental studies when no impact is observed. This might be due to several alternatives (fault was not activated, error masked, etc.); we will come back on this in Section 14.6.1.

When several events are observed within the same experiment, various decisions can be made in order to categorize the outcomes. One usual approach is to give priority to the first event that has been observed. However, it is not always possible to have precise timing measurements for all events. Indeed, in some cases this may require sophisticated and heavy instrumentation (e.g., see [Rodríguez et al. 2003]), which might be out of the scope of the proposal for a dependability benchmark that should be portable, minimally intrusive, and cost-effective.

Other alternatives include giving priority (i) to error notifications [e.g., error codes returned (EC) and exceptions (XC)] or (ii) to the failure modes observed [workload abort (WA), workload incorrect (WI) and Kernel Hang (KH)]. Considering the last two strategies, the first one is clearly optimistic (it assumes that notification will be able to preempt and confine any subsequent impact), whereas the second one is rather pessimistic (the system is assumed to always fail, irrespective of the possible handling of the error ensuing from the notification). In both cases, when multiple events are observed pertaining to the prioritized category, they are recorded for further analysis. The order of occurrence is also highlighted in the table. For example, when priority is given to failure modes, "WI+KH" in row O21 means that WI precedes KH. It is worth noting that, due to the way the considered events are collected, "priority to error notification" closely matches "priority to first event," because error notifications always precede all considered failure modes.

Adopting a classification relying only on end-user perception (i.e., considering only observations made via the API) would have resulted in discarding EC events. For example, in that case O2 would have been merged into O1 and it would not be possible to discriminate O3 from O4, and so on.

14.4.4.2. Viewpoints and Interpretation.

More elaborate interpretations can be defined that feature more dependability-oriented measures. We will consider three of such interpretations that correspond to three distinct contexts: (1) responsiveness of the Kernel (RK), that is, maximize error notification; (2) availability of the kernel (AK), that is, minimize kernel hangs; and (3) safety of the workload (SW), that is, minimize delivery of incorrect service by the application processes. These constitute top-level perceptive viewpoints that support the selection criteria for a system integrator to rank SUBs of interest. This perception follows from the clustering of the detailed outcomes from Table 14.4 (see Table 14.5).

The main rationale for the interpretation associated with RK is to positively consider outcomes gathering both notification events and failure modes. The fact that the kernel is able to report an error is considered as positive, even when failure modes are observed at workload level. Conversely, AK will rank differently the cases in which either a KH or a WA is observed: indeed, the occurrence of a KH has a dramatic impact on the availability of the system, whereas an abort of the workload can be recovered more easily. The measure associated with SW characterizes the case in which safe behavior of the workload is required. Accordingly, we advocate that most favorable outcomes correspond to events prone to induce "fail-safe" or "fail-silent" behaviors, that is, error notifications and kernel hangs, whereas workload abort is assumed to correspond to a critical event, and incorrect completion to an even worse one. Nevertheless, as safety is typically an application-level property, alternative viewpoints could have been devised; in particular, from a "fail-fast"

TABLE 14.5. Viewpoints and dependability measures

Viewpoint: Responsiveness/Feedback of the Kernel		
#	Outcomes [–O1]	Rationale
+ RK1	O2–O4	An error is notified by the kernel before the workload completes correctly
+ RK2	O5–O7, O9–O11, O13–O15, O17–O19, O21–O23	An error is notified by the kernel before a failure is observed
– RK3	O16	No error is notified and the workload is aborted
– RK4	O8, O12, O24	No error is notified and the kernel hangs
– RK5	O20	No error is notified and the workload completes incorrectly

Viewpoint: Availability of the Kernel		
#	Outcomes [-O1]	Rationale
+ AK1	O2–O4	An error is notified by the kernel before the workload completes correctly
+ AK2	O13–O20	The workload is aborted or completes incorrectly
– AK3	O5–O8	The workload completes correctly and the kernel hangs
– AK4	O9–O12, O21–O24	The workload is aborted or completes incorrectly and the kernel hangs

Viewpoint: Safety of the Workload		
#	Outcomes [-O1]	Rationale
+ SW1	O2–O4	An error is notified by the kernel before the workload completes correctly
+ SW2	O5–O8	The workload completes correctly and the kernel hangs
+ SW3	O9–O16	The workload is aborted or the kernel hangs
– SW4	O21–O24	The workload completes incorrectly and the kernel hangs
– SW5	O17–O20	The workload completes incorrectly and the kernel does not hang

perspective, one may well consider that workload abort could be preferred to error notification.

It is worth pointing out that in Table 14.5 several outcomes are grouped into clusters that can be considered as equivalent with respect to a specific measure; each cluster characterizes a relevant "accomplishment level" for the considered measure. These clusters are ranked according to an increasing severity level (i.e., index 1 indicates the most favorable case). We have appended labels (+) and (–) to explicitly indicate what we are considering as positive and negative clusters. However, we recommend keeping the data for each cluster so that a finer tuning of these categorizations is always possible. The rightmost column gives the rationale that defines the various clusters.

14.5. THE EXPERIMENTAL TESTBED: THE RoCADE PLATFORM

Figure 14.3 describes the RoCADE (robustness characterization against driver errors) platform that has been set up for conducting the experiments (only one target machine is shown).

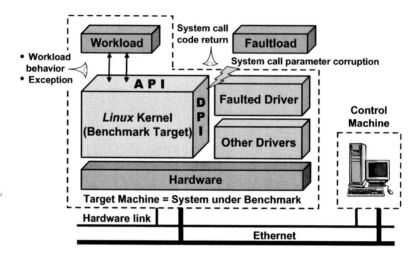

Figure 14.3. Overview of the RoCADE platform.

The experiments were carried out using a rack of four Intel Pentium machines, each featuring 32 Mb of RAM and several commonly used peripheral devices, including a hard disk, a floppy disk, a CD ROM, two network cards, a graphic card, and a keyboard. All four machines run the GNU/Linux distribution. Three of them are the target machines on which faults are injected and behaviors observed; each is supporting two versions of the Linux kernel: 2.2.20 and 2.4.18. The use of three target machines is meant to speed up the conduct of the experiments. The fourth machine (control machine) is connected to the target machines via a private Ethernet network to control the experiments and provide an external means for monitoring these machines. In particular, it is used to restart the target machines, should they be blocked after an experiment. Indeed, for the sake of repeatability, for each experiment the SUB is restored to a specific (fault-free) state.

The injection of faulty parameters into each target machine is carried out via the RAM. The processor uses a stack residing in RAM to store various data, including the parameters of the calls to the functions of the DPI. This stack is accessible via the registers of the processor. At the same time, another area in the memory stores the instructions to be executed. When a DPI function is being used, the processor raises an interrupt. Upon occurrence of this interrupt, the fault injection process takes over; it modifies a parameter in the stack and resumes the execution of the program. When the fault has been applied once, the fault injection process is disabled. The corruptions provoked in this way correspond to transient faults. This choice for the fault model illustrates the kind of pragmatic compromise one has to make among benchmarking properties (e.g., see [Kanoun et al. 2002]), namely here, fault representativeness and low intrusiveness.

In order to recognize the symbols used by the driver, we have developed scripts that automatically extract their names from the driver's object code file. Then, thanks to the list referencing all symbols, we can determine what faults can be injected into these symbols. Hence, all parameters of the selected functions are subjected to fault injection (according to all the fault types defined in Table 14.6). The codes returned after a system call are obtained with similar techniques. The code returned by the symbol subjected to a fault is collected from the stack. In addition to these error codes, the symbols may also display other error messages, such as "blue screen" or "panic." Such error messages are collected at the end of each experiment.

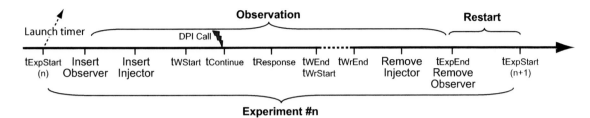

Figure 14.4. Scheduling of relevant events for an experiment.

At the start of each experiment that is indicated by the target machine, the control machine sets a timer. At the end of each experiment, the target machine is rebooted and it is expected to be able to retrigger this timer at the end of the reboot. If the timer overruns, the control machine provokes a hardware restart of the target machine. This situation is interpreted as a hang of the kernel. The hardware exceptions are collected via the log of the target machine. The duration of each fault injection experiment ranges from 2.5 to 5 minutes (the latter when a kernel hang occurs).

The diagram in Figure 14.4 presents the nominal scheduling of a fault injection experiment.

The various important events are identified and described in Table 14.6, where related actions are also detailed.

14.6. RESULTS AND ANALYSES

This section illustrates how the insights one can get from the measurements obtained vary according to the priorities or dependability measures that are considered. We present and analyze a restricted set of results obtained with the RoCADE platform for three representative drivers running on the Linux kernel. Additional results and, in particular, more detailed analyses can be found in [Albinet 2005]. We restrict the presentation of the results to a selected set, in order to facilitate the exposition of the analyses. We voluntarily emphasize two drivers supporting the network card (namely the SMC-ultra and the Ne2000). Network drivers account for the largest part of the code among the drivers whose size is increasing the most [Godfrey and Tu 2000]; we consider also another driver (namely, SoundBlaster) that ranges in the midsize category. An additional set of drivers has been tested (e.g., file system, process memory, etc.).

The main goal that supports the selection of this set of results is to be able to carry out the following types of analyses on:

- Two distinct drivers running on the same version of the kernel: SB + Linux 2.2 and SMC + Linux 2.2
- Two implementations of the same functionality running on the same kernel version: SMC + Linux 2.4 and NE + Linux 2.4
- The same driver* running on two different kernel versions: SMC + Linux 2.2 and SMC + Linux 2.4

---

*It is worth pointing out that the code of the driver is adapted to fit each version of the kernel.

TABLE 14.6.—Detailed description of events and related actions

IDs	Events	Actions
tExpStart Insertion X*	System verification Setup of the modules of the tool and selection of the fault to be injected	Launch of e2fsck utility to check the file system integrity[†] Countdown start (on the control machine) Insertion of a breakpoint
tWStart	Initiation of the workload	Start-up of the workload
DPI call	Injection of the fault on the targeted kernel function call Wait for (error) code returned by the kernel function	Raising of an interrupt and injection of the fault Insertion of the breakpoint for observing the returned code
tContinue	Resumption of the workload after execution of the function being faulted	Observation (internal) of the error code returned
tResponse	Observation of the events perceived externally	Collection of the results provided by the workload
TWEnd	Termination of the workload	Signaling of workload termination
tWrStart	Initiation of the replay workload	Start up of the replay workload
tWrEnd	Termination of the replay workload and observation of the related events perceived externally	Signaling of replay workload termination and collection of the related results provided
TexpEnd Removal X*	End of current experiment	Removal of the modules of the tool and restart

*X= Injector, Observer.
[†]This proved a very useful procedure as in several instances the file system had been damaged due to the corruption of the system call.

Based on the workload and fault types considered, about 100 experiments were carried out for each driver plus kernel combination.

14.6.1. Basic Results and Interpretation

Table 14.7 illustrates the distribution of the basic results obtained when considering the "first event" approach to diagnosing outcomes for which multiple events were collected.

In addition to the specific events previously defined (see Table 14.4), two interesting outcomes are included:

1. Not Activated (Not Act.)—injected faults could not be activated (i.e., the workload was not able to activate the function on which the fault was meant to be injected).
2. No Observation (No Obs.)—none of the notification or failure modes events were observed; of course when the fault is not activated, none of these events can be observed.

The proportion of "Not Activated" cases varies significantly, both among the tested drivers and Linux versions—from 0% (SB + Linux 2.2) to 17% (SMC + Linux 2.4). The fact that in most cases nonnull ratios are observed means that the respective workloads

TABLE 14.7. Distribution of events according to first event collected

Driver + kernel	Not Act.	No Obs.	EC	XC	KH	WA	WI
SB + Linux 2.2	0%	18%	47%	22%	3%	1%	9%
SMC + Linux 2.2	7%	22%	19%	23%	21%	0%	9%
SMC + Linux 2.4	17%	17%	21%	34%	11%	0%	0%
NE + Linux 2.4	14%	10%	15%	30%	17%	0%	13%

Legend—EC: error code, XC: exception, KH: kernel hang, WA: workload abort, WI: workload incorrect.

have to be improved from a *testability* viewpoint—more precisely, *controllability* here. However, these rates are much lower than those reported in related studies on the Linux kernel (e.g., see [Gu et al. 2003]). To our understanding, this better *controllability* is most likely due to the fact that, in our case, faults are targeting the parameters of the system calls made by the driver, rather than the flow of execution of the whole kernel. In the sequel, for further analyses, we will normalize the results presented with respect to experiments in which faults were actually activated.

As already pointed out, the interpretation of the "no observation" cases is highly subject to the specific context in which the analysis is conducted. These outcomes may be counted either as positive or negative depending on the responsiveness, safety, and availability viewpoints. However, as is commonly accepted in testing scenarios, uncertainties still remain about the real situations that such outcomes describe. Accordingly, we have preferred to adopt a conservative approach that consists in ignoring these outcomes. Besides the "replay" mode having been devised to increase the confidence in our analyses, a "No Obs" outcome probably still reveals a lack of *observability* of the tests conducted. But, such an outcome may also be due to controllability-related problems: the kernel does not (or no longer) use(s) the faulted parameter, the faulted parameter has no impact on the kernel, or the error provoked is masked (in our case, injecting a "0" value on a parameter already equal to "0," etc.). However, although the "No Obs." ratios reported are higher than the "Not Act.", the values are significantly lower than the ones presented in [Gu et al. 2003].

Figure 14.5 illustrates the relative distribution among the events observed while considering the "first event" collected, which is a classical approach in most related experimental studies.

A quick examination of these results shows a very low proportion of workload aborts for all tests conducted. The results also reveal that a large percentage of experiments are notified by the kernel (this includes the error code and exception events). Should it be possible to handle equally both types of notifications, then, as the provision of an error code usually features a lower latency, such a notification would be preferable to an exception in order to carry out a successful recovery action. Accordingly, in that respect, the results for SB + Linux 2.2 are more positive than those observed for the experiments concerning network card drivers. However, adopting an end-user perspective would lead to a different assessment; indeed, in that case only exceptions would actually matter.

The comparison of the results obtained for the SMC driver for the two releases indicates clearly an improvement of the robustness for SMC + Linux 2.4 due to the increased percentage of exceptions raised. This results in a reduction of the ratios of kernel hangs and, more importantly, in the "disappearance" of critical cases in which a workload incorrect (WI) event was reported. Indeed, due to the precedence in the collection of the events, the fact that a WI event is counted as a first event means that neither a notification

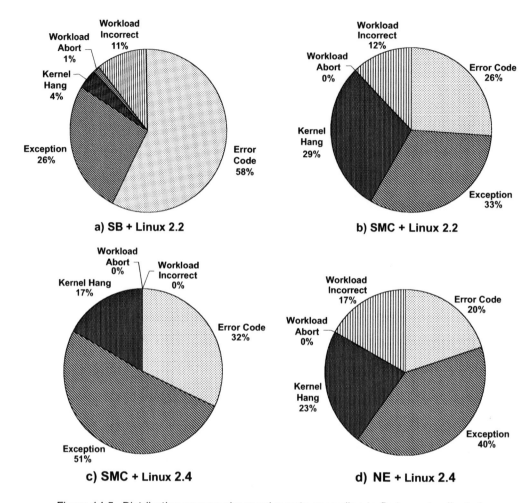

Figure 14.5. Distribution among observed events according to first event collected.

has been made nor an abort has been observed. It is also very likely to be the only event to be collected, unless a hang has occurred after the end of the workload (such cases are actually very infrequent), but, in practice, a deeper analysis of the data collected is necessary to ascertain this statement.

14.6.2. Impact of the Comprehensive Viewpoints

In this section, we revisit the observations made during the conducted experiments in the light of the three comprehensive viewpoints defined in Section 14.5.2. Figure 14.6 summarizes the corresponding measures for the four series of experiments reported here. In each case, the percentages of the various clusters that support the corresponding measure are detailed. It is important to note that the clusters corresponding to the most positive outcomes appear on the top of the histograms (light grey), whereas the critical ones are at the bottom (darker shade). Here we consider the set of outcomes defined in Table 14.4.

Let us consider first the kernel responsiveness (RK) viewpoint. Here we assume that RK1 and RK2 form the most positive outcomes (Table 14.5). The distribution observed for SB + Linux 2.2 indicates a very positive behavior—84% of the outcomes observed correspond to error notifications (RK1 = 43% + RK2 = 41%). However, among the 16% of outcomes for which a failure mode was observed without prior notification, more than two-thirds correspond to WI events (RK5 = 11%). The remaining third is dominated by KH events and few WA events. It is worth noting that this is the only set of experiments for which WA events have been diagnosed without any prior notification. The SMC + Linux 2.2 configuration features a much less positive behavior. For example, the distribution shows that 41% of the outcomes observed correspond to failure modes without prior notification. This is mainly due to KH events; indeed, in that case RK4 = 29%, whereas the RK5 cluster (not notified WI events) amounts to a rather similar value (12%). This also means that almost 30% of the workload failures that are not notified led to an incorrect completion. The results shown for SMC indicate that the evolution to release 2.4 has significantly improved the behavior—the percentage of failures without prior notification is reduced to 17% and corresponds to KH events only. Globally, more than three-quarters (60/77) of the failure modes observed are preceded by an error notification. This confirms the observations already made on the basis of the analysis of the pie charts displaying the distributions of the first event collected (Figure 14.5). The results for NE + Linux 2.4 indicate a much lower error notification ratio, which is similar to the one reported for the SMC + Linux 2.2 case.

For the kernel availability viewpoint (AK), the most critical issue is characterized by a KH event, because this has a dramatic impact on the ability to keep delivering the service. This is why AK3 and AK4 are considered the most critical clusters. The results shown for SB + Linux 2.2 indicate that faults have also a significant impact with respect to availability. Indeed, a KH event is observed in 23% (18% + 5%) of the cases. Moreover, the WI event is observed in more than 78% of these cases (the 18% of the 23%); this means that in most cases, before the kernel hangs, the services that are active in the kernel are no longer able to maintain the proper operation of the application processes. The results also indicate that faults associated with network drivers have consistently a very significant impact—about half of the fault injection experiments conclude with a KH event. For the SMC driver, the results also show that the modifications made between the two releases had no impact from the availability viewpoint.

Concerning the workload safety viewpoint (SW), what matters most is the ability to avoid the delivery of incorrect results. This is why SW4 and SW5 are considered as the most critical clusters. The results shown for SB + Linux 2.2 suggest a much less positive behavior than was deduced from the analysis of the results from the RK viewpoint—the occurrence of the most severe case (cluster SW5 = WI and no KH) amounts to 22%. In addition, it is worth noting that the significant improvement observed with respect to responsiveness (error notification) between SMC + Linux 2.2 and SMC + Linux 2.4 has no impact (actually slightly the opposite) in reducing the WI events. Such a behavior can be explained by the fact that most additional error notifications correspond to exceptions, rather than error code returns (see Table 14.7). As a matter of fact, such exceptions signal already severe erroneous behavior; the erroneous behavior is reported, but no suitable recovery procedure is being launched. The rather poor behavior observed with respect to responsiveness is also confirmed by the analysis with respect to the safety viewpoint; in 53% of the cases (SW5 = 42% + SW4 = 11%) the observed outcome is a WI event, which is the most critical event here.

Figure 14.7 illustrates how these various viewpoints, and the associated properties, can be used by system integrators in making a decision as to whether to incorporate a driver into their system. The histograms plot the percentage for cases in which these properties

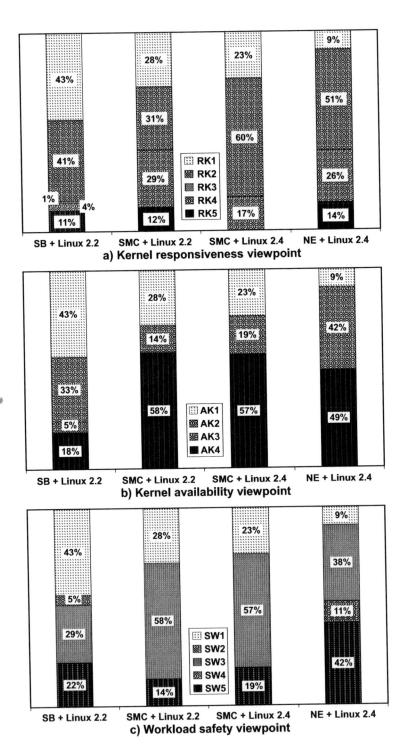

Figure 14.6. Interpretation of the results according to the considered viewpoints.

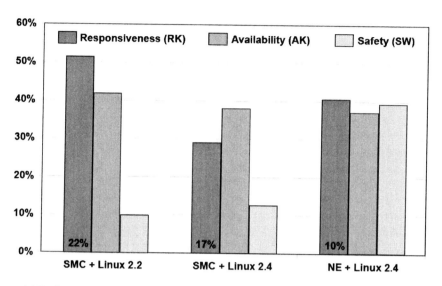

Figure 14.7. Comparison of the property deficiencies induced by the network card drivers.

were not verified (i.e., the cases corresponding to the clusters labeled with index "–" in Table 14.5) when considering the experiments involving the tested network drivers. In this case, the figures being considered explicitly account for the ratios of "No Obs." that appeared in Table 14.7. It is worth noting that these ratios contribute negatively to the evaluation of the responsiveness property (i.e., RK is not verified*); however, they correspond to the verification of AK and SW.

The histograms concerning the two versions of the SMC driver clearly illustrate that the significant decrease in lack of error signaling obtained for version 2.4 does not result in a significant reduction in the weaknesses with respect to the other viewpoints (actually, a slight increase is observed for safety); the improvement in the coverage procured by the error detection mechanisms was not accompanied by an improvement in the handling of error signals. For example, the application of the concept of *shadow driver* reported in [Swift et al. 2004] would help improve the behavior by complementing such a *problem-revealing only* strategy with a specific low-level *recovery* strategy. During normal operation, the shadow driver tracks the state of the real driver by monitoring all communication between the kernel and the driver. When a failure occurs, the shadow driver substitutes *temporarily* for the real driver, servicing requests on its behalf, thus shielding the kernel and applications from the failure. The shadow driver then restores the failed driver to a state in which it can resume processing requests. It is also interesting to observe that, while the network driver NE 2000 features similar or slightly better behaviors than the SMC driver with respect to responsiveness and availability, it exhibits a much poorer behavior with respect to safety. This reflects the fact that very distinct implementation choices were made for these two drivers.

---

*This is consistent with the rationale underlying this viewpoint (i.e., a reaction from the kernel is expected in presence of activated faults). Still, considering the complete "No Obs." ratio as contributing to a deficiency of the RK property might lead to a pessimistic assessment. This is why the related percentages are explicitly shown in the figure.

14.7. CONCLUSION

Popular operating systems (COTS or open source) rapidly evolve into increasingly complex software components. Drivers are known to account for the major part of the increase in terms of lines of source code. These components are often crafted by third-party developers and then integrated within the operating system. This whole process is not always well mastered, as evidenced by the vast consensus that attributes a large proportion of operating system failures to driver malfunctions.

The work reported in this chapter proposed a practical approach to benchmarking the robustness of operating systems with respect to faulty device drivers. In order to facilitate the conduct of fault injection experiments, we have introduced the notion of the driver programming interface (DPI) that precisely identifies the interface between the drivers and the kernel, in the form of a set of kernel functions. In the same way that the API is used to simulate the consequences of faulty application processes, the DPI provides a suitable interface for simulating the potential erroneous behaviors induced by a faulty driver. In practice, we have used a SWIFI technique to corrupt the parameters of these functions. In order to collect relevant outcomes for a detailed characterization of the faulty behaviors, we have considered both internal (error codes returned by the kernel) and external measurements (e.g., exceptions raised, kernel hangs, and workload behavior).

To analyze the experimental results, we have proposed a comprehensive framework for interpreting the results that accounts for several dependability viewpoints. We have considered three viewpoints, namely, responsiveness of the kernel (maximize error notification), availability (minimize kernel hangs), and safety of the workload (minimize delivery of incorrect service). They provide a practical means for analyzing three different facets of the dependability requirements that one can expect from a robust operating system, either simultaneously or individually.

In order to illustrate and assess our approach, we have set up an experimental platform, RoCADE (robustness characterization against driver errors). We have focused here on the series of experiments conducted on two releases of the Linux kernel (2.2.20 and 2.4.18) and on three drivers [sound (sound blaster) and network (SMC and NE 2000)]. The analyses carried out have shown that although the sound blaster driver got a very good rating according to responsiveness, it exhibited poor behavior with respect to the safety and availability viewpoints. The experiments conducted on the SMC driver were able to reveal a significant improvement with respect to responsiveness between the two releases considered, but this did not result in any improvement from the safety and availability viewpoints. Finally, we identified a slightly better behavior concerning availability for the experiments conducted on the NE 2000 driver than for those on the SMC driver, whereas the opposite was obtained for safety and responsiveness.

The results we have obtained and the analyses we have carried out thanks to RoCADE are encouraging with regard to viability of the proposed methodology. The whole approach can thus be considered as a sound basis on which to develop a set of practical dependability benchmarks focusing on the characterization of the impact of faulty drivers on the behavior of an operating system kernel. As witnessed by the insights gained from the measures obtained, although the proposed framework is primarily geared toward the characterization of kernel behaviors, it is also suitable to support the choice of drivers to be associated with a given kernel.

We consider the fact that a large proportion of error codes had been observed (especially as first-collected events) as a positive result in order to perform a detailed characterization of the erroneous behaviors induced by the corrupted parameters. In addition, these codes form a useful basis on which specific error handling could be implemented. Another recommended approach to restrict the impact of faulty drivers would be to enforce a clear separation between the driver address space and the kernel address space (e.g., see [Härting et al. 1997]). The use of specific languages excluding pointer arithmetic and explicitly including IMM (e.g., see [Réveillère and Muller 2001]) is another promising approach to develop more robust drivers. More recently, several proposals have been made to attain a clear separation of concern using virtual machine constructs; for example, see [Fraser et al. 2004, LeVasseur et al. 2004]. The contemporary Nooks approach and its extension in the form of shadow drivers [Swift et al. 2004] offer other attractive approaches.

Finally, it is worth pointing out that the notion of the DPI (driver programming interface) that we have advocated and defined in order to structure the conducted experiments matches very well the concept of separation of concerns that underlies several frameworks that were proposed recently, both by academic studies (e.g., see [Swift et al. 2004]) and by an increasing number of operating system and hardware manufacturers. Let us simply mention the various CDI (common driver interface), DDI (device driver interface), or DKI (driver kernel interface) proposals that have been put forward for several operating systems. Among these initiatives, the Extensible Firmware Interface (EFI) that was recently promoted by the Unified EFI Forum* as an emerging standard deserves special attention. The EFI defines a new model for the interface between operating systems and platform firmware. The UEFI is primarily meant to provide a standard environment for booting an operating system. Nevertheless, the data tables (containing platform-related information, plus boot and run-time service calls) that implements it can be useful also to facilitate run-time access to internal variables and, thus, better structure the design of device drivers. Accordingly, it should be possible to reuse the principles underlying the DPI identified herein and/or to adapt them easily in the forthcoming arena that this emerging standard is promising for structuring the interactions between the operating systems and the related hardware layers, including the device drivers.

ACKNOWLEDGMENT

This work was partly supported by the European Commission (Project IST-2000-25425: DBench and Network of Excellence IST-026764: ReSIST). Arnaud Albinet was supported in part by the Réseau d'Ingénierie de la Sûreté de fonctionnement (Network of Dependability Engineering); he is now with Continental Automotive, Toulouse, France.

REFERENCES

[Albinet 2005] A. Albinet, *Dependability Characterization of Operating Systems in presence of Faulty Drivers,* Ph.D. Dissertation, National Polytechnic Institute, Toulouse, 2005 (in French, also LAAS Report 05-248).

[Albinet et al. 2004] A. Albinet, J. Arlat, and J.-C. Fabre, "Characterization of the Impact of Faulty Drivers on the Robustness of the Linux Kernel," in *Proceedings of IEEE/IFIP International Conference on Dependable Systems and Networks (DSN-2004),* Florence, Italy, IEEE Computer Science Press, Los Alamitos, CA, pp. 867–876, 2004.

*http://www.uefi.org.

[Arlat et al. 1990] J. Arlat, M. Aguera, L. Amat, Y. Crouzet, J.-C. Fabre, J.-C. Laprie, E. Martins, and D. Powell, "Fault Injection for Dependability Validation—A Methodology and Some Applications," *IEEE Transactions on Software Engineering,* vol. 16, no. 2, pp. 166–182, February 1990.

[Arlat et al. 2002] J. Arlat, J.-C. Fabre, M. Rodríguez, and F. Salles, "Dependability of COTS Microkernel-Based Systems," *IEEE Transactions on Computers,* vol. 51, no. 2, pp. 138–163, February 2002.

[Avižienis et al. 2004] A. Avižienis, J.-C. Laprie, B. Randell, and C. Landwehr, "Basic Concepts and Taxonomy of Dependable and Secure Computing," *IEEE Transactions on Dependable and Secure Computing,* vol. 1, no. 1, pp. 11–33, Jan.–March 2004.

[Brown and Patterson 2000] A. Brown and D. A. Patterson, "Towards Availability Benchmarks: A Case Study of Software RAID Systems," in *Proceedings of 2000 USENIX Annual Technical Conference,* San Diego, CA, USENIX Association, 2000.

[Carreira et al. 1998] J. Carreira, H. Madeira, and J. G. Silva, "Xception: A Technique for the Experimental Evaluation of Dependability in Modern Computers," *IEEE Transactions on Software Engineering,* vol. 24, no. 2, pp. 125–136, February 1998.

[Chou et al. 2001] A. Chou, J.-F. Yang, B. Chelf, S. Hallem, and D. Engler, "An Empirical Study of Operating System Errors," in *Proceedings of 18th ACM Symposium on Operating Systems Principles,* Chateau Lake Louise, Banff, Canada, ACM Press, New York, 2001, http://www.cs.ucsd.edu/sosp01.

[Durães and Madeira 2003] J. Durães and H. Madeira, "Mutidimensional Characterization of the Impact of Faulty Drivers on the Operating Systems Behavior," *IEICE Transactions on Information and Systems,* vol. E86-D, no. 12, pp. 2563–2570, December 2003.

[Durães and Madeira 2006] J. Durães and H. Madeira, "Emulation of Software Faults: A Field Data Study and a Practical Approach," *IEEE Transactions on Software Engineering,* vol. 32, no. 11, pp. 849–867, November 2006.

[Edwards and Matassa 2002] D. Edwards and L. Matassa, "An Approach to Injecting Faults into Hardened Software," in *Proceedings of Ottawa Linux Symposium,* Ottawa, ON, Canada, pp. 146–175, 2002.

[Fraser et al. 2004] K. Fraser, S. Hand, R. Neugebauer, I. Pratt, A. Warfield, and M. Williamson, "Safe Hardware Access with the Xen Virtual Machine Monitor," in *First Workshop on Operating System and Architectural Support for the On-Demand IT Infrastructure (OASIS),* Boston, 2004.

[Fraser et al. 2003] T. Fraser, L. Badger, and M. Feldman, "Hardening COTS Software with Generic Software Wrappers," in *Foundations of Intrusion Tolerant Systems—Organically Assured and Survivable Information Systems (OASIS),* J. H. Lala (Ed.), IEEE Computer Science Press, Los Alamitos, CA,pp. 399–413, 2003.

[Godfrey and Tu 2000] M. W. Godfrey and Q. Tu, "Evolution in Open Source Software: A Case Study," in *Proceedings of IEEE International Conference on Software Maintenance (ICSM-200),* San Jose, CA,IEEE Computer Science Press, Los Alamitos, CA, pp. 131–142, 2000.

[Gu et al. 2003] W. Gu, Z. Kalbarczyk, R. K. Iyer, and Z. Yang, "Characterization of Linux Kernel Behavior under Errors," in *Proceedings of IEEE/IFIP International Conference on Dependable Systems and Networks (DSN-2003),* San Francisco, CA, IEEE Computer Science Press, Los Alamitos, CA, pp. 459–468, 2003.

[Härting et al. 1997] H. Härting, M. Ohmuth, J. Liedtke, S. Schönberg, and J. Wolter, "The Performance of μ-Kernel-Based Systems," in *Proceedings of 16th ACM Symposium on Operating Systems Principles (SOSP-16)* Saint-Malo, France, pp. 66–77, 1997.

[Jarboui et al. 2003] T. Jarboui, J. Arlat, Y. Crouzet, K. Kanoun, and T. Marteau, "Impact of Internal and External Software Faults on the Linux Kernel," *IEICE Transactions on Information and Systems,* vol. E86-D, no. 12, pp. 2571–2578, December 2003.

[Johansson and Suri 2005] A. Johansson and N. Suri, "Error Propagation Profiling of Operating Systems," in *Proceedings of IEEE/IFIP International Conference on Dependable Systems and*

Networks (DSN-2005), Yokohama, Japan, IEEE Computer Science Press, Los Alamitos, CA, pp. 86–95, 2005.

[Kalakech et al. 2004] A. Kalakech, T. Jarboui, J. Arlat, Y. Crouzet, and K. Kanoun, "Benchmarking Operating System Dependability: Windows 2000 as a Case Study," in *Proceedings of 10th IEEE Pacific Rim International Symposium on Dependable Computing (PRDC-2004)*, Papeete, French Polynesia, EEE Computer Science Press, Los Alamitos, CA, pp. 261–270, l2004; see also http://www.laas.fr/DBench.

[Kanoun et al. 2002] K. Kanoun, H. Madeira, and J. Arlat, "A Framework for Dependability Benchmarking," in *Supplemental Volume of the IEEE/IFIP International Conference on Dependable Systems and Networks (DSN-2002)—Workshop on Dependability Benchmarking*, Washington, DC, pp. F.7–F.8, 2002; see also http://www.laas.fr/DBench.

[Kanoun et al. 2005a] K. Kanoun, H. Madeira, M. Dal Cin, F. Moreira, and J. C. Ruiz Garcia, "DBench (Dependability Benchmarking)," in *Proceedings of 5th European Dependable Computing Conference (EDCC-5)—Project Track*, Budapest, Hungary, 2005; available as LAAS Report no. 05197, see also http://www.laas.fr/DBench.

[Kanoun et al. 2005b] K. Kanoun, Y. Crouzet, A. Kalakech, A. E. Rugina, and P. Rumeau, "Benchmarking the Dependability of Windows and Linux Using Postmark Workloads," in *Proceedings of 16th IEEE International Symposium on Software Reliability Engineering (ISSRE 2005)*, Chicago, IEEE Computer Science Press, Los Alamitos, CA, pp. 11–20, 2005.

[Koopman and DeVale 1999] P. Koopman, and J. DeVale, "Comparing the Robustness of POSIX Operating Systems," in *Proceedings of 29th IEEE International Symposium on Fault-Tolerant Computing (FTCS-29)*, Madison, WI, IEEE Computer Science Press, Los Alamitos, CA, pp. 30–37, 1999.

[LeVasseur et al. 2004] J. LeVasseur, V. Uhlig, J. Stoess, and S. Götz, "Unmodified Device Driver Reuse and Improved System Dependability via Virtual Machines," in *Proceedings of 6th ACM/USENIX Symposium on Operating Systems Design and Implementation (OSDI '04)*, San Francisco, USENIX Association, pp. 17–30, 2004.

[Madeira et al. 2002] H. Madeira, R. Some, F. Moreira, D. Costa, and D. Rennels, "Experimental Evaluation of a COTS System for Space Applications," in *Proceedings of IEEE/IFIP International Conference on Dependable Systems and Networks (DSN-2002)*, Washington, DC, EEE Computer Science Press, Los Alamitos, CA, pp. 325–330, l2002.

[Marsden et al. 2002] E. Marsden, J.-C. Fabre, and J. Arlat, "Dependability of CORBA Systems: Service Characterization by Fault Injection," in *Proceedings of 21st IEEE International Symposium on Reliable Distributed Systems (SRDS-2002)*, Osaka, Japan, IEEE Computer Science Press, Los Alamitos, CA, pp. 276–285, 2002.

[Mukherjee and Siewiorek 1997] A. Mukherjee and D. P. Siewiorek, "Measuring Software Dependability by Robustness Benchmarking," *IEEE Transactions on Software Engineering*, vol. 23, no. 6, pp. 366–378, June 1997.

[Murphy and Levidow 2000] B. Murphy and B. Levidow, "Windows 2000 Dependability," in *Digest of Workshops and Abstracts of the IEEE/IFIP International Conference on Systems and Networks (DSN-2000)*, New York, pp. D.20–D.28, 2000.

[Réveillère and Muller 2001] L. Réveillère and G. Muller, "Improving Driver Robustness: An Evaluation of the Devil Approach," in *Proceedings of IEEE/IFIP International Conference on Dependable Systems and Networks (DSN-2001)*, Göteborg, Sweden, IEEE Computer Science Press, Los Alamitos, CA, pp. 131–140, 2001.

[Rodríguez et al. 2002] M. Rodríguez, A. Albinet, and J. Arlat, "MAFALDA-RT: A Tool for Dependability Assessment of Real Time Systems," in *Proceedings of IEEE/IFIP International Conference on Dependable Systems and Networks (DSN-2002)*, Washington, DC,IEEE Computer Science Press, Los Alamitos, CA, pp. 267–272, 2002.

[Rodríguez et al. 2003] M. Rodríguez, J.-C. Fabre, and J. Arlat, "Building SWIFI Tools from Temporal Logic Specifications," in *Proceedings of IEEE/IFIP International Conference on Depend-*

able Systems and Networks (DSN-2003), San Francisco, pp. 95–104, IEEE Computer Science Press, Los Alamitos, CA, 2003.

[Swift et al. 2004] M. M. Swift, M. Annamalai, B. N. Bershad, and H. M. Levy, "Recovering Device Drivers," in *Proceedings of 6th ACM/USENIX Symposium on Operating Systems Design and Implementation (OSDI '04),* San Francisco, pp. 1–16, 2004, USENIX Association, http://nooks.cs.washington.edu.

[Tsai et al. 1996] T. K. Tsai, R. K. Iyer, and D. Jewitt, "An Approach Towards Benchmarking of Fault-Tolerant Commercial Systems," in *Proceedings of 26th International Symposium on Fault-Tolerant Computing (FTCS-26),* Sendai, Japan, EEE Computer Science Press, Los Alamitos, CA, pp. 314–323, l1996.

[Vieira and Madeira 2003] M. Vieira and H. Madeira, "Benchmarking the Dependability of Different OLTP Systems," in *Proceedings of IEEE/IFIP International Conference on Dependable Systems and Networks (DSN-2003),* San Francisco, IEEE Computer Science Press, Los Alamitos, CA, pp. 305–310, 2003.

[Zaatar and Ouaiss 2002] W. Zaatar and I. Ouaiss, "A Comparative Study of Device Driver APIs: Towards a Uniform Linux Approach," in *Proceedings of Ottawa Linux Symposium,* Ottawa, ON, Canada, pp. 407–413, 2002.

15

BENCHMARKING THE OPERATING SYSTEMS AGAINST FAULTS IMPACTING OPERATING SYSTEM FUNCTIONS

Ravishankar K. Iyer, Zbigniew Kalbarczyk, and Weining Gu

15.1. INTRODUCTION

The dependability of a computing system (and, hence, of the services it provides to the end user) depends to a large extent on the failure resilience of the underlying hardware (processor) and the operating system. Understanding a system's sensitivity to errors and identifying single points of failure are, thus, of primary importance in selecting a computing platform and in assessing trade-offs involving cost, reliability, and performance.

In this chapter, we discuss our approach to develop technology, methods, and scientifically sound procedures for evaluating dependability attributes (e.g., reliability and error coverage) of computing systems with specific focus on the failure characterization of operating systems. Our goal is to create a *dependability benchmark for operating systems*.

In recent years, several approaches were proposed to evaluate robustness of operating systems, for example, [Arlat et al. 2002], [Koopman and DeVale 2000], [Madeira et al. 2002].* These studies address robustness at the user-visible interfaces and constitute an important component in operating system benchmarking. We believe that a critical aspect in assessing system dependability is the ability to quantify the impact of a broad range of faults that occur in the processor, memory, I/O, and network interfaces of the underlying hardware and the corresponding system and application software. For example, *fault severity,* as measured by the extent of the damage the fault causes to the system, and associated *performance loss* due to recovery are two metrics that characterize system's response to faults and its ability to survive catastrophic events [Tsai et al. 1996, Tsai et al.

---

*Chapters 11, 12, and 13 of this book are devoted to evaluation of operating system robustness at the user-visible interface level, and Chapter 14 evaluates robustness of operating systems at the device drivers' interfaces. Please refer to these chapters for more details.

Dependability Benchmarking for Computer Systems. Edited by Karama Kanoun and Lisa Spainhower

1999]. In this context, sound fault/error injection methods and tools are essential when quantifying these metrics directly or indirectly (as we do by associating performance loss and the severity of faults). Although there are many outstanding issues in terms of how, where, and when faults or errors should be injected so that operating systems can be measured and compared, we believe (and substantiate this claim in this chapter) that fault/error injection should be an integral part of any benchmarking procedure.

Ultimately, a *quest for a comprehensive benchmark* requires one to: (i) evaluate different approaches in assessing system dependability, (ii) analyze their pros and cons, and (iii) use this knowledge to define sound procedures, methods, and tools required to enable experimental OS benchmarking. Unlike in performance benchmarking, it is doubtful that a dependability benchmark completely based on the external characteristics of a system will be satisfying and acceptable. We envisage that a combination of a "black box" and a "white box" approach will emerge.

15.1.2. What Should Be Measured and Why Should We Measure It?

Several measures (or metrics) are identified as useful in quantifying operating system dependability. These include:

- Detection and recovery coverage (for a given set of faults). How useful is the redundancy introduced into the system?
- Recovery time (for each recovery mechanism or strategy)—the contribution of each recovery mechanisms to system downtime
- Fault/error latency (the time between a fault/error occurrence and the time at which the fault/error is activated—the danger of having multiple faults/errors in the system
- Error detection latency (the time between error occurrence and error detection)—the window of system vulnerability (if the error is active, system behavior is unpredictable)

This chapter presents the use of software-implemented fault injection to conduct experimental studies and to derive quantitative dependability measures. Doing so, we can stress a broad range of system components, including operating system code, data and stack sections, and processor registers. The systematic approach allows:

- *Assessing fault severity, efficiency of detection,* and *recovery mechanisms* (present in the system) under variable workloads (real or synthetic applications), which quantifies coverage and ability of the system to recover.
- *Measuring the detection latency,* which is of particular importance in characterizing chances of errors to: (i) propagate between system components and (ii) escape beyond the containment boundaries defined by a computing node, for example, fail silence violations or silent data corruption. For example, our study (discussed in this chapter) of the Linux kernel sensitivity to errors on Pentium and PowerPC-based platforms shows a nonnegligible percentage of cases when crash latency (defined as the time between an error activation and the actual system failure) exceeds hundred of millions of CPU cycles. In other words, the processor can execute millions of instructions in presence of an active error before it finally crashes. During this time, errors can propagate, causing the system to produce bad data or make incorrect decisions.

- Providing insight into how *architectural characteristics* of the target processors impact the error sensitivity of the operating system, which is crucial in selecting a hardware platform.

In addition, by exercising (with faults) critical execution paths within a code one can pinpoint the error-sensitive system components/locations that may become potential dependability bottlenecks. This, in turn, provides a feedback to the developers on potential ways for integrating enhancements.

In order to illustrate our approach, we discuss experience and lessons learned from assessing error sensitivity of the Linux kernel executing on PowerPC G4 and Pentium 4 processors. The goal is to provide methodology and environment that enables: (i) comparing Linux kernel behavior under a broad range of errors on two target processors, the Intel Pentium 4 (P4) and the Motorola PowerPC (G4); and (ii) understanding how architectural characteristics of the target processors impact the error sensitivity of the operating system. Two target Linux-2.4.22 systems are used: the Intel Pentium 4 (P4) running RedHat Linux 9.0 and the Motorola PowerPC (G4) running YellowDog Linux 3.0.

Extensive error-injection experiments are conducted targeting the kernel code, data, stack, and processor system registers while running workload programs. The UnixBench benchmark suite is used to profile kernel behavior and to identify the most frequently used functions representing at least 95% of kernel usage. The responses of the kernel, for example, crash, hang, fail silence violation (or silent data corruption), not manifested on each target system are automatically monitored and logged. Analysis of the obtained data indicates significant differences between the two platforms in how errors manifest and how they are detected in the hardware and the operating system. In addition to quantifying the observed differences and similarities, we provide several examples to support the insights gained from this work.

15.2. RELATED WORK

Failure behavior and characterization of operating systems has been the focus of several studies. This section briefly reviews representative examples.

15.2.1. User-Level Testing by Executing API/System Calls with Erroneous Arguments

CMU's Ballista [Koopman and DeVale 2000] project provides a comprehensive assessment of 15 POSIX-compliant operating systems and libraries as well as Microsoft Win32 API. Ballista bombards a software module with combinations of exceptional and acceptable input values. The responses of the system are classified according to the first three categories of the CRASH severity scale [Kropp et al. 1998]: (i) catastrophic failures (OS corruption or machine crash), (ii) restart failures (a task hang), and (iii) abort failures (abnormal termination of a task).

The University of Wisconsin Fuzz [Miller, et al. 2000] project tests system calls for responses to randomized input streams. The study addresses the reliability of a large collection of UNIX utility programs and X-Window applications, servers, and network services. The Crashme benchmark [Carrette 1996] uses random input response analysis to test the robustness of an operating environment in terms of exceptional conditions under failures.

15.2.2. Error Injection into Both Kernel and User Space

Several studies have directly injected faults into the kernel space and monitored and quantified the responses. FIAT [Barton et al. 1990] was an early fault injection and monitoring environment experiment on SunOS 4.1.2 to study fault/error propagation in the UNIX kernel. FINE [Kao et al. 1993] injects hardware-induced software errors and software faults into UNIX and traces the execution flow and key variables of the kernel.

Xception [Carreira et al. 1998] uses the advanced debugging and performance monitoring features existing in most modern processors to inject faults and monitor the activation of the faults and their impact on target system behavior. Xception targets PowerPC and Pentium processors and operating systems ranging from Windows NT to proprietary, real-time kernels (e.g., SMX), and parallel operating systems (e.g., Parix).

MAFALDA [Arlat et al. 2002] analyzes the behavior of Chorus and LynxOS microkernels in the presence of faults. In addition to input parameter corruption, fault injection is applied on the internal address space of the executive (both code and data segments). In [Buchacker and Sieh 2001], User Mode Linux (the equivalent of a virtual machine, representing a kernel) executing on top of the real Linux kernel is used to perform Linux kernel fault injection via the ptrace interface. In [Gu et al. 2003] the impact in the code segment of the Linux kernel is characterized.

In [Ng and Chen 1999], SWIFI is employed to guide the design and implementation of the Rio File Cache system on top of FreeBSD operating system. Edwards and Matassa in [Edwards and Matassa 2002] use fault injection for hardening kernel-device drivers. A state machine is constructed to track the state of hardware and to support the injection of faults at a specific run-time state.

15.2.3. Other Methods to Evaluate the Operating System

Operating systems have been evaluated by studying the source code, collecting memory dumps, and inspecting the error logs. For example, [Chou et al. 2001] presents a study of Linux and OpenBSD kernel errors found by automatic static compiler analysis at the source code level. Lee et al. [Lee and Iyer 1993] use a collection of memory dump analyses of field software failures in the Tandem GUARDIAN90 operating system to identify the effects of software faults. Xu and coworkers [Xu et al. 1999] examine Windows NT cluster reboot logs to measure dependability, and Sullivan and Chillarege [Sullivan and Chillarege 1991] study MVS operating system failures using 250 randomly sampled reports.

15.3. METHODOLOGY

The objective is to develop sound approach for experimental assessment (benchmarking) of operating systems. The components of the approach include:

1. *Methods* to stress the system; that is, to generate runtime errors
2. *Procedures* to specify a set of measurements in terms of error types, error frequency, and workloads
3. *Metrics* to quantify dependability attributes of the operating system.
4. *Tools* to set up and carry on experiments, collect and analyze the measurement data, and calculate the dependability metrics

Software-implemented error injection is employed to experimentally assess the error sensitivity of the Linux kernel executing on PowerPC G4 and Pentium 4 processors. Single-bit errors are injected into kernel stacks, kernel code sections, kernel data structures, and CPU system registers while running benchmark programs. NFTAPE [Stott et al. 2000], a software framework for conducting fault/error injection experiments, is used to conduct the tests.

15.3.1. Error Injection Environment

A driver-based Linux kernel error injector is developed to enable error injection campaigns. The injection driver (a kernel module) attached to the kernel exploits the CPU's debugging and performance-monitoring features to (i) automatically inject errors; (ii) monitor error activation, error propagation, and crash latency; and (iii) reliably log the data to remote persistent storage (*crash data storage*).

The error injection environment, shown in Figure 15.1, consists of (i) kernel-embedded components (injectors, crash handlers, and data deposit module) for P4 and G4 architectures; (ii) a user-level NFTAPE control host, which prepares the target addresses/registers (to be injected), starts the workload using benchmark (UnixBench; http://www.tux .org/pub/tux/benchmarks/System/unixbench), and logs injection data for analysis; (iii) a hardware monitor (watchdog card) to detect system hangs and crashes in order to provide auto reboot if needed; and (iv) a remote crash data collector that resides on the control host computer to receive crash-data by UDP connections. The latter capability is an important extension to the existing NFTAPE framework and allows reliable collection of the crash data even if the underlying file system (on the target node) is not accessible. The instrumentation to collect data on error latency (cycles to crash) is also added.

15.3.2. Approach

An automated error injection process, illustrated in Figure 15.2, includes the following three major steps:

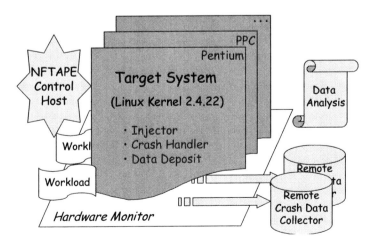

Figure 15.1. Error injection environment.

Step 1: Generate injection targets. The *target address/register generator* provides error injection targets for the following: (i) *code injection*—an instruction breakpoint location based on selected kernel functions, kernel subsystems, and kernel code address ranges; (ii) *stack injection*—the bit patterns to inject at randomly chosen (at runtime) kernel processes; (iii) *system register injection*—system registers to inject; and (iv) *data injection*—random locations in the kernel data (both initialized and uninitialized) section. The error injection targets are generated and stored before an error injection campaign is initiated. As a result, the activation rate may not be 100%, as some of the pregenerated errors are never injected because a corresponding breakpoint is never reached.

Step 2: Inject errors. The kernel injector obtains pregenerated information on the injection target and performs the error injections. This process includes starting the benchmark, enabling performance registers to measure crash latency, and injecting errors.

Step 3: Collect data. Depending on the outcome of the error injection, one of the following actions is taken:

1. *Error Not Activated.* Go to Step 1 and proceed to the next injection without rebooting the target machine.

2. *Error Activated.* (a) (Not Manifested, Fail Silence Violation, System Hang). Log the results, reboot the target system, and proceed to the next injection. (b) (Crash). Collect data on the crash, reboot the target system, and proceed to the next injection. Crash causes, cycles to crash, and frame pointers before and

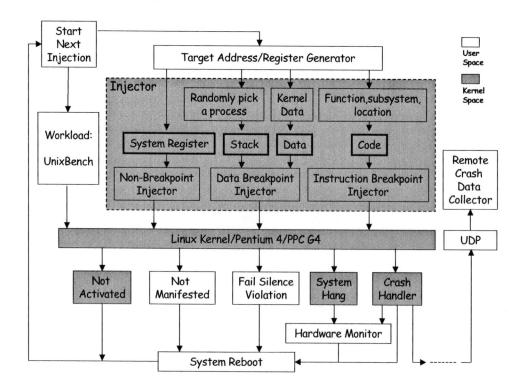

<u>Figure 15.2.</u> Automated process of injecting errors.

after injections are collected using crash handlers embedded in the kernel. This information is packaged as a UDP-like packet and sent to a remote crash-data collector (reliable storage) through a UDP connection. Since the *file system* may not behave properly when the kernel crashes, the crash handler bypasses the kernel's underlying *file system* and supplies these packets directly to the network card's packet-sending function.

15.3.3. Error Activation

The CPU's debugging registers are used to determine error activation. As shown in Figure 15.2, two types of breakpoint—*instruction breakpoint* and *data breakpoint*—are used in the injection campaigns. For code injections, one of the *debug address registers* is used to store a 32-bit linear address to be monitored in the kernel code. When the breakpoint is reached but before the instruction located at this address is executed, an error is injected.* In addition, the performance registers are used to record the latency in terms of CPU cycles.

Kernel data/stack injections use *data memory breakpoints* instead. These breakpoints stop the processor on data reads/writes but not on instruction fetches. The processor reports access to a data memory breakpoint after the target memory location is accessed (i.e., data read/write). Note that an *instruction breakpoint* is reported before executing the target instruction. Consequently, our injector inserts an error before a data memory breakpoint is set. If this breakpoint is not reached, the original value at the location is restored, and the error marked as *not activated.* If the data memory breakpoint is triggered, one of the following actions is taken: (i) *data write access,* in which the injected error is overwritten by the write operation and, thus, needs to be reinjected and is marked as *activated;* or (ii) *data read access,* in which the injected error is not overwritten and is marked as *activated.*

15.3.4. Target System Configuration

Table 15.17 summarizes the experimental setup. To speed up the experiments, three P4 and two G4 machines are used in the injection campaigns. Watchdog cards driven by Linux drivers are embedded in those machines to enable automated system reboot after a hang.

15.3.5. Error Model

The error model assumed in this study is not contingent upon the error origin; an error could have occurred anywhere in the system—the disk, network, bus, memory, or CPU. Single-bit errors are injected into the instructions of the target kernel functions, the stack of the corresponding kernel process, the kernel data structures, and the corresponding CPU's system registers. Previous research on microprocessors [Rimen et al. 1994] has shown that most (90–99%) of device-level transients can be modeled as logic-level, single-bit errors. Data on operational errors also show that many errors in the field are single-bit errors [Iyer et al. 1986].

---

*Although this discussion is in the context of the Pentium 4 processor, the PowerPC G4 injection scheme is similar.

TABLE 15.1. Experiment setup summary

	Hardware		System Software		
Processor	CPU clock (GHz)	Memory (MB)	Distribution	Linux kernel	Compiler
Intel Pentium 4	1.5	256	RedHat 9.0	2.4.22	GCC 3.2.2
Motorola MPC 7455	1.0	256	YellowDog 3.0	2.4.22	

Although in a well-designed system multiple mechanisms for protecting against errors may be available (e.g., parity, ECC,* or memory scrubbing), errors still exist. Errors could, for example, be timing issues due to hardware/software problems, a noise source such as undershoot or overshoot, or noise on the address bus that results in the wrong data being written to or read from the memory. In the latter case, the data maybe unaltered but due to the address bus noise the wrong location is accessed. Our error injection experiments employ memory errors and system register errors to emulate the diverse origins and impact of actual errors. Four attributes characterize each error injected:

1. *Trigger (when?).* An error is injected when (i) a target datum is read/written for stack/data injection, (ii) a target instruction in a given kernel function is reached, or (iii) a system register is used. The kernel activity is invoked by executing a user-level workload (UnixBench) program.

2. *Location (where?).* (i) This can be a randomly selected kernel stack location, a location within the initiated/uninitiated kernel data, or a system register. (ii) For kernel code injection, the location is preselected based on the profiling (http://oss.sgi.com/projects/kernprof) of kernel functions, that is, kernel functions most frequently used by the workload are selected for injections.

3. *Type (what?).* (i) This is a single-bit error per data word in the case of stack, data, and system register injections. (ii) For kernel code injections, it is a single-bit error per instruction.

4. *Duration (how long?).* A bit is flipped in the target to emulate the impact of a transient event, which results in the corruption of data, code, or CPU registers. (i) For data, stack, and system register injections, errors may last as short a time as it takes the corrupted data item to be overwritten due to normal system activities. (ii) For code injections, an error may persist throughout the execution time of the benchmark.

Outcome Categories. Outcomes from error injection experiments are classified according to the categories given in Table 15.2. In addition, the crash category is further divided into subcategories. Table 15.3 and Table 15.4 provide crash subcategories for the Pentium (P4) and PPC (G4) processors, respectively.

Latency (Cycles-to-Crash) is defined as the number of CPU cycles between error activation and the actual crash. (Note that, for system register injections, crash latency represents the time between error injection and the observed crash.) Typically, latency includes three stages, as shown in Figure 15.3.

---

*As indicated by manufacturers, logic failure rates may erode the efficacy of ECC in designs. Hardened logic libraries or schemes to mask logic sensitivity (redundancy on critical paths, spatial and/or temporal) may be needed to account for this deficiency.

TABLE 15.2. Outcome categories

Outcome category	Description
Activated	The corrupted instruction/data is executed/used.
Not manifested	The corrupted instruction/data is executed/used, but it does not have a visible abnormal impact on the system.
Fail silence violation	Either the operating system or the application erroneously detects the presence of an error or allows an incorrect data/response to propagate out. Benchmark programs are instrumented to detect errors.
Crash	The operating system stops working; e.g., bad trap or system panic. Crash handlers embedded into the operating system are enhanced to enable dump of failure data (processor and memory state). Off-line analysis of this data allows determining causes for most of the observed crashes.
Hang	System resources are exhausted, resulting in a nonoperational system, e.g., deadlock.

TABLE 15.3. Crash cause categories—Pentium (P4)

Crash category (P4)	Description
NULL pointer	Unable to handle kernel NULL pointer de-reference.
Bad paging	A page fault. The kernel tries to access some other bad page except NULL pointer.
Invalid instruction	An illegal instruction that is not defined in the instruction set is executed.
General protection fault	Exceeding segment limit, writing to a read-only code or data segment, loading a selector with a system descriptor, reading an execution-only code segment.
Kernel panic	The operating system detects an error.
Invalid TSS (task state segment)	The selector, code segment, or stack segment is outside the limit, or the stack is not writeable.
Divide error	Math error.
Bounds trap	Bounds-checking error.

TABLE 15.4. Crash cause categories—PPC (G4)

Crash category (G4)	Description
Bad Area	A page fault. The kernel tries to access a bad page including NULL pointer, or bad memory access.
Illegal instruction	An invalid instruction that is not defined in the instruction set is executed.
Stack overflow	The stack pointer of a kernel process is out of range.
Machine check	An error is detected on the processor–local bus, including instruction machine-check errors and data machine-check errors.
Alignment	Load/store or other specific instructions' operands are not word-aligned.
Panic	The operating system detects an error.
Bus error	Protection fault.
Bad trap	Unknown exception.

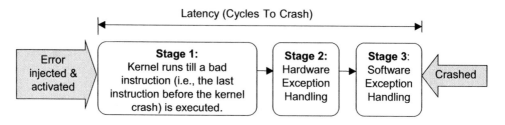

Figure 15.3. Definition of cycles to crash.

Stage 1. A target location is reached, an error is injected, and a performance register is started to measure time to potential crash. The kernel keeps running until a bad instruction is executed, for example, a NULL pointer is referenced; this may take from zero (immediate crash after executing/accessing the injected instruction/data) to millions of CPU cycles.

Stage 2. The CPU's hardware exception handling takes over to determine the exception vector, evaluate correctness, and save and load necessary data; this may consume more than 1000 CPU cycles.

Stage 3. The hardware transfers control to the software exception handler, which typically executes about 150 to 200 instructions.

15.4. OVERVIEW OF EXPERIMENTAL RESULTS

Table 15.5 and Table 15.6 summarize the results of all injection campaigns conducted on P4 and G4 platforms.* The major conclusions from these tables (over 115,000 error injections) can be summarized as follows:

- Although the error activation rates are generally similar for both processors, the manifestation rates for the Pentium 4 are about twice as high.
- For stack errors, there is a significant difference between the two processors in the manifestation rates (56% for P4 versus 21% for G4). A similar trend is observed in the case of an error in the kernel data (66% for the P4 versus 21% for the G4). The observed difference between the two platforms can be explained by the disparity in the way they use memory. The G4 processor always operates on 32-bit wide data items, whereas the P4 allows 8-bit, 16-bit, and 32-bit data transfers. As a result, it is possible for many stack and data errors on the G4 platform to corrupt unused data bits in a target data item.
- For register errors, the trend in manifestation rates is similar to the above, although the manifestation rates for both platforms are lower (5% for G4, and over 11% for P4).[†]

---

*Percentage figures in the third column of the two tables are calculated with respect to all injected errors; all other percentages are given with respect to activated errors.

[†]Register injections target the system registers: flag register, stack registers, and memory management registers. Although we cannot determine the exact percentage of activated errors, the way the system is using these registers creates a high chance that errors will be activated.

TABLE 15.5. Statistics on error activation and failure distribution on the P4 processor

Intel Pentium 4 campaign	Injected	Error activated	Activated			
			Not manifested	Fail silence violation	Known crash	Hang/unknown crash
Stack	10143	2973 (29.3%)	1305 (43.9%)	0 (0%)	1136 (38.2%)	532 (17.9%)
System registers	3866	N/A	3459 (89.5%)	0 (0%)	305 (7.9%)	102 (2.6%)
Data	46000	226 (0.5%)	77 (34.1%)	0 (0%)	96 (42.5%)	53 (23.4%)
Code	1790	982 (54.9%)	308 (31.4%)	13 (1.3%)	455 (46.3%)	206 (21.0%)
Total	61799					

- Although the percentages of FSVs are small (1.3% for P4 to 2.3% for G4) for code segment injection, they have significant error propagation potential and, hence, are a cause for concern. Observe that the P4 data injection does not cause any FSVs, whereas on the G4, 1% of activated data errors manifest as FSVs.

15.5. CRASH CAUSE ANALYSIS

Figure 15.4 and Figure 15.5 show the distribution of the causes of known crashes (i.e., those for which crash dump information was logged). The crash cause distributions for the two platforms have some similarities:

- About 67% (*bad area*) of crashes on the G4 and 71% (sum of *bad paging* and *NULL pointer*) of crashes on the P4 are due to invalid memory access; illegal instructions contribute to 16% of crashes on both platforms.
- As will be discussed in the following section, the P4 does not explicitly report stack overflow (this category is not present in the pie chart in Figure 15.4). On the P4, these stack errors propagate, and most of them manifest as *bad paging* or *general protection fault*. The impact of the propagation is discussed in Section 15.6 in connection with an analysis of error latency.
- On both platforms, about 0.1% of crashes are due to system *Panic* (i.e., the OS detects an internal error).

TABLE 15.6. Statistics on error activation and failure distribution on G4 processor

Motorola PPC G4 campaign	Injected	Error activated	Activated			
			Not manifested	Fail silence violation	Known crash	Hang/unknown crash
Stack	3017	1203 (39.9%)	949 (78.9%)	0 (0%)	172 (14.3%)	84 (7.0%)
System Register	3967	N/A	3774 (95.1%)	0 (0%)	69 (1.7%)	124 (3.1%)
Data	46000	704 (1.5%)	551 (78.3%)	7 (1.0%)	55 (7.8%)	91 (12.9%)
Code	2188	1415 (64.7%)	580 (41.0%)	33 (2.3%)	576 (40.7%)	226 (16.0%)
Total	55172					

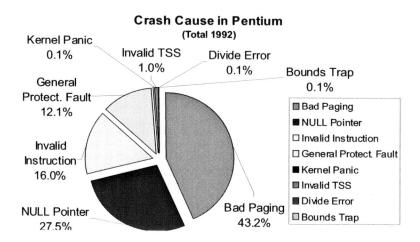

Figure 15.4. Overall distribution of crash causes (*known crash* category on P4).

15.5.1. Stack Injection

In this section, we analyze the manifested stack errors. Stack injections on the G4 primarily result in *stack overflow* (41.9%) and *bad area* (53.5%), whereas *bad paging* (45%) and *NULL pointer* (31%) dominate P4 results (see Figure 15.6).

Stack overflow is caused by corruption of frame pointers stored on the stack. As a result, the kernel attempts to access memory beyond the currently allocated space for the stack, causing an exception to be generated. Although the *stack overflow* category constitutes a significant percentage of crashes (41.9%) on the G4 processor, it does not appear to occur on the P4 platform. One could look for the explanation in the relative sizes of the run-time stack used by the two processors. Although the average size of the run-time kernel stack on the G4 is twice that of the P4 stack, the average number of function frame pointers concurrently kept on each of the two stacks is very much the same (5 to 7 frames).

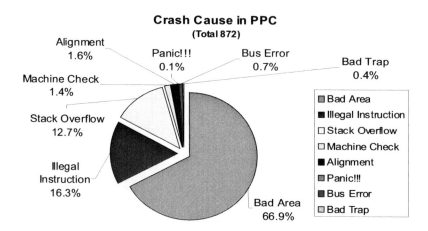

Figure 15.5. Overall distribution of crash causes (*known crash* category G4).

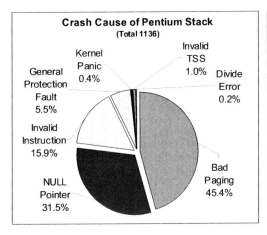
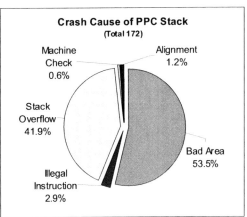

Figure 15.6. crash causes for kernel stack injection.

But the main reason for stack overflows not being reported on the P4 is that the Linux kernel on the P4 platform does not provide an exception to explicitly indicate stack overflow. An analysis of crash data on the P4 platform shows that it is possible to detect error patterns that correspond to a stack overflow (see Figure 15.7). This analysis shows that a fraction of the crashes that manifest as *bad paging* are actually due to stack overflow. Moreover, some of the crashes categorized as *Invalid Opcode* and *NULL Pointer* are also due to stack overflow. In addition, often on the P4 an actual stack overflow leads directly to a *general protection* exception. As will be seen, the fact that the P4 does not indicate

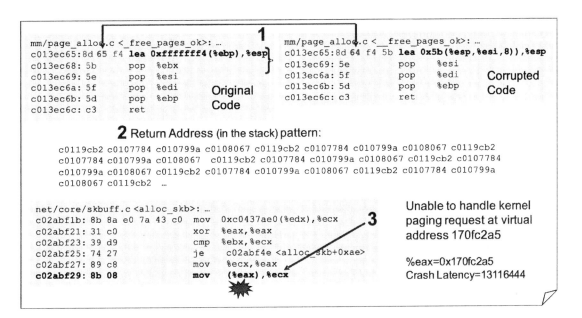

Figure 15.7. Error propagation between kernel subsystems due to undetected stack overflow.

stack overflows has implications for error latency (the time between an error injection and the occurrence of the crash or system detection) as well.

The above observations and analysis also explain the difference in the number of crashes attributed to *invalid memory access* for the two processors: 53% and 76% (the sum of *bad paging* and *NULL pointer* cases) for G4 and P4, respectively. Our analysis shows that some invalid memory accesses on the P4 are actually due to a stack overflow and could have been detected as such if the P4 (or the OS) could explicitly capture such events.

15.5.1.1. Error Propagation Due to Stack Overflow. Figure 15.7 depicts an example of error propagation [between the *memory management (mm)* and the *network (net)* subsystems] due to an undetected stack overflow on the P4. A bit error in the function *free_pages_ok()* in the *mm* subsystem causes the P4 to execute the valid but incorrect instruction *lea 0x5b(esp,esi,8),esp* instead of two original instructions *lea 0xfffffff4(ebp),esp* and *pop ebx*. As a result, the stack pointer (*ESP*) gets an incorrect value (1 in Figure 15.7). Corruption of the stack pointer is not detected by the P4 kernel, which continues executing in the presence of an error. Eventually, the system crashes in the function *alloc_skb()* in the network subsystem (3 in Figure 15.6) when *mov* reads a value from eax register that contains an illegal kernel address (0x170fc2a5). The kernel raises the exception *unable to handle kernel paging request* at virtual address 0x170fc2a5 and crashes. The measured crash latency is 13,116,444 cycles. The crash dump data show a typical stack overflow pattern (2 in Figure 15.7).

15.5.1.2. P4 Stack Error. Figure 15.8 depicts a typical example of the consequences of an error in the kernel stack. The sample source code in the figure shows the function *kupdate()* from the kernel file subsystem. This function is used to flush to disk

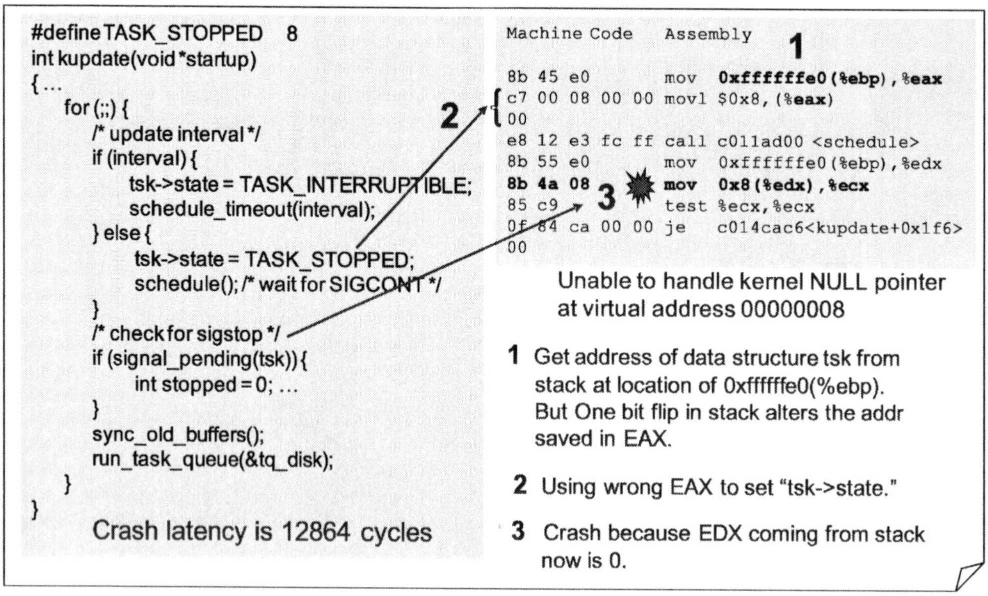

Figure 15.8. Consequences of kernel stack error (P4).

the *dirty data buffers* kept in RAM. The function uses a kernel data structure (*tsk*) stored on the kernel stack. In particular, *tsk→state* is at location *0xffffffe0(%ebp)*, where *ebp* is the stack pointer (1 in Figure 15.8). A bit error inserted and activated at location *0xffffffe0(%ebp)* alters the content of eax so that the state of *tsk→state* is corrupted (i.e., is not set to *TASK_STOPPED (2)*). Thus, incorrect parameters are passed to the scheduler [*schedule()*]. When *schedule()* returns, the content of *0xffffffe0(%ebp)* is 0, which is saved in *edx*. After executing *mov 0x8(%edx),%ecx,* the NULL pointer exception is raised, and the system crashes within the next 12,864 cycles (3 in Figure 15.8).

15.5.1.3. G4 Stack Error. Figure 15.9 illustrates the impact of stack errors on the G4 platform. The sample source code is extracted from *kjournald()* in the kernel file system subsystem. This function manages a logging device journal. At the address *c008d798, lwz* loads the content to the register *r11* from the stack location pointed to by *40(r31)*. Register *r31* is used as a temporary stack pointer. A single-bit error causes an invalid kernel address "1" to be loaded to *r11* instead of a legal address. The kernel crashes (*bad area* exception) trying to access memory at *0x0000004d* (the content of *r11* is used as an address: *76(r11)=0x4d*). In comparison with the P4, the crash latency here is much shorter: 1592 cycles or 210 instructions, clearly a potential advantage in attempting to limit error propagation.

15.5.2. System Register Injection

Register error injection campaigns affect both processors' target system registers. In the P4, the system registers "assist in initializing the processor and controlling system operations" [Intel 2004]. System-level registers targeted on the P4 processor include the flag register (system flags only, e.g., nested task flag), control registers, debug registers, stack pointer, segment registers (*fs* and *gs* only),* and memory-management registers. On the G4, error injection campaigns focus on the registers, which belong to the supervisor model in the PowerPC family (as opposed to the user model) [Motorola 2004]; these include memory management registers, configuration registers, performance monitor registers, exception-handling registers, and cache/memory subsystem registers.

Figure 15.10 shows the distribution of crash causes for system register injections. Out of 99 system registers in the G4 and approximately 20 in the P4, only 15 G4 registers and seven P4 registers contribute to the crashes and hangs observed in our experiments. The key errors observed and their associated registers are as follows:

- *General protection* errors observed on the P4 platform are due to corruption of the control register *CR0* and the segment registers *FS* and *GS*. *CR0* contains system control flags that control the operating mode and states of the processors (11 bits are used as flags; the remaining bits are reserved). In an error scenario, a single-bit error disables protected mode operation and causes a general protection exception. Injections to the P4 stack pointer (*ESP*) cause either *NULL pointer* or *bad paging* errors.
- Few crashes on the P4 are due to *invalid TSS* (*task-state segment*). All these events are caused by the corruption of the *NT* (nested task) bit in the *EFLAGS register*. The

---

*These two segment registers are stored for each context switch as part of the TSS (task state segment).

```
Address     Machine Code   Assembly

c008d794:  4b f8 b8 d9   bl     c001906c <interruptible_sleep_on>
c008d798:  81 7f 00 28   lwz    r11,40(r31)
C code: transaction = journal->j_running transaction
```
Wrong value in stack pointed by r31 is loaded to r11
```
c008d79c:  2c 0b 00 00   cmpwi  r11,0
c008d7a0:  41 82 ff c4   beq+   c008d764 <kjournald+0x178>
c008d7a4:  80 1b 83 68   lwz    r0,-31896(r27)
c008d7a8:  81 2b 00 4c   lwz    r9,76(r11)
C code: transaction->t_expires
```
Crash of "kernel access of bad area"

Figure 15.9. Consequences of the kernel stack error (G4).

NT bit controls the chaining of interrupted and called tasks. Changing the state of this flag results in an attempt to return to an invalid task after an interrupt.

- On both platforms, injections into the system registers can cause crashes due to *invalid instructions:* 6% and 12% on the P4 and G4, respectively. On the P4 platform, invalid instructions occur because of injections into the kernel process instruction pointer (*EIP*), which may force the processor to access memory corresponding to a random place in an instruction binary.

- On the G4, most crashes due to *invalid instruction* are caused by errors in the register *SPR274,* which is one of several registers dedicated to general operating system use and used by the stack switch during exceptions. Corrupting the contents of this register can force the operating system to try to execute from a random memory location that does not contain a valid instruction and to generate an *invalid instruction* exception. A small percentage of *invalid instructions* are due to errors in the register *SPR1008,* which is used to control the state of several functions within the CPU, for

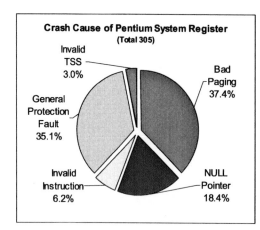
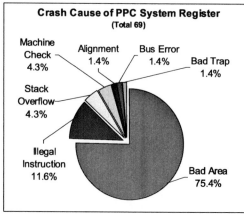

Figure 15.10. Crash causes for system register injection.

example, enabling the instruction cache or branch target instruction cache. In an error scenario (from our experiments), a single-bit error enables the branch target instruction cache when the content of the cache is invalid. As a result, the system crashes due to an invalid instruction exception.

- A small percentage of crashes on the G4 are due to a *machine check* exception being raised. These crashes are caused by corruption of the *machine state register (MSR)*, which defines the state of the processor. In particular, the two bits responsible for enabling/disabling the instruction address translation (*IR*) and data address translation (*DR*) are error sensitive.

15.5.3. Code Injection

The results of the code section injections are shown in Figure 15.11. *Invalid memory access* is a characteristic of code injections on both platforms, although for the P4 they are nearly 20% higher: 50% (*bad area*) on the G4 versus 70% (*bad paging + NULL Pointers*) on the P4. A plausible explanation is that a bit error on the P4 can convert a single instruction into a sequence of multiple valid (but incorrect from the application standpoint) instructions. This is due to the variable length of instruction binaries on the P4 (CISC architecture). On the P4 platform, this error may subsequently lead to an invalid memory access (often a *NULL pointer*); hence, more invalid memory accesses are observed. All instructions on the G4 have the same length (32-bit RISC architecture); hence, a single-bit error (in addition to a invalid memory access) is more likely to result in an invalid instruction.

Stack overflows resulting from code errors are a small fraction (about 5%) on the G4; compare this with the results of stack injections resulting in stack overflow (41.9%). This is most likely because the G4 has a large number of general-purpose registers (GPRs). However, very few of them (often *GPR1* and *GPR31*) are used to operate on the stack (e.g., to keep the stack pointer). Crashes due to stack overflow would require altering a register name used by a given instruction to operate on the stack. Keeping in mind the number of GPRs, the likelihood of stack overflow is low.

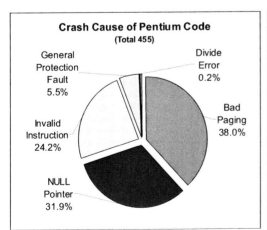
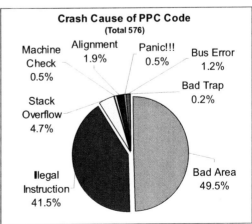

Figure 15.11. Crash causes for code injection.

The *illegal instruction* exceptions detected on the two platforms are also quite different: 24% on the P4 versus 41% on the G4. The difference is due in part to the inability of the P4 to diagnose many of instruction-level faults because of variable-length instructions (as explained earlier).

The preceding sections highlight the role of the hardware in detecting errors. Data injections, discussed next, highlight the operating system's detection capabilities, since the impact of errors in data must be detected at the operating system level.

15.5.4. Data Injection

Recall that only a small percentage of kernel data errors are activated. On both processors, the majority of manifested data errors (see Figure 15.12) result in invalid memory accesses: 89% (*bad area*) and 80% (*bad paging* + *NULL pointers*) for the G4 and P4, respectively. There is also a significant percentage of *invalid/illegal instruction* cases: 9% and 18% for the G4 and P4, respectively.

The key reason that twice as many invalid instruction cases are observed on the P4 platform is that the Linux kernel (for both P4 and G4 architectures) raises the *invalid instruction* exception to handle a variety of error cases, some of which have nothing to do with invalid instructions. Figure 15.13 depicts how the kernel-checking scheme works. The *spin_lock/spin_unlock* function is frequently used to inspect kernel flags and decide whether to set a lock/unlock on kernel objects (e.g., *page_table_lock, journal_tatalist_lock, bdev_lock, arbitration_lock*). The flags are located in the kernel data section (*kernel_flag_cacheline*). In Figure 15.13, a bit error at address *0xc0375bc5* changes *4E* to *0E* (1 in Figure 15.13). As a result, the compare (*cmpl*) instruction detects incorrect data (2 in Figure 15.13), and an invalid instruction (*ud2a*) exception is raised (3 in Figure 15.13). Since *spin_lock/spin_unlock* has a high rate of recurrence, this checking mechanism provides quick error detection.

The original cause of the errors, however, is not an invalid instruction, and the type of the exception raised may mislead the user. The results highlight the need for an operating-system-based checking scheme to provide better detection.

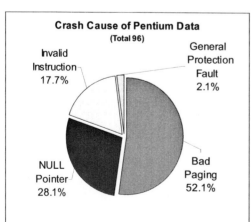
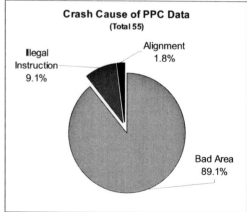

Figure 15.12. Crash causes for kernel data injection.

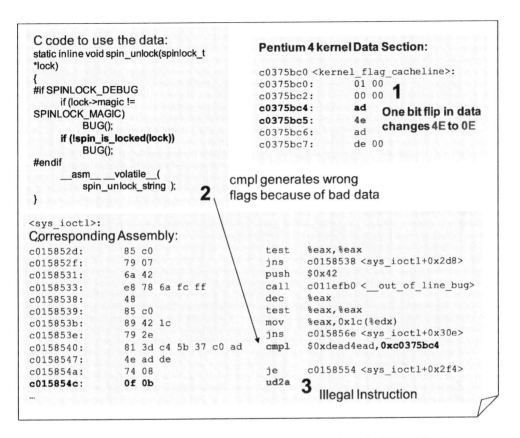

C code to use the data:
```
static inline void spin_unlock(spinlock_t
*lock)
{
#if SPINLOCK_DEBUG
        if (lock->magic !=
SPINLOCK_MAGIC)
            BUG();
        if (!spin_is_locked(lock))
            BUG();
#endif
        __asm__ __volatile__(
            spin_unlock_string );
}
```

Pentium 4 kernel Data Section:
```
c0375bc0 <kernel_flag_cacheline>:
c0375bc0:       01 00
c0375bc2:       00 00        1
c0375bc4:       ad       One bit flip in data
c0375bc5:       4e       changes 4E to 0E
c0375bc6:       ad
c0375bc7:       de 00
```

2 cmpl generates wrong flags because of bad data

```
<sys_ioctl>:
Corresponding Assembly:
c015852d:       85 c0                       test    %eax,%eax
c015852f:       79 07                       jns     c0158538 <sys_ioctl+0x2d8>
c0158531:       6a 42                       push    $0x42
c0158533:       e8 78 6a fc ff              call    c011efb0 <__out_of_line_bug>
c0158538:       48                          dec     %eax
c0158539:       85 c0                       test    %eax,%eax
c015853b:       89 42 1c                    mov     %eax,0x1c(%edx)
c015853e:       79 2e                       jns     c015856e <sys_ioctl+0x30e>
c0158540:       81 3d c4 5b 37 c0 ad        cmpl    $0xdead4ead,0xc0375bc4
c0158547:       4e ad de
c015854a:       74 08                       je      c0158554 <sys_ioctl+0x2f4>
c015854c:       0f 0b                       ud2a    3
...                                                 Illegal Instruction
```

Figure 15.13. Illegal instruction crash (due to data error) on the P4 architecture.

15.5.5. Summary

Several more generic conclusions can be drawn based on the analysis of crash data:

- The variable-length instruction format on the P4 leads to poorer diagnosability because a bit error can change a single instruction into a sequence of multiple valid (but incorrect in the context of the application semantic) instructions. This error may subsequently lead to an invalid memory access and cause, e.g., a *NULL pointer* exception, which can make locating the actual cause of the crash difficult. All instructions on the G4 have the same length (32 bits); hence, a single-bit error is more likely to result in an invalid instruction.

- Though less compact, fixed 32-bit data and stack access makes the G4 platform less sensitive to errors. The sparseness of the data can mask errors. For example, the larger presence of unused bits in data items means that altering any unused bit is inconsequential, even if the corrupted data instruction is used. The more optimized access patterns on P4 increase the chances that accessing a corrupted memory location will lead to problems.

- The data from stack overflow and the lazy detection of instruction corruption indicate that the P4 kernel (and possibly the hardware strategy) reduces the performance overhead that run-time error checks might incur but increases the risk of error propagation and the potential for serious damage to the system. In contrast, the G4 kernel is more likely to perform checking closer to an error's origin. Although this approach may cost performance, it provides early detection and, hence, reduces the chance that errors will propagate.

15.6. CRASH LATENCY (CYCLES-TO-CRASH) ANALYSIS

To explore further differences/similarities in Linux behavior on the two platforms, this section discusses crash latency. Figure 15.16 depicts the crash latency for all conducted error injection campaigns and provides details on crash latency distributions. The major findings can be summarized as follows:

- The majority (80%) of stack errors on the G4 platform are short-lived (less than 3000 cycles). On the P4 platform, the majority (80%) of stack errors result in longer crash latency (3000 to 100,000 cycles). The primary reason for this disparity is the way the two platforms handle exceptions. For example, the kernel on the G4 platform provides quick detection of stack overflow errors, whereas the kernel on the P4 architecture converts stack overflow events into other types of exceptions (e.g., *bad paging*), resulting in inherently slower detection.
- Errors impacting the kernel code show an opposite trend in crash latency (compared to stack errors). Here, 45% of the errors on the P4 platform are short-lived (less than 3000 cycles), whereas about 50% of the errors on the G4 have latency between 10,000 and 100,000 cycles. This dissimilarity is due to the differences in the number of general-purpose registers provided by the two processors (32 on the G4; 8 on the P4).

Most system register errors are relatively long-lived (more than 10,000 cycles). This can be attributed to the fact that most of them are not visible to users and typically are not modified often.

15.6.1. Stack Injection

The crash latency for stack injections is given in Figure 15.16(A). About 80% of the crashes observed on the G4 platform are within 3000 CPU cycles, whereas about 80% of the crashes on the P4 are in the range of 3000 to 100,000 cycles. Crash cause analysis (see Section 15.5.1) indicates that 40% of the G4 crashes are due to stack overflow. The G4 kernel employs a checking wrapper before executing a specific exception handler. This wrapper examines the correctness of the current stack pointer. If the stack pointer is out of kernel stack range (8 Kb), the kernel raises a *stack overflow* exception and forces itself to stop as soon as possible. The wrapper executes before the exception handler is invoked and, as a result, the detection of the corrupted stack pointers is relatively fast. The kernel executing on the P4 does not support this wrapper mechanism. It allows an error to propagate and be captured by other exceptions, for example, *bad paging* or *illegal instruction*, which may lengthen the time before the error is detected.

15.6.2. System Register Injection

As shown in Figure 15.16(B), 35% of the crashes on the G4 platform are within 3000 cycles. This is due mainly to errors in the *machine state register* (MSR), which immediately crash the system. Crashes due to errors in the G4 kernel stack pointer and *SPR274* registers have latencies in the range between 10 M and 100 M cycles. On the P4 platform, 70% of crashes are within 10 K cycles. These crashes are caused by errors in the *ESP* and *EIP* registers corresponding to the kernel process targeted by the injection. The longest crash latency (larger than 1 G cycles) is due to errors in the *FS* and *GS* registers.

15.6.3. Code Injection

Figure 15.16(C) summarizes the cycle-to-crash distribution in kernel code section injections. The P4 architecture has a shorter latency (70% within 10,000 cycles) compared with the G4 architecture (almost 90% above 10,000 cycles). There are several reasons for these differences.

Figure 15.14 shows that a group of instructions in the P4 architecture may be transformed to another, totally different instruction group. Originally, five instructions starting with *mov* are changed to another five instructions starting with *xorl* through a bit flip at address *0xc011e2a6,* which leads the kernel to crash at *0xc011e2b1* ("*crash here*"). Thus, errors in the code section of the P4 architecture may crash faster than those in the G4 architecture. Interestingly, poor diagnosability seems to lead to shorter error latencies in the code section.

The G4 architecture offers a much larger number of GPR registers (32) than the P4 processor (8). Function arguments are often passed using general-purpose registers, for example, *GPR18* to *GPR29.* Registers *GPR3* through *GPR12* are volatile (caller-save) registers, which (if necessary) must be saved before calling a subroutine and restored after returning. Register *GPR1* is used as the stack frame pointer. As a result, values kept in a G4 register can potentially live longer before being used or overwritten. Hence, it may take longer for an error to manifest and crash the system.

Figure 15.15 illustrates a bit error in the *sys_read()* function taken from the kernel code on the G4 platform. The error transforms the *mflr* instruction to *lhax.* The system

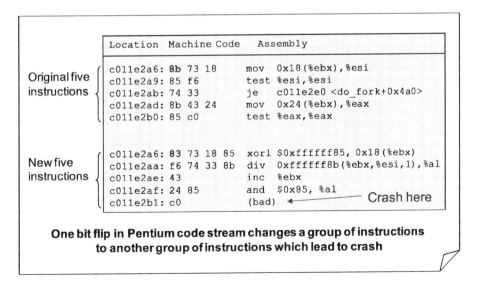

Figure 15.14. Bit error causing change in instruction group (P4).

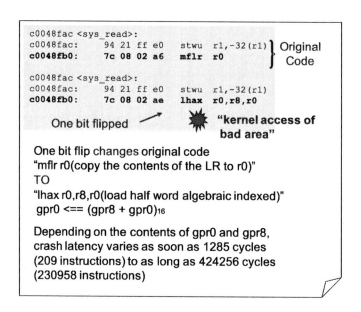

Figure 15.15. Variation in crash latency (G4).

crashes (kernel access of a bad area) due to an illegal address generated by *lhax: r0, r8, r0* *(gpr8 + gpr0)*. Depending on the workload (and, hence, the values in *gpr8* and *gpr0*), crash latency may vary (see Figure 15.15).

15.6.4. Data Injection

Figure 15.16(D) shows that crash latency due to data errors is similar on both platforms. The error activation is small (about 1%) due to the large data space allocated for the kernel despite its rather sparse usage. As a result, the latency distribution has a long tail, indicating that errors can stay in the system for seconds before being activated. Moreover, it is likely that many errors that do not manifest for the duration of the benchmark execution stay latent in memory and may impact the system later. To prevent crashes due to data corruption and to reduce error latency, assertions can be added to protect critical data structures.

15.7. CRASH SEVERITY

In this section, we analyze severity of crash failures. Although the discussion is in the context of the Pentium 4 platform, it also applies to other platforms. The severity of the crash failures resulting from the injected errors is categorized into three levels according to the system downtime due to the failure. The three identified levels are:

1. *Most severe.* Rebooting the system after an error injection requires a complete reformatting of the file system on the disk, and the process of bringing up the system can take nearly an hour.
2. *Severe.* Rebooting the system requires the user (interactively) to run the *fsck* facility/tool to recover the partially corrupted file system, and although reformatting is

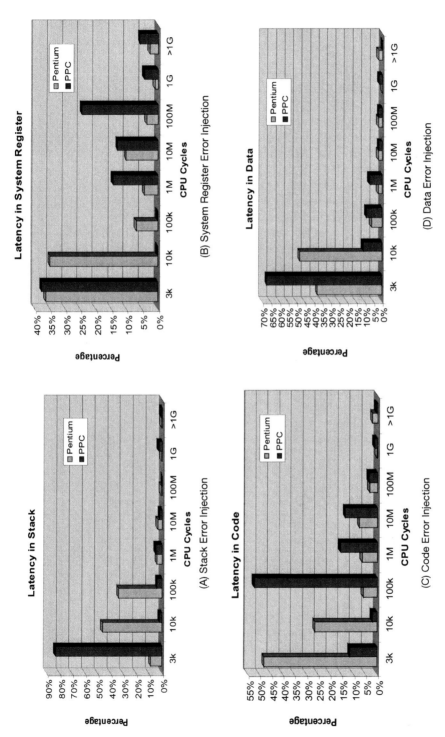

Figure 15.16. Distribution of cycles to crash.

333

not needed, the process can take more than 5 minutes and requires user intervention.

3. *Normal.* At this least severe level, the system automatically reboots, and the rebooting usually takes less than 4 minutes, depending on the type of machine and the configuration of Linux.

An additional set of fault injection experiments has been conducted to enable evalution of crash severity. In all but 34 of 9600 dumped crash cases, the system rebooted automatically. There were 25 cases in the severe level category and nine cases require reformatting the file system. Table 15.7 reports the nine cases, four of which were repeatable and could be traced using *kdb* (kernel debugger). A detailed analysis of one of the repeatable crashes (case 9 in Table 15.7) is provided in Figure 15.17.

A catastrophic (most severe) error is injected into the function *do_generic_file_read()* from the memory subsystem. The restored (using the *kdb* tool) function-calling sequence before the error injection, shown at the bottom right in Figure 15.17, indicates that *do_generic_file_read()* is invoked by the file system as a read routine for transferring the data from the disk to the page cache in the memory. A single-bit error in the *mov* instruction of the *do_generic_file_read()* results in reversing the value assignment performed by the *mov* (see the assembly code at address *0xc0130a33* in Figure 15.17). As a result, the contents of the *eax* register remains *0x00000080* instead of *0x0000b728,* and after executing a 12-bit shift (*shrd* instruction in Figure 15.17), the *eax* is set to 0.

This is equivalent to corruption of the C-code-level variable *end_index* corresponding to the *eax* register; *end_index* is assigned value *0* instead of *0b*. Tracing the C-code shows that another variable (index) in *do_generic_file_read()* is initialized to 0 at the beginning of the for-loop and, hence, the loop executes at least once. However, due to the injected error, the for-loop breaks and *do_generic_file_read()* returns prematurely, causing subsequent file system corruption. Linux then reports: *INIT: ID "1" respowning too fast, 263 Bus error.* Rebooting the system requires reinstallation of the OS.

Additionally, we note that (i) most of the severe crashes happen under the fault injec-

TABLE 15.7. Summary of most severe crashes

No.	Repeat-ability	Injected subsystem: function name	Possible causes for repeatable most severe crash
1	Yes	fs: open_nami()	Error results in truncating the file size to 0. No crash is observed, but on reboot, *init* reports: *error while loading shared libraries: /lib/i686/libc.so.6 file too short.*
2	No	mm: do_wp_page()	
3	No	fs: link_path_walk()	
4	No	fs: link_path_walk()	
5	No	fs: sys_read()	
6	No	fs:get_hash_table()	
7	Yes	mm: do_wp_page()	Error makes the kernel reuse the page (inside the swap area), which is in use.
8	Yes	fs: generic_commit_write()	Error reduces the *inode* size (*inode->isize*).
9	Yes	mm: do_generic_file_read()	Undetected error of an incomplete read of the file (data or executable) to the cache page.

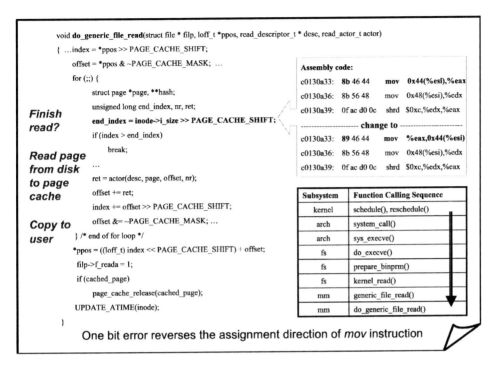

Figure 15.17. Case study of a most severe crash.

tion campaign, where a fault was injected to reverse the condition of a branch instruction; and (ii) although severe damage to the system most often results in a crash, we observed one case in which the system did not crash after an injected error but could not reboot. The availability impact of the most severe crashes is clearly of concern. Although a "valid but incorrect branch" error is rare, it is, in our experience, possible. For example, to achieve five nines of availability (5 min/yr downtime) one can only afford one such catastrophic failure in 12 years, no more than one severe crash in two years, and no more than one normal crash per year.

15.8. LESSONS LEARNED

Lessons learned extend beyond this particular study and provide valuable insight into future development and deployment of dependability benchmarks. Our observations are grouped into two categories:

1. What is the unique value of employing fault/error injection to benchmark computing system?
2. What is expected from benchmarking tools?

15.8.1. Value iof Employing Fault Injection

Characterization of Crash Severity. It is a common assumption that crashes are benign and that there is a mechanism in a system that ensures that when the program encounters an error (that ultimately leads to a crash), the application will crash instantaneously (crash-failure semantics). Although many crashes are benign, severe system failures often result from latent errors that cause undetected error propagation, resulting in file corruption (e.g., corruption of the OS image on the disk), remote process failures, or checkpoint corruption.

Measurement of Detection Latency and Validation of Crash-Failure Semantics. Assumption of crash failure semantics for a program or a system behavior is not good if one cannot provide efficient mechanisms for rapid error detection to ensure that this assumption holds in practice. Measurement of detection latency must be an integral component of the benchmarking procedure. For example, we demonstrated that crash latency can be as large as hundreds of millions or billions of cycles.

Characterization of Recovery Latency. Measurement of recovery time is crucial to assess system downtime and, hence, to quantify availability. Benchmarking must enable validation of system behavior in the case when multiple detection mechanisms are triggered due to propagated error.

15.8.2. Toolset and Benchmark Procedures

Complexity. Benchmarking of fault tolerance requires complex procedures and tools (the process is far more complex than in the case of performance benchmarking). Often, deploying the toolset is more time-consuming than conducting the measurements.

Multiple Platforms (Hardware, Operating System). Using different tools, one runs the risk that the benchmark measures the effectiveness of the tools rather than the dependability of the target system. A key to wide acceptance of a benchmarking toolset is its portability across computing platforms.

Multiple Fault Models. Support multiple fault models and provide well-defined interfaces to enable extensions for new fault models. Evaluation of complex systems benefits from injecting a wide variety of faults such as communication faults, bit-flip faults to memory and registers, and high-level faults specific to an application. The more diverse the fault set, the more that can be learned about the target system.

15.9. CONCLUSIONS

This chapter describes a fault/error-injection-based approach to experimental assessment of operating system dependability. The methodology is applied to characterize and compare error sensitivity of the Linux kernel executing on PowerPC G4 and Pentium 4 processors. Findings from this case study indicate that the proposed approach can provide a solid basis for (i) comparing different platforms and (ii) providing feedback to system designers for removing dependability bottlenecks and integrating potential enhancements to improve robustness of the system. Major findings in the context of comparing Linux kernel running on two different hardware platforms are outlined below:

- Although the activation* of errors is generally similar for both processors, the manifestation percentages for the Pentium 4 are about twice as high.
- For stack errors, there is a significant difference between the two processors in manifestation percentages (56% for P4 versus 21% for G4). A similar trend is observed in kernel data errors, where 66% (for P4) and 21% (for G4) of injected errors manifest as crashes.
- The variable-length instruction format of the P4 makes it possible for a bit error to change a single instruction into a sequence of multiple valid (but incorrect from the application semantic point of view) instructions. On one hand, this leads to poorer diagnosability—executing an incorrect instruction sequence may crash the system and generate an exception, which does not isolate the actual cause of the problem and obstructs diagnosis. On the other hand, the same feature has the potential to reduce crash latency—executing an incorrect instruction sequence is likely to make the system fail fast.
- Less compact, fixed 32-bit data and stack access makes the G4 platform less sensitive to errors. The sparseness of the data can mask errors; for example, a larger presence of unused bits in data items means that altering any unused bit is inconsequential, even if the corrupted data is used. The more optimized access patterns on the P4 increase the chances that accessing a corrupted memory location will lead to problems.

Although there is still a long way to go before we define the dependability benchmark for operating systems, the approach discussed in this chapter constitutes an important step in achieving this goal.

ACKNOWLEDGMENTS

This work was supported in part by Gigascale Systems Research Center (GSRC/MARCO), in part by NSF grant CCR 99-02026, and by Motorola Corporation as part of Motorola Center at University of Illinois.

REFERENCES

[Arlat et al. 2002] J. Arlat, J.-C. Fabre, and M. Rodriguez, "Dependability of COTS Microkernel-Based Systems," *IEEE Transactions on Computers,* vol. 51, no. 2, pp. 138–163, February 2002.

[Barton et al. 1990] J. H. Barton, E. W. Czeck, Z. Z. Segall, and D. P. Siewiorek, "Fault Injection Experiments Using FIAT," *IEEE Transactions on Computers,* vol. 39, no. 4, pp. 575–582, April 1990.

[Buchacker and Sieh 2001] K. Buchacker and V. Sieh, "Framework for Testing the Fault-Tolerance of Systems Including OS and Network Aspects," in *Proceedings of 6th International Symposium on High-Assurance Systems Engineering,* Boca Raton, FL, pp. 95–105, 2001.

[Carreira et al. 1998] J. Carreira, H. Madeira, and J. G. Silva, "Xception: A Technique for the Evaluation of Dependability in Modern Computers," *IEEE Transactions on Software Engineering,* vol. 24, no. 2, pp. 125–136, February 1998.

---

*Error activation cannot be determined while injecting into system registers, as we do not have the ability to monitor kernel access to these registers.

[Carrette 1996] G. Carrette, "CRASHME: Random Input Testing," http://people.delphiforums.com/gjc/crashme.html, 1996.

[Chou et al. 2001] A. Chou, J. Yang, B. Chelf, S. Hallem, and D. Engler "An Empirical Study of Operating Systems Errors," in *Proceedings of 18th ACM Symposium on Operating Systems Principles (SOSP-2001)*, Banff, Alberta, Canada, pp. 73–88, 2001.

[Edwards and Matassa 2002] D. Edwards and L. Matassa, "An Approach to Injecting Faults into Hardened Software," in *Proceedings of Ottawa Linux Symposium*, Ottawa, Canada, pp. 146–175, 2002.

[Gu et al. 2003] W. Gu, Z. Kalbarczyk, R. K. Iyer, and Z. Yang, "Characterization of Linux Kernel Behavior under Errors," in *Proceedings of International Conference on Dependable Systems and Networks (DSN-2003)*, San Francisco, pp. 459–468, 2003.

[Intel 2004] Intel, *IA-32 Intel Architecture Software Developer's Manual, Volume 3: System Programming Guide*, 2004.

[Iyer et al. 1986] R. K. Iyer, D. J. Rossetti, and M. C. Hsueh, "Measurement and Modeling of Computer Reliability as Affected by System Activity," *ACM Transactions on Computer Systems*, vol. 4, no. 3, pp. 214–237, August 1986.

[Kao et al. 1993] W. Kao, R. K. Iyer, and D. Tang, "FINE: A Fault Injection and Monitoring Environment for Tracing the UNIX System Behavior Under Faults," *IEEE Transactions on Software Engineering*, vol. 19, no. 11, pp. 1105–1118, November 1993.

[Koopman and DeVale 2000] P. Koopman and J. DeVale, "The Exception Handling Effectiveness of POSIX Operating Systems," *IEEE Transactions on Software Engineering*, vol. 26, no. 9, pp. 837–848, September 2000.

[Kropp et al. 1998] N. P. Kropp, P. J. Koopman, and D. P. Siewiorek, "Automated Robustness Testing of Off-the-Shelf Software Components," in *Proceedings of 28th International Symposium on Fault-Tolerant Computing (FTCS-28)*, Munich, pp. 230–239, 1998.

[Lee and Iyer 1993] I. Lee and R. K. Iyer, "Faults, Symptoms, and Software Fault Tolerance in Tandem GUARDIAN90 Operating System," in *Proceedings of 23rd International Symposium on Fault-Tolerant Computing (FTCS-23)*, Toulouse, France, pp. 20–29, 1993.

[Madeira et al. 2002] H. Madeira, R. Some, F. Moreira, D. Costa, and D. Rennels, "Experimental Evaluation of a COTS System for Space Applications," in *Proceedings of International Conference on Dependable Systems and Networks (DSN-2002)*, Washington, DC, pp. 325–330, 2002.

[Miller, et al. 2000] B. P. Miller, D. Koski, C. P. Lee, V. Maganty, R. Murthy, A. Natarajan, and J. Steidl, "A Re-examination of the Reliability of UNIX Utilities and Services," Computer Sciences Department, University of Wisconsin, Madison, WI, http://www.suffritti.it/informatica/tco/fuzz-revisited.pdf, 2000.

[Motorola 2004] Motorola, *MPC7450 RISC Microprocessor Family User's Manual*, 2004.

[Ng and Chen 1999] W. Ng and P. M. Chen, "The Systematic Improvement of Fault Tolerance in the Rio File Cache," in *Proceedings of 29th International Symposium on Fault-Tolerant Computing (FTCS-29)*, Madison, WI, pp. 76–83, 1999.

[Rimen et al. 1994] M. Rimen, J. Ohlsson, and J. Torin, "On Microprocessor Error Behavior Modeling," in *Proceedings of 24th International Symposium on Fault-Tolerant Computing (FTCS-24)*, Austin, TX, pp. 76–85, 1994.

[Stott et al. 2000] D. Stott, B. Floering, D. Burke, Z. Kalbarczyk, and R. K. Iyer, "NFTAPE: A Framework for Assessing Dependability in Distributed Systems with Lightweight Fault Injectors," in *Proceedings of 4th International Computer Performance and Dependability Symposium*, Chicago, IL, pp. 91–100, 2000.

[Sullivan and Chillarege 1991] M. Sullivan and R. Chillarege, "Software Defects and Their Impact on System Availability—A Study of Field Failures in Operating Systems," in *Proceedings of 21st International Symposium on Fault-Tolerant Computing (FTCS-21)*, Montreal, pp. 2–9, 1991.

[Tsai et al. 1996] T. Tsai, R. K. Iyer, and D. Jewitt, "An Approach towards Benchmarking of Fault-Tolerant Commercial Systems," in *Proceedings of 26th International Symposium on Fault-Tolerant Computing (FTCS-26)*, Sendai, Japan, pp. 314-323, 1996.

[Tsai et al. 1999] T. Tsai, M.-C. Hsueh, H. Zhao, Z. Kalbarczyk, and R. K. Iyer, "Stress-based and Path-based Fault Injection," *IEEE Transactions on Computers*, vol. 48, no. 11, pp. 1183–1201, 1999.

[Xu et al. 1999] J. Xu, Z. Kalbarczyk, and R. K. Iyer, "Networked Windows NT System Field Failure Data Analysis," in *Proceedings of Pacific Rim International Symposium on Dependable Computing (PRDC-1999)*, Hong Kong, pp. 178–185, 1999.

NEUTRON SOFT ERROR RATE CHARACTERIZATION OF MICROPROCESSORS

Cristian Constantinescu

16.1. INTRODUCTION

It has been known for a significant period of time that radiation has a negative impact on reliability of integrated circuits. In late 1970s, several landmark papers pointed out that single event upsets (SEU) were induced in semiconductor memories by the cosmic ray flux [Guenzer et al. 1979, Ziegler and Lanford 1979] and alpha particles generated during the process of radioactive decay of packaging and interconnect materials [May and Woods 1979]. Spallation reactions occur when high-energy particles penetrate the silicon. Some of the secondary particles generated in this process are highly ionizing and create electron–hole pairs, as they cross the transistor junctions. The particle-induced charge manifests as a current spike. Usually, no permanent damage of the circuit occurs, although data stored in volatile memory may be altered or results of mathematical computations corrupted. The frequency of occurrence of the errors induced by SEU is commonly referred to as the soft error rate (SER).

Neutrons, protons, and pions are the main hadrons emerging from the particle cascades produced by the primary cosmic rays penetrating the atmosphere. The type and the flux of the hadrons is a function of altitude and geographical location. At sea level, neutrons are the main hadrons impairing the proper operation of electronic circuitry. Extensive research has been conducted over the last decades for measuring and estimating the SER of semiconductor devices. For instance, accelerated measurements using neutrons, protons, pions, and heavy ions were presented in [Edmonds 2000, Howard at al. 2001, Ziegler et al. 1998]. Several models were developed for device SEU analysis [Dodd 1996, Palau et

The content of this chapter was presented at the IEEE Dependable Systems and Networks Conference [Constantinescu 2005].

---

al. 2003, Tosaka et al. 1999], simulation of soft errors induced by neutrons [Palau et al. 2002; Tosaka and Satoh 2000] and SER estimation at the system level [Karapetian et al. 2002].

The impact of the SER on computing systems becomes even more significant due to the aggressive scaling of the semiconductor manufacturing processes. Lower transistor features and lower voltages have led to higher performance and, also, have increased circuit sensitivity to particle-induced errors. The impact of SER on the combinational logic has also become a concern [Liden et al. 1994, Shivakumar et al. 2002]. Last but not least, the increased integration and complexity of VLSI circuits, in general, and microprocessors in particular, has been leading to a continuously higher device count per unit of chip area. As a result, SER measurements become paramount for ensuring adequate dependability. The methodology and results of accelerated SER measurements carried out on Intel Itanium® microprocessors at the Los Alamos Neutron Science Center (LANSCE) are presented. Section 16.2 discusses the scaling trends and their impact on neutron-induced SER. The characteristics of the LANSCE neutron beam and the experimental setup are presented in Section 16.3. Results of the experiments are given in Section 16.4. The concluding remarks are given in Section 16.5.

16.2. SEMICONDUCTOR MANUFACTURING SCALING TRENDS

According to the International Technology Roadmap for Semiconductors (ITRS), it is expected that microprocessors (MPUs) and application-specific integrated circuits (ASICs) half-pitch* will drop to 21 nm, by year 2018 [ITRS 2003]. The physical gate length is expected to be as low as 7 nm and 9 nm for MPU and ASIC, respectively. Also, the voltage will drop to 0.7 V for performance and 0.5 V for low-power circuits (Table 16.1). As a result, it is expected that in a decade microprocessor performance will increase to over 100,000 million instructions per second (MIPS). However, higher semiconductor integration and lower supply voltages have led to higher SER. Figure 16.1 shows the scaling trend for neutron-induced SER/bit in the case of static random memories (SRAM). Measurements on test chips were used to derive this data [Hareland et al. 2001]. As the gate length shrinks from 0.35 μm to 0.13 μm, the SER/bit decreases for a constant voltage. The decrease of the voltage leads to significantly higher SER. The explanation of this phenomenon is two-fold. On one hand, shrinking transistor features lowers the probability of collecting the critical charge necessary to upset the circuit. On the other hand, the critical charge itself decreases because of lower cell capacity and supply voltage, increasing likelihood of an upset when a particle strike occurs.

In the future, both transistor size and critical charge will continue to decrease with scaling of the manufacturing processes. The number of particles able to induce errors, for a given die area, is expected to saturate, SER being determined by the actual number of strikes. After the saturation phase, the SER/bit tends to decrease. However, the number of devices will continue to increase, due to the higher complexity and improved functionality of the integrated circuits. This evolution will lead to higher SER/chip. Likelihood of particle-induced multibit errors will also increase, as well as probability of soft errors within combinatorial logic [Shivakumar et al. 2002].

---

*The half-pitch of the first-level interconnect is a representative measure for technology level. One pitch is defined as the width of the metal interconnect plus the width of the space between two adjacent interconnect wires.

TABLE 16.1. ITRS estimates for MPU and ASIC

Year of production	2003	2006	2009	2012	2015	2018
MPU/ASIC half-pitch (nm)	120	85	60	42	30	21
MPU physical gate length (nm)	45	28	20	14	10	7
ASIC physical gate length (nm)	65	37	25	18	13	9
V_{dd} high-performance circuits (V)	1.2	1.1	1.0	0.9	0.8	0.7
V_{dd} low-power circuits (V)	1.0	0.9	0.8	0.7	0.6	0.5

16.3. NEUTRON SER CHARACTERIZATION

The main particles from atmospheric hadron cascades, capable of inducing SEU in electronic devices, are neutrons, pions, and protons. As shown in Table 16.2, neutrons represent 94% of the hadrons reaching sea level; the remaining 6% are equally divided between pions and protons. Although pions and protons play a more significant role at 32,000 feet, an altitude frequently used by commercial aircraft, the neutrons remain the principal component of the hadron cascades. Therefore, this study concentrates on neutron SER characterization.

The LANSCE neutron beam was chosen for accelerated SER measurement as its energy spectrum is very similar to the spectrum of cosmic-ray-induced neutrons [Taber and Normand 1993, Wender 1998]. At LANSCE, high-energy neutrons are produced through spallation. A linear accelerator generates a pulsed proton beam that strikes a tungsten target. The impact produces neutrons with energies up to 600 MeV. In Figure 16.2, the LANSCE neutron energy spectrum is compared with the spectrum induced by cosmic rays, at 40,000 feet. In this figure, the acceleration factor is 10^6 (i.e., the natural cosmic-ray-induced flux is multiplied by 10^6). The LANSCE neutron beam energy spectrum also matches well the natural flux at sea level [JEDEC 2001].

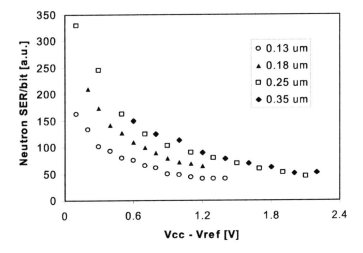

Figure 16.1. Neutron-induced SER in SRAM as a function of voltage and gate length (a.u. = arbitrary units).

TABLE 16.2. Main constituents of atmospheric hadron cascades [Ziegler et al. 1998]

Altitude	Neutrons	Pions	Protons
Sea level	94%	3%	3%
32,000 feet	52%	36%	12%

The system under evaluation at LANSCE consisted of an Itanium-processor-based server, placed in the beam area. Mechanical design of the server chassis allowed only the processor to be exposed to the neutron flux. In order to avoid interruption of the booting process due to neutron-induced failures, the server was moved out of the beam after each processor upset, then slid back into the beam to resume the measurements (alternatively, the beam may be turned on and off). The monitor and keyboard connected to the server resided in the protected user area.

Fluence of the neutrons striking the target is determined with the aid of a fission ion chamber, located in the path of the beam. Neutrons passing through the chamber initiate fissions, which create voltage pulses. Monitoring equipment, located in the user area, counts the fission-induced pulses and determines the number of passing neutrons. A method for calculating SER for semiconductor memories, based on bit-fail cross-section, is provided in the JEDEC JFSD89 standard [JEDEC 2001]. In this study we expand that approach to the case of complex integrated circuits, which incorporate both memory cells and sequential and combinational logic. Equation 16.1 is used for deriving the MTTF induced by the high-energy neutron flux:

$$MTTF = Tua/U = [(Fcp \cdot Nc)/Nf]/U \tag{16.1}$$

where MTTF = mean time to failure due to neutron flux (h), Tua = duration of an equivalent experiment taking place under unaccelerated conditions (h), U = total number of upsets (failures) over the duration of the experiment, Fcp = total number of fission chamber

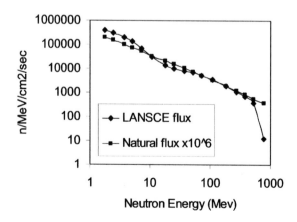

Figure 16.2. Energy dependence of the natural cosmic ray neutron flux and the LANSCE neutron flux [Wender 1998].

pulses over the duration of the experiment,* Nc = average neutron conversion factor (neutrons/fission pulse/cm^2), Nf = cosmic-ray-induced neutron flux at the desired geographical location and altitude (neutrons/cm^2/h).

Fcp and Nc in Equation 16.1 are provided by the LANSCE measurement equipment, which performs the fisson pulse counting and integration over the energy spectrum of the neutron flux. Their product represents the total number of neutrons that pass through one cm^2 of the integrated circuit, over the duration of the experiment. Division by Nf, on the right hand side of Equation 16.1, provides the duration of an equivalent unaccelerated experiment, and division by U gives MTTF due to the neutron flux. MTTF can be determined at any altitude and geographical location by substituting the appropriate Nf in Equation 16.1. A terrestrial neutron flux of Nf = 28.4 neutrons/cm^2/h (sea level, in New York City, neutron energy over 1 MeV) was used in our calculations [JEDEC 2001]. Note that MTTF significantly decreases with altitude (Earth atmosphere plays a shielding role) and slightly varies with geographical location (due to Earth magnetic field). Two procedures for calculating terrestrial neutron flux, at an arbitrary altitude and location, are provided in Annex E of [JEDEC 2001].

16.4. EXPERIMENTAL RESULTS

The results of neutron SER characterization of the Intel Itanium® microprocessors are presented below. A Linpack benchmark [Benchmark 1992] was running on the server. Although designed to measure performance of matrix computations, this benchmark also derives the residues. The value of the residues is an indication of the correctness of mathematical operations and, as a result, the benchmark can capture possible numerical errors, that is, silent corruption of the data. Square matrixes of size 1000 and 800 were used in our experiments. All runs were interrupted by upsets (failures) induced by the neutron flux (i.e., the number of runs equals the number of failures). The main types of failures observed were blue screen and server hang.[†]

Figure 16.3 shows the MTTF as a function of the number of runs. Each data point (the MTTF value) is derived using Equation 16.1. Fcp and U are increasing with the number of runs, while Nc and Nf remain constant. Significant variations of the MTTF, calculated after the first runs of the Linpack benchmark, were observed. This is explained by the fact that the duration of each run varied in a very wide range. As a result, MTTF approaches a stable value only after 40 runs (Figure 16.3). Table 16.3 shows the 80% and 90% confidence intervals of MTTF, after 20, 30, and 40 upsets (failures). As expected, the confidence intervals are narrowing as the number of upsets, that is, the duration of the experiment, increases. An example of interpreting data in Table 16.3 is: after 40 upsets we are 80% confident that MTTF is in the (58, 91) interval. Experiments may be stopped when the MTTF confidence interval is considered narrow enough for the desired confidence level.

Only one silent data corruption (SDC) event was observed. This unique event cannot provide statistically significant data on the frequency of occurrence of SDC. No latch-up events occurred.

---

*The fission chamber counter has to be stopped when the server is out of the beam to avoid underestimation of the MTTF.

†Blue screens provide limited information on error type and location. No error data is available in the case of server hangs.

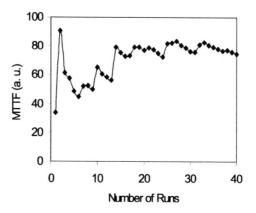

Figure 16.3. Microprocessor MTTF (a.u. = arbitrary units).

Experimental results discussed in this section are specific to terrestrial operating conditions. Heavy ions and proton radiation are commonly used for SER characterization in a space environment. Significantly lower microprocessor MTTF is observed in that case. Details on SER evaluation techniques and estimated failure rates, specific to space applications, are provided in [Karapetian et al. 2002].

16.5. CONCLUSIONS

Impact of semiconductor technology scaling on neutron-induced SER was discussed and the technique used for SER characterization of Intel Itanium® microprocessors was presented. Accelerated measurements, carried out at LANSCE, provided statistically significant estimates of the MTTF due to high-energy neutrons.

The increased level of integration and complexity of the integrated circuits, in general, and microprocessors, in particular, has lead to tremendous performance gains and also to a higher sensitivity to particle-induced errors. The use of fault avoidance and fault tolerance techniques is expected to significantly increase in the future in order to limit the impact of soft errors. Silicon on insulator (SOI), in general, and fully depleted SOI, in particular, have proved to be an effective fault avoidance solution [Baggio et al. 2004; Cannon et al. 2004]. Triple-well [Bhat et al. 2000, Noda et al. 2000, Sato et al. 1999] and circuit design [Gulati et al. 1994, Weaver et al. 1991, Zeng et al. 1999] also lower sensitivity to high-energy particles. Fault tolerance techniques, like space redundancy [Bartlett and Spainhower 2004, Check and Slegel 1999, Slegel et al. 1999] and time redundancy, pri-

TABLE 16.3. Confidence intervals of MTTF induced by the neutron flux

	MTTF (a.u.)*		
Confidence level	20 upsets	30 upsets	40 upsets
80%	52, 103	56, 97	58, 91
90%	44, 110	50, 103	53, 96

*a.u. = arbitrary units.

marily based on multithreading [Rashid et al. 2000, Reinhardt and Mukherjee 2000, Rotenberg 1999], are expected to gain ground. Reduction of instruction vulnerability time [Weaver et al. 2004] and reuse of design for testability resources, to lower SER [Mitra et al. 2005], are attractive solutions. Firmware and software recovery [Quach 2000] as well as the use of error detecting and correcting codes [Chen 1999, Das et al. 2000, Gao and Simmons 2003, Katayama and Morioka 2000, Maamar and Russel 1998] will continue to expand.

As the impact of soft errors becomes more significant, both computer manufacturers and customers need accurate SER measurements. On one hand, manufacturers need to characterize their products from a SER standpoint, in order to validate presilicon, model-based estimates and also compare new designs against the competition and their own previous products. On the other hand, users need to choose from a wide range of products, which employ different circuit design techniques and manufacturing processes, as well as different error handling mechanisms. As a consequence, accelerated SER measurements are expected to become an important element of dependability benchmarking. The presented approach may be employed for benchmarking of microprocessors, as well as any other complex semiconductor devices. No proprietary data about the circuits under evaluation is required, making this technique accessible both to manufacturers and independent evaluators.

ACKNOWLEDGMENT

The author thanks Bruce Takala and Steve Wander of LANSCE, and Nelson Tam and Pat Armstrong of Intel Corporation for their contributions.

REFERENCES

[Baggio et al. 2004] J. Baggio, D. Lambert, V. Ferlet-Cavrois, C. D'hose, K. Hirose, H. Saito, J. M. Palau, F. Saigne, B. Sagnes, N. Buard, and T. Carriere, "Neutron-induced SEU in bulk and SOI SRAMs in terrestrial environment," in *IEEE Reliability Physics Symposium,* pp. 677–678, 2004.

[Bartlett and Spainhower 2004] W. Bartlett and L. Spainhower, "Commercial fault tolerance: A tale of two systems," *IEEE Transactions on Dependable and Secure Computing,* vol. 1, no. 1, pp. 87–96, 2004.

[Benchmark 1992] Benchmark Programs and Reports, http://netlib2.cs.utk.edu/benchmark/.

[Bhat et al. 2000] M. Bhat, S. Shi, P. Grudowski, C. Feng, B. Lee, R. Nagabushnam, J. Moench, C. Gunderson, P. Schani, L. Day, S. Bishop, H. Tian, J. Chung, C. Lage, J. Ellis, N. Herr, P. Gilbert, A. Das, F. Nkansah, M. Woo, M. Wilson, D. Derr, L. Terpolilli, K. Weidemann, R. Stout, A. Hamilton, T. Lii, F. Huang, K. Cox, and J. Scott, "A highly versatile 0.18 μm CMOS technology with dense embedded SRAM," in *Proceedings of VLSI Technology Symposium,* pp. 13–15, 2000.

[Cannon et al. 2004] E. H. Cannon, D. R. Reinhardt, M. S. Gordon, and P. S. Makowenskyj, "SRAM SER in 90, 130 and 180 nm bulk and SOI technologies," in *IEEE Reliability Physics Symposium,* pp. 300–304, 2004.

[Check and Slegel 1999] M. A. Check and T. H. Slegel, "Custom S/390 G5 and G6 microprocessors," *IBM Journal of Research and Development,* vol. 43, no. 5/6, pp. 671–680, 1999.

[Chen 1999] C. L. Chen, "On double-byte error-correcting codes," *IEEE Transactions on Information Theory,* vol. 45, no. 6, pp. 2207–2208, 1999.

[Constantinescu 2005] "Neutron SER characterization of microprocessors," in *Proceedings of IEEE Dependable Systems and Networks Conference,* pp. 754–759, 2005.

[Das et al. 2000] D. Das, N. A. Touba, M. Seuring, and M. Gossel, "Low cost concurrent error detection based on modulo weight-based codes," in *Proceedings of 6th IEEE International On-Line Testing Workshop,* pp. 171–176, 2000.

[Dodd 1996] P. E. Dodd, "Device simulation of charge collection and single-event upset," *IEEE Transactions on Nuclear Science,* vol. 43, no. 2, pp. 561–575, 1996.

[Edmonds 2000] L. D. Edmonds, "Proton SEU cross sections derived from heavy-ion test data," *IEEE Transactions on Nuclear Science,* vol. 47, no. 5, pp. 1713–1728, 2000.

[Gao and Simmons 2003] W. Gao and S. Simmons, "A study on the VLSI implementation of ECC for embedded DRAM," in *IEEE Conference on Electrical and Computer Engineering,* vol. 1, pp. 203–206, 2003.

[Guenzer et al. 1979] C. S. Guenzer, E. A. Wolicki, and R. G. Allas, "Single event upsets of dynamic RAMs by neutron and protons," *IEEE Transactions on Nuclear Science,* vol. NS-26, p. 5048, 1979.

[Gulati et al. 1994] K. Gulati, L. W. Massengill, and G. R. Agrawal, "Single event mirroring and DRAM sense amplifier designs for improved single-event-upset performance," *IEEE Transactions on Nuclear Science,* vol. 41, no. 6, pp. 2026–2034, 1994.

[Hareland et al. 2001] S. Hareland, J. Maiz, M. Alavi, K. Mistry, S. Walsta, and D. Changhong, "Impact of CMOS process scaling and SOI on the soft error rates of logic processes," *IEEE Symposium on VLSI Technology,* pp. 73–74, 2001.

[Howard at al. 2001] J. W. Howard, M. A. Carts, R. Stattel, C. E. Rogers, T. L. Irwin, C. Dunsmore, J. A. Sciarini, and K. A. LaBel, "Total dose and single event effects testing of the Intel Pentium III (P3) and AMD K7 microprocessors," in *IEEE Radiation Effects Data Workshop,* pp. 38–47, 2001.

[ITRS 2003] International Technology Roadmap for Semiconductors (ITRS), http://public.itrs.net.

[JEDEC 2001] JEDEC Standard, JESD89, 2001, www.jedec.org.

[Karapetian et al. 2002] A. V. Karapetian, R. R. Some, and J. J. Beahan "Radiation fault modeling and fault rate estimation for a COTS based space-borne supercomputer," in *Proceedings of IEEE Aerospace Conference,* vol. 5, pp. 5-2121–5-2131, 2002.

[Katayama and Morioka 2000] Y. Katayama and S. Morioka, "One-shot Reed-Solomon decoding for high-performance dependable systems," in *Proceedings of IEEE Dependable Systems and Networks Conference,* pp. 390–399, 2000.

[Liden et al. 1994] P. Liden, P. Dahlgren, R. Johansson, and J. Karlsson, "On latching probability of particle induced transients in combinatorial networks," in *Proceedings of 24th FTCS Symposium,* pp. 340–349, 1994.

[Maamar and Russel 1998] A. Maamar and G. Russel, "A 32 bit RISC processor with concurrent error detection," in *Proceedings of 24th Euromicro Conference,* vol. 1, pp. 461–467, 1998.

[May and Woods 1979] T. C. May and M. H. Woods, "Alpha particle induced soft errors in dynamic memories," *IEEE Transaction on Electron Devices,* vol. ED-26, p. 2, 1979.

[Mitra et al. 2005] S. Mitra, N. Seifert, M. Zhang, Q. Shi, and K. S. Kim, "Robust system design with built-in soft-error resilience," *IEEE Computer,* vol. 38, no. 2, pp. 43–52, 2005.

[Noda et al. 2000] K. Noda, K. Matsui, S. Ito, S. Masuoka, H. Kawamoto, N. Ikezawa, K. Takeda, Y. Aimoto, N. Nakamura, H. Toyoshima, T. Iwasaki, and T. Horiuchi, "An ultra-high-density high-speed load less four-transistor SRAM macro with a dual-layered twisted bit-line and a triple-well shield," in *Proceedings of IEEE Custom Integrated Circuits Conference,* pp. 283–286, 2000.

[Palau et al. 2002] J. M. Palau, R. Wrobel, K. Castellani-Coulie, M. C. Calvet, P. E. Dodd, and F. W. Sexton, "Monte Carlo exploration of neutron-induced SEU-sensitive volumes in SRAMs," *IEEE Transactions on Nuclear Science,* vol. 49, no. 6, pp. 3075–3081, 2002.

[Palau et al. 2003] J. M. Palau, M. C. Calvet, P. E. Dodd, F. W. Sexton, and P. Roche, "Contribution of device simulation to SER understanding," in *Proceedings of IEEE International Symposium on Reliability Physics Symposium,* pp. 71–75, 2003.

[Quach 2000] N. Quach, "High availability and reliability in Itanium processor," *IEEE Micro,* vol. 20, no. 5, pp. 61–69, 2000.

[Rashid et al. 2000] F. Rashid, K. K. Saluja, and P. Ramanathan, "Fault tolerance through re-execution in multiscalar architecture," in *Proceedings of IEEE Dependable Systems and Networks Conference,* pp. 482–491, 2000.

[Reinhardt and Mukherjee 2000] S. K. Reinhardt and S. S. Mukherjee, "Transient fault detection via simultaneous multithreading," in *Proceedings of the 27th International Symposium on Computer Architecture,* pp. 25–36, 2000.

[Rotenberg 1999] E. Rotenberg, "AR-SMT: A microarchitectural approach to fault tolerance in microprocessors," in *Proceedings of 29th FTCS Symposium,* pp. 84–91, 1999.

[Sato et al. 1999] H. Sato. T. Wada, S. Ohbayashi, K. Kozaru, Y. Okamoto, Y. Higashide, T. Shimizu, Y. Maki, R. Morimoto, H. Otoi, T. Koga, H. Honda, M. Taniguchi, Y. Arita, and T. Shiomi, "A 500-MHz pipelined burst SRAM with improved SER immunity," *IEEE Journal of Solid-State Circuits,* vol. 34, no. 11, pp. 1571–1579, 1999.

[Shivakumar et al. 2002] P. Shivakumar, M. Kistler, S. W. Keckler, D. Burger, and L. Alvisi, "Modeling the effect of technology trends on the soft error rate of combinatorial logic," in *Proceedings of IEEE International Conference on Dependable Systems and Networks,* pp. 389–398, 2002.

[Slegel et al. 1999] T. J. Slegel, R. M. Averill, M. A. Check, B. C. Giamei, B. W. Krumm, C. A. Krygowski, W. H. Li, J. S. Liptay, J. D. MacDougall, T. J. McPherson, J. A. Navarro, E. M. Schwarz, K. Shum, and C. F. Webb, "IBM's S/390 G5 microprocessor design," *IEEE Micro,* vol. 19, no. 2, pp. 12–23, 1999.

[Taber and Normand 1993] A. Taber and E. Normand, "Single event upset in avionics," *IEEE Transactions on Nuclear Science,* vol. 40, no. 2, pp. 120–126, 1993.

[Tosaka et al. 1999] Y. Tosaka, H. Kanata, T. Itakura, and S. Satoh, "Simulation technologies for cosmic ray neutron-induced soft errors: Models and simulation systems," *IEEE Transactions on Nuclear Science,* vol. 46, no. 3, pp. 774–780, 1999.

[Tosaka and Satoh 2000] Y. Tosaka and S. Satoh "Simulation of multiple-bit soft errors induced by cosmic ray neutrons in DRAMs," in *Proceedings of IEEE International Conference on Simulation of Semiconductor Processes and Devices,* pp. 265–268, 2000.

[Weaver et al. 2004] C. T. Weaver, J. Emer, S. Mukherjee, and S. K. Reinhardt, "Reducing the soft-error rate of a high-performance microprocessor," *IEEE Micro,* vol. 24, no.6, pp. 30–37, 2004.

[Weaver et al. 1991] H. T. Weaver, W. T. Corbett, and J. M. Pimbley, "Soft error protection using asymmetric response latches," *IEEE Transactions on Electron Devices,* vol. 38, no. 6, pp. 1555–1557, 1991.

[Wender 1998] S. Wender, "Accelerated neutron testing of semiconductor devices," *LANSCE Activity Report 1995-1998,* pp. 52–53, 1998.

[Zeng et al. 1999] C. Zeng, N. Saxena, and E. J. McCluskey, "Finite state machine synthesis with concurrent error detection," in *Proceedings of IEEE International Test Conference,* pp. 672–679, 1999.

[Ziegler and Lanford 1979] J. F. Ziegler and W. A. Lanford, "The effect of cosmic rays on computer memories," *Science,* vol. 206, p. 776, 1979.

[Ziegler et al. 1998] J. F. Ziegler, M. E. Nelson, J. D. Shell, R. J. Peterson, C. J. Gelderloos, H. P. Muhlfeld, and C. J. Montrose, "Cosmic ray soft error rates of 16-Mb DRAM memory chips," *IEEE J. Solid-State Circuits,* vol. 33, pp. 246–252, 1998.

INDEX